P9-CDL-629

Post New Wave Cinema
in the
Soviet Union
and
Eastern Europe

Post New Wave Cinema
in the
Soviet Union
and
Eastern Europe

Edited by
Daniel J. Goulding

Indiana University Press
Bloomington and Indianapolis

Visual Studies Workshop
Research Center
Rochester, N.Y.

September 1990 gift
of the publisher

© 1989 by Indiana University Press

All rights reserved

No part of this book may be reproduced or utilized in any form or by
any means, electronic or mechanical, including photocopying and
recording, or by any information storage and retrieval system, without
permission in writing from the publisher. The Association of American
University Presses' Resolution on Permissions constitutes the only
exception to this prohibition.

Manufactured in the United States of America

Library of Congress Cataloging-in-Publication Data
Post new wave cinema in the Soviet Union and eastern
Europe.
Bibliography: p.
Includes indexes.
Contents: Toward a new openness in Soviet cinema,
1976–1987 / Anna Lawton—Testing the borders /
Sigrun D. Leonhard—Czechoslovakia / Peter Hames—
[etc.]
1. Motion pictures—Europe, Eastern. 2. Motion
pictures—Soviet Union. I. Goulding, Daniel J.
PN1993.5.E82P65 1988   791.43′0947   87-46247
ISBN 0-253-34559-6
ISBN 0-253-20486-0 (pbk.)
1 2 3 4 5 92 91 90 89 88

Contents

ACKNOWLEDGMENTS

The preparation of this book required intense intellectual collaboration and agreement among the contributors on the overall purpose and basic organization of the work, as well as a mutual willingness to meet a tight schedule of deadlines. I am very grateful to my fellow collaborators for their efficiency and cooperation in meeting and often exceeding the expectations and demands placed upon them.

While it would be impossible to name all of those who have served as generous and expert guides in preparing my own chapter on Yugoslav film, I would be remiss not to mention certain key institutions and individuals without whom the work could have not been completed. Milomir Marinović, Head of International Films for Jugoslavija film, offered valuable advice, set up special screenings of recent films, and provided me with film illustrations. Gorka Ostojić-Cvajner, Director of the Annual Festival of Yugoslav Feature Films at Pula, extended every courtesy to me while I was a guest of the festival in 1986 and 1987, and made available valuable materials from previous festivals. Dušan Stojanović, professor of the Faculty of Dramatic Arts in Belgrade and one of Yugoslavia's leading film critics and theoreticians, read the manuscript and made numerous helpful suggestions. I am also grateful to a wide circle of film critics, artists, and directors of film enterprises in Belgrade, Zagreb, Sarajevo and Ljubljana for their lively discussions, hospitality, and generous support in providing interviews and arranging for screenings of important films.

Margaret S. Jennings, senior writer-editor for the MITRE Corporation in Bedford, Massachusetts, provided detailed and expert editorial assistance in the preparation of all the manuscripts for the book. Priscilla Scott and Thelma Kime typed the manuscripts and their many revisions with unfailing efficiency and cheerfulness.

DANIEL J. GOULDING

Introduction

Daniel J. Goulding

The late nineteen seventies and eighties have witnessed a remarkable out-pouring of stylistically varied and sociopolitically significant films from the Soviet Union and the socialist countries of Central and Eastern Europe. Film directors and other gifted film artists who made their international reputations in the sixties and endured a period of comparative neglect, political harassment, and bureaucratic interventions throughout most of the seventies, have once again begun to make films of startling originality and depth. Already established film artists have been joined recently by a newer generation of filmmakers, superbly trained in their craft—who reached maturity after the cataclysmic events of the Second World War and the Stalinist aftermath of socialist reconstruction, and who are bringing fresh perspectives to historical themes and contemporary realities. The new spirit of resurgence and pluralistic cinematic expression which has taken place in the Soviet Union and the so-called Eastern European countries (a geographic and cultural misnomer which the title of the present book perpetuates for lack of a more convenient label) has expressed itself in highly variable ways within the national and multinational cinemas analyzed in this volume.

The Gorbachev-inspired policies of *glasnost* (openness) and *perestroika* (restructuring) have, at the time of this writing, led to a profound reorganization of the Soviet film industry and to the completion of a growing number of impressive new films as well as the release of previously censored or shelved films made in the late seventies and early eighties. In her chapter "Toward a New Openness in Soviet Cinema, 1976–1987," Anna Lawton masterfully surveys these recent developments, placing them in relationship to the earlier "thaw" (late fifties and early sixties) and within the important political and sociocultural transitions which have taken place in Soviet cinema from the end of the Brezhnev era to the present.

The culturally rich and sophisticated cinemas of Poland and Hungary had already gone through their own versions of *glasnost* well before the Soviet Union. In Poland, the rebirth of a "cinema of moral concern" was signaled by the international critical and popular success of Andrzej Wajda's *Man of Marble* (1976) and its sequel *Man of Iron* (1980), the latter of which won the *Palme d'or* for best feature film at Cannes in 1981. The new mood of Polish cinema was richly confirmed by Krzysztof Zanussi's complex cinematic and philosophical meditations *Camouflage* (1976), *Spiral* (1978), and *The Constant Factor* (1980). After the crackdown on the Solidarity movement in late 1981, it was widely assumed by Western film critics and international film festival goers that the recently reborn Polish cinema would be strangled in the cradle. Such gloomy prognostications did not fully take into account the moral and intellectual tough-mindedness of the Polish film community and the unique and complex relationship which exists between the Polish intelligentsia and regime authorities. As Frank Turaj amply demonstrates in his chapter, the last few years have witnessed an impressive number of artistically well-made and socially relevant Polish films.

Beginning in the late seventies, Hungarian cinema has enjoyed a sustained and often brilliant period of creativity. Several Hungarian films have won major international awards and widespread critical acclaim: Márta Mészáros's *Women* (1977), Pál Gábor's *Angi Vera* (1979), István Szabó's *Mephisto* (1981)—a Hungarian-West German coproduction which captured the Academy Award for best foreign-language film in 1982—and *Colonel Redl* (1984). Miklós Jancsó, the best-known Hungarian film director in the sixties, has continued to make cinematically complex experimental films which have often perplexed both foreign and domestic film critics. In his chapter "The Magyar on the Bridge," David Paul provides a sensitive reading of Jancsó's recent films, and relates them to his earlier *oeuvre* and to the other important creative currents which are coursing through contemporary Hungarian cinema.

The extraordinarily versatile and gifted Czechoslovakian film community continues to labor under the tight bureaucratic and ideological controls imposed after the fall of Dubček in 1968. Despite these constraints, there are unmistakable signs of artistic renewal and resurgence. Jiří Menzel *(Closely Watched Trains,* 1966, and *Capricious Summer,* 1967) has made a well-deserved comeback with several important films in the late seventies and eighties, including his most recent international success, *My Sweet Little Village* (1986). Věra Chytilová has also directed several recent films which exemplify the same artistic vitality and uncompromising integrity which characterized her work in the sixties. Peter Hames provides a cogent analysis of recent film trends in Czechoslovakia and appraises them in relation to current ideological conditions and in relation to the wider and deeper Czechoslovak *new wave* period of the sixties.

East German filmmakers have also made impressive films in the late seventies and eighties despite a framework of ideological and aesthetic constraints which, if anything, is even more rigorous than that in Czechoslovakia. While these recent trends are followed closely in the brother state of

West Germany, they are little appreciated in the rest of Western Europe and the United States. In her chapter, "Testing the Borders: East German Film between Individualism and Social Commitment," Sigrun Leonhard makes a detailed and well-documented contribution toward filling this gap in our understanding.

Bulgarian cinema has followed its own unique rhythms of upward and downward cycles of resurgence and decline which are not always synchronous with similar cycles in neighboring socialist countries. Participating fully in the period of the "thaw" in the late fifties and early sixties, Bulgarian cinema experienced a rapid decline in the mid-to-late sixties—at the very time when the cinemas of Poland, Hungary, Czechoslovakia and Yugoslavia were reaching the highest creative peaks of the *new wave* period. By contrast, the revival of a significant and interesting Bulgarian cinema began in the early seventies (when other socialist cinemas were stagnating) and was maintained into the early eighties. The last few years, however, have been comparatively sterile and represent a complex period of readjustment and struggle toward recovery. Ronald Holloway, whose intimate knowledge of Bulgarian cinema has been formed over many years, provides an astute and convincing analysis and overview of these developments.

Among the internationally significant national cinemas of Central and Eastern Europe, only Romania has shown little sign of renewal. Her gifted community of film artists is caught between the twin millstones of a prolonged and deepening economic crisis on the one hand, and an unrelentingly conservative ideological climate on the other. At the time of this writing, film developments in Romania do not seem to warrant separate treatment in a book focusing upon resurgence and new cinematic breakthroughs.

Romania's neighboring state, Yugoslavia, however, is experiencing an unusually fecund and impressive revival of its multinational cinema which was most dramatically confirmed by the award of the *Palme d'or* for best feature film at Cannes in 1986 for Emir Kusturica's film, *When Father Was Away on Business*—a substantial international critical and popular success. Kusturica's film represents only the tip of a broadly based film revival, the full dimensions of which are described and analyzed in the final chapter, "Yugoslav Film in the Post-Tito Era."

Even within the confines of such a brief overview of the contents of this book, it should be obvious that the rich and varied cinemas of the Soviet Union and of the Central and Eastern European socialist states are not cut from the same cloth nor stitched together by threads woven from looms made in Moscow. It is equally valid to observe, however, that all of these countries (including Yugoslavia, which does not belong to the "eastern bloc") have shared, in varying ways, a turbulent and sometimes tragic contemporary history characterized by revolution, war, and socialist reconstruction. These "common" experiences have provided a rich source of filmic themes which cut across cultural boundaries. There also exists an important socialist legacy of assigning to film a larger political and sociocultural status than it typically enjoys in the West. The best of the films from the "East" are characterized by a high level of artistic "seriousness" and sociocultural and political significance. They often yield distinctive, valuable, and unique perspectives on the contemporary human condition. Seriousness, of course, does not imply unrelieved somberness and tragedy. Some of the best recent films exemplify a lively sense of the comic, which ranges from slapstick to the mordant, surrealistic, and Kafkaesque—revealing a sense of humor and of the absurd which is deeply rooted in Central and Eastern European historical experiences and cultural traditions.

Many of the best Soviet and East European films never make it past the festival circuit into networks of commercial film distribution which would expose them to a wider audience. There has been much discussion recently about opening the windows of the East more widely to the flow of Western news, thought, and culture. Perhaps we need to think more deeply about opening more windows in the West to influences from the East. It is hoped that the present volume will make a small contribution in that direction.

Post New Wave Cinema
in the
Soviet Union
and
Eastern Europe

1

Toward a New Openness in Soviet Cinema, 1976–1987

Anna Lawton

Soviet cinema from its inception has been strictly connected with the national political reality. It has been a sensitive recorder of socio-economic changes and of shifts in cultural policies. The beginning of the Gorbachev era, with its broad program of reforms, its dynamic foreign policy, its media awareness, its openness, and its sophisticated public relations, has also been the beginning of a new orientation in the cinema industry. To mark this new stage of development the Soviet filmmakers called it the *new model*.

After the Golden Age of the twenties and the subsequent Stalinist freeze, Soviet cinema experienced an artistic renaissance at the time of Khrushchev's cultural "thaw." In the late fifties and early sixties, the change in the political leadership and the emergence of a new generation of talent brought fresh energies into film production. Creativity was allowed a freer hand and new themes and styles, inspired by a general concern for the individual and his inner world, made their way to the screen. In addition, there was a modest revival of formalistic experimentation, most notable in the "poetic" style of several directors from the southern republics, and in the works of Andrei Tarkovsky. The trend of the sixties reflected to a great extent the filmmakers' aesthetic and moral concerns, as well as the public's demand for engaging subject matter and films with emotional appeal. After two decades of make-believe, audiences yearned for a measure of truth. How large that measure could be, no one knew for sure. Notwithstanding the relaxation in cultural policies, Party directives could not be ignored. Filmmakers had to test their limits and operate within the realm of the permissible. The revival of film art in those years brought Soviet cinema to the attention of international audiences and critics, and, as it did in the twenties, it scored high marks. Soviet cinema underwent such a radical renewal that the conservative aftermath of the "thaw" could not erase what was gained, much less turn the clock back to the forms of the Stalinist years.

1

However, for more than a decade there were no significant aesthetic and thematic developments. The Brezhnev era was a period of cultural stagnation. The prevalent policy aimed at suppressing creativity and favored entertainment genres that supported the status quo. Commercial considerations became an important factor. The increasing availability of television required cinema to become commercially competitive. To fill the movie theaters and fulfill the yearly financial quota established by the Ministry of Culture, film producers, distributors, and exhibitors had to cater to public taste. The genre repertoire widened considerably, and the commercial film directors became increasingly skillful at presenting ideology as entertainment. Public expectations for engagé films of the previous decade were dulled by the prevailing consumeristic atmosphere, which was expressed by light genres and simplistic morals. There were no troubling discoveries; rather, self-complacency and benign irony created a comfortable psychological setup. Within this general trend, however, there were isolated achievements. A few talented directors were able to rise above the level of greyish mediocrity and stand up for humanistic values and artistic integrity. Most of them belonged to the generation that emerged in the sixties as an innovative force, others were no-less-talented newcomers. Unfortunately, a number of remarkable films made in the seventies were either shelved or, at best, had limited circulation. Only now, as a result of the change that is reshaping the Soviet film industry, are those films beginning to come out.

Following a brief period of transition, the eighties mark the end of an era and the beginning of a new phase in the history of the Soviet Union. The parallels with Khrushchev's "thaw" are numerous, as are the differences. Cinema is undergoing a creative revival similar to that of the sixties. However, the upsurge of creativity during the sixties occurred as the by-product of a general policy of liberalization and soon had to be contained, while this more recent artistic renaissance has been planned and sustained by the Party. Furthermore, the new regime has created the conditions for a radical restructuring of the cinema industry's administrative apparatus, which will ensure a long-term commitment to the goals of today and make it difficult to reverse the process. This is not to deny the role of the filmmakers. In fact, a creative ferment has been building for more than a decade, and Gorbachev's policies provide a much needed outlet.

This essay illuminates the recent changes in the context of the developments of the past ten years, through the decline of the Brezhnev era and the period of transition, to the new phase of glasnost and perestroika.

THE BREZHNEV ERA, 1976–1982

The year 1976 was a middle point in the Brezhnev administration and marked the beginning of its decline. The Ninth Five-Year Plan (1971–

1975) had produced rather disappointing results. Designed as the first plan to provide for faster growth in the consumer sector (rather than in the producer), its projections foresaw a dramatic rise in the standard of living through a combination of scientific and technological innovations, greater managerial efficiency, and increased labor productivity.

Several factors intervened to thwart those optimistic goals. The automation of factories and industries depended to a great extent on the steady input of new technology and expertise from the West. However, there were already signs that detente would not last forever. Even more damaging to the process of modernization was internal opposition from conservative economists and Party ideologues. Unable to come to terms with revisions of the Marxist-Leninist doctrine, they defeated the Kosygin reforms of 1965 and subsequently fought against any deviations from pure Communist orthodoxy. They denounced such innovations as system analysis, economic forecasting, and decentralized decision-making, and opposed a plan to assign priority to the consumer sector. Even a passive and corrupt managerial class was eager to defer to the conservative view in order to avoid responsibilities and unnecessary stress.

To worsen the situation, the country suffered two major crop failures, the first in 1972 and the second in 1975. Grain imports alone could not make up for the food shortages, and the standard of living, which had been slowly improving in the early seventies, took a turn for the worse. Even before the latest crop disaster the average family spent 40 to 50 percent of its income on food. After it, prices rose and the state had to intervene with massive subsidies in order to stifle public discontent. However, the revenues from energy exports temporarily compensated for the mismanagement of the nation's economy. The catastrophic results of two decades of government passivity became painfully obvious in the early eighties and inflicted a mortal blow on the Party and state gerontocracy. But, for the time being, the old guard still held firmly to their key positions.

The twenty-fifth Congress of the CPSU, held in February 1976, did not offer new perspectives. On that occasion Brezhnev criticized failures in the economy, but found many achievements to praise and restated the same goals for the next Five-Year Plan with an even more optimistic forecast. He stressed the need for an immediate restructuring of the economy and exhorted scientific and technical personnel at all levels to improve efficiency and quality. But the guidelines he issued did not translate into action.

Younger leaders of the new generation were needed to carry out the plan. They were slowly rising through the ranks and impatiently awaiting their day. Meanwhile, more of Brezhnev's cronies were appointed to the Central Committee and the Politburo. The consequences were disastrous for the political, economic, and cultural life of the nation. As the ailing leadership clung stubbornly to their chairs and to each other, refusing to relinquish power and demanding order and stability, the granting of privileges to extended family became a common practice and corruption was rampant. During his last years, a direct ratio can be observed between Brezhnev's failing health and his accumulation of honors and titles. This was apparently an attempt to sustain the leader's prestige which was rapidly fading, both nationally as well as internationally.[1]

After the honeymoon with the Nixon and Ford administrations which allowed the Soviet Union to modestly improve its standard of living and to rise to an international position of strength, Brezhnev clashed with Carter over the Soviet policy on Afghanistan and Poland. Ratification of the SALT II treaty by the U.S. Senate was suspended, the American athletes boycotted the Moscow Olympic Games, the Soviet Union closed the doors to Jewish emigration. The era of detente came to an end and was replaced by a Cold War syndrome that plunged to severely low temperatures with the incoming Reagan administration. The deterioration of international relations was paralleled by a domestic atmosphere of cultural reaction and rapid economic decline.

The Cinema Industry

The general political trend of the period was reflected in the administrative structure of the cinema industry as well as in film production and distribution. From the time cinema was nationalized, in 1919, by a Lenin decree, film production and distribution had been regulated by a government institution, the State Committee for Cinematography (Goskino),[2] which gradually gained complete control over the film industry. In the seventies, Goskino suffered from the widespread national epidemic of bureaucratic growth. Its inflated cadres, securely entrenched behind their desks, ran the film industry as a state chancery. They dealt with the artistic sector as they would with an unfortunate nuisance. The newly appointed head of Goskino, Filipp Ermash (1972–1986), came from the Central Committee's Department of Culture and enjoyed high connections in the Politburo as a relative of Andrei Kirilenko, one of Brezhnev's closest personal and political associates.

Brezhnev's foreign and domestic policies had brought about a measure of material comfort, especially perceptible toward the middle of the decade. Mounting corruption in the higher echelons and an increasing preoccupation with material goods trickled down to the middle and working classes.[3] The current atmosphere favored the breeding of a consumer mentality. The public taste in entertainment turned "bourgeois." Goskino was quick to exploit this conjuncture. Under Ermash's leadership, the Soviet film industry moved decidedly in the direction of commercial films which met the public demand and increased profits for the Soviet government. The educational function of cinema, however, could not be neglected. Conveniently, the commercial genres were labeled as "popular." Unlike the "elite" films that indulge in aestheticism, popular films were supposed to sustain orthodox ideology and socialist moral values. This combination found its most successful expression in the film that crowned the decade, *Moscow Does Not Believe in Tears* (*Moskva slezam ne verit*, 1980), and which was hailed in equal measure by Party ideologues, Soviet audiences, and, ironically, the Hollywood Oscar prize givers. But most of the time commercial considerations worked against not only artistic endeavors but also ideology. Toward the end of his tenure, Ermash was despised by the film artists and disapproved by the ideologues.

Cinema in the Soviet Union has been for decades the main filler of leisure time. As television became available to a larger number of the population, movie theatre attendance registered a sharp decline. While in the late sixties ticket sales were close to 5 billion a year, in 1977 they had dropped to 4.2 billion, with a per capita sale of 16.4,[4] still sizable figures when compared to those in any Western country. Very revealing of the public taste is the breakdown of the attendance figures per film, which show that a mere 15 percent of all Soviet feature films released in a given year (the yearly output is approximately 150 films) account for 80 percent of all ticket sales. A comparison of the already-mentioned *Moscow Does Not Believe in Tears*, which drew 75 million viewers over the first twelve months of its circulation, to Andrei Tarkovsky's philosophical parable *Stalker*, which was seen by a mere 3 million over the same period, shows where the people's preferences lie. True, *Stalker* did not enjoy the support of Goskino's competent (or, incompetent?) authorities, and it had limited circulation. Nevertheless, there are indications that it would not have fared well in any case. Research conducted at the State Institute for Cinematography (VGIK) ranked some common film features in the order they appealed to the masses:

1. Contemporary theme.
2. Russian production (as opposed to other republics).
3. Adaptation of a popular book.
4. Fast tempo.
5. Continuity (no flashbacks).
6. Simplicity.
7. Spectacular (special effects, crowd scenes, and costumes).
8. Active and attractive leading characters.
9. Appealing title.[5]

By adding sex and violence, and substituting "American" for "Russian" in point No. 2, this list could be used to characterize most U.S. box office successes of the past decade. Not without foundation was Ermash known to be a secret admirer of the Hollywood motion picture industry.

Thus, Goskino promoted the production of films that suited the public taste. In order to do so, it needed the cooperation of film workers. This meant the studios and the Filmmakers Union, which supposedly represented the interests of workers in the field. However, the Union supported its members only nominally. In effect, throughout the seventies and up to

1986, the Union was burdened by a very conservative and passive leadership, which provided material assistance but did not stand up for creative freedom and decentralized decision-making.

Lack of support from the Union was reflected in the studios where the actual creative process took place. Of all the studios of the 15 republics, Mosfilm was, and still is, by far the largest and most prestigious, followed by Lenfilm (Leningrad studios), and at a considerable distance, the Georgian, Ukrainian, Armenian, and Kirgizian studio. The production of the Baltic republics was negligible.[6] In the seventies, both the head of Mosfilm, Nikolay Sizov, and his deputy in charge of scriptwriting, Leonid Nekhoroshev, were well regarded by the filmmakers as rather sensitive intellectuals, authors of several books. They were also well connected politically. Sizov had been a Party functionary and was currently a member of the Moscow City Council and a deputy chairman of Goskino. Nekhoroshev was a graduate of the Social Science Academy of the Central Committee. Both were seasoned politicians not devoid of intellectual sophistication. Mosfilm therefore managed to satisfy the requirements of Goskino while giving elbow room to the most creative directors. In fact, besides the bulk of commercial films, known as "greyish" films from an aesthetic as well as a political point of view, Mosfilm produced a good number of stimulating pictures. However, the best films were not always released, and if they were, only a few copies were printed.

The tendency toward the mass genres enlarged the traditional repertoire with a considerable number of melodramas, comedies, detective stories, science-fiction films, and musicals. Because of their poor quality, however, the majority of these films were not well attended. The audiences demanded light genres, but they had reached an average level of sophistication (at least in the major urban areas) and would not put up with facile plots and sloppy techniques. Often, but not always, the films that rose above mediocrity were also the most successful with the public.

"Bytovoy" Film

One trend revived from the repertoire of the late twenties/early thirties became predominant: the *bytovoy* film. The term can be approximately translated as "slice-of-life" film. These are stories about contemporary society, individual lives and relations, current problems, and human values. The *bytovoy* film could be anything from comedy to "problematic melodrama."[7]

The preoccupation with economic growth and reforms was reflected in a long series of *bytovoy* films concerned with factory problems—the so-called "production movies." The prototype of the trend, many times imitated but hardly ever matched, was *The Bonus (Premiia,* 1975) by Sergei Mikaelian.[8] It marked a new approach to the worker and the work place. This film does not follow the traditional socialist-realist model where enthusiastic shock-brigade workers, inspired by their infallible leader, overcome the challenges of enemies and saboteurs, fight against all odds with superhuman strength and moral stamina to overfulfill the plan, and in the end happily applaud the brigade leader, who, with much fanfare, is awarded the decoration of hero of socialist labor. In *The Bonus* there are no far-fetched dramatic situations, no heroics. Most of the action unfolds in one room during a meeting of a construction enterprise's Party committee. The only dramatic device that gives the screenplay the tension necessary to sustain the action is the conflict which arises between workers and management when a construction team refuses to accept their yearly bonus.

The situation seems odd in a society accustomed to accepting whatever benefits they can get without questioning. What is the workers' motivation? Is this another edifying example of self-abnegation resurrected from movies more than thirty years old? The screenwriter, Alexander Gelman, is not so naïve. His numerous works, primarily for the stage, have won him a solid reputation as a writer of psychological dramas with popular appeal. In *The Bonus* the reasons behind the workers' behavior turn out to be complex and engaging in their apparent simplicity. The construction team refuses the bonus because they feel cheated. The workers think that bad management and poor work organization were responsible for low productivity and personal financial losses which were not adequately compensated with the bonus.

However, the workers' motivations are not totally materialistic. The token bonus becomes a symbol of the hypocrisy and concealment which surround the country's problems, hinder economic growth, and thwart the possibility of healthy social development. The film does not provide a solution to the problem, but it raises the viewer's awareness of a life based on complacency and devoid of spiritual values. It also suggests that it is the people's responsibility to denounce the current situation both in their own interest and in the interest of the nation.

The confrontation takes place between the brigade leader, Potapov, and three executives of the construction enterprise, while the Party representatives preside over the meeting. It is clear from the outset who is the villain and who is the hero. The attribution of roles, however, was bound to generate uneasiness. This perhaps explains why the film's authors, although breaking important ground in this direction, stopped short of carrying the denunciation of management to the very top. The main villains are the senior engineer, Lyubaev, a weak, servile man with an unctuous smile, and the assistant director, Shatunov, a ruthless careerist whose main pleasure in life is to carry out the director's orders. However, the director himself, Batartsev, is not devoid of redeeming qualities. A pragmatist versed in the art of compromise, he comes to the meeting with the self-assurance of an experienced negotiator convinced of an easy victory. But Potapov's tough stance and unshakable convictions make it difficult for him to score with his usual ease. Actually, the values of youth, which had been dulled by the requirements of a managerial career, are reawakened, and allow him to make a moral choice.

On the opposite side, fighting for truth and justice, stands the brigade leader Potapov. No knight in white armor, he is a stocky middle-aged man, slightly overweight, with a round, good-natured face and a bald pate. The role is performed, brilliantly, by Evgeny Leonov, better known to the audiences for his numerous comic characterizations. But already in the film *Byelorussia Station* (*Belorusskii vokzal*, 1972) there were signs of a change toward serious, engaged roles. Nevertheless, when director Mikaelian cast him as Potapov the choice made more than one eyebrow rise among the members of the production team, including the screenwriter. In fact, the script called for "a young Communist," assertive, principled, with high morals—in other words, a traditional "positive hero." Leonov does not fit the exterior model, but the inner qualities he gradually displays are worthy of his role. The hero Potapov, at first awkward, somewhat bashful and ineffective, looks like an easy contender to his opponents and a disappointing champion to the audience. But in the course of the meeting it becomes abundantly clear that Potapov's modest appearance conceals a lively mind, sound common sense, and the courage to stand up for his co-workers' rights and for basic truths. Because of these qualities Potapov turns out to be stronger than his more powerful and sophisticated adversaries, a true folk hero who strikes a deep sentimental chord in the viewer's heart.

How does the transformation take place? Mikaelian explains:

> In the shooting of *The Bonus* everything was subordinated to the actors. Therefore, down with cinemascope, no music with eternal "accents," no contrast of colors. It was not necessary to vary the place of the action (oh, how they insisted on that!). Let the camera follow the actors, let it come closer to the actor in the course of the film, closer and closer . . . In this film an old truth triumphed: the depth and strength of a person's character are revealed by the totality of the smallest features."[9]

Another variant of the *bytovoy* film is the light comedy involving a love story, humorous situations, and vignettes of social and private life. One of the most successful directors of this genre is Eldar Ryazanov, who, since the mid-fifties, has worked both in cinema and the theater. He co-wrote a large number of stage plays together with Emile Braginsky, as well as many scripts for his own films. The first movie comedy that brought them fame and popularity was *Beware of Automobiles* (*Beregis' avtomobilia*, 1965) starring the actor known abroad as the Russian Hamlet, Innokenty Smoktunovsky. One of the hits of the mid-seventies was *Irony of Fate, or Have a Good Sauna* (*Ironiia sud'by, ili S legkim parom*, 1975), originally made for television and based on a play which itself was staged in more than one hundred theaters all over the country. This film has been called a "comic-musical-psychological-fantastic tale."[10] Its appeal comes from the use of a classical comedy-of-errors plot device in a modern urban context. A man, after a drink too many, goes home to what seems to be his apartment only to discover that he is in another city and in the apartment of an unknown woman. The residential outskirts of the big cities, and the lives of their dwellers, have become so uniform and depersonalized that this sort of mix-up, with a little stretch of the imagination, is conceivable. It is even conceivable to use the key to one's own Moscow apartment to open someone else's door in Leningrad. But the encounter of the two strangers, after a first moment of fear and hostility, leads to the discovery of love and brings magic back into everyday routine. By a wide margin of its readers, *Irony of Fate* won a popularity contest held every year by the journal *Soviet Screen*.

A few years later, another comedy by the same authors, *An Office Romance (Sluzhebnyi romans,* 1978) became a box office success and scored the highest mark in the *Soviet Screen* contest for 1979. In many ways this film resembles its predecessor. In an ordinary environment (a statistical bureau) and among ordinary people (middle-aged clerks whose zest for life has been dulled by years of office routine) a "miracle" suddenly takes place. The bureau director, a stern, colorless woman, falls in love with one of her subordinates and, as if by magic, she is transformed into a sensitive, elegant, young-looking beauty (an easy feat for the make-up artist, since the role is played by the indeed beautiful Alisa Freindlikh). Similarly, the initially frightened petty clerk turns into a self-assured, attractive man. What is more, the love that radiates from the happy couple gives a rosy coloration to the office and its drab occupants.

Some Western feminist critics have read the transformation process as a male affirmation of traditional sex roles.[11] This is a possible reading, given the general social context of male chauvinism in the USSR. Nevertheless, it seems that in these films transformation works primarily as a traditional fairy tale element. Ryazanov and Braginsky have snobbishly been criticized for creating contemporary urban fairy tales meant to "reassure" the viewer, to which Ryazanov answers:

> First of all, to reassure, to encourage the viewer, in order to make it easier for him, to cheer him up, to help him believe in himself, it's not such a sin in my opinion. And secondly, when I work with Braginsky on our stories we do not force a happy ending on them. Perhaps, we are so disposed that it's more interesting to us to talk about what unites people, rather than what separates them.[12]

Perhaps, but are Ryazanov's "fairy tales" as innocent as they seem? From the very beginning, satirical elements were interspersed in the text, although offset by the general tone of good-natured humor. In the following film, *Garage (Garazh,* 1980), good-natured humor decisively turned into biting satire and the film's overall effect was quite unsettling.

This was a departure not only from Ryazanov's and Braginsky's dominant style but from the common practice of Soviet screenwriters and directors. Satire was virtually effaced in Soviet cinema by the non-conflict theory of socialist realism. One of the characters in *Garage*, having learned that the woman he is talking to is a scholar doing research in satire, says: "You have an odd profession. You're studying a subject which does not exist."[13]

In *Garage*, conflict and contrast, both on the narrative and the stylistic levels, are the main structural elements. A group of citizens, the staff of the Research Institute for the Protection of the Animals against the Environment, has entered as a cooperative into a contract with the state to build a number of garages (a commodity in very short supply) under the supervision of a Committee. Halfway toward completion of the work, the state changes the plan, and four garages have to be scratched from the project. The Committee chairman calls a meeting to decide which staff members will lose their garages. The film starts at this point. The action is static, developing in one place at one time, and the subject is banal. The meeting takes place in the Research Institute's exhibition hall, which hosts an array of stuffed animals in danger of becoming extinct. Through a clever *mise en scène* and skillful camera work, the Institute staff blends with the fauna, and in the viewer's eyes, becomes an endangered species itself—one that needs "protection against the environment." In fact, under a veneer of democratism mixed with self-congratulatory pomposity, the Committee chooses as victims the four most harmless and helpless of the "animals." Although they are aware of the injustice being perpetrated, the decision is supported by a collective that turns against its kind in order to ensure their own survival (or, more appropriately, the survival of their garages). Ryazanov himself plays the role of Sleepy, one of the four victims who sleeps throughout the entire meeting. Another victim, Mute, is the only one who is ready to protest the decision, but unfortunately, he has no voice because he is suffering from a case of laryngitis. And so, the meeting is adjourned.

What follows is a turning point which, according to conventional dramatic rules, should radically affect the outcome of the story. As the participants are about to leave, they discover that the door is locked and the key is lost. They are totally cut off from the rest of the world, entrapped in a grotesque menagerie of mummified mammals. What is worse, in a desperate act of protest, Mute has swallowed all the documents relative to the garage project, which means that the organization no longer exists, since within a bureaucratic structure identity depends on papers. Having lost their official status, the members of the group gradually reacquire some human characteristics, or so it seems, if one reads the film on the narrative level alone. They go through a night of mea culpa speeches, confessions of wrongdoing, stories of corruption, hypocrisy, and callousness. Finally, the Committee is disbanded and the cooperative members resolve to decide their destinies by drawing lots instead of relying on arbitrary decisions. All seems fair and good: repentance and catharsis.

With the light of a new day the door opens and, as the tired protagonists leave the building, the viewer is confronted with an open ending. Is this the beginning of a new life based on moral principles? Or, is this a return to routine law and order, and the usual mores, after the nightly carnival? The sustained grotesque that runs throughout the film heavily tips the scales in favor of the second option by undercutting all the conventions of the socialist realist model structure, including a moralizing happy ending.

Ryazanov had to pay a price (however small) for depriving the viewer of fairy-tale psychological comfort. Although *Garage* was held in great esteem by the educated public and the liberal critics, and was well attended, it turned up in ninth position in the popularity contest, whose first place that year (1981) was stolen by the great favorite, *Moscow Does Not Believe in Tears*.

Menshov's film has been widely seen and discussed in the United States, and it is not necessary to go into details about it here. It is sufficient to say that by portraying a conventional literary plot in a classical cinematic form (in the sense of "Hollywood classical"), the film reiterates traditional values as the foundation of society, while effacing the disturbing problems connected with the disappearance of those values. In other words, in this film the hero is a hero and the heroine is a heroine; success and happiness await them at the end of the road because they are dedicated to work, moral rectitude, and human compassion. Obviously, average viewers (and not only in the USSR) are willing to suspend their disbelief in order to identify themselves with the "winners"—successful, respected, loved—rather than with Ryazanov's pathetic specimens of an endangered species. Curiously enough, according to Western theories of Marxist criticism, *Moscow Does Not Believe in Tears* may be easily classified as a "bourgeois" film, insofar as it sustains the *status quo* by reaffirming that everything is for the best in the best of all possible worlds, while *Garage* falls into the category of "revolutionary" films, which are meant to disturb the established ideology and challenge the viewers' self-satisfied perception of themselves.

Another son of the sixties, Georgi Danelia, made his debut with the remarkable film *A Summer to Remember* (*Serezha*, 1960), codirected with Igor Talankin. He then proceeded alone with a steady flow of good movies, among them *Afonia* (1975) and *Mimino* (1977). By the end of the seventies he put on screen the very successful and highly praised *Autumn Marathon* (*Osennii maraton*, 1980).

This film is a sympathetic but ironic portrait of a gentle university professor in his mid-forties, entering the "autumnal" phase of his life. Incapable of turning down anyone's requests, Professor Andrei Buzykin (interpreted with extreme sensibility by Oleg Basilashvili) has spread himself so thin that he can no longer cope with the increasing demands in his professional and private life. Although meaning well and trying to please everyone, he ends up causing great unhappiness to both his wife and his mistress, and disappointing his greedy colleagues as well as his concerned friends and neighbors. At one point Andrei seems to have found a way out of the impasse. But it is only a brief delusion; life then returns to the normal routine. He is trapped in a vicious circle which he has helped to create. In fact, his positive qualities—intelligence, sensitivity, kindness of soul—are offset by one dominant trait: total passivity. He does not act in life; he simply reacts to people and events as best he can, without any protest and with a resigned smile. This is what he does every morning when his foreign colleague, a Danish professor and a physical fitness devotee, rings his doorbell and drags him out to go jogging.

The structure of the film is circular. It starts and ends with a jogging session in the dark morning hours. In the northern city of Leningrad, where the action takes place, darkness is a sign of autumn and the oncoming winter. The visual metaphor does not suggest the possibility of a new spring in Andrei's life. In the final sequence the jogging path is punctuated by a row of street lamps leading to infinity. This delicate comedy of manners—whose basically elegiac tone is enlivened by a measured sense of humor—seems to find its inspiration in the cultural tradition of the past century by proposing an updated version of a typical literary figure, the so-called "superfluous man." Certainly, it is not by accident that Danelia chose to set the story in Leningrad, the city that since Pushkin's time has bred a vast fictional progeny of gifted and inept anti-heros.

Although a Mosfilm production, *Autumn Marathon* shares many features of the "Leningrad school," which emerged in the mid-seventies. This group includes directors such as Alexei German, Gleb Panfilov, Ilya Averbakh, Vitaly Melnikov, and Dinara Asanova, whose films are characterized by stylistic restraint in treating the "eternal questions" of the human predicament. And yet, they probe deeply into the complexity and ambiguity of everyday life.

While most of those filmmakers are practically unknown abroad, Alexei German and Gleb Panfilov in the last year have suddenly come to the attention of foreign audiences and critics with the release of films previously censored. However, the sensationalism attached to the films' belated release is less important than their intrinsic value.

Panfilov started his career with the film *No Ford in the Fire* (*V ogne broda net*, 1968), followed shortly by *Debut* (*Nachalo*, 1970). In both films, as in those which followed, his wife Inna Churikova played the leading role. An extremely gifted actress, Churikova has been called a Soviet Giulietta Masina because of "her touching and comical facial expressions, and awkward movements."[14] But to Panfilov she has "a face, a personality, marked by God."[15] She very aptly embodies the central theme of these two movies: the idea that the divine gift of artistic inspiration resides in an unsophisticated and sensitive soul. In the first film a young peasant woman turns out to be a naif painter of great talent, and in the second a simple worker is chosen to play the role of Joan of Arc in a movie and reveals the same spiritual strength of the French heroine.

Panfilov's next film, *May I Have the Floor* (*Proshu slova*, 1977) continues to develop that theme, although the heroine here has superficially changed. She is now the mayor of a provincial town and, therefore, a middle-class lady, with a middle-class family and a mid-level education. But her purity of soul, inner strength, and creative potential remain those of the simple women of the previous films. It is to Panfilov's credit that he succeeded in presenting true heroines while denying the heroic genre through both stylistic and narratological devices.[16]

After this film, and some disagreement with the local authorities, Panfilov moved to Moscow to work at Mosfilm where he obtained approval for his next picture *Theme* (*Tema*, 1979). Upon completion, however, *Theme* was shelved for seven years. When it was finally released, in 1986, it brought the director international fame and awards. It is once more the problem of artistic creativity which constitutes the main "theme" of this film, and it is once more Churikova who represents the source of spirituality. She is contrasted with the figure of a renowned and solidly established playwright whose artistic vein is drying out, played by the seasoned and talented Mikhail Ulyanov. The central character, by the ironical name of Kim Esenin,[17] has reached a creative impasse. Accompanied by a colleague—a hack writer more interested in the comforts of life than in the pangs of creation—Esenin takes a trip to the ancient town of Suzdal to find inspiration for the historical theme of his new play. There, immersed in the atmosphere of old Russia, in touch with the land and the people, he rediscovers the traditional values which he had lost, and realizes that his highly acclaimed works and his very life are a sham. What precipitates Esenin's spiritual crisis is the encounter with the local museum guide, Sasha Nikolaeva, who is the quintessential expression of the Russian soul and the custodian of the national cultural heritage.

An interesting counterpoint to Esenin is provided by the character of Borodaty, with whom Sasha is in love. Borodaty is a disaffected Jewish writer who, having suffered some injustice, seeks to emigrate. The issue of emigration is discussed in a dramatic confrontation between Sasha and Borodaty—he maintaining that he must leave in order to seek creative freedom, she maintaining that he would no longer be able to create in a foreign land after having severed his cultural roots. In the end, Esenin's crisis, as well as the other characters' destinies, remain unresolved, as the film focuses on the human drama and avoids easy solutions. The camera work underlines the human turmoil by contrasting expressive close-ups of the characters with lyrical longshots of Russia's vast expanse, her snowy plains, and her serene medieval settings.

When *Theme* was completed it did not pass the last censorship scrutiny. Obviously the subject of emigration was still considered too sensitive at that time. Panfilov may have staked his chances on the fact that Jewish exit visas had been steadily increasing to reach the record number of 51,320 in 1979. He could not have foreseen that a combination of unfortunate international events would prompt the Soviet Union to reverse its policy and drastically curtail emigration (the decline reached its lowest level in 1984, when only 896 people left). But another, less topical reason may have played a role as well. The portrayal of an official playwright doubting the value of his own work, and consequently the values of the writers' community and of society at large, may have been seen as a threat to the cultural establishment. The fact that *Theme* has now been released and presented at international festivals testifies to a healthy change of policy and a willingness to face the nation's problems. Thus, while *Theme* is a film of the seventies, reflecting the nation's issues in those years, its release is a phenomenon of the eighties, which will later be discussed in more detail.

The work of another representative of the "Leningrad school," Dinara Asanova, is interesting in many respects. She was a Kirgiz who moved to Leningrad and worked at Lenfilm from the early seventies until her untimely death in 1985. Her ethnic background is not apparent in her films, as she was able to assimilate the mood and the habits of her adoptive Russian city. Her films, in fact, fit well in the frame of the "Leningrad school," with their dry, unadorned style, and their difficult questions left unanswered. Asanova's style reveals her interest in the documentary, an interest that she inherited from her teacher Mikhail Romm, and which, in 1983, manifested itself in a TV series on juvenile delinquents.

She made her debut with the film *Woodpeckers Don't Get Headaches* (*Ne bolit golova u diatla*, 1975) from a screenplay by Iuri Klepikov, who wrote most of the scripts for her subsequent films. With this first work Asanova established the theme that became a constant feature of her films— the world of adolescents, with all the uncertainty and uneasiness of a time of transition, and their troubled relations to adults. In *Woodpeckers*, Asanova focuses on the idyll of two fourteen-year-olds, their discovery of unknown feelings, their awkward behavior, their naïve happiness, their comic "serious" talks, and in the end, their all-encompassing grief. A train takes the girl away. The boy runs after it. The idyll ends, and with it, childhood. In the background, Asanova shows the adult world, self-centered and often insensitive to the adolescents' precarious state of mind. Besides providing a dramatic tension, it also provides a backdrop of unromanticized everyday reality.

The gap between generations came to the foreground in her subsequent films, and Asanova did not conceal her contention that most of the blame lies with the parents. Referring to her film *The Restricted Key*

(*Kliuch bez prava peredachi*, 1977), set in a high school and dealing with the relationships between teachers and students, she said: "At sixteen . . . the human soul is especially fragile, defenseless, it needs to be treated extremely cautiously and tactfully. . . . It is very painful to tenth-graders when they feel they are not trusted, looked down upon, patronized."[18] Following one of her favorite practices, in this film she mixed professional actors of a high caliber, such as Lidya Fedoseeva-Shukshina and Alexei Petrenko, with nonprofessional teenaged performers. During the shooting, it turned out that the young people actually imposed their own point of view, giving the film a truthful ring. This, obviously, happened with the director's blessing. According to Asanova: "We had to give them freedom. . . . This group of kids put us in a situation which excluded all lies, all taboos, even the slightest expedients which may be forgivable in a different situation."[19] Given the subject of this film, which hinges on the right to privacy versus obedience to authority and poses the question of what constitutes honesty, the attitude of the adolescents seemed to fall perfectly in line with the director's design.

Asanova had been rather outspoken about social problems even before the age of *glasnost*, and yet none of her films were shelved. She made eight films in ten years, through which she has left a portrait of a generation, puzzling in its taste for Western music and punk attire and its honest search for a new identity.

Asanova was not the only one to treat the theme of contemporary youth. The subject became a trend, sometimes attaining excellent results (for example, Sergei Solovev's *A Hundred Days after Childhood* [*Sto dnei posle detstva*, 1975]), but more often producing undistinguished films for mass consumption (for example Pavel Lyubimov's box-office success *School Waltz* [*Shkol'nyi val's*, 1979]). The trend assumed more dramatic accents in the eighties, as discussed later.

Women directors are rather scarce in Soviet cinema (as elsewhere). Educated women in Soviet society usually reach a comfortable mid-managerial level of employment but are rarely allowed to operate at the top of any industrial, cultural, or political establishments. In the film industry there are many female editors, costume designers, make-up artists, and actresses, but very few directors. Those few are, therefore, the best of the best.

Lana Gogoberidze, like Dinara Asanova, is one of those few. Before graduating from the State Film Institute she already had a background in philosophy and poetry. A Georgian working in the Tbilisi studio, she made documentary and feature films throughout the sixties and seventies. But it is with the film *Some Interviews on Personal Matters* (*Neskol'ko interv'iu po lichnym voprosam*, 1979) that she gave full expression to her talent as a director and co-screenwriter. Her previous film, *Commotion* (*Perepolokh*, 1977), had already drawn praise, although of a peculiar kind, as she ironically reports: "After viewing my film . . . a well-known director told me: 'This is your first truly manly film,' assuming that to be 'manly' is the ultimate goal of a woman's art—manly films, manly poems, manly paintings. I smiled to myself at that boundless male presumption (can you imagine the opposite case, of a woman saying to a man: 'This is your first truly womanly film'?!).''[20]

And so, *Some Interviews* is the film of a woman about a woman. The part of the protagonist, Sofiko, was written expressly for the beautiful, sensitive, intelligent Sofiko Chaurieli, who distinguished herself in numerous Georgian films, including Paradzhanov's *The Colors of the Pomegranate* (*Tsvety granata*, 1968). The fictional Sofiko is a woman in her early forties, a professional journalist, a devoted wife, a loving mother, an affectionate daughter, and an overall caring human being. She has it all, like the heroines of the many third-rate movies which exalt the woman as the keeper of family unity and as the model of civic responsibility, at the cost of her personal happiness. This detail, however, did not bother anyone because the sacrifice was presented as the ultimate virtue. But something unusual happens with Sofiko. She reaches a point where she is no longer able to reconcile all the different aspects of her life, to satisfy all the demands placed

I–1   *Some Interviews on Personal Matters (Neskol'ko interv'iu po lichnym voprosam)*

on her. One solution her husband suggests is to get a less demanding job, perhaps as a secretary. But Sofiko is not the kind of heroine willing to suppress her creativity. She can only live one kind of life, a life which involves all of herself. And so, her marriage falls apart as her husband finds himself a more convenient companion. This film, therefore, does not end with the apotheosis of the heroine, rather with a question: Who is to blame? The admirers of "manly" films would have no trouble pointing a finger at Sofiko. The script allows this presumptuous interpretation. But the camera does not. Throughout the film it conveys Sofiko's point of view, or penetrates into her inner world by closing up on her expressive, dark eyes. There is sadness and happiness in those eyes, there is compassion, curiosity, humor, disbelief, pain, but not defeat. Sofiko is a feminine creature of extraordinary strength, because she has found a solid anchor in herself. And so, who is to blame? Perhaps the habits and conventions of a society which places on the woman too many demands and expects too much from her. This point is also conveyed by the women Sofiko interviews as part of her assignment. Gogoberidze, through the journalist Sofiko, offers the viewer a fascinating and challenging gallery of women's portraits and, while focusing on "personal matters," points out a general social problem.

The director continued to focus on the woman's world view in her next film *The Day Is Longer than the Night (Den' dlinnee nochi,* 1984). Much more ambitious in scope, and aesthetically uneven, this film covers the life of the heroine from early youth to old age, tying it to half a century of recent national history.

These films reflect a general thematic trend. Since the early seventies, short stories and novels about women have become more and more frequent. The press started debating women's issues, mostly concerning the double workload women had to carry—on the job and at home—and the problems connected with shopping hours, queues, and poor service. By the middle of the decade the "woman theme" in film became fashionable. The titles were worded to appeal to the masses: *A Sweet Woman (Sladkaia zhenshchina,* by V. Fetin, 1977), *A Young Wife (Molodaia zhena,* by L. Menaker, 1979), *A Strange Woman (Strannaia zhenshchina,* by Iu. Raizman, 1978), *The Wife Has Left (Zhena ushla,* by Dinara Asanova, 1980). Most of these films focused on the psychology of the new woman, independent and self-sufficient, and the way her new status affected the traditional woman/man relationship. While simplistic films offered simplistic solutions, films like *A Strange Woman* and *The Wife Has Left* raised troubling questions. Are independence and love incompatible? What is the role of the man? Is woman going to find happiness within herself? Other films without the specific "woman trend" touched on the same problems. For example, *Five Evenings (Piat' vecherov,* 1979) and *Kinfolk (Rodnia,* 1982), both by Nikita Mikhalkov, reflect women's material responsibilities and spiritual frustration.

Historical Dramas and Literary Classics

At the opposite pole from the *bytovoy* pictures, historical periods and exotic settings were prominent in the seventies. Some of the most popular films in this category were foreign imports from India, which excited the popular imagination, especially in the provinces, with inflated tales of love, death, magic, and heroic pursuits. The national production displayed a more serious approach to the genre. Nikita Mikhalkov, who had been acting in film since the early sixties, made his debut as a director in 1975 with the film *At Home among Strangers, Stranger at Home (Svoi sredi chuzhikh, chuzhoi sredi svoikh)* which, after the "spaghetti Western" attribution of worldwide fame, can aptly be called a "pirozhki Western." Unlike other Westerns, however, here train robberies, horseback chases, and shootouts are set against the backdrop of the Reds and Whites in the Civil War. Mikhalkov himself plays the main role in a duster and hat à la Clint Eastwood. Mikhalkov's second film, *A Slave of Love (Raba liubvi*, 1976), is set in the same period and, like the previous one, indulges in playing with cinematic genres. The self-reflexivity of genre is here even more explicit, since this film, in a Felliniesque vein, portrays the shooting of the silent melodrama, *"A Slave of Love."* But filmmaking is not the only concern of Mikhalkov, who intermingles with the melodrama the political events of the day—the conquest of the Crimea by the Red Army—and the tragic destinies of the protagonists. Because of a construction *en abîme* (a film within a film) the boundary between illusion and reality is blurred and, in the end, it is not possible to rely on facile assumptions.

Mikhalkov moved slightly back in time with his third film, *Unfinished Piece for a Player Piano (Neokonchennaia p'esa dlia mekhanicheskogo pianino*, 1977). The basis for the script was Chekhov's play *Platonov*, which lent the film the decadent atmosphere of a collapsing culture.[21] Disregarding class ideology, Mikhalkov transferred to the screen the neuroses of an aristocratic and *nouveau riche* milieu which were relevant to the upper circles of contemporary Soviet society. What the director emphasized was the spiritual bankruptcy and isolation of every character. The disintegration of society as a meaningful agglomerate was conveyed by placing particular emphasis on group games as an illusory means of keeping the social fabric together. But what is particularly important to Mikhalkov is neurotic alienation as a direct consequence of estrangement from nature and gradual identification with the machine. The player piano, with its mechanical, soulless performance, is obviously the central metaphor of the film. This theme recurs in *Some Days in the Life of I. I. Oblomov (Neskol'ko dnei iz zhizni I. I. Oblomova*, 1980). The film is based on excerpts from the novel by Ivan Goncharov, *Oblomov* (1859), which raised heated debate among contemporary critics, and whose protagonist became, in Russian radical criticism, the quintessential example of the "superfluous man."[22] Mikhalkov, rather than following the official negative interpretation of Oblomov as the product of a parasitic aristocratic country estate, stresses his child-like poetic nature, his inclination toward daydreaming, his ties with nature and with the feminine life principle—the mother. By contrast, maleness, energy, progress, productivity, and technology are attributes of Oblomov's childhood friend, Andrei Stoltz. Born of a German father, Stoltz has inherited these "non-Russian" features, which were hailed by the progressive socialist critics of the past century, but are looked upon with apprehension by Mikhalkov's post-positivist, post-Stalinist generation.

A film with a vast historical background, *Siberiade (Sibiriada, 1979)*, was made by Mikhalkov's older brother, Andrei Mikhalkov-Konchalovsky. An outspoken sustainer of the "American model" both in terms of filmmaking and marketing techniques, Konchalovsky wanted to produce an epic with popular appeal. The film did very well at the box office. Then, suddenly, it was withdrawn from circulation when Konchalovsky traveled to the West and rumors began that he was going to defect.[23]

Siberiade, first conceived as the story of the development of Siberian oil wells, turned into a much more complex work, intertwining history and fiction. This "cine-epos" covers the events connected with the lives of two families in a small Siberian village, from the beginning of the century through the sixties. The major historical events that shook the nation are presented in select documentary inserts, which introduce the fictional episodes as, so to speak, epigraphs. Besides chronicling half a century of the country's history, the film also raises questions of universal significance, as vast as the scope of the epos. These are questions about the eternal struggle of man against nature—man's drive to conquer and nature's power to annihilate, man's suffering and nature's impassivity, and most of all (as metaphorically conveyed by the character of Afanasy) man's irrepressible need to cut a road through the wilderness for no other reason than to pursue a dream.

Many historical films did not score high marks despite the efforts of reputable directors of the old guard, such as Sergei Iutkevich who made *Lenin in Paris (Lenin v Parizhe, 1981)* with all sorts of "poetic" embellishments. However, worthy of mention in the historical category is Elem Klimov's *Rasputin (Agoniia, 1975)*, which was released only in 1984. The version that has been circulated in the USSR and abroad was drastically cut, and it is, therefore, difficult to judge the film with fairness. What remains is a glimpse of the Romanov family and their empire on the verge of collapse. The film offers an intriguing portrait of the two main figures, Rasputin and Tsar Nicholas, who, according to the original plan, would have functioned as each other's doubles. As the film stands, this point is unfortunately lost.

World War II Films

Films about World War II have been the staple of Soviet cinema since the early forties. So many pictures have been made on this theme that they soon constituted a genre with its own peculiar conventions. The treatment of war changed over the years in the works of a few creative directors who ran against the conventions of the genre. The turning point came at the beginning of the sixties when there developed a new sensibility for the personal lives of human beings caught in the war catastrophe. Nevertheless, dozens of conventional and insufferably flat war movies continued to be made throughout the seventies. One exception was a film by Larisa Shepitko, *Ascent* (*Voskhozhdenie*, 1977)—a stylized parable heavy with biblical metaphors. Here, the war situation is used to test the moral stamina of the protagonist. The logic of the film, and the implacable will of the director, require that the protagonist ascend his "Golgotha" in order to restore mankind's hope in spiritual rebirth. Although rather obvious in its symbolism, this film has been acclaimed by both domestic and foreign critics.

The best war movies of the seventies undoubtedly belong to Alexei German, whose latest film *My Friend Ivan Lapshin* (*Moi drug Ivan Lapshin*, 1983; released in 1985) finally revealed him to be one of the most brilliant and innovative directors of his generation. German made only two films in the seventies, *Trial on the Road* (*Proverka na dorogakh*, 1971; released in 1986), based on motifs from the war stories of his father Iuri German, and *Twenty Days without War* (*Dvadtsat' dnei bez voiny*, 1976), loosely adapted from a novel by a classic author of Soviet literature, Konstantin Simonov. Only the second film was released upon completion, and therefore German remained virtually unknown among the public-at-large until now. However, with that one film he already caught the attention of the critics.[24]

Although made in the early seventies, *Trial on the Road* belongs in a discussion of the past ten years of Soviet cinema because of its recent release and also because it shows German's progression toward his latest brilliant achievement. The time is the winter of 1942; the setting, a Nazi-controlled region in northwestern Russia. Sergeant Lazarev (played by V. Zamansky), a POW suspected of having been a collaborator with the Nazis, lets himself be captured by a partisan division (as his name suggests, he comes back from the "dead"). As a reformed traitor, he must undergo several tests of courage and loyalty in order to win the trust of the officers and his comrades-in-arms. The leadership is represented by two officers whose opposite world views constantly clash and provide the plot's dramatic tension. The stiff-necked Major, played with cold precision by the gifted (now deceased) Anatoly Solonitsyn, is a fanatical doctrinaire who places ideology above human lives, while the commander of the partisan division, played with compassion and a touch of humor by

I–2   *My Friend Ivan Lapshin (Moi drug Ivan Lapshin)*

I–3   *Trial on the Road (Proverka na dorogakh)*

Rolan Bykov (one of the audience favorites), is a simple man who relies on basic human feelings rather than military rules. After several trials and humiliations, Lazarev finally redeems himself in a hyperbolic war-action sequence, where he single-handedly guns down a detachment of Germans and dies in the process. Clearly, the censors objected to the unconventional treatment of the protagonist—the "traitor" turned "hero." This was a bold violation of the Soviet narrative canons, which showed German to be an innovator even in those early days. However, the style of the film does not match the boldness of its conception. German still uses the traditional stylistic devices of the Soviet war genre, albeit applied to unorthodox characters and situations. The director at that time had not yet found his true cinematic language.

With his second film, *Twenty Days without War*, German leaves the combat zone to concentrate on the lives of ordinary people in the rear. By moving away from the war, he also moves away from the rhetoric of the genre and displays an admirably restrained realistic style. It is December 1942. The newspaper correspondent Lopatin (Iu. Nikulin), on a roundabout route to the Caucasus front, stops in Tashkent, an evacuation point overcrowded with war refugees. There he has a brief and meaningful affair. It is a fleeting encounter of two human beings brought together and soon separated by the cataclysm of war. Contrary to the melodramatics of the genre, this encounter is devoid of the fateful overtones which typically bear on the destinies of lovers. In German's film, the encounter is a serene pause in a difficult journey, a poor but hospitable refuge to share the intimacy of each other's bodies and feelings. To avoid trite sentimentality, the camera maintains a controlled detachment throughout the film. One example is the scene of the morning after, where the two lovers are enjoying a chat over a cup of tea, containing their sadness with laughter before saying good-bye, and the camera discretely remains outside, watching them through the window panes and preventing the viewer from overhearing their conversation. Another example is the scene on the train, where Lopatin meets a pilot who tells him a long and melodramatic story of love and betrayal, involving himself, his wife, another man, and an illegitimate child. The story has all the elements of an ordinary tearjerker, and that is what it would have been, had German exploited it cinematically. But he did not. The pilot pronounces his monologue in a static close-up of ten minutes' duration. The melodramatic effect is destroyed, and by dint of the interview-type shot the story acquires a ring of verisimilitude. After all, melodramatic stories do happen in real life; they only look unreal when placed within certain narrative conventions.[25]

On his journey Lopatin meets many victims of the war who share with him their personal tragedies, thus weaving the canvas of a larger common tragedy. The gloomy picture of life on the home front, shot in greyish tones and from neutral angles, is contrasted to Lopatin's visit to a movie set where they are shooting a typical war film of the period, imbued with phony heroism. The juxtaposition of the two styles makes a statement both about true heroism and true cinema. This introduces the theme of the interplay of reality and illusion which is central to German's next film, *Ivan Lapshin*.

The "Poetic" Film

Several films with a tendency toward lyricism and a highly metaphorical style left a mark on the sixties and continued to be produced in the seventies, although on a smaller scale. Their structure, based on analogical images rather than narrative logic, resembled that of a poem. In fact, this trend was known as the "poetic school." It was also characterized as the "archaic school," because these films were often based on folk tales and legends. The directors belonging to this school were mostly from the Caucasus or the Ukraine, and regarded themselves as the heirs to Alexander Dovzhenko and the "poetic" style of his early films. Among them were the controversial Sergei Paradzhanov,[26] himself an Armenian but occasionally working at the Ukrainian studios named after Dovzhenko (*Shadows of Our Forgotten Ancestors* [*Teni nashikh zabytykh predkov*, 1965], *The Colors of the Pomegranate*, and most recently, *The Legend of the Surami Fortress* [*Legenda o Suramskoi kreposti*, 1984; released in 1986]); the Ukrainian Iuri Ilenko (*On the Eve of Ivan Kupala* [*Vecher na kanune Ivana Kupaly*, 1969] and *White Bird with a Black Mark* [*Belaia ptitsa s chernoi otmetinoi*, 1972]); the Georgian Tengiz Abuladze (*The Prayer* [*Mol'ba*, 1969] and *The Tree of Desire* [*Drevo zhelaniia*, 1978]); and later Otar Ioseliani, also from Georgia (*Pastorale* [*Pastoral'*, 1977]) and the Kirgiz Bolotbek Shamshiev (*The White Ship* [*Belyi parakhod*, 1977]). These films were never box-office successes, though they were highly regarded among cinema connoisseurs. Some critics expressed deep appreciation, but others attacked them in the press for being "difficult" and self-indulgent. As a consequence, those directors were only allowed to make a few films over the years.

Such was the case with Andrei Tarkovsky, who may be regarded as a northern offshoot of the poetic school. The poetic elements clearly present in his early film, *Andrei Rublev* (1965), came to full bloom in his movies of the seventies, *Mirror* (*Zerkalo*, 1975) and *Stalker* (1980). *Mirror* reflects the director's search into his childhood for those fragments of experience which determined the course of his life. Memory brings into focus disconnected episodes, events out of chronological sequence, flashes of relationships charged with intense emotion, or simply visual and aural impressions. Recurrent images and poetry on the soundtrack (by Tarkovsky's father) connect the protagonist's childhood to his adult life. The same actress (Margarita Terekhova) plays both the role of the young mother and later the wife, while Tarkovsky's real mother (M. Vishniakova) appears briefly at the end of the film. This poetic autobiogra-

phy conveys the inner world of the child in relation to the surrounding
reality—the parents' divorce, the hardships of war, life in the countryside, the mother's struggle for economic and political survival—as well as
the effect of the child's experience on the adult protagonist. Tarkovsky
fills his *Mirror* with a delicate canvas of aesthetic images and human emotions which both challenge and fascinate the viewer. Actually, the director himself was not totally pleased with the result, judging by the following interview:

> Many think that *Mirror* is my favorite film. But it's not my very favorite. . . .
> It was very difficult to make it, almost impossible to edit it. . . . I had to make
> nineteen versions of the editing, each one fundamentally different from the
> others, where each episode was moved back and forth before we achieved
> a satisfactory version. . . . To me *Mirror* is too motley a picture to say it ex-
> presses my aesthetic taste.

For his next film Tarkovsky found different formal solutions, as he stated
in that same interview: "In *Stalker* . . . it seems to me that I achieved a sim-
pler form, asceticism as a narrative form."[27]

We have to agree with Tarkovsky's statement, especially in view of the future developments of his "ascetic" style, which matured through *Nostalgia* (1983) and achieved the perfection of a Japanese haiku in his last
film, *The Sacrifice* (*Zhertvoprinoshenie*, 1986). These two films do not belong to the history of Soviet cinema. They were made abroad and are connected with Tarkovsky's last few years of painful exile and fatal illness.[28]
A few words about *Stalker*, however, must be added to point out the
main theme that runs through most of Tarkovsky's films: the discrepancy between the spiritual and the material in the human being. The director's
main concern is moral as well as philosophical. Tarkovsky goes beyond
questions of ethical behavior to touch on the deeper problem of the spiritual essence of the human being. The protagonists of his films are engaged in a quest for a return to a state of grace, a recovery of the soul
that was suffocated by matter. The Stalker is one of those marked crea-
tures, blessed with a special sensibility (fools in Christ, or "poets"), that allows them to find the path to the hidden truth—the essence of things beyond their material appearance. The Stalker feels that he has a mission to
help mankind achieve the ultimate vision. The characters in the film are
symbolic of three states of mind: the Stalker as the visionary, the Professor as the positivist, and the Writer as the skeptic. The action is a metaphoric voyage through a dangerous and mysterious "zone" filled with the
material debris of our civilization, in order to reach the Chamber of Desires where the pilgrims would have their most intimate wishes fulfilled.
Eventually, the mission fails because the Professor and the Writer do not undertake the quest with a pure heart, and are unable to enter the Chamber. The film ends with the Stalker crushed by failure. But a final note of

hope is conveyed by the Stalker's daughter, whose glance is so powerful as to be able to impress a kinetic force on inanimate objects (an allusion to the "kino" artist?). *Stalker* was based on a science-fiction story by the brothers Strugatsky, but Tarkovsky departed from the genre and created a philosophical parable of stunning visual beauty.

The Ecological Theme

A major figure in the cinema as well as the literature of the early seventies was Vasily Shukshin (deceased in 1974). First popular as a movie actor, he then had a large following as a writer and film director. His best films—*Strange People (Strannye liudi,* 1970); *Shop Crumbs (Pechki-lavochki,* 1973); *The Red Guelder Rose (Kalina krasnaia,* 1974)—are based on his own stories. As a writer, Shukshin belonged to the trend of so-called "country prose," whose practitioners look at village life as an alternative to the loss of traditional values and spirituality caused by the big city. Their lifestyles, based on natural life cycles and folk rituals, are opposed to the dehumanizing effects of technology. Himself from a Siberian village, Shukshin transferred to the screen the thrust of his books, which emphasized going back to the roots in search of the real man. He did so in an unconventional style with many suggestive images and ingenious camera work. His film *The Red Guelder Rose,* the only one which has been widely seen abroad, was extremely popular in the USSR and won the *Soviet Screen* contest for 1974. It tells the story of an ex-convict (played by Shukshin himself) who, after serving time, goes back to his native village in order to cleanse his spirit of urban corruption. Eventually he is hunted down by his old gang and killed. Notwithstanding the unhappy ending and the symbolic style, Soviet audiences sympathized with the protagonist's longing for spiritual rebirth. His tormented soul-searching is all the more poignant as it is set against a backdrop of petty bureaucrats and indolent workers.

Close to Shukshin's works because of the ecological theme is the film *Farewell (Proshchanie,* 1982), completed by Elem Klimov after the tragic death of Larisa Shepitko, who initiated the project. Loosely based on a novel by the "country prose" writer Valentin Rasputin, *Farewell* is a moral-philosophical tale concerned with the biological (and sacred) ties between the human being and the place he calls home. The film has practically no plot. The action consists of the evacuation of the small island of Matyora, which, according to government plan, is going to be flooded to create a water reservoir. We are again confronted with the dilemma of industrial progress disrupting the natural environment. But the film does not pretend to offer a solution, or even to argue against the advancement of civilization. Its purpose is to focus on the other side, to show the villagers who live not *on* the island but *together with it.* With a stylistic restraint which defies the facile idealization of the peasant, Klimov conveys the organic, and at the same time reverent, relation of the people to the land (Daria praying in the woods), the water (the ritual of communal bathing in the lake), the house (Daria washing and decorating her room). Conversely, he puts more dramatic pathos in the scenes depicting the violence perpetrated on the land (the furious attack on the "tree of life" by the driver of the bulldozer). *Farewell* is ultimately a film about death. Whether it is justified in the name of progress, the flooding of Matyora is shown in the last sequence as the entombment of life under a still, cold, marble-like, black liquid expanse.

THE YEARS OF TRANSITION, 1983–1984

When the Brezhnev era came to an end it seemed that the country was headed for a period of moral and economic regeneration. Brezhnev's demise was expected and the new leadership had been positioning itself for at least a year.[29] The new General Secretary, Iuri Andropov, an enigmatic, ascetic man with the methods of a KGB chief and the mind of an intellectual, was quick to crack down on corruption and privilege. Many heads fell, including some that were very close to the Brezhnev family.[30] Andropov sought to renew Party and government cadres, at the highest as well as the lowest levels, and to inject energy and purpose into the stagnating economy. The country was at a turning point. Economic indicators were alarming, due in part to American punitive measures, and in part to another disastrous harvest, the fourth in a row. Furthermore, the war in Afghanistan, the Polish engagement, and other foreign misadventures were draining financial resources needed for domestic use. A new elite of technocrats, economists, and intellectuals was painfully aware of the current situation and looked to Andropov for leadership. The other two main sustainers of the new leader were the KGB, which Andropov had refurbished and brought to a new level of sophistication, and the armed forces. As a measure of social uplift, Andropov promoted campaigns against alcoholism, petty theft, and black marketeering, and encouraged discussions of these problems in the press. While censorship was firmly maintained in the arts, a movement towards constructive social criticism was favored. Cinema picked up on this trend, and the most notable films of those years fell within these parameters.

When speaking of the period of transition, we cannot strictly rely on chronology because films which appeared in 1983 had to have been started at least a year earlier, before Andropov. Conversely, films planned under Andropov came out in 1984, when Chernenko was already trying to turn the clock back to the ways of the old regime. Nevertheless, Chernenko had little impact on cultural life. The films discussed here, therefore, characterize the end of the Brezhnev era and the dawning of a new period which later acquired more defined features under Gorbachev.

The Underground Economy

Cinema turned its attention to the underground economy and offered the audience a gallery of portraits of a new social type: the enterprising middleman, or, depending on the point of view, the black market profiteer. The film that anticipated this trend was *Train Station for Two (Vokzal dlia dvoikh*, 1983), by Ryazanov and Braginsky. Extremely popular, and mostly well-received by the critics, the film introduced black marketeering as a secondary motif. The focus of the story is on the encounter between a provincial waitress (interpreted by Liudmila Gurchenko, unfailingly good in all her roles) and an intellectual from the big city (played by Oleg Basilashvili, the protagonist of *Autumn Marathon*). Both have serious problems with their lives and eventually find in each other love, compassion, mutual support, and the hope for improvement. The sentimental strand was responsible for the film's success. Nevertheless, like all of Ryazanov's works, this was a comedy (perhaps a tragi-comedy, as it was called in the Soviet press) with biting satirical elements. The action unfolds in a railroad station, a symbol for transitoriness, disorderly life, superficial relations, vagrancy, underground deals—in a word, anarchy. In that railroad station, it seems, social rules and the moral imperative are no longer operative. The target of the satire is a train conductor, masterfully played by Nikita Mikhalkov with the cocky self-assurance of a successful rogue. He has established a profitable (and illegal) cantaloupe trade with the help of the waitress from the station

I–4   *Train Station for Two (Vokzal dlia dvoikh)*

café. When the train arrives from the south, the flamboyant macho conductor dumps a couple of suitcases full of cantaloupes on his waitress and even manages hurriedly to enjoy her favors in an empty compartment. This half-willing, half-misguided woman eventually finds a way out of the demeaning situation through her encounter with a gentle and sensitive man, himself the victim of unfortunate circumstances. Because of a car accident caused by his wife—a materialistic woman representative of the *nouveau riche* mentality—he is serving time in a penal colony, and is, in fact, hurrying back to prison after a brief leave. The penal colony setting, with its rules, rigidity, law and order, conformism, and discipline is a metaphorical opposite to the train station; both are seen as dehumanizing environments. Between is the private space of the two lovers, where they find the spiritual nourishment necessary to their survival.

Several films subsequently picked up on the rogue theme and offered an interesting social commentary, however superficial and wanting on the artistic side. Among them, *The Blonde Girl Around the Corner* (*Blondinka za uglom*, 1984), directed by Vladimir Bortko, tells the story of a pretty and frivolous food shop clerk who affords a life of affluence by privately trading state-owned groceries. Viktor Tregubovich's *A Rogue's Saga* (*Prokhindiada*, 1984) is a satirical "epic poem" about the modern rogue. An amiable wheeler-dealer, an energetic, hard-working entrepreneur, he neglects his regular job in order to pursue his private business of trading favors, establishing connections, and providing services— placing someone's son in graduate school in exchange for a vacation on the Black Sea, in exchange for a role on stage, in exchange for a good deal on a car, and so on. As a result, he lives "above his salary," which means that his apartment is a consumer goods showcase. To press their case against the swindler (who, by the way, is able technically not to break the law, but to operate on the edges), the film's authors suggest a parallel with the prototype of all Russian rogues: Chichikov from Gogol's *Dead Souls*.[31] Like Chichikov, who evades his chasers in a flying troika, our contemporary speeds away in his white Mercedes and vanishes into thin air.

A similar character is the protagonist of *Sincerely Yours . . .* (*Iskrenne vash . . .* , 1985), by a woman director, Alla Surikova. The character's personality, the comedy situations, the consumeristic paradises, the bonanza of imported clothes and electronic gear, the petty concerns of a materialistic society—all of these are characteristic of the rogue trend. However, we must note that in all these films the rogue is a person of medium social status, an average citizen in no position of power. The causes for the social malaise—the inefficiency of the economic system itself and the self-serving attitude of Party and government functionaries—are not discussed. The films simply show alarming symptoms, leaving it to the viewer to figure out the causes and the cure. Obviously, the filmmakers were testing the new parameters of censorship, and, at the same time, pushing for their expansion.

To soften the critical discourse and to make it more acceptable, many filmmakers added to their films elements of the fantastic. The extent of this practice led Soviet critics to develop a new term with which to characterize these films: "social fiction" (*sotsial'naia fantastika*), analogous to "science fiction" (*nauchnaia fantastika*). The fantastic element may be more or less prominent in certain films (*The Blonde Girl* and *A Rogue's Saga* both have "fantastic" endings), but is rarely absent. In *One of a Kind* (*Unikum*, directed by Vitaly Melnikov, 1985), an employee of a scientific research center discovers that he has the mental power to transmit his dreams; he goes into show business, so to speak, and establishes a profitable enterprise selling his dreams to a sleeping audience.

One of the best achievements in this genre is the film by Eldar Shengelaia, *Blue Mountains, or An Improbable Story* (*Golubye gory, ili Nepravdopodobnaia istoriia*, 1985). The "improbable story" occurs in an unidentified institution (a publishing house, a magazine's headquarters?) where extremely busy employees attend to their business with meticulous scrupulousness day after day. Unfortunately their business is not the same as the institution's. They study French, grind coffee, knit, play chess, or

I–5 *Blue Mountains (Golubye gory, ili Nepravdopodobnaia istoriia)*

run between absorbing activities taking place elsewhere. As a result, the young writer who submits his manuscript, "Blue Mountains," has to wait a year, only to learn that the manuscript has been lost. In the end, because of neglect, the institution's building collapses on the heads of its oblivious staff. No one is hurt (after all, this is a fantastic story), and the institution is moved to a modern building of glass and concrete. There everything is new—except for the institute's operations, which resume their usual activities—knitting, coffee grinding, chess playing, French spelling, etc.

The fantastic in this film extends beyond the narrative level. It is also conveyed through a style which is hyperbolic in its realism of detail. The discrepancy between the hyperrealism of the environment and the triviality of the action attains a level of absurdity. The institution becomes an empty shell, and the characters become grotesque masks without souls.

Outside the realm of the fantastic, but within the trend of social criticism, is the winner of the popularity contest for the year 1984. Once again, it was a film by Eldar Ryazanov, *A Ruthless Romance (Zhestokii romans)*, which is based on the nineteenth-century play by A. Ostrovsky, *Without a Dowry*. The merchant milieu, materially rich but spiritually poor, served Ryazanov well as a parallel to certain circles of the contemporary Soviet "bourgeoisie." But the audience was probably attracted by the tragic destiny of the heroine, who succumbs to the requirements of a tyrannical environment and to the romantic glamour of a refined swindler (another superb interpretation by Nikita Mikhalkov).

To a certain extent the film *Vassa* (1983), by Gleb Panfilov, belongs to the same genre, inasmuch as it is about an industrialist's family of the early twentieth century and is based on the play *Vassa Zheleznova*, by Maksim Gorky. However, as in all of Panfilov's films, the figure of the heroine here is strong and positive. Notwithstanding the fact that she is the representative of the capitalist world on the verge of collapse, she fulfills her destiny with dignity and responsibility.

Chamber Films

Corruption and disillusionment in public life had a counterpart in films concerned with personal problems, family, and love. The peculiar themes of the so-called "chamber films" are reflected in titles such as *Private Life (Chastnaia zhizn'*, directed by Iuli Raizman, 1983) and *Without Witnesses (Bez svidetelei*, directed by Nikita Mikhalkov, 1983). The former is about an executive going into retirement and discovering his true self through closer contact with his family; the latter, about a divorced husband who visits his ex-wife and engages her in a bitter confrontation in order to gain psychological revenge.

Another film by Iuli Raizman, *Time of Desires (Vremia zhelanii*, 1984), is interesting as a sequel to the "woman films" of a few years earlier. The character type epitomized by the heroines of *Strange Woman* (also by Raizman) and *Moscow Does Not Believe in Tears* (Vera Alentova played the leading role in both *Moscow* and *Time of Desires*), independent but romantically disposed and seeking a true love relationship, has turned into a practical, efficient, energetic provider of material comfort, a woman of useful connections, whose aim is to fit her own and her husband's lives into the fashionable mold of her desires—needless to say, with catastrophic consequences.

Quite different in tone are the films of Petr Todorovsky, *Waiting for Love (Liubimaia zhenshchina mekhanika Gavrilova,* 1983) and *A Wartime Romance (Voenno-polevoi roman,* 1984). These are delightfully unpretentious comedies, humorous and touching at the same time. A *sui generis* "chamber film" was *Success (Uspekh,* 1984), by Konstantin Khudiakov, telling the story of a strong-willed stage director possessed by a fanatic dedication to the theater and determined to achieve artistic perfection at all costs—even at the cost of trampling on human feelings.

The film *Look Back (Oglianis',* 1984), by Aida Manasarova, touches on the specific problem of the generation gap. More precisely, it portrays the drama of a mother whose teenage son has turned into an egotistical monster full of repressed fury. Although the film hints at the causes for the young man's troubles by vaguely suggesting that the mother in earlier years did not give her infant son enough love and attention, it finally seems to exonerate her because of her suffering and honest efforts to correct her mistakes. The viewer is left without a solution and with the uneasy feeling that a young life will be wasted.

The Problem of Youth

The issue of difficult youth, and often of outright juvenile delinquency, once a theme to be avoided, was singled out by the press in the early eighties as one of the main social problems to be addressed without delay. Newspapers, especially in the provinces, frequently reported stories of brutality among teenagers and showed that juvenile delinquency was on the rise. Both the stage and the screen reflected this trend.[32]

One film that had a vast following all over the country, but also raised a chorus of indignant protests, was *Scarecrow (Chuchelo,* 1984) by Rolan Bykov, a veteran actor eventually turned director. *Scarecrow* tells the story of a twelve-year-old girl, Lena Bessoltseva, who becomes the target of her schoolmates' vicious attacks. Because of a banal incident she is unjustly accused of having betrayed the group, and after a period of ostracism and psychological abuse she is burned at the stake, in effigy. The metaphor of the burning dummy, with Lena watching it, is more eloquent of her suffering than any scene of explicit violence. Bykov probes an issue which is often hidden behind a neat facade of respectability. In this film the setting is a small provincial river town, with its pretty old houses, a church, a model school. It is, in fact, a tourist attraction. The school children look as neat and pretty as the surrounding environment, but under the surface they hide disquieting personalities. They have a tendency to act as a collective, no doubt instilled by official education and upbringing and aggravated by the disintegration of the family. This would not be a bad thing per se, except that this collective, in order to have a *raison d'être*, needs a victim to hate and torment.

Thus, besides denouncing a current youth problem, this film carries deeper implications. Artistically woven into its texture is the idea that the collective can become a tyrant. In this teenager microcosm one can observe familiar patterns of denunciation, purge, demagoguery, lack of moral stamina, and loss of individual integrity typical of behavior that, although most prominent in the Stalinist years, is not completely obsolete. One image that functions as a metaphorical link between past and present is that of the marching band. The omnipresent bands of the thirties used to play their martial tunes in parks, city squares, workers' clubs, steamboats, train stations, and every other public place, in order to lift the people's morale and cover up the drab reality of the day with a cheerful note of optimism. In *Scarecrow*, the marching band, with its smart uniforms and shining brass, blends well with the rest of the neat town's facade. One would hardly notice it, were it not for its conductor. Bykov himself makes a brief appearance in this role, and his simple expression of embarrassment and shame at performing the usual upbeat tune upon Lena's final departure, provides the viewer with the key to the entire film.

Another great success was the film by Dinara Asanova *Tough Kids* (*Patsany*, 1983). Based on real-life episodes and characters (Asanova eventually turned her research materials into a documentary for television), this film is set in a correctional institute, more precisely a summer camp for male teenage offenders. The camp director, Pavel Antonov (simply Pasha to the boys), rejects abstract pedagogical principles in favor of spontaneous human relations. In other words, he believes that his young friends can be reformed not through regulations, but through love and understanding. He establishes a big-brother relationship with each of the boys and pursues his mission with total dedication. Eventually, the experiment fails when the kids suddenly go on a rampage of violence and vandalism.

One of the merits of Asanova's films is that they never idealize heroes or vilify villains. Pasha is neither a saint nor a guru, just a decent man with strengths and weaknesses. His weakness, in fact, is brought into focus when he vents his rage and frustration on the youths for having failed him. In a dramatic scene, where the boys—sincerely sorry for their deeds of the previous night—come to Pasha to apologize, he repeatedly shouts at them in a crescendo of fury: "I will *not* forgive you!" In the end, it is clear that Pasha will not give up his mission. But it is also clear that he is shaken and does not have any concrete answers. Thus, the film raises once more the problem of the generation gap, and poses the ques-

I–6   *Tough Kids (Patsany)*

tion of how to reach out to youth and reestablish the missing link.

Asanova's next and last film, *Dear, Dearest, Beloved . . . (Milyi, doro-goi, liubimyi, edinstvennyi . . . ,* 1984),[33] touches on the same problem, but in a different setting and mood. This film was not as popular as *Tough Kids* because of its "difficult" structure—allusions, innuendoes, bits and pieces of information that the viewer had to reorganize in order to make sense of the story. One can even say that the film borders on "social fiction," given the absurd (and yet, totally believable) mind set of the young heroine. A nineteen-year-old, in the eccentric attire of the latest counter-culture fad, holding an infant in her arms, jumps into the car of a stranger and asks him to "rescue" her. The driver, a good-natured fellow a generation older, is taken by surprise and willing to help. Driving around Leningrad in the course of the night, he tries to establish a dialogue with the young woman. He wants to understand her problems, to assist her and the baby. But all he gets is a confused story about her "dear, dearest, beloved" who kicked her out of the house. Ultimately, it turns out that she is being chased by the police for having stolen the baby from another woman. Her motive? To blackmail her estranged lover by having him believe that the baby was their own. The kind "rescuer" (played by Valery Premykhov, who also played Pasha in *Tough Kids* and wrote the script for this film) in the end is totally baffled and, while discussing the incident at the police station, he offers the audience a question to ponder:

What can I teach them? You, yourself, do you understand anything about these . . . kids? For me this is the first time I have run into one of them. Who are they? What do they want? Before, when there was famine around, they engaged in theft, vandalism . . . this can be understood, justified. But now, what do they want? Do you, yourself, know?[34]

Asanova does not pretend to know what they want, but in the course of the film she suggests what is wanting: a family environment, loving parents, and the transmission of values—all things that the pitiful heroine of this story did not get.[35]

Escapism and Politics

To balance the serious genres engaged in social criticism, the Soviet audiences were offered a good number of light musicals. Some of them were bound to be popular in spite of weak plots and poor production values, simply because they featured celebrities from the musical world. Among them were *Don't Get Married, Girls (Ne khodite devki zamuzh,* directed by Evgeny Gerasimov, 1985), with the pop singer Valery Leontiev, and *I Came to Talk (Prishla i govoriu,* directed by N. Ardashnikov, 1985), with the rock queen Alla Pugacheva. Others had more substance and were made with taste and ingenuity; for example, the films of Karen Shakhnazarov, *Jazzman (My iz dzhaza,* 1983) and *A Winter Evening in Gagra (Zimnii vecher v Gagrakh,* 1985).[36]

Escapist, but with a clear political slant, was a series of movies belonging to the detective genre. In the early eighties, when the period of international detente came to an end, the Soviet leadership intensified anti-Western propaganda (anti-American, in particular) in the mass media and in film. This marked the beginning of a new trend which exploited the entertainment value of the detective genre borrowed from the West, while presenting an image of the West that suited the current political mood. And so, the audience got a taste of James-Bondism Soviet style, with less explicit violence and no sex, but with enough intrigue, chases, stunts, and karate chops to please the popular taste. Eloquent examples of this genre are *Unmarked Freight (Gruz bez markirovki,* directed by V. Popkov, 1985), *Cancan in English Garden (Kankan v Angliiskom Parke,* directed by V. Pidpalyi, 1985),[37] *Two Versions of One Accident (Dve versii odnogo stolkno veniia,* directed by V. Novak, 1985), *European Story (Evropeiskaia istoriia,* directed by Igor Gostev, 1984), and the television series *TASS Is Authorized to Announce (TASS upolnomochen zaiavit',* directed by Valery Fokin, 1984).[38]

Less adventurous but just as propagandistic were the films *We Accuse (My obviniaem,* directed by T. Levchuk, 1985), a dramatization of the trial of the American pilot, Gary Powers, in the sixties; and *Flight 222 (Reis 222,* directed by Sergei Mikaelian, 1985), based on a real-life incident involving a Soviet ballerina who, upon departure from New York, was detained by the Immigration Service, together with an Aeroflot jet full of passengers, in order to ascertain whether she was going back of her own will. As expected, in these films the Americans are the villains. However, one must note that the targets of Soviet criticism are generally government officials or people somewhat connected with the "military-industrial complex." Not infrequently, the average American citizen comes across as a good fellow, although naïve and misguided. On balance, the Hollywood producers of recent hits have concocted a much more monstrous image of the enemy.[39]

The Abdrashitov-Mindadze Team

The works of Vadim Abdrashitov (director) and Alexander Mindadze (screenwriter) do not fall neatly into any of the trends discussed above. Both Georgian but working at Mosfilm, Abdrashitov and Mindadze have been collaborating for ten years and their co-signature has always been a guarantee of aesthetic achievement and moral commitment. Their early films include *Speech for the Defense* (*Slovo dlia zashchity*, 1977), *The Turning Point* (*Povorot*, 1979), and *Fox Hunt* (*Okhota na lis*, 1980). Each in its own way is concerned with the protagonist's sudden awareness of a reality that transcends the illusory world of social conventions. The consequences of the awakening are not pleasant, as the individual in question is alienated from what was previously his/her own environment.

This theme has remained a constant in more recent films, such as *The Train Stopped* (*Ostanovilsia poezd*, 1982). Here, an investigator pursuing the causes of a train accident struggles to break through a shield of lies and indifference in the working community where the accident occurred. The search for the truth becomes the focal point of his life, but he has to give up when he realizes that the community resents the investigation—the results of which are bound to disturb the quiet flow of life. Hypocrisy and comfort are preferable to turmoil and truth. The next film, *Parade of Planets* (*Parad planet*, 1984), treats the same theme in an allegorical form. In the opening titles, the authors announce that this is "a quasi-fantastic story." Indeed, the story, although justified on a realistic level, is set in environments which destroy the perception of everyday reality. Not only the viewers, but the film's protagonists themselves, have the impression of having stepped into an uncanny world. The six protagonists are forty-year-old reservists who were called upon for the last time to play war games. In the course of the maneuvers (a perfect stylization of the classic Soviet war movies, which reinforces the illusionist motif), they are "killed," and subsequently dismissed. Wanting to prolong the game for a couple of days before going back to their jobs and families, the "ghosts" set out on a journey that takes them first to "the city of women" (a textile factory town), an idyllic and sensuous spot inhabited exclusively by charming and hospitable females, and then to the "old people's world" (an institution for senior citizens), where semi-surrealist figures of gentle octogenarians bring them in touch with history. The voyage for the six reservists has been an exploration into the self, the experience of a reality which seems illusory only from an ordinary point of view. Now they know that the illusion is on the other side, the positivist world of social conventions and conformism. Will they be able to readjust? The viewer does not know. At parting, the men disperse in the woods shouting nonsensical playwords at each other.

Besides being very successful at home, *Parade of Planets* was screened at the 1985 Venice Film Festival, and later received the first prize at the Avellino Festival. Together with *The Train Stopped,* it has been shown in the major European capitals, and was highly praised by the critics.

GORBACHEV IN POWER

With the general atmosphere of cultural renewal that has spread throughout the USSR since the spring of 1985, perhaps no other field has responded to the Party directives for *perestroika* and *glasnost* with more enthusiasm and concrete action than the cinema industry. All the art fields were shaken by a sudden creative upsurge and the urge to reshape their administrative structures. While change occurred randomly and on individual initiatives, the film industry was the first to institutionalize the new policy in order to ensure continuity.

A major administrative shakeup took place in May 1986, at the Fifth Congress of the Filmmakers Union. On that occasion, three-fourths of the conservative Union's Secretariat was replaced with younger members from the creative ranks rather than the bureaucratic apparatus. For the first time, nominations to official posts were not prearranged by the incumbent leadership, which allowed the up-to-then-controversial film director, Elem Klimov, to be elected First Secretary of the Union, ousting Lev Kulidzhanov who had afflicted the filmmakers with two decades (1965–1986) of superconservative policies. This event has been characterized in some Western circles as a small revolution. Actually, Klimov's election was the result of a backstage strategy devised by the new political forces. His nomination was sustained, if not suggested, by Alexander Yakovlev, who at that time was the head of the Central Committee's Propaganda Department, and who is credited with being the main architect of *glasnost.*[40] In line with Gorbachev's policies, therefore, the Filmmakers Union acquired a dynamic and progressive leadership. Nevertheless, for all its progressiveness, the new Secretariat, like the previous one, consists of men alone.

Six months later, in December 1986, it was the turn of Goskino to have its director replaced. Another old pillar of conservatism, Filip Ermash, was replaced by Alexander Kamshalov. Kamshalov comes from the Central Committee's Department of Culture and represents the Party policy on the cinema industry. He is expected to establish a viable relationship with the Filmmakers Union and to foster a policy that favors artistic expression. Where in the past, Goskino was responsible for all aspects of film production and exercised ideological and financial control, the latest reorganization has tipped the scales a bit by increasing the Filmmakers Union's decision-making power. Individual studios may now decide on scripts, shooting schedules, and film releases, and, more important, they may move toward self-financing. Censorship is being dismantled as an institution, although Goskino can still influence decisions. The process of decentralization means greater autonomy and greater responsibility on the part of the filmmakers, most likely resulting in a greater number of films of artistic value and public appeal.

The resolution of the Fifth Congress was reaffirmed less than a year later, in February 1987, at the plenary session of the Filmmakers Union. In his opening speech, Elem Klimov made it clear that "the first plenary session after the Fifth Congress must be devoted . . . to the most complex and the hottest issue of our cinematography—the issue of its fundamental, radical *perestroika*."[41] With this in view, he proposed to work toward a "new model" of film production and distribution. A few days later, an article in *Pravda* officially sanctioned the filmmakers' position. It read:

> The new model is a moral one. . . . Although in our Constitution there are good pronouncements on creative freedom, this freedom has not yet been implemented in practice. As soon as the studios become autonomous and self-supporting . . . the artist whose thoughts are shaped through suffering and who is in touch with his time will acquire a greater weight. . . . The Fifth Congress of the Filmmakers has started a struggle against routine thinking . . . and has marked a change of style in Soviet cinema.[42]

One cannot help but note that "the change of style" has been remarkable in journalism as well. Actually, the *new model* tag can be applied to Gorbachev's leadership in general. Filmmakers have made explicit references to the fact that they were following the "revolutionary" directives announced by Gorbachev at the Twenty-Seventh Congress, which "created the political, ideological, and psychological preconditions" for a sharp turn.[43]

There has been a great deal of speculation in the West about Gorbachev's motives in fostering the policy of *glasnost*. The most convincing argument is that for his program of general reforms he needs the support of the intelligentsia and the consensus of the people. By making concessions to the artists, Gorbachev seeks to make faithful allies and, at the same time, to open a dialogue with the people. This is particularly true for a medium as far-reaching as cinema.[44]

It is too early to talk about *new model* cinema (although it is easy to predict that this term will become a historical landmark, like *new wave* or *neorealism*). It will take more than one year before today's productions are released. But one can talk about a new mood in which old films, previously censored, are now distributed, and provocative recent ones are appearing. The first measure taken by the newly elected Union leader was to appoint a Conflict Commission to screen all the films which had been shelved over the years because of censorship. As a result, Alexei German's *Trial on the Road* was finally released. This followed the release, one year earlier, of his most recent film, *My Friend Ivan Lapshin* (*Moi drug Ivan Lapshin*, 1983; released in 1985), which was distributed on the regular circuit and broadcast on national television, becoming the subject of heated debate among the public.

The controversial success of *Ivan Lapshin* was due primarily to the fact that it dealt with an extremely sensitive period of Soviet history—the thirties, the years of forced collectivization, famine, the purges. Although this background is absent from the film, the realistic portrayal of ordinary life in those days, so different from the propagandistic films of the period about the marvels of industrialization, was in itself a sensation to the Soviet viewer. Since then, the theme of Stalin has been profusely treated in the media and in fiction as part of the Party policy to restore a historical period that was virtually erased, and to come to grips with its problematic legacy.

The action takes place in a northern provincial town, and is related by a narrator who "witnessed" the events as a child. The main plot hinges on the struggle of the head of a small police unit, the NKVD officer Ivan Lapshin, against a gang of bloodthirsty criminals who terrorize the local population. But this movie is more than a simple detective story. In fact, its slow-paced rhythm and fragmentary structure deny the conventions of the genre. Rather, the film is the evocation of a forgotten past—a past marked, on the one hand, by brutality, lawlessness, prostitution, and the hardships of life, and on the other, by lofty as well as naïve ideals. The grim reality of life in the provincial town is juxtaposed to the idealized world of a play which is being staged in the local theater. In the play, criminals can be reformed through labor, and prostitutes can be redeemed through love and compassion.[45] Lapshin knows that in real life criminals are often shot in cold blood (as he eventually does with the gang's chief), and love is an elusive dream (the actress of the local theater rejects him for a friend of his). And yet, as a simple man with a basic faith in the human being, Lapshin accepts the illusion of the theater as the depiction of the ideal toward which he is striving. The motif of illusory reality runs through the film as a reminder of the Stalinist myth that was being built in the thirties. By juxtaposing these two planes, German succeeds in removing all naïveté from his film while preserving the substance of the ideal.

My Friend Ivan Lapshin has troubled some Western critics, who perceived a certain nostalgia for those years and questioned the intentions of

I-7   *Repentance (Pokaianie)*

the director. Indeed, there is an aura of nostalgia, deliberately conveyed through the film's structural and stylistic devices, but it is not nostalgia for the Stalin regime. On the contrary, it is nostalgia for a lost dream. The year of the film's action, 1935, was the last moment before the beginning of the great terror (right after the murder of Kirov), a moment when it was still possible to believe in the Communist utopia.[46] After that, one had to face the reality of the purges, the Gulag, collectivization, and famine, and the dream was destroyed forever. With this film German acknowledges a loss of innocence typical of his generation. There is more cynicism now. True, this accounts for a more realistic and mature attitude—precisely the responsible attitude that informs German's film. The director looks back at the early thirties and at the naïve heroes of the country's childhood from the vantage point of an adult, with tenderness and a bit of nostalgia.[47]

Besides the thematic level, this film is extremely interesting for its innovative form. German is undoubtedly one of the most original directors of his generation, whose creative talent has developed in spite of the fact that he was not allowed to work for many years. The simultaneous release of two films separated by a fifteen-year lapse testifies to the evolution of his style, from a traditional romantic form to a post-structuralist open text.

Another film dealing with the thirties, *Repentance (Pokaianie*, 1984; released in 1986) by Tengiz Abuladze, brings the viewer face-to-face with the years of terror. *Repentance* is a production of Gruziafilm—the Georgian film studio. The fact that it was possible at all to get this film past preliminary censorship (script approval, etc.) and into production was due in part to the personal support of the Georgia Party Secretary, Eduard Shevarnadze (now, Foreign Minister), and in part to the geographical location. Georgia is far removed from the center and enjoys a certain degree of autonomy, thanks to the official policy of support for ethnic cultures. According to this policy, Georgian television can use a three-hour period daily for local broadcasting, unsupervised by the central Gosteleradio administration. Hence, *Repentance* was made for Georgian television. Because the film is on its way to becoming an international hit, and one of the most sensational productions in the history of Soviet cinema, the circumstances of its making become almost anecdotal. At the same time, they testify to the talent, inventiveness, and expediency of the Georgian filmmakers who are regarded as being among the best in the Soviet Union.

Repentance is dominated by the grotesque figure of Varlam, the incarnation of the quintessential dictator. Varlam is a composite caricature of Stalin, Hitler, and Mussolini, as his features and behavior suggest. But to a Soviet audience he is also the effigy of Lavrenti Beria, who headed Stalin's secret police. This surrealist tale of horror is set in an imaginary time and place, so that by its abstraction from history it could be endowed with a more profound and universal significance. However, no matter how generalized the characters and the situations are, the symbolism of the film cuts very close to the bone for a Soviet viewer.[48] *Repentance* not only explores the past, but it also relates the past to the present and warns that the legacy of Varlam is still alive and has to be confronted in order to be exorcised. The film moves back and forth in time without any marked transition, and the same actor (Aftondil Makharadze) plays both the dictator and his son Avel, who is not able to face the past and tries to justify it. By so doing, Avel perpetuates his father's legacy. In a dramatic finale Avel's son, disgusted with hypocrisy and injustice, commits suicide, and this tragedy prompts Avel to unearth Varlam's body and throw it over a cliff. Now the viewer, having been delivered from evil, can sigh with relief; except that all of this was a daydream—a fantasy going on in the mind of the film's heroine, whose family was destroyed by the tyrant Varlam. Thus, the viewer, deprived of a catharsis, is left with the uneasy feeling that he is the one that has to perform the exorcism.

The latest film by Abdrashitov and Mindadze, *Plyumbum, or A Dangerous Game* (*Pliumbum, ili Opasnaia igra,* 1987) probes deeply into the philosophical roots of evil. The film's protagonist is a sixteen-year-old boy who, in his spare time, helps the police in their fight against robbers and other outlaws, while he works under the pseudonym of Plyumbum. He becomes involved in this "dangerous game" through a sense of justice, having himself been robbed. But the game Plyumbum plays proves to be dan-

I–8   *Plyumbum, or A Dangerous Game (Pliumbum, ili Opasnaia igra)*

gerous, first of all, to his spiritual well-being. His original motivation gradually turns into an obsession, and the moral idea that was the basis for his actions becomes evil. Plyumbum's mechanical pursuit of "justice," devoid of love and human compassion, leads him to betray his father and to cause the death of his devoted girlfriend, Sonia. There are ominous echoes of Dostoevsky's characters in this film (primarily Raskolnikov in *Crime and Punishment*), which remind the viewer that the moral foundation of ethics is not an abstract principle of justice but the human feeling of brotherly love.

The year 1985, the fortieth anniversary of the victory in World War II, called for an extraordinary number of war movies. Most of them were mediocre productions; some were spectacular but shallow.[49] Only one is worthy of note, *Come and See (Idi i smotri*, 1985) by Elem Klimov. This film, based on an actual event, depicts the brutality of the Nazi invaders in the Byelorussian village of Khatyn. It was awarded the first prize at the Moscow International Film Festival, and since then has attracted millions of viewers in the Soviet Union. The sparse American audiences that saw it were profoundly disturbed; they either loved it or hated it. Indeed, this film does not allow the viewer to remain indifferent. The viewer's senses are relentlessly attacked by the powerful camera work, combined with striking imagery, a harrowing soundtrack, and even a palpable illusion of smell. The medium itself, more than the narrative, conveys the horror of the war by taking the viewer through a painful physical experience. This is supposed to parallel the ordeal of the film's protagonist, Flyor, who is able to preserve his human dignity amid violence and destruction.

Klimov's film suggests two levels of meaning. While focusing on violence and brutality, its symbolism is intended to transcend the physical experience and raise the viewer into the realm of spiritual values. Evocative in this respect is Mozart's cathartic *Requiem*, underscoring the final camera tilt toward the sky. Therefore, while portraying the war, *Come and See* wants to spread a peace message. In line with the Soviet policy of arms control, the film with its apocalyptic title warns the viewer about the possibility of a nuclear holocaust.[50]

This theme is treated more directly in *Letters of a Dead Man* (*Pis'ma mertvogo cheloveka*, 1986), by the young director Konstantin Lopushansky. The film portrays life in an underground shelter after a nuclear explosion. The dominant brownish coloration corresponds to the somber emotional tone of the movie. The central figure, a scientist (played by Rolan Bykov) who feels he has contributed to the destruction of mankind, carries the philosophical theme throughout the film. Contrary to positivistic logic, this ex-scientist believes that although the genetic base of life has been destroyed, the human spirit will survive and be able to regenerate

I–9   *Come and See (Idi i smotri)*

mankind. Therefore, the film is an affirmation of hope—crystallized in the image of the Christmas tree which the scientist builds from fragments of scrap metal for a group of traumatized children condemned to die in the nuclear winter.[51]

Lopushansky is representative of a generation of promising young directors whose works have attracted the attention of the critics at home and abroad. Among them is Alexander Sokurov with the film, *A Lonely Man's Voice* (*Odinokii golos cheloveka*, 1978; released in 1987). He is considered to be a disciple of Andrei Tarkovsky, and to be just as uncompromising as his mentor was. This film is the story of Nikita, a lower-class man who after the revolution marries a woman who once belonged to a higher class. The mismatched couple cannot overcome their differences. Nikita retreats to a small town where he is able to find the meaning of his existence. The film is based on Andrei Platonov's stories, but the central theme is very Tarkovskian. As Sokurov himself put it: "In the context of the young man's lofty spiritual claims, the erotic motivation reveals how the lonely voice of the spirit dies in the face of matter."[52] Sokurov's latest movie *Solemn Heartlessness* (*Skorbnoe bezchuvstie*, 1987) is based on George Bernard Shaw's play *Heartbreak House*.

Another new voice is that of Sergei Ovcharov, who emerged with the film *Believe It or Not* (*Nebyval'shchitsa*, 1983). It is a comic fairy tale based on folkloric motifs and stock characters, such as the peasant, the blacksmith, the soldier, the housewife, and the devil. The style wavers between the surrealism of the images and the slapstick of the situations. Ovcharov's fascination with the rich Russian cultural heritage is also evident in his latest film, *Lefty* (*Levsha*, 1987) from a nineteenth-century tale by Nikolay Leskov.

From Georgia comes an original film by Nana Djordjadze, one of the youngest representatives of the small pool of women film directors. Her film *Robinsonada, or My English Grandfather* (*Robinzonada, ili Moi angliiskii dedushka*, 1986) won the Golden Camera award at the Cannes Film Festival (1987). It is both a political satire and a romantic comedy—the story of a British engineer who comes to Soviet Georgia in the twenties to help with the construction of a telegraph line. He falls in love with the sister of the local Party chief, and gets involved in a series of comic situations in an effort to be with his beloved.

Many more young directors are worthy of mention—Yuri Mamin, *Neptune's Holiday* (*Prazdnik Neptuna*, 1987); Timur Babluani, *The Sparrow's Flight* (*Perelet vorob'ev*, 1986); Mikhail Belikov, *The Night Is Short* (*Noch' korotka*, 1981), but it is sufficient to note that the new spirit which informs the Soviet cinema industry is supportive of young talent; and that there are plans to increase experimental workshops and offer the young broader opportunities. Special festivals devoted to the work of young filmmakers have been organized for the first time in Riga (the cineforum "Arsenal," 1986) and Leningrad ("Leningrad Young Cinema," 1987).

I–10   *Believe It or Not (Nebyval'shchitsa)*

Besides nurturing a new generation of filmmakers, the film industry pays a great deal of attention to today's teenagers. This concern is reflected in the latest hit films, *The Burglar* (*Vzlomshchik*, 1987; director, Valery Ogorodnikov), *Is It Easy to Be Young?* (*Legko li byt' molodym?*, 1987; director, Iuris Podnieks), and *The Courier* (*Kur'er*, 1987; director, Karen Shakhnazarov).[53]

The Burglar focuses on modern youth subculture, specifically that of rock music. It is the story of a "difficult" teenager who tries to give meaning to his life by participating in an illegal deal in order to help his brother. *Is It Easy to Be Young?* is a documentary produced by the Latvian studio, which presents a compassionate but disturbing picture of alienated and disaffected youth. Hard rock, punk attire, drugs, the me-generation syndrome, mystical flights into the world of Hare-Krishna—it seems that they have caught up with the West, at least in this sphere. However, the causes of the phenomenon are domestic, as a candid review of the film suggests: "What they say from the screen is: 'You made us the way we are with your duplicity, your lies.' . . . Let us recall one of the many tragedies in *Repentance*. One, but perhaps the most severe . . . Varlam's grandson putting a bullet through his heart."[54] And so, it is all

I–11   The Burglar (Vzlom-shchik)

I–12   Is It Easy to Be Young? (Legko li byt' molodym?)

the parents' fault. A young viewer in a newspaper commentary reinforces this opinion:

> Our generation . . . grew up in an atmosphere of pompous ceremonies, at the sound of prerecorded ovations and 'Hurrah!' shouts. . . . Many of those words which we heard from childhood . . . became a habit . . . lost their meaning, and their utterance became a ritual. We were obedient and observed the rituals . . . did our homework without asking about its purpose, its meaning. . . . We lost our illusions incredibly fast, and at 17–18 years of age we feel completely powerless. What can we change? We cannot escape those decades. . . . That's the way they have shaped us.[55]

But if Soviet teenagers cannot escape their legacy they are nevertheless trying very hard to submerge it in the latest musical fad. *The Courier*, like Shakhnazarov's other films, is a musical. While the previous films were devoted to jazz and then tap dancing, this one hinges on break dance. The director, sympathizing with the youth, draws a parallel between the illogicality, absurdity, and bold spontaneity of break dance and the mental setup of today's teenagers. Break dance is a metaphor for the deep-set antagonism to the values of the parents' generation, an antagonism which, in the protagonist's normal life routine, is expressed through mute, hostile passivity. Who can blame him? At the end of the movie the seventeen-year-old hero is drafted into the army. The last shot shows him pensively staring at a comrade who has just come back from Afghanistan.

So, "the *new model* is a moral one," and the Soviet filmmakers are taking it seriously. They are not only exploring troubling problems, they are pointing at the causes. They are no longer glossing over the surface of the social malaise, they are going to the roots. They are not remaking history according to the heroic code, they are uncovering dark spots. This is a new type of discourse which cannot be sustained by old-fashioned aesthetics. Formal experimentation is an instrinsic part of it, as some of the most recent films have already shown. And so, the *new model* is also an aesthetic one. The next few years will determine how and to what extent it is possible to implement it.

NOTES

I want to thank the Hoover Institution, which provided me with a six-month fellowship for this project. I also want to thank my colleagues Richard Stites and Denise Youngblood for their close reading of this essay, their expert suggestions, and insightful comments. Finally, I want to express my appreciation to all the colleagues who at different times over the past two years were willing to engage in discussions of the aesthetic and social contexts of Soviet cinema.

1. He was promoted to marshal of the Soviet Union (among the politicians only Stalin held that military rank) and chairman of the presidium (not even Stalin

held both the presidency and the Party secretaryship simultaneously). He was also awarded the Lenin prize for literature, for his memoirs and collected works, most, if not all, of them written by a professional writer.

2. Before being called Goskino, it had several other names. A detailed description of Goskino and other institutions pertaining to the movie industry can be found in Val Golovskoy, *Behind the Soviet Screen* (Ann Arbor, Michigan: Ardis, 1986). This book covers the years 1972–1982, and does not reflect the changes that have taken place more recently in the administrative structure of the movie industry.

3. It is viable to use class terminology to describe Soviet society, if one replaces the concept of property with that of power and privilege.

4. Golovskoy, p. 59. The data that follow come from this same source.

5. Ibid, p. 61.

6. The most prestigious studio of the Caucasian republics is Gruziafilm, in Georgia. An interesting case is that of the Kirgizian studio, which acquired a reputation through the works of a few talented film directors (Tolomush Okeev, Bolotbek Shamshiev), but primarily because of the studio's director, Chingiz Aitmatov, a novelist known and appreciated nationwide. Many Kirgiz films were based on his literary works. Furthermore, he produced the first films of young directors from other republics, such as Andrei Mikhalkov-Konchalovsky and Larisa Shepitko.

7. This term was used by Maya Turovskaya in "Why Does the Viewer Go to the Movies?" *Zhanry kino*, (Moscow: Iskusstvo, 1979), pp. 138–154 (all translations are mine).

8. The subject was actually broached in an earlier film by Yuli Raizman, *Your Contemporary* (*Vash Sovremennik*, 1967, which anticipated this trend.

9. Sergei Mikaelian, "The Bonus," *Sovetskii ekran*, No. 21 (1977), p. 21.

10. Inna Levshina, "A New-Year Tale by Eldar Ryazanov," *Sovetskii ekran*, No. 24 (1975), p. 10.

11. Franboise Navailh, "La femme dans le cinéma soviétique contemporain," *Film et Histoire*, ed. Marc Ferro, (Paris: Editions de l'Ecole des Hautes Etudes en Sciences Sociales, 1984). pp. 155–161.

12. *Sovetskii ekran*, No. 5 (1977), p. 11.

13. Quoted in an article which castigates Ryazanov's grotesque style. Andrei Zorky, "Standing in Line for Garages,"! *Sovetskii ekran*, No. 11 (1980), p. 7.

14. Jeanne Vronskaya, *Young Soviet Filmmakers* (London: George Allen and Unwin Ltd., 1972), p. 49.

15. Alla Terber, "Actress," *Sovetskii ekran*, No. 24 (1976), p. 7.

16. The subtext of *May I Have the Floor* is the film, *Member of the Government* (*Chlen pravitel'stva*, 1940) by A. Zarkhi and I. Kheifits, an apotheosis of the heroine who honestly and laboriously works her way up from worker to leader.

17. All Soviet citizens from their school years are acquainted with Sergei Esenin (1895–1925), a "peasant" poet who represents a nostalgic attachment to the land and folk traditions (his bohemian life and formalistic experimentation with verse are usually glossed over). The name Kim is an acronym for Communist International of Youth (*Kommunisticheskii Internatsional Molodezhi*). Many people born in the twenties and thirties were given similar names by zealous idealistic parents.

18. Dinara Asanova, "The Diarector Presents Her Film," *Sovetskii ekran*, No. 3 (1977), p. 10. Soviet children begin school at age seven.

19. Ibid.

20. Lana Gogoberidze, "Some Interviews," *Sovetskii ekran*, No. 2 (1979), p. 16.

21. Another director, Emile Loteanu, transferred a Chekhov story into luscious images of a decaying world in his film *The Shooting Party (Moi laskovyi i nezhnii zver'*, 1979).

22. The radical critic Nikolay Dobrolyubov (1836–1861) started this trend with his famous article "What Is Oblomovitis?"

23. Since the early eighties, Konchalovsky has been living in Hollywood, where he directed a number of movies. Among them, *Maria's Lovers, Runaway Train, Duet for One*, and *Shy People*.

24. Insightful observations on German's style in *Twenty Days* were published in N. Dymshits, "Under Another Name. The Metamorphoses of the Melodrama," *Zhanry kino*, pp. 155–170; and V. Mikhalkovich, "Cinema Style and Film Style," *Iskusstvo kino*, No. 1 (1979).

25. Another significant deviation from the cliché in this film was to cast Iuri Nikulin, a clown of the Moscow circus, in the leading role. Nikulin turned out to be an excellent interpreter of the compassionate, sensitive, intelligent Major Lopatin.

26. Very controversial has been the case of Sergei Paradzhanov, who was arrested on a charge of homosexuality and given a seven-year sentence. He was released after four years, partly because of pressure from the West. He resumed his work as a director in the early eighties.

27. Andrei Tarkovsky, "Confession," *Kontinent*, No. 42 (1984), p. 400.

28. Tarkovsky was given permission to go to Italy, in 1982, to work on the film *Nostalgia*. When, in 1984, he decided to extend his stay, the Soviet authorities stripped him of his citizenship. Tarkovsky died of cancer in Paris, in December 1986. Contrary to practice, and thanks to the new policy of *glasnost*, the major Soviet newspapers carried obituaries, and the film magazines published several articles on the deceased artist. The Moscow Film Festival (July 1987) hosted a retrospective of Tarkovsky's Soviet films.

29. After the death of Mikhail Suslov, in January 1982, old Communists started dying one after another, leaving a void in the top echelons which Andropov's men proceeded to fill.

30. The crackdown on Brezhnev's extended family began even before the leader's death. In January 1982, the KGB arrested a ring of diamond smugglers and black marketeers which was headed by a senior official of the Ministry of Culture, Anatoly Kolevatov, his deputy Viktor Gorsky, and Boris Buryatia (alias Boris the Gypsy), a flamboyant ex-circus performer and the lover of Brezhnev's daughter, Galina. About the years of transition, see Dusko Doder, *Shadows and Whispers* (New York: Random House, 1986).

31. Alexander Kalyagin, who played the rogue in the film, also portrayed Chichikov in a dramatization of Gogol's novel which was aired on national television close to the time of the film's release.32. Examples of plays dealing with juvenile delinquency were *Dear Elena Sergeevna (Dorogaia Elena Sergeevna)*, by Lyudmila Razumovskaya, staged at the Lenin Komsomol Theater in Leningrad; *The Little Carriage (Vagonchik)*, by N. Pavlova, produced at the Little Stage of the Moscow Art Theater; and *Bait Size 46, Medium Short (Lovushka No. 46, rost vtoroi)*, by Iuri Shchekochikin, staged at the Central Children's Theater in Moscow.

33. Dinara Asanova died of a heart attack in April 1985, during the shooting of the film *The Stranger (Neznakomka)*, which remained incomplete.

34. See V. Antonova, "A Call in the Night," *Iskusstvo kino*, No. 7 (1985), p. 84.

35. Other films dealing with youth were *In Broad Daylight . . . (Sred' bela dnia*, by V. Gurianov, 1984); *The Cage for Canaries (Kletka dlia kanareek*, by Pavel Chukhrai, 1984); *Overheard Conversation (Podslushannyi razgovor*, by

S. Potopalov, 1985); and the documentaries *First Sorrow* (*Pervaia bol'*, 1985), *It Is Painful to Draw Mama's Portrait* (*Mne strashno risovat' mamu*, 1985), *The Most Beautiful* (*Samaia krasivaia*, 1985), *The Kids Get Even* (*Rasplachivaiutsia deti*, 1985.)

36. Special mention must be made of two very recent films devoted to the figure of the poet and balladeer, Vladimir Vysotsky. In life, he was loved as no other cultural figure for his simple and straightforward protest songs, and he became an object of veneration after his death (August 1980). He was tolerated by the authorities because of his extraordinary popularity at home and abroad, but he had no access to print or broadcast. Now, the director Alexander Stefanovich has produced the movie *Begin at the Beginning* (*Nachni snachala*, 1986), which features some of Vysotsky's songs and stars another controversial musician, Andrei Makarevich. A long video entirely devoted to Vysotsky, *Remembrance* (*Vospominanie*, 1987), has been produced by director Vladimir Savelev for the Ukrainian studio.

37. The title refers to Englischer Garten in Munich, where the headquarters of Radio Liberty and Radio Free Europe are located.

38. This TV series won the KGB movie award for 1984. The Soviets have numerous contests and festivals sponsored by various institutions, including the KGB.

39. In the escapist genre we should also list the "disaster movies," such as *The Crew* (*Ekipazh*, by Alexander Mitta, 1979), which was rated third on a list of the ten greatest box-office successes. *Literaturnaia gazeta* (January 14, 1987), p. 8.

40. Yakovlev became a Politburo member in June 1987.

41. "Toward a New Model for Cinematography," *Sovietskii ekran*, No. 6 (1987), p. 2.

42. S. Freilikh, "The New Model Is New Thinking," *Pravda* (3/7/1987), p. 3.

43. "Toward a New Model for Cinematography," p. 2.

44. Television, too, has undergone dramatic changes and is being skillfully used to the same end.

45. It is easy to recognize in that provincial production the much acclaimed play *The Aristocrats* (*Aristokraty*), by Nikolay Pogodin, which premiered in 1935 at the Moscow Realistic Theater.

46. This is suggested by the strategic placement of the portraits of two political figures. The portrait of Kirov is shown at the beginning of the movie, in the communal apartment where Lapshin lives. As a counterpoint, in the final sequence, a tram carrying a marching band (again, the marching band!) toward "the future" is decorated with a smiling portrait of Stalin. I am grateful to my colleague, Richard Stites, for his insightful observations concerning the historical setup of this film.

47. From an interview with Aleksei German:

> The story I'm telling is about the real life of these people, their faith, their melancholy, the fact that they go straight ahead toward Communism without understanding that the road is long and dangerous. Maybe these people included my father and my mother. Some people understand that. Others don't.

> *Catalog of the 30th International San Francisco Film Festival* (April 1987), p. 37.

48. This is what the poet Robert Rozhdestvensky had to say about *Repentance:*

> And so, 'Once upon a time. . .' No, no more make-believe and pretending that nobody understands and remembers anything! Yes, all this happened in our country! Our country, mine and yours . . . But the lessons of the past, even the most difficult and painful ones, do not disappear. It is necessary to learn them, to get to know them to their full extent. Otherwise, what kind of lessons are they?—*Literaturnaia gazeta* (January 21, 1987), p. 8.

49. For example, *Victory (Pobeda)*, directed by Evgeny Matveefv; *The Shore (Bereg)*, directed by Alexander Alov (recently deceased) and Vladimir Naumov; *The Battle for Moscow (Bitva za Moskvu)*, by Iuri Ozerov, who also directed the 1972 epos *Liberation (Osvobozhdenie)*.

50. Klimov himself made that connection: "After the premiere of the film . . . a Japanese film critic told me: "Your Khatyn is our Hiroshima'," *Iskusstvo kino*, No. 12 (1985), p. 38.

51. The documentary *The Bell of Chernobyl (Kolokiol Chernobylia*, 1987), which won much praise at the 1987 West Berlin Film Festival, is another poignant warning against a nuclear catastrophe.

52. Press materials of the Museum of Modern Art, New York. Festival "New Voices from the Soviet Cinema," November 1987.

53. *The Courier* was awarded the Special Prize at the Moscow Film Festival (July 1987) together with the Polish film *The Hero of the Year*.

54. Alexander Egorov, "These Are Our Problems," *Sovietskii ekran*, No. 6 (1987), p. 9.

55. Tatyana Maksimova, "We Are Your Children," *Literaturnaia gazeta* (June 3, 1987), p. 8.

2

Testing the Borders: East German Film between Individualism and Social Commitment

Sigrun D. Leonhard

SOCIALIST AESTHETICS AND POLITICAL CONSTRAINTS

The history of the German Democratic Republic's (GDR's) relationship with its artists has been a long, sometimes productive, sometimes frustrating, but always intense process of negotiation about the responsibilities and the liberties of the artist in a socialist society.[1] In agreement with the official credo that art should support and inspire development towards the perfection of socialism, artists have suffered from various degrees of pressure to conform to their role as it was designed by the state's cultural officials. As recently as 1980, member of the Central Committee Gregor Schirmer reinforced the notion that art should submit to socialist values, since the very possibility of art depended on the conditions created by the socialist state:

> Even today, the socialist system cannot renounce power and the means to enforce it, as long as aggressive imperialism exists, and as long as the rules of social life are broken by some individuals. In socialism, power has a deep moral justification.[2]

While one has to understand all manifestations of art in the GDR as taking place under conditions of censorship and the constant awareness of potential personal drawbacks as a result of undesired cultural activities, it is equally important to keep in mind that the ties work both ways: artists need public and political approval to get the necessary funding for their work, but at the same time, the state needs the creative potential of its people to create a cultural self-definition, especially in a country as young as the GDR, which for the longest time had to fight for acceptance as an independent state. Also, restrictions on art, resulting from the attempt to bind it into the sphere of well-defined social responsibilities, have not had only negative effects for the artists themselves. In contrast with West Germany, the rival brother state, where market value and market strategies determine publication and distribution of art, and where the abundance of new cultural products is often met with indifference, the GDR grants its cultural elite the social importance their colleagues in the West sorely lack.[3] They know that they play a crucial role—not only performing the "official" task of working on a national self-image for their country, but also fulfilling the need for communication about important current social and political issues; for in the GDR, art has also taken over the function of informing citizens about the latest crucial events, which in the West are covered by a variety of papers and magazines.[4] This has given to artists and intellectuals the conviction that they share with the government the responsibility for the development of their country, and some of the power to direct it.

In the short history of the GDR, there have been times of great closeness between the state and its creative community, such as the years from 1959 to 1963, following the Bitterfeld conference and its ensuing, relatively liberal, attitude towards and encouragement of new directions in the arts.[5] But the brief periods of thaw after significant events which produced the wish, on the part of the government, to assure itself of the cooperation of the intellectual elite, were always followed by new restrictive measures, resulting in disorientation, discouragement, and anger on the part of the victims of the respective clean-ups.

When Honecker took office in 1971 as the party chief of the Sozialistische Einheitspartei Deutschlands (SED), i.e., the Socialist Party, great hopes arose for the beginning of a more liberal era in politics, social life, and art. His first statements seemed to confirm this expectation. At the famous Eighth Party Congress of the Sozialistische Einheitspartei Deutschlands in December of 1971, he declared:

> If one comes from a firm socialist position, there can, in my opinion, be no taboos in the realm of art and literature. This applies to questions of content as well as style—briefly: questions of what one calls artistic mastery.[6]

This announcement came as a great relief, especially since it followed the very restrictive last years of the Ulbricht era, culminating in the 1965/66 clean-up which also affected film directors Kurt Maetzig and Frank Beyer of DEFA (Deutsche Film Aktiengesellschaft, i.e., the "German Film Corporation").[7] Ironically, those two victims of the effort to redefine the political course counted among the most ardent representatives of the new state, and had contributed, with their famous antifascist films, to building up the DEFA film right after the war. The punitive measures following the infamous Eleventh Plenum of the SED resulted in the interruption of many artists' work, its disappearance into archives, and a crisis of faith on the part of the reprimanded artists.[8]

The great hopes for liberalization caused by Honecker's taking the political lead came crashing down only five years later, when singer Wolf Biermann was expatriated while giving a concert in Cologne, West Germany. He had supposedly maligned his own country and thus lost the right to GDR citizenship. Biermann, a committed socialist, but—to the dismay of his political superiors—also committed to discussing, with uncomfortable candor, social problems and scandals in his own country, had been asked to leave the GDR earlier, and had indignantly refused. He settled down in Hamburg, West Germany, where he lives now, still mourning the loss of his chosen fatherland which has treated him so harshly.[9] The incident resulted in an alarming exodus of artists and intellectuals to the West. A letter, written by some of them, protesting the decision, provoked further expatriations and emigration applications (*Ausreiseanträge*), which were, on the whole, granted with unusual swiftness. The letter written on Biermann's behalf, and signed during the following days by more artists who declared their solidarity with the protesters, became further politicized by the fact that the writers had given it to the West German press, which meant, to the GDR government, cooperation with the class enemy.

What the Biermann case showed—and it represented only the most drastic of many punitive measures against artists in the GDR—was that while a greater willingness to accept a variety of themes and artistic expression existed, taboos continued to operate. The vast grey areas made it only more difficult for artists to orient themselves, and may account for the vagueness and tentativeness that characterizes so many contemporary GDR films, for example.

When comparing today's East German literature to film, one cannot help but marvel at how differently the two media deal with form. All art in the GDR labors under the late effects of the prescribed aesthetic program, socialist realism, uncompromisingly enforced in the fifties, then increasingly modified to accommodate changing aesthetic needs and concepts.[10] At the same time, however, the definition of art as a social activity in the service of socio-political progress continued, and continues to this day, to be the core of socialist aesthetics, just as formalism—that is, all art in which the question of form becomes more important than its content—is still rejected. In the eyes of the committed socialist critic, formalist art loses its humanistic and democratic character.

The degree to which an art form is subjected to censorship is directly proportionate to the degree of its availability to the public. Not all the arts suffer equally from limitation of themes and restrictions on artistic expression. While a sculptor is permitted to work rather freely, the writer must deal with a tighter net of constraints. Literature, however, enjoys more freedom than film, which in turn, is granted greater freedom of expression than TV. As a result of TV's total accessibility, it has become entirely the mouthpiece of state propaganda.[11] If film has been much less able than literature to emancipate itself from the tight frame of socialist realism (as advocated, for example, by critic and theoretician Georg Lukács, who served for a while as the official spokesman on aesthetic value), it was because of its capacity to reach a mass audience. This illuminates the paradoxical situation created by the interdependence of art and politics in the GDR, in that, after having curtailed the evolution of film (resulting in a drastic decrease in public interest), official criticism expressed concern about the crisis of contemporary film.[12]

The formal conservatism of art and its promoted alliance with the ideological tenets of the GDR version of Marxism-turned-socialist realism, as Eberhard Lämmert remarked, into a "monstrous mixture . . . : In terms of its ideological content, it followed the [schematized] materialist concept of history; aesthetically, it sanctioned the canon of forms of a specific step in the development of bourgeois art as valid beyond history."[13]

The contradictions inherent in this concept of art reflect those of GDR politics. On the one hand, the government claims to adhere to a materialist concept of history according to which class differences and evolving social conflicts will eventually dissolve in the dialectical process. In reality, however, this process is channeled by the government in all aspects of social and political life.[14]

In its view of the perfectibility of the human race, in its belief in a movement towards the solution of social conflicts and the control over the natural world, in its limitation of the importance of religion and its affirmation of reason as the prime instrument and source of insight, the ideology of socialism shows itself indebted to enlightenment philosophies. The parallel extends to the definition of art. In both systems, it was subordinated to philosophy, which it served by expressing difficult and abstract ideas in a useful and pleasing way. In times that assign a higher rank to philosophy/ideology than to art, the formal side of art is neglected, and little experimentation takes place.

In this context, it is not surprising that the norms for art in the GDR today seem to belong to late eighteenth-, early nineteenth-century aesthetics. Art serves the purpose of propagating ideas and values. In contrast with the artistic movements of the early bourgeois age, however, this state-imposed aesthetic value system lacks the former revolutionary impulse. It cannot be progressive in the context of the GDR in the late twentieth century. The way the GDR treated Bertolt Brecht, the pioneer of a Marxist aesthetics, after his return to the "new Germany" clearly shows the commitment to a traditional concept of art.[15] Brecht's iconoclastic rebellion against the closed form, the concept of the work of art as an organic whole, and the theory of empathy was, after all, deeply political. He meant to restructure the aesthetic experience by turning it from an essentially passive one to a thought-provoking, liberating one. At least during the early years of the GDR, when the necessity to survive as a separate state overwhelmed all other needs, the Brechtian version of Marxist aesthetics seemed too dangerous to be supported.

While literature had freed itself rather early from the constraints of some very limiting concepts, such as the "positive hero," it took much longer for film heroes to turn into more complex and believable human beings. Even today, the term is still an issue, as the titles of recent publications on contemporary film prove, for example: "Helden gesucht!," *Ist der positive Held in unseren Filmen in Verruf geraten?*, *Die jungen Helden*, etc.[16] To the extent that films move away from the old aesthetics, critical voices make themselves heard, expressing concern about the disintegration of aesthetic principles and, along with them, moral values. As my later analysis of specific films will demonstrate, a new system of reference that could deal with art forms not oriented towards the classical/enlightenment tradition has hardly been developed yet. This results in confusion and helplessness, sometimes in outright rejection of works of art that do not fit the known patterns.

Along with the dubious statement on the freedom of art from all sorts of taboos, Honecker gave another signal at the Eighth Party Congress. In contrast to his predecessor, Ulbricht, who had insisted on the social development of the GDR as being one towards the realization of a "socialist community" (*sozialistische Menschengemeinschaft*)—that is, a society of individuals by-and-large on the same educational and cultural level, with similar living conditions and the same cultural expectations—Honecker adjusted to the demands of the times by projecting a new image for his country as a "non-antagonistic class society."[17] Such a system, he argued, would allow for, and even encourage, a variety of social and cultural interests and aesthetic tastes among the population. One general level could not meet the demands and the specific needs of all.

Politically, this signified a step away from the socialist ideal of a unified society, and might well be considered, if not a sell-out of socialist values, at least a significant and alarming concession to bourgeois individualism. What it meant for the arts was, however, potentially positive. True, the new course opened the doors to a lowering of standards, and it has been observed that this was, in fact, a consequence.[18] On the other hand, the partial suspension of judgment on aesthetic tastes and forms also meant greater freedom from the very narrow and often simplistically moralistic standards which critics and cultural officials applied to works of art. If film, literature, painting, and music could and should direct themselves to specific subgroups of society, fulfilling their needs for entertainment, education, and aesthetic experiences, it followed that the great pedagogical task of leading everyone to the same level of "Bildung" was suspended, and that the educational function of art was dispersed, watered down. The change would also necessitate a redirection of criticism which would now have to be applied in a more relativistic way from the viewpoint of the audience at which it was aimed. Honecker's change of political course meant, for the practice of art, a partial escape from the value system that had held it down until then. Of course, this applied only to aesthetic values; political censorship functioned much as it had before, and continued to limit the development of art.

TOWARD AN AESTHETIC OF EVERYDAY LIFE

Film directors and script writers reacted to the greater permissiveness at the beginning of the seventies with a fervent turn to the representation of socialist everyday life (*sozialistischer Alltag*). At first glance, this may seem surprising, since all through the fifties and sixties the claim had been that art presented socialist society on its way to perfection. But many films of those years had been deformed by the wishful thinking engendered by the official ideology, and the result was a group of works structured according to the same mechanical principles of conflict and conflict resolution which turned the films into packages of socialist values.[19] The public recognized the inauthenticity of these films and stayed away from the movie theaters.

The trend towards producing works unproblematic enough to receive funding continued through the seventies, but the decade also saw a new kind of film which led to a short blossoming of the DEFA production in the late seventies and early eighties. The creators of these successful films worked within the larger framework of realism, but went their own way within it, sometimes stretching it to the limit. Some of these films even break the realistic framework from the inside, by inserting dreams and fantastic elements while still grounding the unaffected narrative in the realistic setting, or in the psyche of individual characters. Without questioning the realist structure in principle, they shift the importance of individual elements so much that the films appear to go in a new direction.

A New Style of Realism

One of the representatives of that category is Heiner Carow's *The Legend of Paul and Paula (Die Legende von Paul und Paula,* 1973).[20] Carow, born in 1929, belongs to the middle generation of GDR film directors who went through schooling at the DEFA-Nachwuchsstudio from 1950–1954. He started by making documentary films, but it was a totally different kind of work that made him famous. *The Legend of Paul and Paula* turned into a cult film unrivaled in its importance by any other DEFA film since the beginning of the seventies, except maybe Konrad Wolf's *Solo Sunny* (1979). The film owes its great success to a number of qualities, the most important one being the appeal of the youthful and temperamental heroes, the image and the claim of young people who want

II–1   *The Legend of Paul and Paula (Die Legende von Paul und Paula)*

to break the mold.[21] It made long hair and blue jeans acceptable, celebrated the invincibility of true love, and at the same time managed to show, in an ironic, sometimes even parodistic style, GDR reality in both its endearing and its less appealing aspects. Based on a screenplay by Ulrich Plenzdorf, author of the novel *The New Sufferings of Young W,* which had been originally conceived as a film but was not accepted by the DEFA,[22] it tells the story of two young people who, having known each other from childhood on, must go through the experiences of unhappy relationships before they find each other. By that time, Paul is married to an empty-headed beauty who has married him for his professional status, while Paula is busy raising two children by herself. It is not until she loses her son in a car accident that Paul realizes how much he loves her, and after overcoming her objections, he finally moves in with her. The film ends with Paula's half-intentional death as she gives birth to another child—Paul's—which she knew would probably cost her life.

Where does the explosive material of this love story lie? First of all, its entertainment value made it much more attractive than many contemporary products. With a great sense of the theatrical and the comical, Carow juxtaposes relatively realistic scenes—such as one that shows Paula hauling coal into her basement, a job everyone in the GDR is familiar with from his or her own experience, but one that also describes how she has to manage her life all by herself—with playful scenes that glow with the enjoyment of self-expression, especially on the part of Paula, who is played with great verve by Angelica Domröse.[23] The back and forth between serious and comical scenes and modes of presentation creates a tension which causes spectators to stay alert and try to orient themselves.

Interestingly, the Western press reacted to this film—one of the few to receive any attention on the other side of the Wall—with bafflement and a lack of understanding. The reviewer of a conservative Christian paper even used it to demonstrate just how bad life must be in the GDR: "If this nothing of individual freedom demanded in 'Paul and Paula' provokes such a scandal, the freedom to move in that state must be smaller than one has believed so far."[24] But the film was released and it contributed, within its limited means, to a liberalization of everyday life. The strong reaction it provoked reveals its meaning when one looks at its position within the aesthetic system of which it was a part.

The aggressive impetus of this "legend" actually must be considered quite strong: it absolutizes love and personal fulfillment; it even neglects to consider the role of the individual in the social sphere, reality being only an obstacle. Accordingly, the film met with criticism from the official press, such as this comment by Horst Knietzsch, who is the reviewer for the party paper, Neues Deutschland:

> While didactic elements weighed down some of our other contemporary films and therefore bored us, this film bears signs of isolation from society, it leads to a lack of personality of the characters. . . .[25]

He also criticizes Paula's death as not sufficiently motivated and refers to a recent discussion in the "Verband der Film- und Fernsehschaffenden"[26] during which one top official arrived at the conclusion that "death in the work of art needs profound reasons and must be, if it is to be used at all, of social relevance."[27] Of course the connection between love and death, a deeply romantic idea, had to raise suspicion on the part of the guardians of socialist morality. Carow's "legend" not only defends irrationality, the status of the outsider, a sensuous life style, but also celebrates these new values with great enthusiasm. It also contains an indirect blow to the ruling class by making Paula, a child of the people, superior in her humanity to Paul, who holds a high position in the government. This is probably the first portrayal of a top official as a person whose human shortcomings are directly related to his high social and political position.

Formally, the film presents a break with socialist realism in the strict sense.[28] The montage of realistic scenes and fantastic ones often has a parodistic effect. Carow's film is consciously, sometimes glaringly, theatrical. That this was his intention can be derived from a series of interviews, including one in which he pointed out that in the original version of the screenplay, Paula was able to perform magic when inspired by love.[29]

II–2   *The Legend of Paul and Paula (Die Legende von Paul und Paula)*

All of Carow's films deal with, and are designed to evoke, strong feelings. Hermann Herlinghaus observed that what made Carow's films of the seventies so explosive was the choice of young heroes and their energetic striving for self-realization, a psychological perspective, and an effective use of the actors that brought out the dynamics of interpersonal relationships.[30] I would add that the success of his films also results from a romantic attitude towards the world which expresses itself in a criticism of, or at the very least a supplement to, the enlightenment view: reason is not the ultimate authority; what motivates human beings is the totality of their desires, fears, and thoughts, which can neither be predicted nor prescribed. What meets human needs must consequently be equally complex. Carow's modern "legend" not only picks up the romantic idea of life as a mystery and of love as a force that will fulfill itself at the expense of death which it thus transcends, but it also uses a romantic aesthetic by introducing a mixture of genres—the realistic, the comic, and the tragic—with the inclusion of rock music and dream scenes.[31] The very title suggests an homage to the romantic appreciation of genres that belong to the Middle Ages and their religious and mystical world view.

Interestingly, Carow has consistently refused the repeated assumption that his cinematic style is one of "romantic realism."[32] In an interview he gave at the time he was working on this film, he answered the question of whether he saw a preference for romantic motifs as characteristic of his films, by saying that "I would totally deny that. On the other hand, poetry plays a role for me in film today, more than ever before. But that has nothing to do with romanticism."[33]

I understand Carow's protest against the label as a reaction to connotations the term "romanticism" carried in the GDR fifteen years ago. At that time, the romantic poets were considered bourgeois reactionaries, pathological individuals, and were carefully excluded from the cultural effort of *Erbeaneignung* (appropriation of the heritage). It was only in the seventies that a reevaluation of the romantic movement and its representatives took place, once again a process started by literature, taken up with considerable delay, and still not admittedly, by the visual arts.[34]

The most successful films of the late seventies assumed some of the elements introduced by Carow's film. In the works that followed his big success, *Ikarus* (1975) and *Until Death Do Us Part (Bis dass der Tod euch scheidet,* 1978), he went back to a more realistic technique, while preserving an emphasis on the exploration of the characters' inner lives. *Ikarus* is the story of a young boy whose hopes for a first plane trip with his father are shattered, a story of betrayal followed by disillusionment. Like Carow's other films, it makes a case for the validity and the value of young people's hopes and dreams.

Carow's films, as one critic put it, are all controversial.[35] *Until Death Do Us Part* stimulated a nationwide discussion as to whether the film actually reflected present trends in the GDR; it met with a high degree of criticism and disapproval. But it was precisely the controversial nature of Carow's films that made them famous and turned them into public issues.[36] This rebelliousness of intention characterizes all the films released between 1978 and 1982 that enjoyed great popularity. Like Carow's *Until Death Do Us Part,* all of them can be interpreted as studies on the situation of women as it evolved during the process of state-supported emancipation.[37] The public wanted, and accepted as figures of identification, the strong and sometimes aggressive female protagonist. With their films on women, filmmakers were able, for once, to attract great numbers of viewers to the movie theaters.

A Special Case: Rebellious Women

In 1979, Konrad Wolf, the GDR's best-known and internationally renowned film director, surprised his admirers and critics alike by making a film, *Solo Sunny,* about the problem-ridden life of a nightclub singer. This film became one of the most famous and most discussed films of the decade.[38] Wolf had made a name for himself with his excellent anti-fascist films, which were devoted to the analysis of Nazism, and with films that creatively explored the possibilities and the problems the new state had to face. Embracing the philosophy of the new beginning, he saw his task and his contribution as one of providing films that stimulated discussion; he thus found himself in agreement with the official mission of the artist.

The son of a Communist writer and doctor who had left Germany in 1933, and a convinced Communist himself, Wolf had spent his formative years in the Soviet Union, which he reluctantly left to help build up the new Germany. The films that brought him national and even some international acclaim, like *Lissy* (*Lissy*, 1956/57), *Professor Mamlock* (*Professor Mamlock*, 1960/61), *The Divided Sky* (*Der geteilte Himmel*, 1963/64), *I Was Nineteen* (*Ich war neunzehn*, 1967), and *Mama, I'm Alive* (*Mama, Ich lebe*, 1976) all deal with either the Nazi past or the formative period of the GDR. In the seventies, he made two films about the relationship of the artist with society, *Goya* (1970/71) and *The Naked Man in the Stadium* (*Der nackte Mann auf dem Sportplatz*, 1973). The difference between these two films and *Solo Sunny* lies in the treatment of art. While the two earlier films revolve around the central question of the freedom of art and the responsibility of the artist towards society (both artists are males), the later one focuses on the individual (a woman) and what art means to her—an instrument of self-realization. Sunny does not see herself as serving art, which in turn would be serving society, but art becomes her means of striving for an identity. The reversal of perspective in favor of the individual is another indication of the shift in contemporary GDR culture from the demands of society to the demands of the individual.

In his earlier films, Wolf had been known to dramatize great historical moments, in which the individual became the exponent of certain social and political changes. Asked why he had turned from his patriotic and at the same time cosmopolitan commitment to making a film about the problems of everyday life, and the marginal existence of an unfortunate starlet at that, he replied that the response, or lack of response to his latest film, *I'm Alive, Mama,* had alarmed and convinced him "that we must not avoid the debate on immediate, real, everyday life of the present, which is full of conflicts and questions."[39] Wolf's unfailing sensitivity to the needs of the historical moment led him to choose as the protagonist a woman whose struggles (for recognition, for a balance between her personal needs and her professional demands, and for an improvement of interpersonal relationships in general) managed to synthesize elements that had preoccupied the population at large.

The appearance of *Solo Sunny* signifies a turning point in Wolf's career—which was sadly cut short by his unexpected death in 1982—and testifies to a changing social and political climate in the GDR. Barton Byg, who considers Wolf's cinematic oeuvre "a useful indicator of trends in the cinema and cultural policy of the GDR over three decades," argues that *Solo Sunny*, his last film, attests to a more relaxed attitude on the part of the cultural bureaucracy towards socially critical art:

It [*Solo Sunny*] reflects the fact that the GDR has achieved a degree of historical and political legitimacy. Its artists can participate in contemporary social
criticism. The fact that a film such as *Solo Sunny* was not threatening to the
state shows that GDR film has begun to function as popular culture does in
any highly organized mass society.[40]

The film unfolds in a series of episodes characterized by Sunny's
search for a meaningful life, for being accepted as who she is. "Why, it
should be possible to be a personality without being famous" she tells a
friend, thereby admitting that artistic success alone would not be enough
to make her feel valued. Sunny's life does not meet her demands. She constantly finds herself in conflict with her environment, which discredits her
claim, or at least the aggressiveness with which she fights for it. At the beginning, we see her in a police office where she has to justify her lifestyle;
in her private life, two men, the bully in the orchestra who later tries to
rape her and the nice but singleminded taxi driver Harry, try to convince
her to throw in her lot with them, which she refuses to do in spite of occasional loneliness. When she finally meets a man she can respect and
love, the philosopher Ralph, he is so removed from her world, and in
fact so unable or unwilling to understand her demands, that the relationship ends with Sunny's failed attempt to murder him. Her own death
seems to be the only alternative left to her, but she is brought back to life
after a suicide attempt. The psychologists who offer support prove to be
of no help, either. After a brief return to the factory where she had
worked before being discovered as a singer, she pulls herself together
and auditions again, this time possibly better equipped with her own
song, which Ralph has written for her and which gives the film its title.

The episodic character of *Solo Sunny* as well as many other contemporary films has been a point of contention with the critics, because it was frequently understood as a technical failure. It constitutes, however, the stylistic correlative to the fact that Sunny's song remains incomplete, her
needs unsatisfied. Just as life in the GDR withholds personal fulfillment, synthesis of the various facets of life, from Sunny, the film withholds from
the viewer the satisfying traditional structure of a story that is organized according to the need for wholeness and completion. In the openness of
the quest, as in numerous other characteristics, the film is paradigmatic of
the many other films on women at that time. It presents a heroine who
goes through various situations, tries them out, as it were, without finding
one that would be right for her.

The strong and lively response to *Solo Sunny* confirmed that Wolf had indeed addressed a great need for the discussion of issues that crystallize
around the question of self-realization in the contemporary GDR. While
there were voices that sharply criticized, even condemned outsider figures like Sunny and their glorification in film, the majority of the letters,
even those from viewers who characterize themselves as conducting "or-

derly lives," reveal a strong identification with the heroine. "Sunny—that could be me!" one (female) reader wrote.[41] The reason so many spectators were able to project themselves into Sunny's character does not lie in her appealing profession, but in her quest for a meaningful place in society, and in her refusal to give in, even in the face of seemingly insurmountable obstacles.

The film also questions the idea of a "normal" life and suggests a new definition: normal must be considered what is essential, appropriate to an individual. This redefinition legitimizes individuality in the search for self-realization, and this is why so many viewers could put themselves in Sunny's place. As script writer Wolfgang Kohlhaase said, Sunny wants something "quite normal," namely to be needed, not just as someone to fill a place, but as the unique person she is.[42]

Along with the support of the individual goes an indirect, silent criticism of social reality. It manifests itself in the paradigms, in the oppositions the film sets up, which play off the "normal" versus the "unusual," the citizen versus the outsider, the new apartment buildings versus the old houses on Prenzlauer Berg, order versus creative disorder, reason versus feeling. *Solo Sunny* derives its potential for provocation from the fact that what was previously considered desirable, like having a secure job and living in one of the much-coveted new apartments, now appears to be the expression of a contemptible, petty-bourgeois attitude towards life. This paradigmatic shift was what many reviewers and critics found alarming.[43]

Konrad Wolf not only wanted to defend characters like Sunny, but also to recommend them and everything they embody as model figures for the future development of socialism. In an interview printed in *Neue Zeit*, he said that in socialism it is not enough merely to accept a person such as Sunny:

> In the long run, it [socialism] depends on such individuals. The real conditions under which socialism must develop and assert itself do require a long breath. . . . We must encourage the public to accept such people, encourage them and ourselves.[44]

Another reason for the film's great appeal lies in its poetic stylization, which distinguishes it from other works with the same topic and the same radical attitude. Naturally, this stylization serves the purpose of emphasizing the new values. For example, the grubby neighborhood of Prenzlauer Berg is depicted in a romanticized fashion so that it attains a slightly rundown, but alluring aura. This softening of the hard edges has caused even those critics who appreciated the film to complain about the inauthenticity of those scenes, and the implicit suggestion that in the recent DEFA films, worthwhile life only seemed to take place in the "rear buildings" (*Hinterhaus*).[45]

On the other hand, Wolf destroys the illusion of glamour in Sunny's life over and over again. At the beginning, the film seems to dive into the glossy existence of a star. It uses Hollywood appeal—Sunny is made up to look like Liza Minnelli—totally uncharacteristic of Wolf's previous films. But already the opening scene contrasts the seeming splendor with the real cheapness of Sunny's artistic world. A closer look at the primitive working conditions, the slimy announcer with his tactless introductions, the "boys" from the band called "The Tornadoes," convinces the spectator that this is a milieu that does not give much reason to be proud of being an artist. Eberhard Geick's camera work intensifies the effect of these contrasts by abruptly moving back and forth between long (establishing) shots that preserve the illusion of glamour, and close shots or even closeups which reveal the whole dishearteningly shabby reality of Sunny's workplace. Thus Wolf cunningly uses the Hollywood technique and the effect of show business to capture the spectator's attention, only to dismantle the first impression by a "closer analysis" of the milieu. Even in the disillusioning shots, however, Wolf remains faithful to the principle of a well thought-out composition, which gives the film its unified look in spite of the unsettling visual and thematic jumps.

Sunny's song helps viewers to understand the seeming contradiction between a romanticizing and a disillusioning technique as interrelated elements of a greater conception. Her solo, which Ralph has written for her in bits and pieces during their relationship, epitomizes her claim for recognition as an individual. "She's Sunny, they will say/some day," she sings, in English—a concession to the goals of (Western) individualism? The song portrays her hope, her longing, as a dream not yet realized. Some day she will be recognized and accepted for her own self.[46] It therefore unfolds, like the film as a whole, as a dream; the vision of beauty and wonder which we sometimes see is as yet a figment of our imagination.

The films that analyze the situation of women share some basic structural and thematic patterns with *Solo Sunny*. The protagonists find themselves in an existential crisis, because of seemingly insurmountable personal and professional problems, because of illness or because they have come in conflict with the law, and this crisis moves them to rethink what is important in their lives and to consider turning everything upside down. They go about their search with great energy and the conviction that to look for personal happiness is their inalienable right. Their enthusiasm for experimentation goes hand in hand with a deep and sometimes aggressive skepticism towards traditional values. Compared with the lively and colorful heroines, whose portraits, however, do not always escape the stereotype, the male counterparts in these films are frequently pale and passive observers of all the turmoil around them, and more often than not, fail to rise to the occasion of a new start in life. This accounts for some of the heroines' frustrations, for while they are more than willing to take the responsibility for their lives into their own hands, they cannot change the colleagues and partners with whom they work. The position

II–3   *Solo Sunny*

of the woman in these films is so prominent that one critic felt inclined to draw the conclusion that the "heroines are representatives of human possibilities for development in socialism as such. . . ."[47]

Most of these films are made by men, and the few women directors like Iris Gusner and Evelyn Schmidt have not been successful.[48] Even Schmidt's *The Bicycle* (*Das Fahrrad,* 1982), which treats the same subjects as the other films on women, did not manage to elicit the same lively and strong response. The neglect it experienced on the part of the public and critics alike is not quite justified, for it adds to the typical features of the women's film an analysis of class conflicts which were hinted at in Carow's *Legend of Paul and Paula* but not really examined, and were not brought up as a topic in the later films. Susanne, a young worker with a child, meets an engineer who has just passed his exam and has drifted from the distinguished party "upstairs" to the smoke and rock music-filled disco scene "downstairs" where she spends her evenings, aimlessly hanging out with her friends. The young engineer tries to get to know her, but she remains distant, so that for most of the film the relationship remains tentative. This leads to an atmosphere of hesitation and a lack of action much criticized by reviewers.[49] The reasons for the difficulties in getting together for two people from such different backgrounds be-

come obvious, though, when Susanne has falsely claimed her bicycle
was stolen and the fraud is discovered. Her friend's first reaction is concern over what the people in his company will say. The resulting fight polar-
izes and defines them as representatives of the two value systems mentioned before; his success-oriented life, his commitment to order and
reason, stand in contrast with her disorderly existence. Schmidt does not ro-
manticize the heroine's lifestyle but, on the contrary, shows her poverty
and lack of options as limiting and depressing; yet she has Susanne leave
the man who could lift her out of her old milieu because she refuses to
live according to the value system to which he adheres.

It is an indication of the profound paradigm shift in the films on
women between 1978 and 1982 that a social outsider, a person turned
criminal, becomes the model against which society is measured. This applies also to Erwin Stranka's *Sabine Wulff,* which appeared one year before *Solo Sunny.* It describes the start in life of an eighteen-year-old
woman who has spent time at the *Jugendwerkhof*—a juvenile correction
house where the youngsters work and receive an education—for her early
years of rebelliousness and petty larceny. During the credit section of the
film, we see scenes in rapid succession and without diegetic sound that
give an impression of the process of socialization she has just gone
through at the "Werkhof." The film and the protagonist's new free life

II–4   *Sabine Wulff*

begin with the moment she passes through the prison gate—the weight of her past on the one hand, and her hopes and dreams for the future on the other.

Faced like many of his colleagues with the question whether he would label *Sabine Wulff* an outsider film, Stranka replied: "No, and I wouldn't want to make such a film. I only make the premise that an eighteen-year-old girl leaves a "Jugendwerkhof" and then ask: How is such a person accepted by us, what happens to her . . ."[50] This makes it sound as though Stranka's main interest lay in the way socialist society deals with young people who have turned criminal, in the adequacy or inadequacy of social reintegration. In my opinion, however, Sabine's former transgressions of the law seem so poorly motivated and appear so insignificant that it is difficult to see her as a criminal youth who needs to be reformed. Instead, she comes across as a very positive character who embodies many of the qualities that make Sunny and various other protagonists powerful models of identification; honesty, an unwillingness to compromise her ideals, commitment to improving living and working conditions in the socialist state, and depth of feeling. Therefore the film transforms Stranka's question of how socialist society reintegrates those individuals who have gone astray into a reflection on how this society deals with creative, energetic individuals whose insistence on their personal visions often proves uncomfortable. This is the reason *Sabine Wulff* belongs to those films that represent a quest, as the title of the book upon which it was based suggests.[51] When we see Sabine decorate her new room by covering the walls with her fingerprints, we also know that it is herself, her own creative and productive potential, that she tries to find. The last long sequence that shows her wandering down the street, still looking for her own story, emphasizes the openness and the feeling of being in limbo between so many choices that do not seem quite right.

The structural and atmospheric affinity between the movies of this kind sometimes even manifests itself in details. Thus, Stranka considered calling his film "Blues for Sabine," thereby highlighting, as Konrad Wolf does in *Solo Sunny*, the elegiac, poetic mood of these women's life stories. The title of one West German reviewer's article on Hermann Zschoche's *One Year's Probation* (*Bürgschaft für ein Jahr*, 1981) was "Solo Nina," an indication that the author placed it in what was by then a tradition of the cinematic exploration of women's often very lonely way to self-realization. Their wish for a "solo," the expression of the totality of their dreams and desires, must often be bought at the price of loneliness and social rejection.[52]

Nina Kern, the protagonist of *One Year's Probation*, struggles to reclaim her children, who were taken away from her by public welfare because of her unreliability and her irresponsible life style. In the eyes of the community, she drinks too much, and a series of lovers make her unfit to ade-

II–5   One Year's Probation (Bürgschaft für ein Jahr)

quately take care of her young children. Again, the introductory scene
sets up a basic opposition that will structure the entire film; the contrast between the accused mother, sitting in front of an educational board, sulk-
ing, struggling with shame and pride, and the self-satisfied group of good
citizens who deny the woman the right to raise her children because she
does not conform to the values and the rules of society. The camera
moves from character to character, from face to face, and brilliantly tells
the story of irreconcilable differences in world view and moral attitude.
While the guardians of bourgeois values condemn the heroine, the camera does not.

Just as Wolf and Stranka had to justify their pleas for an outside figure—
who, after all, did not deserve so much attention, let alone sympathy—
Zschoche was criticized, for example by Fred Gehler in the intellectuals'
magazine Sonntag, for having constructed a universe of a petty bourgeoisie all of whose members had deteriorated to mere caricatures.[53] However, while the film works with very strong oppositions, the story prevents
a mechanical confrontation between bourgeois world and antibourgeois
heroine. One of Nina's "tutors," who is supposed to help her get back
on the right track, turns into a real friend. In structuralist terms, she "crosses
the boundary" and moves over to Nina Kern's side. Interestingly, in the
novel, which served as a point of departure for the film, this tutor is the
central figure and her inner change is the focus of the narrative.[54] It gives

another sharp edge to the story that true understanding and support come from a woman (!) who is a practicing Christian, not from the socialist community.

The reader-response column of *Sonntag*, in which viewers ask themselves and the filmmakers whether this movie truly reflects GDR "Alltag," again indicates that the function of cinema in the GDR consists in providing a means of communication about the social reality of the country.[55] Some of the viewers find the end (Nina gets her children back but, of her own accord, gives one of them up for adoption because she cannot manage to raise three children as a single working mother) negative and full of resignation. They see her as giving up, defeated, forced into a society she does not whole-heartedly accept. Their disappointment illuminates that they have, if unconsciously, sided with the value system of the film. *One Year's Probation* is certainly a successful plea for outsiders, and a call for more understanding and fewer prejudices, as West Berlin DEFA specialist Heinz Kersten argued.[56]

A different and thought-provoking commentary comes from Günter Sobe who writes for the *Berliner Zeitung*. Like many other critics, he grants that this is Zschoche's best film so far, and that the director's claim of giving an authentic picture of contemporary reality is fully met; but he raises the question how much further the cinema can move in the direction of the documentary.[57] Nothing, he argues, could be gained from a more intense exploration of documentary realism. Instead, Sobe wishes to see an artistic world in film, and quotes Goethe's theater director at the beginning of *Faust* who wants "the entire radius of creation" to be covered in the play.[58] This means the demand for a wholly different aesthetic, which the GDR art scene has only been able to meet in bits and pieces. The wonderful, the miraculous, and a certain radicalism of feeling will be noticeable in some of the films of the mid-eighties.

Even more so than Zschoche, whose careful composition of visual images reminds one of Wolf's cinematic style, Lothar Warneke subscribes to the documentary method; in fact, he has the reputation of being a fetishist of everyday life.[59] In *The Disturbance* (*Die Beunruhigung*), which appeared the year after Zschoche's film, he describes a day in the life of a woman—framed by the early morning hours of a day one year later—who finds out she has cancer and must have one of her breasts removed. The film is in black and white, to emphasize the sober and somber atmosphere. Lay actors were hired to heighten the authenticity of the narration, and the camera man, Thomas Plenert, who comes from documentary film and has worked extensively with Warneke, shot almost all of the scenes on location, some in the apartment of Helga Schubert, the author of the book on which the film was based.

While responses to *The Disturbance* were largely positive, praising it as Warneke's best film and as a gripping account of the situation, there have also been voices to point out that using particles of reality such as, in this in-

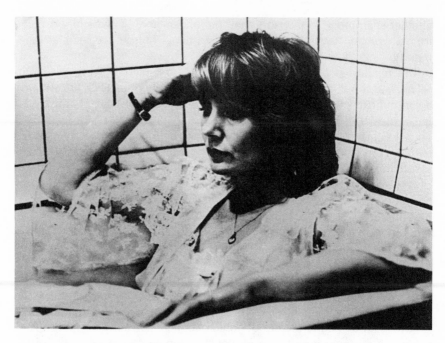

II–6   *The Disturbance (Die Beunruhigung)*

stance, a "real" doctor in the hospital and a lay actor for the heroine's son, does not necessarily increase the "truth of art."[60] Fred Gehler argues that the painstaking collection of realistic details does not add up to a true image of reality, and he quotes Bela Balaz's protest against a "fanaticism of the facts."[61]

Another objection to the film concerned its happy ending, which, to some viewers and critics, made it look as though a solid-functioning human relationship were the answer to all problems, cancer included. Thus the new man in the heroine's life, the right one to wake up with in the morning, seems like a *deus ex machina* who makes it possible for her to go through the ordeal of her illness and face the fear that it might recur. Why such a positive outlook, some spectators wondered; how does that relate to the claim of giving a realistic picture, even insofar as content is concerned?[62] But Warneke sees it differently:

> A positive ending often is rejected and considered unartistic, but I believe that is wrong. We should have the courage to look for a life-affirming solution, even with topics like these, and I see these possibilities in partnership between human beings.[63]

Warneke's comment reveals a basic contradiction in his work; only formally can he be called the fetishist of reality. The content of his films, however, proves heavily influenced by a moral attitude that may be governed by wishful thinking. A former theology student, Warneke has changed the field of his activity, but not the belief system within which he works. This is why all his films, of which *The Disturbance* is the best one, suffer from an unwillingness to delve deeper into the problems he analyzes, thus remaining superficial. In his earlier films, *Dr. med. Sommer II* (1969), *It Is an Old Story* (*Es ist eine alte Geschichte*, 1971/72), *Life with Uwe* (*Leben mit Uwe*, 1973), and *The Incorrigible Barbara* (*Die unverbesserliche Barbara*, 1976), Warneke had been able to use the hunger for *Alltagsgeschichten* (stories from everyday life) as a source of interest. These films fully explored the liberation from having to present the great subjects of history. His relative popularity was founded on the novelty of his approach, and in the attraction of cinematic works in which everybody could recognize familiar surroundings, lifestyles and characters. The surface realism of his works, however, usually lacks the sharp edge and skeptical insight that characterize Zschoche's and Carow's films, and accounts for the fact that Warneke has had few problems with the bureaucracy, and usually managed to realize his projects.

Walking a Fine Line: Films on Young People

Films about and for young people have the potential to address some of the same pressing issues which the films on women present.[64] In fact, in some cases, like *Sabine Wulff* and *Until Death Do Us Part*, the two categories overlap. Heiner Carow and Hermann Zschoche, as well as other filmmakers, have repeatedly chosen youthful heroes for their idealism, their purity of motivation and as yet unbroken hopes and desires. But the implied criticism that lies in the necessary comparison of the young hero's vision to reality as he finds it, and the suspicion that such films might inspire a whole generation with unrest and rebelliousness, makes them highly vulnerable to censorship. The notion that not enough is being done for the youth of the country is unacceptable to the GDR because it goes entirely against its proclaimed goals, and its self-definition. Understandably, there is no equivalent in terms of the youth film, or any other genre, for that matter, to the successful films on women who rethink and completely restructure their lives.[65]

Attempts to walk the fine line between a work too provocative to be admitted and one too lukewarm to attract attention, have often resulted in the production of so-called "small films," that is, very personal oeuvres that deal with noncontroversial issues and renounce the claim to great social relevance. Some of them are admirable, humorous miniatures about life in the GDR, such as *Ete and Ali* (*Ete und Ali*, 1985) by one of DEFA's youngest film directors, Peter Kahane, while others lack any substance worthy of artistic conception. Several of Roland Oehme's comedies belong in this last sad category, like *Je t'aime, chérie* (1986), as well as Gunther

Scholz's *Grown Up as of Today* (*Ab heute erwachsen*, 1985) and Erwin Stranka's *The Shark-Feeder* (*Der Haifischfütterer*). The latter represents an especially interesting case, since it touches on an important political issue without truly dealing with it. The young protagonist has committed himself to a voluntary three-year service in the army, instead of going for the required minimum of eighteen months, because, as he confesses at one point, he believes in his country's side. But this remains the only reference to this controversial subject, and the main part of the film revolves around how the hero can get his first sexual experience before taking off to serve the fatherland. To assume that the need for sexual conquest indicates a psychological displacement of his pre–military service anxiety would be giving the film too much credit. It may be impossible, as I have frequently been told, to make a truthful film about service in the army, but it is certainly avoidable to make one that, while seemingly addressing the issue, clouds and sentimentalizes it.[66]

Among the few films that tackle problems of the young generation head-on is Zschoche's *Island of the Swans* (*Insel der Schwäne*, 1983), for which Plenzdorf, a sure bet for explosiveness, wrote the screenplay. It shows the world of early teenagers as totally indifferent, if not hostile to

II–7   *Island of the Swans*
(*Insel der Schwäne*)

their needs—virtually deserted by grownups, except for brief moments when they give advice, admonition, or warnings.

Stefan, the thirteen-year-old protagonist, moves from an idyllic, but technologically backward place in the country, to one of the much-coveted modern apartments in Marzahn, one of the particularly disfigured new residential districts of East Berlin. The dichotomy works the same as in more recent films which, with the help of an outsider/criminal/victim figure, turn around the familiar value system of old versus new, anarchy versus order, feeling versus reason, and so on. The old country house, complete with a grandmother and a view of the lake over which the swans fly in slow motion, stands for a better, full life, while city planning, in the spirit of maximum efficiency, has left no room for children, the guardians of humankind's creative and imaginative potential.

In this case, Plenzdorf and Zschoche went too far. A fake reader response instigated by the youth organization Freie Deutsche Jugend (FDJ), as well as the official critics, rejected the film for its supposed distortion of socialist reality, implausibilities of plot, and a generally negative mood.[67] Horst Knietzsch in *Neues Deutschland* summarized the criticism of the ideological content when he asked, rhetorically, "how much narrow-mindedness or ignorance" it took to make a film about young people which devalues their own contribution to the building of new settlements by making the buildings look like "a frightening and oppressive 'world of concrete.' "[68] The complaint about the negative attitude towards the blessings of socialist civilization, which is still striving to catch up to Western standards of living, strikes the reader as predictable and understandable, as does the formal criticism of the rigidity with which the world of the old and the new are contrasted.[69] To the initiated friend of GDR film, however, the attack on the story's implausibility must appear as the devious victory of the cultural bureaucracy that has mutilated the film in the first place.

The film that provoked such a violent reaction was already a watered-down version of an earlier concept. In the original script, Stefan develops an adversary relationship with a boy slightly his elder, who blackmails the weak Hubert and tyrannizes the whole group of youngsters. This youth, called Windjacke, tries to show to his grandparents that, contrary to their wishful thinking, evil still exists. Having spent part of the war in a concentration camp, the grandparents believe that, with socialist society, paradise has come to earth.[70] Windjacke's extreme case of "acting out" is thus related to a denial of reality on the part of his family. A committee of resistance fighters who previewed the film declared that this was a distortion of the views and attitudes of former members of this movement, to which the grandparents had belonged, and insisted that the scene be taken out.[71] The understandable reaction on the part of the critics was the complaint that Windjacke appears "way too much as the incarnation of evil."[72] By cutting out the grandparents who insisted that all evil had been banned from the (socialist) earth, the censors cut out themselves, and undermined a more adequate understanding of the story. It is due to this attitude—closing one's eyes to the problems and dangers of the present—that the roots of such problems become invisible and the bad turns demonic. Robbed of its context, Windjacke's meanness must appear as diabolical; that disqualifies him as a character for socialist realism which has no use for the demonic.

Unnoticed by the self-absorbed adults, the fight between the two boys grows more and more serious, until it reaches its climax in a deadly duel, which takes place in one of the half-finished buildings on the vast construction sites in Marzahn. In the final scene we see Stefan threatened from behind by his enemy who tries to push him down a shaft. In a brief struggle, Stefan manages to move back, and now it is Windjacke who falls and can only hang on to the wall of the shaft with the tips of his fingers. This was supposed to be the final scene, suggesting Windjacke's fatal fall. But the censors required a "positive ending," and now the last shots of Stefan pulling Windjacke up, which is physically almost impossible, and then the screen going dark, seem like an intentionally unbelievable, abrupt ending.[73]

CONTRADICTIONS OF AESTHETIC NORMS: THE CRISIS OF THE HERO

When comparing the reception of very recent films like *Island of the Swans* (1983) and, say, *The Shark-Feeder* (1985), one cannot help but feel sympathy for the filmmakers who move between the Scylla of prohibitions and the Charybdis of requirements, between trying to address issues of some importance and themes that are taboo. As one prominent film director said in a personal interview, you are encouraged to present social conflicts and thus to contribute to their resolution, but persecuted if you really do.[74]

The current debate over the contemporary hero exemplifies this dilemma as perhaps no other issue does in the debate about aesthetics in the GDR. After 1983, a virtual panic seems to set in about the lack of characters that would qualify as true heroes. According to the critics who responded to the situation with their desperate SOS calls—save our heroes!—the protagonists seem to stumble through socialist reality, partly content, partly dissatisfied, not fully conscious, and certainly not aware of their opportunities to shape history. Even though the writers approach the problem from different angles, most of them agree that contemporary GDR films lack the following ingredients necessary to being successful: 1) A central hero who can evoke empathy and invite identification on the part of the spectator—a hero who actively participates in the larger social development of his time;[75] 2) A story that has social relevance and does not apply only to outsiders, or to highly idiosyncratic individuals, but that tackles the great social and political questions of the age. These criteria are reiterated or varied at every one of the many symposia and conferences and in a number of academic articles, such as Horst Knietzsch's contribution to the discussions of the hero in the films of 1983/84. In *Prisma*, the GDR's TV and film almanac, Knietzsch writes that he welcomes

> the artistic individuality of authors and film directors, but with introverted stories and narrative techniques, the reflection of their own modes of existence, the path to the spectator will be hard to find. The best works in the history of the DEFA have always been those that reflected the social changes of our time, the transformed socialist relationships in socialist society, [films] that gave artistic expression to the new human experiences, interests, thoughts, feelings and modes of behaving.[76]

Then Knietzsch goes on to identify his viewpoint as the official one, referring to party chief Honecker's address in 1984 that celebrated the artists of the country as "active and reliable co-producers [*Mitgestalter*] of the developed socialist society."[77] Honecker once again defines what kind of art the state expects, and his words make clear that while a greater generosity in accepting a wider range of themes and styles in art has become the norm, no institutional changes have occurred that would free the artist from his or her commitment to a specific ideological viewpoint:

> Our time needs works of art which strengthen socialism, which call into consciousness the beauty and greatness of what has been achieved, often with difficulties. [We need] works of art in the center of which stands the active hero who shapes history, the working class and its representatives. Naturally, for such achievements we need, especially in our struggle-filled time, a firm position. The attitude of an observer or critic of our society cannot do justice to this.[78]

Obviously, socialist art as Honecker promotes it does not allow for a critical analysis of the truly problematic issues of "our problem-ridden time," such as the so-called German question and everything connected with it; the idea of reunification, the spectre of continuing attempts to escape to the West, the difficulty of travel, as well as anything that touches on internal problems of the GDR and the unfinished edges that its short history has impressed upon the country's self-image.

Thus, for art, Kohlhaase's observation in 1972 about the "continuity of unsolved questions" is still valid.[79] Film directors are caught in a vicious circle of having to present the great conflicts of the age without adopting "the attitude of the observer or critic." This dilemma itself, however, can hardly be called by name at the many conferences and in the research articles devoted to the improvement of GDR film, since to do so would uncover the impossibility that underlies such a claim. In the booklet entitled *Ist der positive Held in unseren Filmen in Verruf geraten?*, however, two contributions contain at least some crucial questions that do not turn all of the attention to issues of aesthetics (genre, choice of characters, etc.), but place them in a larger context. Rolf Richter wonders why such issues as *Republikflucht* (attempted escape) and other political themes never make it into the contemporary DEFA film. Hans Müncheberg reflects on the preconditions that comprise a good work of art, and comes to the conclusion that it needs a great, authentic conflict. However,

> A conflict is great and profound when the hero's freedom of decision is great and believable. There must be two ways for the hero to go, and both ways must be possible, also in our society.[80]

Müncheberg then invents a situation he might want to dramatize in a film, and shows at what point "utilitarian thinking"—here a euphemism for censorship—would come into play.[81] If a film had enough explosive material, Müncheberg argues, the critics would start to worry about which group of people might be made to feel insecure or get some wrong ideas. Also, the question would arise as to whether the film would "discredit the real existing socialism."[82] But Müncheberg's is the only contribution among several dozen that raises the question of censorship. Most filmmakers and their critics go on looking for the roots of the crisis of GDR film within the artists' domain of aesthetics, and most artists continue to withdraw into small private worlds, mirroring in their films the general trend toward hiding in one's own little niche, which has led the West German diplomat Günter Gaus to talk about GDR society as a "society of niches."[83] While unwanted cultural activity can be suppressed, the desired work of art cannot be forced into existence, and the aesthetics of the small form may well constitute an indirect way of rebelling against a state-enforced concept of art.

NEW TENDENCIES IN ANTI-FASCIST FILMS

Anti-fascist films occupy a special position within the DEFA production. They belong to its longest and possibly best tradition, which started right after the war. DEFA was the first German film company to begin producing again after 1945, and continued to produce anti-fascist films, after a period in the seventies when public interest in the topic declined due to the intense involvement with questions of everyday life, right into the eighties. According to Wolfgang Kohlhaase, scriptwriter for the film *Held for Questioning* (*Der Aufenthalt,* by Frank Beyer, 1983), a direct line leads from the earliest films, such as Wolfgang Staudte's *The Murderers Are Among Us* (*Die Mörder sind unter uns,* 1946) and Kurt Maetzig's *Doomed Marriage* (*Ehe im Schatten,* 1947), to the film he made with Frank Beyer.[84] The older generation of film directors especially—those who had experienced the war as teenagers, who were young enough to remain innocent, and old enough to have known the horrors of war—repeatedly returned to the artistic representation of the historical period that led to the collapse of the Weimar Republic and the division of Germany into two separate states.

More than its Western counterpart, the GDR has followed the policy of "de-Nazification" to ensure that a repetition of mass seduction by a fascist regime would be impossible. It spent great energy on educating the population about the political and social causes and strategies of Nazism, offered from a socialist perspective, and made sure that no former Nazi officials attained positions in the government. In this context it is not surprising that the GDR welcomed and encouraged the attempts of writers and filmmakers to contribute their share of *Vergangenheitsbewältigung* (coming to terms with; working through the past). Thus the anti-fascist film became a sort of state-protected genre, in contrast with its counterpart in the FRG, where the works of Fassbinder, Kluge, Sanders-Brahms, von Trotta, and others who made films about the Nazi era, belong to an intellectual counter-culture that is eyed with suspicion or disregarded by the conservative majority.

The special status of the anti-fascist film within the DEFA tradition, which, in my opinion, relates directly to its success, results from the fact that on the topic of *Faschismusanalyse* (analysis of fascism), the interests of the government and those of the filmmakers met and merged. Taboos, if they existed in this realm, did not come into effect. This relative freedom from constraints produced a sense of control, assertiveness, and directness that is absent from many films dealing with the more sensitive contemporary issues. This fruitful meeting of interests also applied to matters of form. The official aesthetic doctrine of socialist realism was relatively easy to combine with Italian neorealism, the declared model for many GDR film directors in the fifties and sixties. Kohlhaase's following remarks about the beginning of his fascination with the cinema elucidate this situation:

> My interest in film arose from the experience of the destroyed city of Berlin towards the end of the war. These sights, the landscapes of ruins [*Trümmerlandschaften*], fascinated me, and I thought that it was absolutely necessary to capture them. At that time, I was very much fascinated with Italy's Neorealism while before that time, cinema had been, for me, something totally separate from reality, with splendor, pomp and glory; now I started to imagine a totally different cinema.[85]

While the genre of the anti-fascist film constitutes the one with the longest and most famous tradition in the GDR, it has undergone substantial changes in the forty years of its existence. After a period of hibernation during the seventies, when interest in the topic declined as a result of the intense involvement with questions of everyday life, the tradition resurfaced in the eighties, newly transformed by demands for self-expression in artistic work.

It may seem surprising that the anti-fascist film should have taken a turn towards the subjective; that it should have incorporated the same claim for individualism which had become the previous decade's main concern. But this is precisely what happened, and it may account for the profundity of change that the shift from a political to a psychological perspective also took place within the historical analysis of fascism. The anti-fascist films of the eighties tend not to deal so much with the war and its causes; instead, they focus on the effects it had, and continued to have, on the individual who was neither a hero of the resistance, nor an active member of the National Socialist Party. This turn to the average citizen as the protagonist had a great effect on the way the audience experienced anti-fascist films, since the majority could now identify with the heroes as characters who had, like them, just tried to survive the war.[86] The move away from the (Communist) resistance fighter and the evil Nazi as central figures in the films also allowed for a greater differentiation in the portrayal of the characters. Imagining ordinary people's daily struggles to survive and cope with the ordeals of the war, the uncertainty of the future, and the weight of their share of the responsibility for what was happening politically, led to such questions as: What is the guilt of the individual who has "only" played the part of the passive bystander? How much can a person bear to see and go through before he or she breaks down? How can one go on living a normal life after experiencing the holocaust, or the awareness of collective guilt?

Predictably, the official press reacted to the new type of anti-fascist film with mixed feelings. On the one hand, it welcomed the renaissance of the genre as a new stage of *Vergangenheitsbewältigung*. On the other hand, it viewed the preeminence of personal questions with suspicion, afraid that the historical dimension might be sacrificed. In some cases, a skeptical attitude towards the "privatization of fascism" proves to be well-founded. For example, Michael Kann's debut film *Stielke, Heinz, 15* (1987) uses and abuses the sensational aspects that can be derived from a story about the Nazi years. As the director candidly confesses, his goal was not to contribute to the understanding of fascism, but to make an adventure story.[87] This lack of concern for the historical dimension of the time period combined with an uninhibited exploitation of sensational, cliché-ridden situations, seems to reveal the questionable attitude towards fascism that Susan Sontag describes in her article "Fascinating Fascism."[88] In other cases, however, the rejection of films like *Olle Henry* (1983) by critics who claim that limiting a film to the personal perspective produces an unhealthy pessimism and a defeatist world view, strikes me as itself limited, and as an anachronistic insistence on a cultural optimism which totally ignores the truth of this particular film.[89]

Usually, however, the audience was aware of the fact that the new kind of anti-fascist film did not exclude the historical dimension, but rather incorporated it into the individual stories of average citizens. Frank Beyer's already-mentioned film, *Held for Questioning*, is a good example of a successful close-up of history. Based on Hermann Kant's novel of the same title, it tells the story of a young German soldier who, in 1945, is mistaken for an SS officer and detained in a Polish prisoner-of-war camp for having murdered a child. The time he spends there before his release becomes an ordeal and an unforgettable learning experience for him. While the Polish officials try to figure out whether he is guilty of the crime the mother of the murdered child has accused him of, he begins to think differently about guilt, and comes to realize that even his brief participation in the war as a simple soldier assigns to him his part of the collective guilt.

In contrast with the novel, which, like all of Kant's prose, is very complex, rich, and multi-layered, the film does not and cannot analyze the story from a number of different perspectives, but concentrates on the hero's limited view. The fact that the young German does not speak Polish, and that he soon finds himself in conflict with the other prisoners, further limits the spectator's verbal acquaintance with him.

While Beyer and Kohlhaase renounce the verbal richness of Kant's text, they gain a breathtaking intensity. Niebuhr, the hero, anxiously watches his environment for traces of meaning; so we search his face and physical expression to find out who he is and whether, in fact, we can trust him. The film thus captures the claustrophobic atmosphere and the hostility of the environment to which Niebuhr is exposed, but at the same time it transcends the totally subjective view, which would leave us with no text at all, by including the interpersonal dynamics of the group of real Nazi criminals with whom Niebuhr shares his prison cell. In their company, he begins to understand some of the psychological conditions that make people susceptible to totalitarian regimes. While they look harmless enough in their state of defeat and humiliation, they soon exhibit, through the games they play, through their pathological concern with hierarchy, order, and punishment, their strange mixture of sentimentality and heroism, the same sadomasochistic tendencies that qualified them for the role they played in the Nazi regime.

In an interview, Beyer refers to *Held for Questioning* as a cinematic "novel of education," thereby placing it in the context of the German tradition of classicism.[90] He furthermore emphasizes the film's trans-historical significance by explaining that what first attracted him to the book and to the story,

> has nothing to do with war or post-war time. It is the story of a nineteen-year-old who gets into the crisis of his life. One cannot choose at what time one is born. . . . We demonstrate that someone must make an effort to understand under which conditions he lives. This is not a given.[91]

II–8   *Held for Questioning (Der Aufenthalt)*

With all its subjective perspective, Beyer's film still achieves an interpenetration of the personal and the historical. With all its commitment to psychological analysis, it arrives at a tentatively positive conclusion. This gives the film a balanced, classical character, which has made it attractive to a variety of audiences.[92] More drastic, and more pessimistic in tone are Günter Reisch's *The Fiancée* (*Die Verlobte*, 1980), and *Your Unknown Brother* (*Dein unbekannter Bruder*, 1980/81) by Ulrich Weiss. The former resembles Beyer's film in the depiction of a menacing, claustrophobic environment and its effects on the human psyche. *The Fiancée*, too, plays in a prison where a previously apolitical woman has to spend ten years, after having been caught trying to deliver sensitive material for her lover who is active in the resistance. If it is love that has thrown her into this situation, it is also the power of love and hope that prevents her from breaking down under the strain of the brutal and inhuman treatment she endures during her long period of imprisonment and slave labor.

Your Unknown Brother actually does give the portrait of psychic disintegration. It documents the crisis of faith and the final breakdown of a man in the resistance who is betrayed by his own comrades, a topic that made the film unpopular with the official critics, since it admitted the possibility that the spirit of solidarity might not be enough to sustain a person in times and crises like these. Weiss also encountered resistance to his film because of his unorthodox aesthetic approach. He is one of the few DEFA film directors for whom visual composition carries as much importance as content, and he has been one of the few to openly ridicule, and even debate, such concepts as the positive hero.[93] In *Your Unknown Brother*, Weiss works with strong visual metaphors to express the protagonist's alienation, his growing sense of fear and despair as he realizes there is no longer anyone whom he can trust. The emphasis on visual images, combined with the fact that the events are seen entirely from the hero's perspective, transforms the film into a study of the mental and emotional breakdown of any outcast under any dictatorial system. The abstract nature of its presentation contributed to making the film susceptible to official criticism.

We find the same reliance on visual imagery in Weiss' subsequent work, *Olle Henry*, a portrayal of the emotional and economic sell-out of the "hour zero." The wasteland (*Trümmerlandschaft*) of Germany figures as the true protagonist, dominating the characters' pitiable attempts to create new lives for themselves. Realism and expressionism coincide here, in that the starkest visual images of burned-out cities and human beings are reality itself. Henry Wolters, formerly called Olle Henry, and Xenia, the woman who attaches herself to him, are so damaged by their experiences during the war that neither Xenia's affection for Henry, nor the glimpses of possibilities for them to build an existence together have the power to carry them through this time. All their efforts concentrate on survival, and prevent them from examining their previous beliefs and attitudes, which have since become obsolete. Xenia, especially, hangs on to her fantasy of reversing the division of human beings into winners and losers by becoming a winner for once. Projecting her wish onto Henry (who was a boxer before the war and wishes to return to his profession) Xenia tries to make a "killer" out of him by preparing him for his first big fight. She provides him with good food and lavishes him with attention, but the bitter end shows Henry as a beaten man whose last fight has left him in a stupor from which he is not likely to recover.

In 1983, the year that saw the release of *Held for Questioning* and *Olle Henry*, a third film on the Third Reich came out: *Fariaho* (the word is the refrain in a song about the joys of gypsy life) by Roland Gräf. This film gives the spectator a very subjective view of history—one so idiosyncratic, in fact, that many reviewers claimed they could not make much sense of it.[94] Indeed, the story is nearly as exotic a story as any in GDR film. It is the story of former concentration camp victim, Sebastian Fussberg, who tours the GDR in a decrepit old van, and tries to offer his hopelessly old-fashioned puppet shows to an uninterested audience. The film starts when Fussberg picks up the grandson of a friend who was in Buchenwald with him and died there, promising him a free life on the road and many adventures. To the youth's disappointment, this life turns out to be strenuous and unexciting, except for his new acquaintance with

II–9   *Fariaho*

a young woman who decides to travel with them. In the end we see
Fussberg alone once again, as he drives into the devastatingly monoto-
nous and sterile landscape of a new settlement.

The film connects several important interrelated issues, that prove to
be difficult to discover. Thus Günter Sobe acknowledges that Gräf's film
is about a particular view of the artist as a gypsy—an eccentric individual
at the periphery of life—but he cannot understand why the director
added the political dimension of Fussberg's holocaust past.[95] Fussberg's insistence on symbolic art, however, is deeply connected with his emphasis on the ineradicability of the past; it is not just an obsession with his
time in Buchenwald where he used to entertain the other inmates with
more success than nowadays. He believes that realism, as he hears it promoted at a conference he attends, not only gives a one-sided view of reality, but also constitutes a kind of betrayal; the same kind of betrayal if he
were to make a late profit from his past in Buchenwald, accept the pen-
sion he is entitled to, and make a comfortable life for himself. This is
what a high official, who has also spent time in a concentration camp, suggests to Fussberg, provoking only his angry insistence that "nothing could
be done about it" (i.e., the past). Gräf's film is thus a plea for artistic and
emotional structure, for the symbolic versus the realist mode of thinking.
His own very complex and difficult work, to which a brief analysis like

this cannot do justice, is itself an example of the kind of art that would neither lose itself in social irrelevance, like Fussberg's, nor compromise itself
by submitting to the "Bitterfeld option" so sarcastically treated in the film.

RECENT FILMS: TESTING THE BORDERS

The most recent productions of DEFA films do not offer a clear picture.
There are no major trends, no favorite topics, no films that have gained
the popularity of those of earlier periods. Contrary to some of the official
GDR press, however, which seems to me to be inappropriately harsh in
its criticism of the "small" and idiosyncratic film, I would like to argue
that already-existing trends are emphasized, which leads to a degree of experimentation and variation that pushes the boundaries of the respective
genres. Thus, the individualism and romanticizing attitude of some films
are taken to the extreme, while staying within a very personal realm,
which confirms Gaus's speculation about the development of the GDR towards a *Nischengesellschaft*. The more realist films focus on this increasingly smaller details of reality until the perspective dissolves and the picture seems strangely unreal, or unexpected. This is the case with films
related to, but not necessarily in the mainstream of, the comic genre. In
the last part of this analysis, I examine three groups of films that embody
these subtle trends of the eighties.

Stretching Comedy

Comedy has always been a stepchild of GDR film. Apart from Frank
Beyer's *Carbide and Sorrel* (*Karbid und Sauerampfer*, 1963) and Günter
Reisch's *Anton the Magician* (*Anton der Zauberer*, 1978), few films have
been released that go beyond the unimaginative confrontation of clichés
and the resulting cheap slapstick effect. With the so-called small forms, unpopular with the press and the general public alike, a new kind of film
has evolved that is related to comedy, but often has either a devious, an enigmatic, or a very bitter edge to it, so that one has a hard time classifying
it at all.

Anton the Magician is still a classical comedy, firmly grounded in GDR
reality, and on the whole, on good terms with it. Reisch shows the development of the likeable but slightly corrupt auto mechanic, Anton Grupske,
"from the I to the we." Though the narrator displays a moral tendency in
his commentary, didacticism is pleasantly counteracted by the vitality of
the story, by Anton's earthy character and his charming unscrupulous-
ness. Audiences did in fact recognize him as "one of us," and responded af-
fectionately to this portrait of a real, down-to-earth person, and to his development at a time of social change which many remembered from their
own experience.[96] The story of the auto mechanic, to whom the renuncia-

tion of his very successful private business comes hard, was one of the films that did not make the audience feel cheated. While so many films of socialist persuasion claimed to present the *GDR* citizen and hero, but really offered an idealized type, Reisch's film introduces a character whose very weakness for women, cars, and the good life, offers qualities with which to identify. What adds to the complexity and the quality of the film is the slightly ambiguous attitude of the narrator when it comes to evaluating the true nature and the extent of Anton's "conversion." The comments about his moral improvement are all tongue-in-cheek, and in the end the narrator fictionalizes the story by toasting everybody—"even those who believe that Anton has really died!" Since Anton's death was connected to his conversion, to "superhuman goodness," as the legend of the evil knight has it—another parallel to Anton's life, we may venture that his conversion is mere fiction, too.

Music and voice are effectively used in *Anton the Magician*, not just to emphasize certain moods, but also to place them in relative relationships vis-à-vis each other. A variety of different types of music—rock, opera (Wagner!), songs, dance—sometimes exaggerate the atmosphere of a given moment, as when the hero and his "business friends" ride up the mountain on horseback to the monumental and voluptuous music of Wag-

II–10   *Anton the Magician (Anton der Zauberer)*

ner, so that a comic willfulness becomes apparent. The contradiction between the soft, gentle voice of the narrator, his euphemistic description
of what Anton is doing, and the visual correction of the image, further
helps to create a comic contrast. It also seems to suggest a secret conspiracy between narrator and protagonist, as does the title, which refers to
the latter's illegal activities not as crime, but as "magic."

Anton is still a hero, even in the strict sense of GDR cultural politics,
which require the hero to be a positive character who takes an active
part in the social processes of the present. This ceases to be the case for
the central figures of those films in the eighties that received criticism for
their small or highly specialized subjects and situations. Roland Gräf's *Research in the March* (*Märkische Forschungen*), which appeared only one
year before *Fariaho* and resembles the later film in its complexity and
high artistic demand, certainly belongs in this category. The story, an adaptation of Günter de Bruyn's novel and very close to the original, especially in the extremely witty, eloquent and well-delivered dialogue, revolves around a famous professor, expert on the poet and political writer
Max von Schwedenow, and his friend-turned-enemy, the village teacher
and Schwedenow-enthusiast Ernst Pötsch. During the time of their cooperation following their accidental acquaintance on the occasion of Professor
Menzel's trip to the country, Pötsch slowly and painfully, very much

II–11   *Research in the March (Märkische Forschungen)*

against his own desire to see the professor as an extraordinarily wise man, realizes that the latter will sacrifice the truth to the success of his book on Schwedenow. Menzel does not care to hear, let alone admit for publication, what Pötsch has discovered about the supposed revolutionary Schwedenow; that, after a rebellious phase, he turned conservative and actually worked as a censor employed by the king. The fight between Pötsch and Menzel turns into one of truth against greed, but the portrait of the two characters does not fall into a black and white representation. For all his commitment to truth, Pötsch seems too wrapped up in himself—like Fussberg, another obsessed man—to attract the affection of the viewer, while the professor, with all his egotism which he would be the first to admit, is shown as a likeable man.

The press agreed on the high artistic niveau of the film, while pointing out that it would fail to attract a large audience, but was divided over generic questions; the film seemed too bitter to be a comedy—the end does in fact have a desperate touch, and it did not qualify as a "tragic comedy," since tragedy, as one reviewer stated, requires a fall from greatness which he was unable to detect.[97] The discussions about the film's genre reflect the uneasiness of the press vis-à-vis new paths in art, and also the inability to deal with works that move away from the traditional aesthetics.

This applies even more to Karl-Heinz Heymann's second film, *Unnatural Father* (*Rabenvater*, 1985). It is a study of divorce and its effects on the relationships between parents and children—and yet it is not that at all. The story, about a man who renews contact with his son after a two-year absence from his family, leads to an exploration of interpersonal relationships that leaves traditional "studies" of divorced families far behind, especially from the "problem film' supported by GDR cultural politics.[98] The negative response to perhaps one of the best films in GDR cinema during the last ten years may be attributed to the fact that it does not provide the same basis for discussion as the controversial films of the late seventies and early eighties. In an interview, Heymann emphasized that it was not his intention to make a film in which one could assign the labels of right and wrong to the different parties.[99] The balanced view of all the characters has caused critics to complain about their lack of emotion, the fact that they never lose their composure, and that they carry on conversation as if completely governed by reason all of the time.[100] By searching for conflict in Heymann's films, critics have failed to realize that his work follows a totally different course.

The film plays with the spectator's expectations. Every situation, which at the outset resembles those of other "problem films," takes a new and completely unexpected turn. The agonies of divorce do play their rightful role, but Heymann goes beyond the usual situations of shared custody, the overworked mother, and so forth, by showing how people arrive at places they never thought they would. This can be taken literally. When Jonathan finds out that his son has left for camp, he follows the bus and,

with the victim's active cooperation, kidnaps the child. Totally unpre-
pared for the trip, they spend an improvised vacation together; their motor-
cycle gets stolen, they begin to look like tramps, they live on dried
cookies—but they get closer to each other in a surprising and touching
way. What started out as a socially critical film turns into a GDR variation of the road movie—destination uncertain and really irrelevant.[101]

Unnatural Father is a particularly good example of a cinematic style typical of the GDR. Like many other films (even the less convincing ones) *Unnatural Father* surprises the viewer with the great care and gentleness in individual character study and the development of interpersonal relationships.
The camera approaches the characters with a curiosity that is at the same
time attentive, inquisitive, and respectful of their personal aura.[102] On the
story level, a corresponding gentleness of basic attitude expresses itself
through characters that usually deal with each other in an accepting and respectful manner, even if they happen to be in conflict with each other.
The cases where communication breaks down completely, as in
Zschoche's *Island of the Swans* and Frank Beyer's *Ram's Horn*
(*Bockshorn*, 1984), are the exception. The admirable humaneness which
the films embody and, at the same time, suggest as a way of dealing with
other people, constitutes a distinguishing feature of GDR film which remains—undeservedly and inexplicably—unnoticed in its country of origin.

II–12   *Unnatural Father (Rabenvater)*

Women's Issues Revised

While women's striving for the realization of their dreams continues to play a prevalent role in GDR cinema, none of the latest films on this subject manage to project the momentum, the sharpness, and aggressiveness of earlier works. Warneke's *A Strange Sort of Love* (*Eine sonderbare Liebe*, 1984) and Gunther Scholz's *Grown Up as of Today* (*Ab heute erwachsen*, 1985) have not contributed anything new to the picture and even fall behind what had already been achieved.

The year 1986 saw the release of two stronger, but highly problematic explorations of this favorite subject. Both Heiner Carow (who had not made a film in seven years) with *So Many Dreams* (*So viele Träume*), and Siegfried Kühn in *The Dream of the Elk* (*Der Traum vom Elch*) clearly assume the paradigms established by the older films. The women are the guardians of unrest whose dissatisfaction with their lives and social relationships leads them to question themselves and others.

But there are also differences, a stronger emphasis on some elements and a decrease of importance in others. Hope, the great stimulus for the earlier heroine (combined with the self-assurance of knowing that one's claims are legitimate), has lost its forcefulness. At least this applies to the hope for realizing their wishes in society—something that deeply connected the heroines of the late seventies and early eighties with the basic philosophy of socialism. What has moved into its place?

As the titles of the two films suggest, dreams play an important part in their stories; they move into the empty space created by the loss, or partial loss, of hope for the creation of a society in which the individual could completely express himself/herself. In Kühn's film, we encounter Anna, a competent, reliable anaesthetic nurse in her late twenties, and a group of her friends drifting through life. Anna is in love with a man whom, for his fierce love of freedom, she calls the elk, and whom she sees only once a year when he appears out of nowhere to spend a few blissful days with her. She spends the rest of her time working, confiding in her friend Anette, and dreaming about the absent Markus.[103] This is something the earlier heroines would not have done. They were geared towards real life, like the outsiders they embodied. They looked for experiences in the social world, even if at the outskirts of society; and if they nurtured dreams, it was to transform them into reality as quickly and as thoroughly as possible. Anna's substitute for a day-to-day relationship, on the other hand, seems to have turned into an end in itself. During her long times alone, she recites to herself, over and over again, the romantic poetry she shared with her lover. She writes letters to him which, instead of mailing, she collects in her closet; and she has no real hope of changing this situation. The alarming commentary on Anna's story is that the subplot of her friend Anette's painful but daily relationship with the egotistical and eccentric painter Ludwig, a story that could function as an alterna-

II–13   *The Dream of the Elk (Der Traum vom Elch)*

tive to or a corrective of Anna's unhappy attachment, ends fatally. Anette kills herself and thus destroys—within the context of this film—the only viable alternative to Anna's life. Anna's dreams still prove to be healthier than the one other relationship we see in the film, which is grounded in "reality." This does not speak well for the reality portrayed.[104]

As far as outrageous situations and relationships are concerned, *So Many Dreams* can hardly be surpassed. Christiane Klüver, who has just received distinction for her long and faithful work as the head midwife of a big hospital, meets her daughter, whom she had abandoned as a small child some twenty years previously, on the train back home. Unaware of who the young woman is, and elated and somewhat confused by the events of the day, she takes her home, where the young woman meets Christiane's boyfriend who is of the daughter's age and very much affected by her presence. The film culminates in the two women's self-revelations to each other, to a number of stupefied witnesses, and to the spectator who can hardly believe what these two have gone through. As it turns out, Christiane has an abusive marriage behind her, while her daughter, whose traumatic childhood development put her on the wrong track, has been through a sentence at the juvenile delinquent home and a marriage with a man of homosexual inclinations—a first in GDR film.

The emotional chaos resulting from these shattering confessions was more than many spectators could handle. East and West German critics agreed, for once, in their observation that Carow had "crammed all the conflicts which the DEFA usually likes to avoid into this one film," and that he must have conceived of it as a "kind of anti-film to the many DEFA productions" whose overriding characteristic is moderation in all respects.[105]

What is also new and interesting about Carow's most recent film is its use of dreams. It begins with a series of images that belong to Christiane's daydream on the train, fusing faces and events from the past with those of the present. At this time, the spectator has no way of understanding these images in the context of her life, and some of them do not "translate" easily even later, when they recur and reveal their connection with certain parts of the heroine's past. While they still function within the narrative as "real" dreams, they also begin to dissolve the realistic texture of the plot from the inside. With this film, Carow is closer to his 1973 *Legend of Paul and Paula* than to the other films he made in between.[106]

Still, even this film does not entirely leave the aesthetics of socialist realism behind. Accordingly, the two main women characters are grounded in the context of their historical situation, which lends to the film a curious double perspective and to the women a split existence. In spite of the importance of their dreams, both of them occupy very responsible positions. They work in the health profession, they are extremely reliable and competent, and they enjoy the respect and the affection of their co-workers, more so, in fact, than the earlier heroines. This split between day and night existence, between social reality and the dream that has become totally separate, is itself a romantic concept.

Does this suggest a move away from the "great subjects?" Not necessarily. In an interview about his latest film, Carow places Christiane Klüver in the tradition of great women in the GDR and expands:

> Her biography is at the same time a piece of history of our country; she started, like many others of her generation, to help create a different, a better world and has, in the process, lived a life full of contradictions, conflicts and hardship, and she has also become guilty. It is this question of her guilt that interests me.[107]

If one takes the analogy between Christiane Klüver and the GDR seriously, and if one imagines the woman as representing the country, the assumption of Christine's split existence acquires a new level of meaning. What has become, Carow asks, of the dreams, the initial enthusiasm, the innocence of the state that was supposed to be the better of the two Germanies? How much have we suppressed that emerges again in our dreams-turned-nightmares, and in which forms will the denied fears and desires eventually surface?

Private Films, Cultural Visions

That these questions can only be asked indirectly may account for the curious confusion in these films, their emotional hysteria, and thematic over-
determination.[108] It also alerts the spectator to suspect similar political implications in other seemingly "private" films. Thus sensitized to a subtle
system of underground communication, the viewer in fact discovers fragments of cultural and political self-portraits of the GDR in works of art
which at first glance do not appear to embody any self-reflection at all. In
the following three films, the new system of oppositions so characteristic
of the women's film is at work again, this time, however, transposed
from its application to different groups within society to different cultures.
In this value system, the GDR is associated with the less desirable side, another good reason for the film directors to make their point as subtly, yet
with the retreat into the surface story as open, as possible.

Zschoche's *The Middle of Life* (*Hälfte des Lebens*, 1985) traces the life
of the German romantic poet Friedrich Hölderlin, who spent the second
part of his life in an insane asylum and was, until recently, one of the out-
casts of GDR literary history. His academic resurrection is connected
with the recent acceptance of the romantics into the canon of the traditional heritage, so that the choice of subject matter was no longer a prob-

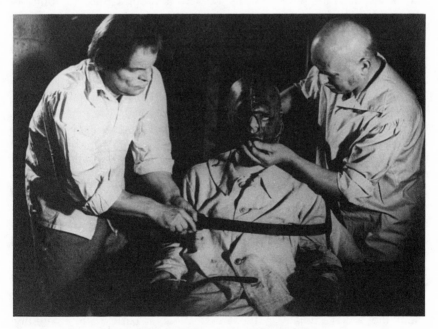

II–14   *The Middle of Life (Hälfte des Lebens)*

lem. The main complaint about the film was that it concentrated too heavily on the unhappy love between Hölderlin and Susette Gontard, and omitted the whole political context and the fact that "Hölderlin was undone by reality in general—the absence of the desired social progress, the failure of the revolutionary movements in his native land, daily life with its oppressive conditions. . . ."[109] Zschoche has confirmed the mainly romantic reading by saying that the love story was the element he wanted to emphasize.

But the general rule, that historical films function as an indirect commentary on the present, also applies to this film. The de-emphasis of the *specific* political situation only highlights the basic roots of Hölderlin's malaise; the discrepancy between reality and his personal poetic and philosophical ideal, and the national character of the Germans. In a revised binary system of oppositions, we see the ideal, the dream, played out against reality, a synthesis of feeling and thought against reductionist reason, the sphere of art against the sphere of politics. Hölderlin's idealist vision of the world demands the transcendence of such oppositions, and the freedom of the artists—claims that Zschoche had reason to express with poetic or even sentimental vagueness.

In Hölderlin's world view, the Germans are a people whose high standard of civilization has done nothing to improve its deep barbarism; so much so that in his novel *Hyperion* (whose protagonist has autobiographic features) the author makes the hero a young Greek; the outsider has now literally become a foreigner, someone who looks at society from the point of view of the "observer and critic" which Honecker had no use for in late twentieth-century GDR. In the film, we see and hear Hölderlin recite to his lover precisely a merciless condemnation of the German character.[110]

In his latest film, *Blond Tango* (*Blonder Tango*, 1986), Lothar Warneke makes the comparison between two cultures explicit. The plot describes the difficulties of a Chilean refugee with his new chosen fatherland, the GDR, which has become a home for him, but one so hard to love that on one cold day he sits down at the snowy beach of the Baltic in order to stare into the ocean and literally freezes to death. What better image can there be of the coldness of his new home, especially when compared to the close-knit community of which he was a part? Again, we witness the discussion of GDR culture by an outsider who associates the northern country with coldness, order, obsession with work and efficiency, and his native community with warmth of interpersonal relationships, imagination, and the pleasure-oriented life of the south.[111] The frame of the story—the fact that on the larger political level the GDR came to Rogelio's rescue—may have made it possible to bring up such unpleasant observations about the social climate in the GDR. What is particularly interesting about this portrayal is that the characterization of the East Germans rests on stereotypes that were applied to the Germans centuries ago, like

II–15   *Blond Tango (Blonder Tango)*

Hölderlin's of the early nineteenth century. This makes it particularly hard to understand why none of the criticism challenges Warneke's outrageous assumption that the German national character of the nineteenth century basically has not changed in the "new Germany."

The same abstention of the press from discussing such implicit statements on contemporary GDR society applies to the film on Hölderlin, and also to Frank Beyer's latest work, *Bockshorn*. The latter is the filmic adaptation of West German writer Christoph Meckel's fairy tale–like story about two youngsters' odyssey in an (unspecified) capitalistic country; a road movie with a fatal ending. The two boys meet the mysterious and evil Mr. Landolfi who tells Sauly, the younger of the two, that he has sold his guardian angel. While the older Mick manages to shrug off Landolfi's words as nonsense, Sauly begins to believe in them, falls ill, and finally dies after a fight with Landolfi, whom they have tracked down right before reaching the ocean, the destination of their trip. The film ends with the image of the weekend house, where Mick has taken his dead friend, going up in flames.

The film has confused critics and audiences alike. Since the beginning scenes were shot in the Bronx, the viewers assumed that Beyer was giving a picture of the United States, which, as he emphasizes, was not his in-

II–16   *Bockshorn*

tention.[112] As a portrait of the United States, the film was rejected, since it should be, as one critic said, up to the Americans to analyze their own culture.[113] But if the film is not a portrayal of any one capitalistic country and its neglect of and cruelty towards its youth, what is Beyer trying to say? While many have assumed that the film forms a universal parable, and that its story could also unfold in the GDR, it meets with violent resistance in the official criticism. All the negative attitudes of a world of grownups hostile to the needs and the dreams of children and adolescents— once again, the guardians of creativity and imagination—would apply to contemporary GDR society if Beyer had intended his film to be politically unspecific. The image he conjures up is too dark. In contrast to the other very critical films, this one has no corrective, no positive pole against which the bad can be pitted, and from which redemption can be expected—except for the moving friendship between the two boys, which dies with Sauly's death. The one redeeming perspective of the film may lie in the possibility of the boys' friendship and mutual support.

Conclusion

It is not surprising that the last films discussed here are only half successful and must live with the obscurities and ambiguities that are the preconditions of their existence. I would argue, though, that they count among the most interesting ones, because they represent an attempt to look at contemporary reality from a point "outside"—from precisely the distance that is still politically suspect, and at the same time, essential to artistic creation. Thus they contribute their share to redefining the role of the artist and the intellectual in the GDR; mediating between the productive demand for social participation and the need for artistic freedom. It is this kind of film from which we can expect the most interesting developments in the future.

NOTES

1. For an overview of the relationship between politics and culture in the GDR, see Manfred Jäger, *Kultur und Politik in der DDR.* (Köln: Wissenschaft und Politik, 1982); Hans-Jürgen Schmitt, ed., *Die Literatur der DDR,* in the series: *Hansers Sozialgeschichte der deutschen Literatur,* Band 11 (München: dtv, 1983); Dietrich Staritz, *Geschichte der DDR 1949–1985* (Frankfurt/Main: Suhrkamp Verlag, 1985).

2. *Sonntag,* 11/1980 ; as quoted in Jäger, p. 179. (All translations are mine.)

3. For an evaluation of the radically different starting points of the two German cinemas, see Jean Roy and Jacques Petat, "Les Cinémas des Deux Allemagnes," in *Cinéma* 249, 1979; pp. 13–47.

4. Reader responses in papers like *Sonntag, Wochenpost,* etc. show that films indeed serve the purpose of initiating discussions on relevant issues. Compare also Christiane Lemke's article "New Issues in the Politics of the German Democratic Republic: A Question of Political Culture?" in *The Journal of Communist Studies,* Vol. 2, Number 4, December 1986, p. 344.

5. The main periods of short-lived thaws were after the workers' uprising in 1953, after the building of the wall in 1961, and at the beginning of the Honecker era.

6. As quoted in Wolfgang Emmerich, *Kleine Literaturgeschichte der DDR* (Darmstadt, Neuwied: Luchterhand Verlag, 1985[3]), p. 178. Already in 1972, however, Honecker qualified his earlier promises on the freedom of art: "If we decidedly speak for the breadth and variety of all the possibilities of socialist realism, . . . this excludes any concession to bourgeois ideologies and imperialist concepts of art." In Jäger, p. 136.

7. Maetzig's *The Rabbit Is Me (Das Kaninchen bin ich,* 1965) and Beyer's *Trace of the Stones (Spur der Steine,* 1966) were among the most criticized films, but a large part of the DEFA production of the year 1965/66 was destroyed or taken to the archives.

8. As scriptwriter Wolfgang Kohlhaase, who had worked together with Gerhard Klein on *Berlin Around the Corner (Berlin um die Ecke,* 1965)—another film never shown—said years later, the break of confidence between him and the cultural bureaucracy had paralyzed him for years and made him question the notion that the artist shared power and responsibilities with the politicians of his country. See: Manfred Jäger, *Kultur und Politik in der DDR* (Köln: Wissenschaft und Politik, 1982), p. 122.

9. Biermann had grown up in Hamburg, West Germany, and had moved to the GDR in 1953 to help build up socialism. His problems with the SED had started in 1962.

10. For a good overview of the GDR version of socialist realism, see Emmerich, pp. 77–82.

11. Compare Hans Drawe, "Literatur in Film," in Hans-Jürgen Schmitt, ed., *Hansers Sozialgeschichte der deutschen Literatur* (München: Carl Hanser Verlag, 1983), p. 220.

12. For example, see Horst Knietzsch in "Helden gesucht! DEFA-Spielfilme der Jahre 1983/84," in *Prisma,* vol. 16 (Berlin: Henschelverlag, 1985); also various publications of discussions on aesthetic questions published by the "Verband der Film—und Fernsehschaffenden," such as: *Die jungen Helden* (*The Young Heroes,* Berlin, 1986) and *Ist der positive Held in unseren Filmen in Verruf geraten?* (*Does the Positive Hero Have a Bad Reputation in Our Films?,* Berlin, 1985).

13. Emmerich, p. 79.

14. The concept of the work of art as organic, as a totality reflecting the inclusiveness of reality, as a "whole" whose parts were interrelated in a complex and necessary way—this conservative, traditional concept of art was designed to appeal to the non-proletarian groups in society, and to give the audience figures of identification who were industrious, responsible individuals willing to give their whole energy to the state (see Emmerich, p. 80). Understandably, the "positive hero" with his commitment to the common cause fits right into this program.

15. Jäger, p. 48ff.

16. Compare footnote 12.

17. Compare Jäger, pp. 135–58, especially p. 138.

18. While the writers of rock music, for example, used to come from an academic background, studied poetry, and produced highly demanding texts, the latest development shows a decrease in the quality of contemporary popular songs. (Gabi Stiller, in an unpublished interview 12 April 1987.)

19. For example Lothar Warneke's *The Incorrigible Barbara* (*Die unverbesserliche Barbara,* 1976), a film that thematizes and advocates women's emancipation, but it is such a model case, so soberly constructed, that it failed to engender the lively response which characterized the reception of the other women's films which appeared only a few years later.

20. For biographical information on individual film directors, as well as interpretations of their works, see *DEFA-Spielfilm-Regisseure und ihre Kritiker,* ed. Rolf Richter, vols. 1 (1981) and 2 (1983) (Berlin: Henschelverlag); see also Heiko R. Blum, et al., *Film in der DDR* (München, Wien: Carl Hanser Verlag, 1977).

21. Many of Carow's films, like *Ikarus* (1975), deal with the lives of very young people or even children. Asked whether it was his main goal to tell stories about the youth of his country, Carow replied that that was not the point, but rather "the high and ideal demands which young people generally have on life." He goes on to characterize his hero Matthias, who represents Ikarus, as "suited to represent this high morality, which our society must expect from everyone." See Heiner Carow, *Filmkunst, die alle angeht, Aus Theorie und Praxis* 3, 1983, p. 67.

22. Plenzdorf turned *Die Neuen Leiden des jungen W.* into a play, which was successfully performed all over the GDR, and later into an equally popular novel (1972). The book turned out to be unique and controversial at the time because it introduced the colloquial language of young people into literature, which immediately endeared it to the younger generation, and because of the spontaneity with which the youthful hero propagates his own view of the world, i.e., his society. Plenzdorf, author of numerous other film scripts, continues to dramatize the way of life of young people and receives as much enthusiastic response from them as he gets criticism from the authorities.

23. In an interview with Hartmut Albrecht, Carow describes the process of

working on this film which, as he says, had not been planned to the last detail, but evolved as they were working on it. Carow admits that one of his basic considerations when making the film had been how one could attract more people into the movie theaters, and that during the filming process, the crew as well as the actors had been carried away by the charm and the creative potential of the story. Carow, *Filmkunst, die alle angeht, Aus Theorie und Praxis* 3, 1983, p. 21f.

24. Eckhart Schmidt, in *Christ und Welt*, 22 March 1974. Also Siegfried Schober in the West German magazine *Der Spiegel* totally pulls the film to pieces (4 January 1974).

25. 3 March 1973.

26. The term is virtually untranslatable and means as much as the collective of all of those working with film and TV.

27. As quoted in Knietzsch, "Helden gesucht! DEFA-Spielfilme der Jahre 1983/84," *Prisma*, vol. 16 (Berlin: Henschelverlag, 1985).

28. Konrad Wolf's film *The Divided Sky* (*Der geteilte Himmel*, 1963/64) is even more experimental in the way it joins together different levels of narration, just like Christa Wolf's novel (1963) with the same title, on which it was based. But the film met with disapproval and was labeled manneristic and unintelligible; neither Wolf nor any other film director has tried, in later films, to take up and develop the formal techniques with which Wolf had experimented in this film.

29. Carow, *Filmkunst, Aus Theorie und Praxis* 3, 1983, p. 44.

30. "Heiner Carow; Leidenschaft und Charakter," in Rolf Richter, ed., *DEFA-Spielfilm-Regisseure und ihre Kritiker*, Bd. 1 und 2 (Berlin: Henschelverlag, 1981, 1983), p. 52.

31. Hans-Jörg Rother identified the "logic" of Paula's death as the result of a dangerous "idyllic thinking." *Forum* (Berlin), 1 April 1973.

32. Hans-Dieter Tok, in *Leipziger Volkszeitung*, 30 March 1973.

33. *Berliner Zeitung*, 10 September 1972.

34. Christa Wolf's novel *No Place on Earth* (*Kein Ort. Nirgends*, 1979) and her scholarly work on the German romantics are among the most important and most influential examples of "Erbeaneignung."

35. Rosemarie Rehahn in a review of Carow's *So Many Dreams* (*So viele Träume*, 1986) in *Wochenpost* (Berlin), 10 October 1986.

36. About the reception of *Until Death Do Us Part*, Carow said that: "The most important thing about it was the almost relieved openness, the need to speak one's mind, to communicate." (*Filmkunst, Aus Theorie und Praxis* 3, 1983, p. 73). He understands the function of his story as a therapeutic one and claims that even though a film may have technical and conceptual problems, it can be a great success in terms of its potential to make people talk about issues they usually suppress.

37. The GDR is the most advanced country in the Eastern block in terms of actively supporting women's emancipation by creating the social network necessary for a woman to combine family life with a professional career. See Gisela Helwig's study *Frau und Familie: Bundesrepublik Deutschland—DDR* (Köln: Verlag Wissenschaft und Politik, 1987²), especially chapters 3 and 4. However, while the institutional foundation has been laid, attitudes and ways of thinking are much slower to change, and so the expectation that women contribute their share to the economic growth of the country by being part of the work force has led to double duty for them, the negative results of which are addressed, for example, in contemporary women's literature and in film. Many of the heroines of the films I am discussing, such as the mother in *Grown Up as of Today*, and Nina Kern in *The Disturbance* are single mothers who struggle to make a living for their families and have time left for their children.

38. A compilation of articles under the title " 'Solo Sunny'—ein Film von Wolf und Kohlhaase," appeared in the GDR's esteemed literary journal *Weimarer Beiträge* 6, 1980, containing contributions by Lothar Bisky, Irene Dölling, Lutz Haucke, Artur Meier, Ingeborg Münz-Koenen, Hans Richter and Silvia Schlenstedt, pp. 90–110. The monthly journal on film and TV, *Film und Fernsehen (FF)*, published an extensive review by Dieter Wolf (*FF* 6, 1980, pp. 3–7), followed by further discussions, often in the context of other DEFA films on women, such as Maja Turowskaja's article, "Auf der Suche nach einer 'freundlichen Welt,' " in *FF* 1, 1981, pp. 20–24, and Hans-Rainer Mihan's contribution "Sabine, Sunny, Nina und der Zuschauer," in *FF* 8, 1982, pp. 9–12.

39. *Freiheit* (Halle), 25 January 1980.

40. Barton Byg, "Konrad Wolf: From Anti-Fascism to *Gegenwartsfilm*," in *Studies in GDR Culture and Society*, Selected Papers from the Tenth New Hampshire Symposium on the German Democratic Republic, ed. Margy Gerber et al. (New York: University of America Press, 1985), pp. 115–124; p. 115, p. 122.

41. *Wochenpost* (Berlin), 21 March 1980.

42. *Wochenpost* (Berlin), 25 April 1980.

43. Konrad Wolf embraced this quality of the film, saying it would bother him if it were not alarming. *Wochenpost* (Berlin), 25 April 1980.

44. *Neue Zeit* (Berlin), 19 January 1980.

45. Ingeborg Münz-Koenen in her contribution to " 'Solo Sunny'—ein Film von Wolf und Kohlhaase," *Weimarer Beiträge* 6, 1980, p. 106. She concludes that "The protest against an equation of new building and socialist quality of life threatens to become a new cliche."

46. This prompted Lutz Haucke, in his contribution to the discussion in *Weimarer Beiträge* 6, 1980, to reject the film on the basis of its negative evaluation of contemporary reality: "The present here becomes a negative post in the historical development (" 'Solo Sunny—ein Film von Wolf und Kolhaase," p. 98). He also finds fault with what he calls the film's undialectical perspective, resulting from the director's and scriptwriter's uncritical acceptance of Sunny, and the unquestioned assumption that society will not be able to give her what she needs. Haucke's criticism, the most negative evaluation of the film I have seen, culminates in his observation that Wolf has fallen behind the constructive dialectical/historical approach of his earlier films in favor of a less complex and truthful moralizing one, p. 95ff.

47. Hans-Rainer Mihan, "Sabine, Sunny, Nina und der Zuschauer," *FF* 8, 1982, p. 12.

48. "I see little risk, and lots of resignation," said Margit Voss in her review of Iris Gusner's *Kaskade rückwärts* (untranslatable, a backward somersault in horseback-riding), in *FF* 3, 1984, p. 12.

49. See Margit Voss's review in *FF* 8, 1982, p. 14.

50. In *Freiheit* (Halle), 21 November 1978.

51. Heinz Kruschel, *Gesucht wird die freundliche Welt* (Halle-Saale Mitteldeutscher Verlag, 1976). The title of the book also seemed suited to characterize the totality of films dealing with women's quest for a better, a "friendly world," and inspired, for example, Maja Turowskaja's article "Auf der Suche nach einer 'freundlichen Welt,' " *FF* 1, 1981.

52. Heinz Kersten, "Solo Nina," in *Frankfurter Rundschau*, 25 November 1981.

53. *Sonntag*, 11 October 1981.

54. The change also reflects a shift of interest: while the protagonist of Tine Schulze-Gerlach's novel of the same title (1978) sympathizes with the outsider, the heroine of the film *is* the outsider. What intensifies the implicit social criticism is that the other tutor, the good socialist "Herr Müller," is the epitome of the

petty bourgeois who gives up on Nina when he feels that she cannot be sufficiently reformed according to his narrow moral principles.

55. *Sonntag*, 1 November 1981.

56. *Frankfurter Rundschau*, 25 November 1981.

57. *Berliner Zeitung*, 29 September 1981.

58. As quoted in *Berliner Zeitung*, 29 September 1981.

59. East Berlin film critic Regine Sylvester in an unpublished interview, 7 April 1987.

60. Fred Gehler in *Sonntag*, 7 March 1982.

61. Ibid.

62. *Thüringische Landeszeitung* (Weimar), 28 October 1982.

63. Ibid.

64. My following remarks on films about and for young people exclude children's films, which have to answer completely different needs and for which totally different conditions of production exist. In fact, the DEFA is famous for its sensitive and ambitious films for its youngest audience, and many renowned film directors like Hermann Zschoche and Rolf Losansky have repeatedly made films of that genre.

65. See Emmerich, *Kleine Literaturgeschichte der DDR* (Darmstadt und Neuwied: Luchterhand Verlag, 1985³), p. 195: "Again and again young people take over the function of making obvious, by articulating their individual needs, the gap between (their) claims and reality, and it turns out that the GDR cannot stand the unintentionally estranging glance of children and juveniles."

66. Even Claus Dobberke's film *Drost* (1985) about Lieutenant Colonel Drost who, after thirty-five years of service to the People's Army, leaves to become mayor of a small town, and for whom this transition becomes an opportunity to think about his life, is, while not really satisfying in its analysis of Drost's attitude towards the army, a better film than *The Shark Feeder*.

67. See the reader response in *Junge Welt* (Berlin), May 1983.

68. *Junge Welt* (Berlin), 4 May 1983.

69. In *Island of the Swans*, two systems of reference are at work: on the one hand, there is the contrast between country and city, on the other hand, within the city of Berlin, that between "Altbau" and "Neubau," between the old houses and parts of town (like Sunny's Prenzlauer Berg) and the new settlements with their anonymity and uniformity (like Stefan's Marzahn).

70. The original version of the script is printed in Plenzdorf's compilation of a number of film scripts: *Filme* (Rostock: Hirnstorff Verlag, 1986).

71. It is common practice to have every film previewed by a number of committees who are responsible for accuracy and appropriateness of presentation; thus a film may "lose" a number of elements, even entire scenes, on its way from the cutting room to the viewer, based on the decisions of the respective committees.

72. Hans-Dieter Tok, in *Leipziger Volkszeitung*, 30 April 1983. Compare also Klaus Hannuschka's criticism in *Märkische Volksstimme*, 25 May 1983, and the West German Wilhelm Roth's commentary in *Süddeutsche Zeitung*, 20 May 1983; all the reviewers agree on the insufficient motivation of Windjacke's meanness.

73. It would be interesting to know if GDR audiences can draw the conclusion from occasional unevenness and thematic gaps in a film that something— and possibly even what—has been cut out.

74. For political reasons, the director cannot be identified by name.

75. For Carow, for example, this definition of the hero is still tied up with the notion of participation in a larger social process. See *Ist der positive Held in unseren Filmen in Verruf geraten?* p. 18. This Verband der Film booklet (see note 12) will be referred to, from now on, as *Positiver Held*.

76. *Prisma, Kino- und Fernseh-Almanach* 16, ed. Horst Knietzsch, (Berlin: Henschelverlag, 1985), p. 7.

77. Ibid., p. 11.

78. Ibid., p. 12.

79. As quoted in Jäger, *Kultur und Politik in der DDR*, p. 151.

80. In *Positiver Held*, p. 65.

81. Ibid.

82. Ibid., p. 66f.

83. Günter Gaus, *Wo Deutschland liegt* (München: dtv, 1986²), pp. 115–169.

84. From an unpublished interview with Wolfgang Kohlhaase, 3 April 1987.

85. Ibid. In this interview, Kohlhaase also explained his early commitment to socialism as the combined effect of youthful enthusiasm and the rejection and abhorrence of Nazism. For further reference, see also "What Film Can and Cannot Do in Society," an interview with Wolfgang Kohlhaase by Lenny Rubenstein and Shelley Frisch, in *Cinéaste* 13/4, 1984, pp. 34–35, 53.

86. Frank Beyer in an unpublished interview, 26 March 1987.

87. In *Progress Pressebulletin Kino DDR* 2, 1987, p. 11f.

88. In Susan Sontag, *Under the Sign of Saturn* (New York: Farrar, Straus and Giroux, 1980); pp. 73–105.

89. Horst Knietzsch rejects the film for its "small, subjective view of the world." See "Helden gesucht! DEFA-Spielfilme der Jahre 1983/84," *Prisma* Vol. 16 (Berlin: Henschelverlag, 1985), p. 22.

90. *Progress; Filmblatt DDR*, 1982.

91. *Sonntag*, 2 January 1983.

92. It should be noted, however, that the film was initially withdrawn from the Berlin film festival upon the request of the Polish government.

93. As an introduction to his remarks on the positive hero, he said: "When I read about the topic, I had to laugh, because a discussion about it reminded me of the Middle Ages when the monks in the monastery wrote voluminous books about whether or not angels have wings or how one has to imagine the soul's ascension into heaven. The concept of the positive hero never had a truly serious meaning for me. . ." *Positiver Held*, p. 54.

94. See Günter Sobe in *Berliner Zeitung*, 8 September 1983; Raymund Stolze in *Junge Welt* (Berlin), 3 September 1983; and Regine Sylvester in *Tribüne* (Berlin), 6 September 1983.

95. *Berliner Zeitung*, 8 September 1983.

96. See Hans-Dieter Tok's summary of reader responses, and his commentary in *Leipziger Volkszeitung*, 6 October 1978.

97. Fred Gehler in *Sonntag*, 23 May 1982.

98. Roland Oehme, in *My Wife Inge and My Wife (Mrs.) Schmidt (Meine Frau Inge und meine Frau Schmidt, 1985)*, by contrast, is an ironic social utopia that shows the gradual change from a nuclear family to a classical triangle to the dissolution of both in favor of a kind of extended family. In comparison with Heymann's film it seems rather noncommittal, focused more on the sensational aspects of the story and its comic potential than on the subtle analysis of interpersonal relationships.

99. *Progress; Pressebulletin Kino DDR* 5, 1986, p. 8.

100. See Rosemarie Rehahn in *Wochenpost* (Berlin), 9 May 1986, Günter Sobe in *Berliner Zeitung*, 3 May 1986, Peter Claus in *Junge Welt* (Berlin), 6 May 1986, etc.

101. Trips and traveling are important ingredients in many GDR films, an expression at once of the difficulty and the desire to travel, and of a restlessness of mind that fits with the quest character of many films. Traveling also plays a crucial role

in . . . *and Next Year at Lake Balaton* (. . . *und nächstes Jahr am Balaton,* 1980) by Hermann Zschoche, in Carow's *So Many Dreams,* Kühn's *The Dream of the Elk,* and many others.

102. The DEFA has an ensemble of excellent actors, many of whom hold a double engagement with the theater. Unfortunately, some very fine artists, such as Angelica Domröse and Hilmar Thate, have left the GDR following the scandal about Wolf Biermann.

103. Most of the films on women contain, as a structural and thematic element of extreme importance, the heroine's friendship with another woman which offers the closeness and support the women can not seem to find with their male partners.

104. At one point in the film, Anna takes a lover, but that does not interfere with her dream life. It seems as though the two levels of experience, dream/love and reality, are totally separate. Only in the end does she appear to be ready to give up her dream of the "elk."

105. Heinz Kersten, in *Der Tagesspiegel* (West Berlin), 23 November 1986, and Rosemarie Rehahn in *Wochenpost* (Berlin), 10 October 1986.

106. See Fred Gehler in *Sonntag,* 13 October 1986. However, Gehler argues that the attempt to reach a metaphorical level does not make this film a success.

107. In *Das Volk* (Erfurt), 21 August 1986.

108. These are the charges brought against the film by Fred Gehler in *Sonntag,* 13 October 1986, by Helmut Ullrich in *Neue Zeit,* 17 September 1986, and others.

109. Axel Geiss, in *Thüringische Landeszeitung* (Weimar), 23 May 1985.

110. In Hölderlin, *Gesammelte Werke,* vol. 3 (Stuttgart: Kohlhammer Verlag, 1957), p. 153. In the film, Hölderlin quotes the text literally.

111. There has been no response, on the part of the reviewers, about the stereotypes involved in this confrontation.

112. In an unpublished interview with Frank Beyer, 26 March 1987.

113. Horst Knietzsch, in *Neues Deutschland,* 16 April 1984.

3

Czechoslovakia:
After the Spring

Peter Hames

In his 1987 Report to the Central Committee of the Soviet Communist Party, Mikhail Gorbachev referred variously to "the all-round development of the democratism of the socialist system . . . ," to "the vital inner link between socialism and democracy . . . ," and to the need to "allow complete freedom to the creative faculties of the masses. . . ." During his visit to Prague in April, he alluded to the new policies in the USSR, hoping that the Soviet experience would be of value to Czechoslovakia. Before the visit, President Husák announced support for the new Soviet policies. After his visit, the Prime Minister, Lubomír Štrougal, spoke of the urgent need to follow the Soviet lead in economic restructuring.

Of course, neither Husák nor Štrougal meant to imply anything like a return to the Prague Spring of 1968. Both referred primarily to economic restructuring; Štrougal had already been identified with that cause for some time. But, in the Soviet Union, alongside *perestroika* (restructuring) has come *glasnost* (openness) and alongside that, the reinstatement of Pasternak, the publication of Nabokov, Tenghiz Abuladze's film attacking Stalinism, the reissue of banned films by Elem Klimov, and others, a reassessment of the role of the Old Bolsheviks, including Trotsky—in fact, a genuine liberalization in the field of culture. Reform has a habit of spreading from one area of society to another and, if Gorbachev's policies are right for the Czechoslovak economy, might they not also be right for culture? By the time this chapter appears, we may have some answers.

The parallels between the Gorbachev reforms and the Prague Spring of 1968 when Alexander Dubček was leader of the Czechoslovak Communist Party have often been noted. Despite differences, the economic reforms, the promotion of democratization, and the abolition of censorship all have elements similar to the changes currently envisaged in the Soviet Union. Dubček, it has been remarked, was the right man at the wrong time. Not surprisingly, the Czechoslovak reformers sometimes discussed their proposals for reform with their opposite numbers in the Soviet Union.[1]

If a policy of *glasnost* were to be applied in Czechoslovakia, it is impossible to assess the ultimate implications. It is no doubt Utopian to expect the Warsaw Pact invasion of 1968 to be seen as a "mistake" or to await the rehabilitation of the thousands in exile or associated with the reform movement. However, it is not unreasonable to suppose that the Prague Spring would no longer be deemed counter-revolutionary or that many of its reforms would be seen as having been, in certain senses, correct. The crisis would probably be seen increasingly as the result of political and tactical error. What is certain is that the Gorbachev line, if applied, would result in an inevitable and progressive move beyond the restrictive policies that have prevailed in the seventies and early eighties.[2]

The Warsaw Pact invasion was, of course, designed to liquidate the reforms of the late sixties. As such, it had wide-ranging effects on culture, and not least on the cinema. The international success of the Czechoslovak *new wave* in the sixties, said the novelist Jiří Mucha, did more to attract international attention to his country than any previous industrial or cultural endeavor.[3] Directors such as Miloš Forman, Ivan Passer, Ján Kadár, Jan Němec, Věra Chytilová and Jiří Menzel, were—all too briefly—international figures. Yet they remained only the tip of the iceberg, the creative range and diversity of the period being scarcely recognized to this day. Unfortunately, the policies of "normalization" that followed the invasion led to exile, silence, or accommodation. International interest in Czechoslovak cinema (and Czechoslovakia itself) faded after the sixties.   In order to understand both the achievements and failures of the seventies and eighties, it is necessary to understand something of the society that has emerged, a society in itself part of the continuing tragedy of Central Europe.

In the past seventy years, the former Austro-Hungarian provinces of Bohemia, Moravia, and Slovakia (present-day Czechoslovakia) have undergone what can only be regarded as a traumatic experience. After 300 years of Hapsburg domination, they have experienced a democratic state, Nazi domination, a briefly reinstated democracy, Stalinism, the Prague Spring, and the period of normalization that has lasted since 1969. On two occasions, the government has capitulated to superior force without a struggle—in the case of the Munich *Diktat* of 1938 and the Soviet invasion of 1968. Some would also single out the Communist *putsch* of 1948—although that is an altogether more complicated case.

Democracy cheaply won, it has been argued, can also be cheaply surrendered. A leaning towards policies of "realism" and accommodation with superior powers has often been condemned as destructive of pride, spirit, and self-confidence, yet it can equally be argued that the creation of the new state in 1918 was a gift of the Great Powers. As such, the interests

of Czechoslovakia (and indeed, other Central and East European countries), have always remained subservient to wider strategic interests. The
view of British Prime Minister Neville Chamberlain at the time of Munich, that Czechoslovakia was "a faraway country of which we know nothing," was not, unfortunately, historically specific.

Despite its position as "the bastion of democracy" in Central Europe,
Czechoslovakia was callously dismembered by the 1938 Munich agreement when Britain and France sacrificed their democratic ally in the
cause of appeasement. If the Yalta Conference of 1945 did not actually di-
vide Europe into "spheres of influence," it was conducted in the context
of such a strategic reality. When Churchill urged an allied advance into
Central Europe in early 1945, General Eisenhower replied for Washington, "Why should we endanger the life of a single American or Briton to
capture areas which we will soon be handing over to the Russians?"[4] Before the Soviet invasion of 1968, President Johnson reaffirmed his adherence to the Yalta and Potsdam agreements. When one is without powerful allies, a strategy of survival and accommodation can seem remarkably
rational.

The suppression of the Prague Spring, with its attempt to further the democratic and human face of socialism in the face of bureaucracy and
power politics, was a tragedy not only for Czechoslovakia. While it confirmed the fact of *realpolitik* as the governing principle of international relations, it also confirmed the conservatisms of both Left and Right. In Eastern Europe, any attempt to reform the system could be presented as the
creeping face of counter-revolution while, in the West, all forms of socialism could be presented as steps on a slippery slope leading to neo-
Stalinism. It reaffirmed the political simplifications on which continuing
Cold War politics depend.

But what of the society that now exists in Czechoslovakia? As one of
the most economically advanced of the Eastern bloc countries, its standard of living is high—in some respects indistinguishable from West European countries. Also, its tradition of progressive social legislation has
been maintained. As Vladimír Kusin puts it,

> A Czechoslovak citizen is reasonably satisfied with his material standing. . . .
> He has, relatively, enough money, and he does not have to work too hard
> to earn it. He is assured of his job as long as he does not show deviation
> from the official political line. He knows that for his money he can buy rela-
> tively good food and adequate merchandise. . . .[5]

However, the political and cultural repression that followed 1969 cannot
be seen as a necessary accompaniment.

If one accepts that the policies of normalization were aimed at restoring the situation that prevailed before the Prague Spring, then a variety of
tactics were possible. It was not inconceivable that, as many members of

the government argued in 1968, some aspects of the reforms might be preserved, and that, with the confirmation of the "leading role of the Party," moderate progress might be possible while recognizing the new political realities.

The extreme form that normalization, in fact, took has been variously blamed on Dubček's successor, Gustav Husák, his right-wingers, and the Soviet Union. The rumor in 1969 that the Soviet defense minister, Marshal Grechko, had threatened a second invasion and even military rule, was clearly significant. The removal of Dubček at that time, and the triumph of the conservatives, led to the elimination of the progress achieved by the Prague Spring and to official affirmation that the Soviet invasion was the correct tactic.

Normalization proved a massive task. Between 1968 and 1970 it has been estimated that 170,000 people left the country. In order to cleanse the Communist Party of reformist elements, 70,000 were expelled (while another 400,000 were removed from the list of members).[6] An interesting statistic from the period is that Departments of Marxism-Leninism in the universities were reconstituted, and in the process, 60 percent of their staff were lost.[7] Similarly extensive purges extended to all walks of life. The reformist virus, it seemed, was so deep rooted that it had to be eliminated at every level.

The political scientist Milan Šimečka has pointed out that normalization, as it affected the Party, was not aimed at the creation of an ideologically right-minded membership. On the contrary, it aimed "simply to turn the membership into what it used to be: a political conglomerate of the most varied concealed denominations, united only by obedience and a readiness to fulfill its role as a trustworthy receiver of instructions and directives."[8]

This exercise in screening led to a system in which "the ruling party of existing socialism became the vanguard of mediocrity, obedience, and fear." The screening boards were not made up solely of what was termed the "healthy core," but also those being given a chance to prove their loyalty, and even "supposedly decent people."[9] Thus the burden of guilt was spread and an atmosphere of distrust and fear encouraged. If this was the case in the Communist Party itself, it was entirely logical that similar tactics would be applied throughout society, particularly in the professions, the arts, and the media, including the cinema.

With the desire to institute a model of society in which directives were obeyed, the regime inevitably promoted a depoliticized culture, one in which the only political expression allowed reflected that of the Party itself. Alongside this, people were encouraged to concern themselves with material benefits, private life, and cottages in the country. It is a situation well dramatized in Václav Havel's play, *Private View* (*Vernisáž*, 1975), where the dissident hero is entertained by an affluent and materialistic couple who want to help him adjust. However, the confrontation only serves to make them face the hollowness and evasions of their own "adjustment."

After domination by the oppressive Austro-Hungarian bureaucracy before the First World War and a sequence of nearly fifty years since the Munich *Diktat* where democracy has been, at best, intermittent or nascent, it might be argued that a particular kind of society or psychology may have developed—a society forced to accept oppression as a fact of life. Of course, one can point to Charter 77, the human rights group set up to monitor the Helsinki agreement, but even that has remained scrupulously legalistic in its approach and in no way aims at confronting the Party. In the Czechoslovak context, of course, this still rates as dangerous subversion. While Charter 77 has an influence far beyond its signatories, the fact remains that most of those who agree with its position keep their views to themselves. The public expression of such views is regarded as self-indulgent and even foolish.

The unique nature of the Czechoslovak experience has led to two quite remarkable works of political philosophy. The first, based on the experience of the fifties and sixties, was Karel Kosík's Marxist analysis, *Dialectics of the Concrete*.[10] The second, based on the post-1968 experience, is Václav Havel's non-Marxist *The Power of the Powerless*.[11] The wider significance of both is that they see the Czechoslovak experience as but merely an extreme manifestation of tendencies present in all advanced societies, but more effectively masked or less completely developed.

Describing the Czechoslovak situation as "post-totalitarian," Havel sees it as only one aspect, albeit a particularly drastic one, "of the general inability of modern humanity to be the master of its own situation. The automatism of the post-totalitarian system is merely an extreme version of the global automatism of technological civilisation."[12]

For Havel, the good/evil and Right/Left polarities of the Cold War are increasingly without meaning. Instead, he argues that we should focus much more on issues of "right" or "wrong," on personal morality, and a commitment to living in truth; "the issue is the rehabilitation of values like trust, openness, responsibility, solidarity, love."[13]

Havel's view of Czechoslovak society as an extreme version of tendencies present in Western societies indicates why it is not helpful to regard it solely as a kind of Kafkaesque aberration. Despite the extraordinary process of normalization, it is a society of complexity and contradiction where the truth is rarely simple. If many follow Havel in his commitment to morality, others hold to the bureaucratic conformity to which they have been forced to adjust. Inevitably, the position of most people is between these extremes or a mixture of both. Perhaps this is not too unlike the kind of adjustments made in more open societies.

The effect of normalization on culture and, in particular, literature, has been described by Charter 77 as one of "systematic suppression . . . a frontal attack threatening the very spiritual, cultural, and thus also national identity of the Czechoslovak society."[14] In 1982, Charter 77 issued a list of 282 Czech writers alone who were unable to publish. To a Western observer the reasons for this often appear to be trivial or incomprehensible.

If, as was certainly the case, the aims of the new regime included the liquidation of the intelligentsia's traditional role as "the conscience of the nation," then the banning of all but captive intellectuals can be seen as logical. On the other hand, recantation has often meant no more than a formal rejection of past views and has become a form of Švejkism.[15] Thus, while a significant number of works were banned because of their content, others are banned because of the current attitudes and/or exile of the authors.

Attitudes to the cinema have reflected those in other areas. In view of the international success of the sixties movies, they have proved somewhat difficult to disown. On the other hand, they have been successfully marginalized and only a select few are revived with any regularity. Internationally, many of the films have been withdrawn and, like the problems of Czechoslovakia itself, virtually forgotten. In this connection, it is worth noting that many Western film histories now minimize and simplify the contribution of the sixties wave often to little more than a reference to the work of Miloš Forman.

In Czechoslovakia, the work of directors who left the country has been largely disowned and banned, and their names eliminated from the history of Czechoslovak cinema.[16] These included Forman, Passer, Kadár, Němec, Jasný, and Weiss. Among leading filmmakers who remained behind, a veil has been drawn over the work of Ladislav Helge, Evald Schorm, and Pavel Juráček, and they have been unable to make films. Ester Krumbachová, whose scripts and design contributed so much to the sixties films, has completed a script for only one film—Chytilová's The Very Late Afternoon of a Faun (Faunovo příliš pozdní odpoledne, 1983).

Under the policies adopted after the invasion, the management of the film industry was changed and the autonomous production groups that had given birth to the sixties achievements were abolished. The objects of the newly centralized industry were, according to the then executive producer at the Barrandov Studios, Ludvik Toman, dedicated to an art "which rejects and criticises scepticism, feelings of alienation, desperation, inconsiderate sexuality, egoistic bourgeois individualism. We want to support by our films those properties which strengthen our society and not those which break it up."[17]

These views clearly reflected official policy. The production schedule therefore reintroduced orthodox movies about the Second World War, industrial heroes, films based on classics and fairy stories, and an endless chain of domestic and detective comedies. The objectives could be described as ones of official optimism, support for the status quo and the role of the Soviet Union, and a reassertion of the threat from the West.

In the immediate post-invasion period, very few leading filmmakers were able to make films but, gradually, most have made a reappearance. Thus the mid-seventies saw the return of František Vláčil, Jan Schmidt, Antonín Máša, Dušan Hanák, Věra Chytilová, Jiří Menzel, and Juraj Jakubisko. No doubt they were all required to give a satisfactory account of their attitude to the sixties—witness Jakubisko's denunciation of his own films at the 1983 Venice Festival—but that was par for the course. What is certain is that they were now required to work within the guidelines of normalized Czechoslovak cinema.

A number of the sixties films were considered controversial for their political content and, in 1973, four films were apparently banned "forever." These were Forman's *The Firemen's Ball* (*Hoří, má panenko*, 1967), Němec's *The Party and the Guests* (*O slavnosti a hostech*, 1966), Jasný's *All My Good Countrymen* (*Všichni dobří rodáci*, 1969), and Schorm's *End of a Priest* (*Farářův konec*, 1969), scripted by Josef Škvorecký.

In fact, the directly political film was relatively rare, Schorm's *Everyday Courage* (*Každý den odvadhu*, 1964) and Jasný's *All My Good Countrymen* being two of the few. When they were made, they were never crude and frequently sympathetic and ironic. In *Everyday Courage* the Stalinist central character is virtually a tragic hero.

What is striking about many of the condemned films of the sixties is that they can be seen as allegorical—either intended as a direct political comment or capable of being interpreted that way. This leads to a major problem—the tendency of Czech audiences to interpret everything as political. Since both the artists and the regime share in this atmosphere, it is only a short step to the banning of anything remotely suspect.

The distrust of the allegorical was inevitably linked to a rejection of the avant garde and anything that smacked of intellectualism or elitism. Writing in 1967 in the context of the banning and subsequent release of Němec's *The Party and the Guests* and Chytilová's *Daisies* (*Sedmikrásky*, 1966), Jan Žalman indicated that these films were not alone in being at the center of controversy.[18] Other films that met official criticism included Němec's *Martyrs of Love* (*Mučedníci lásky*, 1966), Antonin Máša's *Hotel for Foreigners* (*Hotel pro cizince*, 1966) and Štefan Uher's *The Miraculous Virgin* (*Panna zázračnica*, 1966). Complex, poetic and surreal, none were susceptible to an easy interpretation. They were accused of being unintelligible, pessimistic, undisciplined—even of being deceitful and constituting "ideological sabotage." One is reminded of the reputed attitude of the British censor when banning Buñuel's *L'Age d'Or*—that the film was meaningless but, if it had a meaning, it was doubtless objectionable. Žalman also noted the official preference for conventional narrative and an increasing concern with the real or imagined tastes of the audience. A preoccupation with accessibility and the box office in the seventies and eighties was not therefore a simple product of normalization—even if it was facilitated by it.

The times have rigorously excluded formal innovation, and political films in any way equivalent to Polish and Hungarian movies like Wajda's *Man of Marble* (*Człowiek z marmuru*, 1976), Zanussi's *Camouflage* (*Barwy ochronne*, 1976), Gábor's *Angi Vera* (1978) or Sándor's *Daniel Takes a Train* (*Szerencsés Dániel*, 1983) have not been produced since the sixties. In these circumstances, should films be judged for their achievement in world cinematic terms or should allowances be made for the ideological straightjacket? Should filmmakers be judged by their movement in new directions or by an ability to preserve at least some of the critical edge and formal freedoms of a forbidden past? Are we not also looking at the rise and fall of talent quite independently of the socio-political situation?

If we consider films more obviously produced to meet the government's ideological objectives, it is difficult to find anything very persuasive. The most productive area has been that of the war film, which, functioning much like a Hollywood genre, allows a diverse range of products. At its most conventional it has produced films of considerable banality. It is perfectly possible to regard films like Vladimír Čech's *The Key* (*Klíč*, 1971) or Otakar Vávra's *The Liberation of Prague* (*Osvobození Prahy*, 1976) simply as bad films. However, the same cannot be said of a more recent example, Juraj Herz's *I Was Caught by the Night* (*Zastihla mě noc*, 1986). Herz is best known in the West for his nightmarish black comedy *The Cremator* (*Spalovač mrtvol*, 1968), the story of an employee in a crematorium who rises to power and insanity through cooperation with the Nazis. Although he had previously managed to avoid films with an explicit propagandist purpose, here he takes the true story of a Communist journalist in wartime concentration camps and treats it with a great deal of technological and dramatic brio. But conviction, it seems, exposes the creaking ideology of the formula as much as its opposite.

Films adopting correct attitudes towards industrial initiatives are no more impressive. Films such as Jaromil Jireš's *People of the Metro* (*Lidé z metra*, 1974) or Menzel's comeback film *Who Looks for Gold?* (*Kdo hledá zlaté dno?* 1975) share the vestigial qualities of the scripts filmed in the early seventies. Perversely, both films attain a kind of purely formal beauty with Jireš making a poem about underground trains and Menzel introducing a waltz of the trucks.

A more sophisticated example of the genre is Jaroslav Balík's *Nuclear Cathedral* (*Atomová katedrála*, 1985), which at least developed its characters with domestic and work situations leading to dramatic conflict. However, its idealized hero, fighting careerism at work and lack of understanding at home, is too obviously a moral symbol and too remote from recognizable reality to carry much conviction. If the schematic quality of the film is apparent to a foreigner, how much more apparent is it to those who have a lifetime of familiarity with the stereotypes?

The trouble with these kinds of simplified productions is that they have not moved much beyond the formula established by the Vasiliev brothers'

Chapayev of the thirties. They are films in which the policies and role of the Party can never be questioned, where the role of the Soviet Union is like that of the Seventh Cavalry, where simple working men overcome difficult odds. Even if the analysis offered were correct, their schematic nature inspires disbelief. When films manage to transcend the formulae, they encourage a response on quite a different intellectual and aesthetic level that invalidates the very restrictions within which they have been conceived.

Although the threat to the nation's cultural identity has been genuine, the government has clearly allowed the promotion of national culture at a certain level. There seems to have been fairly systematic support for Czech traditions and achievements in the field of classical music, while older literary traditions have not been found as subversive as their modern equivalents. Nationalist work, provided it is respectable, historical, and preferably traditional in style, has not been considered a threat.

The veteran director Otakar Vávra, despite some embarrassments and a heavy-handed style, has remained true to his commitment to Czech literature and history. Working with established writers like the historical novelist Miloš Kratochvíl and the novelist and playwright Jiří Šotola, he has made two films centered on nineteenth-century literature. The first, *A Meeting with Love and Honor* (*Příběh lásky a cti*, 1977) was a dramatization of the relationship between the poet Jan Neruda and the novelist and pioneer feminist Karolina Světlá. The second, *Veronika* (1986), focused on another famous woman novelist and patriot, Božena Němcová. He also filmed a screenplay he had written in conjunction with a leading poet, František Hrubín. A major lyric poet of the older generation, Hrubín had often championed the role of the intellectuals and had previously scripted two of Vávra's best films, *The Golden Rennet* (*Zlatá reneta*, 1965) and *Romance for a Bugle* (*Romance pro křídlovku*, 1966). The new film, *Oldřich and Božena* (*Oldřich a Božena*, 1985), filmed fourteen years after his death, was set in the tenth and eleventh centuries and concerned the consolidation of the Czech state under the Premyslid dynasty and the resistance to foreign intrigues. Hrubín's work had originally been a successful play in 1968 and carried the subtitle *A Bloody Plot in the Czech Lands*. No doubt, the fact that audiences took the play allegorically at the time accounted for its slow transition to the screen.

Other historical films by Vávra worth noting would include his careful reconstruction of the Munich crisis, *Days of Betrayal* (*Dny zrady*, 1971) and his *Jan Amos Comenius* (*Putování Jana Ámose*, 1983), about the seventeenth-century Czech educator condemned to a lifetime of exile. The first was remarkably honest for the time and in its treatment of democratic leaders such as President Beneš and Jan Masaryk, and the second was not without irony in its reference to an intellectual community forced abroad for its failure to conform.

The traditions of Czech music have been well served by a number of screenplays by Zdeněk Mahler, nephew of the composer. František Vláčil's *Concert at the End of Summer* (*Koncert na konci léta*, 1979) was a tribute to the work of Dvořák, while Jiří Krejčík's *The Divine Emma* (*Božská Ema*, 1979) was an old-fashioned biographical film about Emmy Destin, a successful opera star in the United States before the First World War. Her refusal to act as an agent for the Austrian secret police was considered by some to offer political parallels. Mahler, who acted as a consultant on Miloš Forman's *Amadeus* (1984), which was filmed in Prague, also wrote the script for Miloslav Luther's *Forget Mozart* (*Zabudnite na Mozarta*, 1986). Similarly, Jaromil Jireš made a two-part documentary on Janáček in 1973 and supplemented this with his biographical feature, *Lion with a White Mane* (*Lev s bílou hřívou*, 1986).

Given the restrictive situation described earlier, the preservation of artistic identity and a personal perspective in itself becomes an achievement. Věra Chytilová and Jiří Menzel are widely seen as directors who have survived without compromising their artistic integrity and, not surprisingly, continue to attract international attention. However, if one makes allowances for generic limitations, a whole range of films are of interest, in particular, the work of Jaromil Jireš and František Vláčil and the Slovak directors Štefan Uher, Dušan Hanák, and Juraj Jakubisko.

III–1   Božidara Turzonovova as Emmy Destin in *The Divine Emma*

Jireš, whose contribution to the *new wave* has sometimes been underestimated, made one of *new wave's* most important early films with his formally innovative *The Cry* (*Křik*, 1963). Two of the most significant films of its later phases were his adaptation of Milan Kundera's novel *The Joke* (*Žert*, 1968) and the kaleidoscopic surrealist fantasy, *Valerie and Her Week of Wonders* (*Valerie a týden divů*, 1969).

In the early seventies, Jireš made one of a select group of convincing films set against a Second World War background with his *And Give My Love to the Swallows* (*A pozdravuji vlaštovky*, 1971). The story of a Communist resistance heroine, Maruška Kudeřiková, it was a morally uplifting story about imprisonment and sacrifice in the name of a better future. Reduced to its essentials, it differs little from a film like Herz's *I Was Caught by the Night*. Under Jireš's poetic control, however it was given a spiritual emphasis that transcended the sterility of the genre to produce a film of genuine conviction and humanity. Subsequently, his work has failed to attain the same aesthetic level—although he can scarcely be blamed for the limitations of *People of the Metro*!

Two of his more recent films, *Young Man and the White Whale* (*Mladý muž a bílá velryba*, 1978) and *Catapult* (*Katapult*, 1983), both based on novels by Vladimír Páral, shared a new engagement with social realities.

III–2   Poetic emphasis in Jireš's *And give My Love to the Swallows:* Magda Vašáryová

Páral, one of the leading writers of the sixties, has written a whole sequence of novels based on the frustrations of life in industrial society. *Private Hurricane (Soukromá vichřice*, 1965), his damning portrait of the alienation of provincial life, the apathy of work in a factory, and a lack of both public and private morality, was filmed by Hynek Bočan in 1966.

According to Alfred French,[19] Páral's novels almost exactly match the environment of the fifties' novels of "socialist construction" but, in place of forced optimism, offer a disillusioned world of alienated horror. *Catapult*, first published in 1967, tells the story of a modern Don Juan, who locates a series of mistresses along the route of his commercial journeys. His sexual exploits are a means of filling the emptiness in his everyday life but finally lead to self-destruction. However, rather like Bočan and *Private Hurricane*, Jireš makes his points without the film becoming the dreadful lesson implied by the book. What is interesting, however, is the fact that the films should have been made at all.

Jireš's other recent films could perhaps be characterized as exercises in mild social criticism. *Payment in Kind/The Rabbit Case (Causa králík*, 1979) tells the story of an eminent lawyer forced by ill health to retire to the country. There, he wins a case against the odds only to lose out in the final analysis to a world of manipulation and influence. Other recent films focus on subjects such as blindness (*Incomplete Eclipse [Neúplné zatmění]*, 1980) and cancer (*Prolonged Time [Prodloužený čas]*, 1985). While none of them present world-shaking themes, they do dramatize problems crucial to everyday life. If Jireš often approaches them with a spirit of lyrical optimism, one suspects it may have as much to do with his own predilections as official policy. His pleasure in making films is evident, even if his subjects since the sixties have never really matched his obvious ability.

In contrast to Jireš, the films of František Vláčil present a rather bleak view of human nature. He first attracted attention with his visual poem, *The White Dove (Holubice*, 1960), and confirmed his reputation with a remarkable series of historical films, of which his adaptation of Vladislav Vančura's *Markéta Lazarová* (1966) is the best known. Even in the sixties, he tended to select simple, oblique, sometimes allegorical themes that allowed him maximum creative flexibility. This experience has stood him in good stead in the seventies and eighties, where he has produced a number of films of integrity.

The atmospheric but low-keyed *Smoke on the Potato Fields (Dým bramborové natě*, 1976) concerns itself with the late middle age of a doctor and his friendship with a young girl expecting an illegitimate child. Both are victims of misfortune, but, despite the positive relationship between the two, there is a tragic ending. A touching film that offers only oblique social analysis, it can best be seen as a sad and rather fatalistic account of a reconciliation with the disappointments of life.

A contrast in style, his dramatic World War II film *Shadows of a Hot Summer (Stíny horkého léta*, 1978), shared the Grand Prix at Karlovy Vary. A

III–3   Juraj Kukura as the father in Vláčil's *Shadows of a Hot Summer*

group of Banderite guerrillas (Ukrainian nationalists), fleeing the Russian advance, occupy a Moravian farm. Although the film simplifies historical reality by turning the Banderites into little more than surrogate Nazis, the subject—the defense of the home against foreign occupation, has a wider resonance. The theme has obvious parallels with Sam Peckinpah's *Straw Dogs*, with the difference that Vláčil's hero is finally destroyed by the occupiers. It is a powerful movie that provides an ultimately pessimistic view of human nature.

In 1985, Vláčíl adapted a pre-war novel by the painter Josef Čapek, brother of Karel, with whom he wrote *The Insect Play*. *The Shades of Ferns (Stín kapradiny)* is the tragic story of two youths who go on the run after shooting a gamekeeper. Their search for escape and adventure is doomed as they are hunted by an unsympathetic society and destroyed by their own contradictions. The theme of pursuit has marked parallels with Němec's adaptation of Arnošt Lustig's *Diamonds of the Night (Démanty noci,* 1964) but, though made with his usual sensitivity, Vláčil's film lacks the same degree of dynamism. But he has again made a rather morose personal statement with none of the redeeming optimism of a Jireš.

Conditions in the smaller Slovak industry have sometimes seemed less restrictive than those in its Czech counterpart. Štefan Uher, for instance, is one of the few directors who has been able to maintain a continuity of work without compromising his sixties reputation. His pioneering and poetic work, *Sunshine in the Net* (*Slnko v sieti*, 1962) may look less radical than it did at the time and, while there has been no repetition of the surrealist exaggerations of *The Miraculous Virgin*, he has maintained work of a formally and thematically interesting level. In 1972, when most of his Czech colleagues were producing films of unbelievable banality, he made *If I Had a Gun (Keby som mal pušku)*. A film about the last days of the fascist regime in Slovakia, it was a remarkable and authentic portrait of children growing up in wartime. One of the most interesting of his recent films is *Concrete Pastures* (*Pásla kone na betóne*, 1982), adapted from her own short stories by the film's leading actress, Milka Zimková. Set in a remote village in Eastern Slovakia and filmed largely in dialect, it examines the problems of the unmarried mother across two generations. The setting allows for a dramatization of the process of social change and evolving moral attitudes while emphasizing the truth of the repeated maxim, "There's no roof without a man."

Two Slovak directors who originally made their reputation in the sixties but did not return to features until the late seventies were Hanák and Jakubisko. Hanák made the Mannheim prizewinner, *399* (1969), never released in his home country, while Jakubisko's trio of films, *Crucial Years* (*Kristove roky*, 1967), *The Deserter and the Nomads* (*Zbehovia a pútnici*, 1968), and *Birds, Orphans, and Fools* (*Vtáčkovia, siroty a blázni*, 1968) rank among the most controversial of the sixties, both for their content and their provocative style. As mentioned earlier, he recently denounced them and commended his critics during an interview at the Venice Festival.

Hanák's return to feature films, *Rose-Tinted Dreams* (*Růžové sny*, 1976), a love story involving a Slovak and a gypsy girl, steered just the right side of sentimentality through its gentle humor, poetic sensibility, and awareness of social realities. The more polemical *Silent Joy* (*Tichá radosť*, 1985) attracted attention with another examination of the changing role of women, this time dramatized through the story of a woman who gives up her marriage in order to follow an independent career.

Jakubisko's comeback picture *Build a House, Plant a Tree* (*Postav dom, zasad strom*, 1980), while extremely well made, hardly equals his achievements of the sixties. Still, its tragic story of a dropout truck driver who decides to build his own house and a life outside of the community is sympathetic and emotionally involving. *The Millennial Bee* (*Tisícročna v čela*, 1983), an epic about the life of a Slovak village from the turn of the century to the end of the Second World War, varies in level but includes several scenes showing the folk inspiration of Jakubisko's earlier work. The most impressive is during a village funeral. As a funeral party carries a coffin through the snow, it slips from their grasp and the whole event is converted into a wild toboggan ride. Visually, the episode is remarkable and evokes an enormous sense of liberation.

As the work of Menzel and Chytilová is clearly considered the most sig-

III–4   Dušan Hanák's *Rose-Tinted Dreams:* Iva Bittová and Juraj Nvota

nificant of the seventies and eighties, it is worth discussing in rather more detail.

After a striking debut with his Oscar-winning film of Bohumil Hrabal's *Closely Watched Trains* (*Ostře sledované vlaky*, 1966) and an adaptation of Vladislav Vančura's *Capricious Summer* (*Rozmarné léto*, 1967), Menzel directed Škvoreckýs *Crime in the Nightclub* (*Zločin v šantánu*, 1968) and Hrabal's *Larks on a Thread* (*Skřivánci na nitích*, 1969). *Larks on a Thread* was never released and seems to be regarded as one of the most controversial of the sixties films.

Not surprisingly, Menzel had difficulty in reestablishing his film career, and it was not until 1974, after a recantation, that he was allowed to direct *Who Looks for Gold?*, a conventional socialist realist film that presumably indicated contrition. Since then, he has directed five comedies, most of which stand well above the general level of production. They also belong to the classic tradition of film comedy, owing a clear debt to silent comedy and its various descendents from Tati to Tashlin. His love for early cinema is made explicit in his homage *Those Wonderful Movie Cranks/ Those Wonderful Men with a Crank* (*Báječní muži s klikou*), 1978, and in his references to Lupino Lane in *Cutting It Short* (*Postřižiny*, 1981).

The two films he has made with Bohumil Hrabal are probably the most substantial. One of the most popular writers of the sixties, Hrabal's work de-

III–5   Jozef Króner (star of *The Shop on Main Street*) in Jakubisko's *The Millennial Bee*

rived its impact from his depiction of scenes from everyday life. However, it is an everyday life full of eccentricity and illogicality and a far cry from socialist-realist stereotypes. In the seventies his work was banned, but he was later reinstated after reaching an accommodation with the authorities.[20]

Cutting It Short was the most successful film of 1981 but has not achieved the international recognition it deserves. Set at the turn of the century, and based on Hrabal's novella about his mother, it is no exercise in conventional nostalgia. Rather, the heroine is seen as the personification of female sexuality. But despite flirting outrageously with men, Maryška is in no danger of becoming a latter-day Lulu. Her presence—and more especially her long hair—give quiet pleasure to the inhabitants of a provincial town dominated by the local brewery.

Maryška's husband, Francin, is a shy and rather straight-laced young man who travels the country checking on the quality and cleanliness of the brewery's clients. His careful and respectable dress is complemented by an absurd juxtaposition with the motorbike and sidecar in which he travels.

The film's comedy is triggered by the arrival of his brother, Pepin, an uncouth cobbler given to shouting and ear-splitting monologue. In particular, he is full of typical Hrabalian tales about pet raccoons, Austrian officers, aunts and uncles, and dentists who pull out one another's teeth. His disrup-

III–6   A scent of freedom: Menzel's adaptation of Bohumil Hrabal's *Cutting It Short:* Jaromir Hanzlik and Magda Vašáryová

tion of the brewery executives' meeting prompts the comment: "This is not a Charlie Chaplin comedy with Lupino Lane." When he and the beautiful Maryška are rescued from the top of a factory chimney by the local fire brigade, they observe: "We are a voluntary fire brigade, not a Keystone Kops comedy with Lupino Lane."

Apart from the references to Lupino Lane, one is irresistibly reminded of Forman's satire on bureaucracy, *The Firemen's Ball* (1967), where the firemen were frequently posed in compositions reminiscent of the Keystone Kops. Of course, Menzel's respectable organized groups are also bureaucrats, and there is one uncomfortable scene, following a pig-slaughtering sequence, in which the gluttonous brewery committee gorge themselves on pig fat like caricatures from an early film by Eisenstein.

Despite its glancing but uncomfortable attacks on bureaucracy, the film is primarily an assertion of the values of sexuality and nonconformity. Magda Vašáryová's tender beauty is filmed lyrically, with a predictable emphasis on her billowing dress as she cycles through town or stands on a phallic chimney in the wind above the town. There are a number of explicitly erotic scenes—Maryška's night-time bath in the brewery, the marital massage with a strange piece of medical equipment, the public spanking of her backside. In another chauvinist scene, her beautiful hair turns out to be a horse's tail. When her hair is cut, one of the references of the film's

III–7   A scene from married life: Jiří Schmitzer and Magda Vašáryová in Menzel's *Cutting It Short*

title, it is a symbol of inevitable change and a move beyond the film's frozen fantasy.

The uncouth Pepin's role as protagonist mirrors that of Tati's Hulot as he sows chaos about him—particularly in the running gag where one of the workers at the brewery becomes permanently accident-prone after meeting him.[21] The film is also full of references to silent comedy, right down to the systematic use of the iris throughout.

In many ways, *Cutting It Short* is the best post-Tati comedy. However, as with *Closely Watched Trains*, Hrabal's occasionally bitter humor turns it into something else—and Tati would never have included the slaughter of a pig. But there is no doubt that it is Menzel's best film since the sixties and, on every level, the most successful Czech film of the post-invasion period.

With *The Snowdrop Festival* (*Slavnosti sněženek*, 1983), Menzel and Hrabal sounded a more somber note. Set in the countryside near Prague, it examines the conflict between two villages in their dispute over the right to the corpse of a wild boar. The initial incident with the boar is filmed as silent comedy until the unfortunate beast is tracked down to a classroom at the local school and shot dead in front of the children. As the dispute over the carcass begins, the children sing "My Bohemia."

Menzel's portrait of Czech village life is here somewhat removed from the idylls he portrays, albeit satirically, in his other work. His camera travels past houses at night, each echoing to the sound of television and identical banalities. It is a countryside where the vegetation is tipped by the white of junkyards and penetrated by a regular influx of joggers and motorcyclists. Hrabal's expected gallery of reprobates and misfits, despite comic procedures, seem to lack the redeeming qualities of their equivalents in *Pearls of the Deep* (*Perličky na dně*, 1965) and *Closely Watched Trains*. The scene in which one of the characters plays a flute to his goats only seems to emphasize the bitter nature of much of the comedy. The film's one optimistic character, the delivery boy, is killed in a road accident following the drunken celebration at the Snowdrop Inn. Perhaps the film is not quite as grim as this implies, but it is certainly some way from the publicity handout's reference to a tale of ordinary folk exhibiting "a profound awareness of man's part in the wondrous range of the beauties of nature."

The role of Hrabal in Menzel's success should in no way be underestimated—it is the considered amalgamation of the abrasive and the lyrical that has produced a unique combination in which access to a wide audience involves no sacrifice of aesthetic level. Although Menzel's tribute to the early Czech cinema, *Those Wonderful Movie Cranks*, the story of a filmmaker and a traveling picture-show man, has been considerably underestimated, the absence of a strong script allowed the domination of a rather hermetic exercise in nostalgia.

Menzel's second major collaborator has been the actor and playwright Zdeněk Svěrák, who has made a multi-level contribution to Czech film culture in recent years. His scripts for *Seclusion Near a Forest* (*Na samotě u lesa*, 1976), co-written with Ladislav Smoljak, and *My Sweet Little Village* (*Vesničko má, středisková*, 1986) share many characteristics, and are both satirical and critical while lacking the more abrasive elements of the Hrabal collaborations. *Seclusion Near a Forest* was a film of social relevance produced at a time when Czech production was emerging from its most banal and simplistic period, while *My Sweet Little Village* was one of the smash hits of 1986.

Seclusion Near a Forest deals with the subject of a Prague family in search of a country cottage to which they can retreat during holidays and weekends. This has every appearance of being a national obsession and the film concentrates on the conflicts between the city dwellers (the "Praguers") and the local inhabitants. The Praguers try to buy up the property, while the locals set up as landlords and building consultants.

The central situation is based on that of a nice middle-class family who want to buy a country cottage but find they must share the accommodation with its aging owner. He shows little sign of either moving or dying and, when they discover that his father is still alive at the age of 92, they recognize that the future must be based on compromise.

III–8   A Czech idyll: Ladislav Smoljak and Nada Urbánková in Menzel's *Seclusion Near a Forest*

The happy conclusion may be a case of wishful thinking, but the film makes some sharp observations on the weekenders. One successful couple lives in a working replica of a flour mill and keeps a stuffed stork that can only go out in the fine weather. Another visiting Praguer tries to smoke out the occupant of his weekend retreat by bricking up the chimney.

The search for a "Czech idyll" not only involves social conflict but also the obverse of the romantic dream. Behind the picturesque house secluded near woods lies the reality—of rotting floorboards, mildew, snakes, and marauding goats.

The preoccupation with private life and material possessions has been encouraged by the regime in the post-1969 period. However, it nominally disapproves of the growth in petty bourgeois preoccupations. The criticism is, therefore, permitted criticism—even if it is relevant and apt. At the same time, Menzel's nostalgic and visually romantic treatment asserts the reality of the dream.

My Sweet Little Village is an obvious complement to the earlier film, albeit with a more complex script amid ambiguous mood. The film begins with a lyrical and nationalistic music theme as two men walk to work in a fog and meet (or rather come together) at precisely the same point outside the gate of the second. There is a physical discrepancy between the short, fat truckdriver and his long and lean assistant. The second breaks into a marching pace in time with the first. We hear the vain efforts of car ignition and come across the local doctor in a rusty and battered old Škoda. The truckdriver gets him started.

As the doctor drives through the countryside, he launches into a romantic and pseudo-poetic commentary on its delights as the images both reflect and contradict what he is saying. As in *Seclusion Near a Forest* and *The Snowdrop Festival*, Menzel seems anxious to draw a distinction between the fantasy Czechoslovakia and the reality, even if he loves the fantasy.

What follows is a simple but multifaceted comedy, a portrait of characters and of a community with a rich variety of intertwining subplots. The story of Otík, the truckdriver's simple-minded assistant, provides the lynchpin for the film. After Otík has provoked a series of minor disasters, his friend tries to get rid of him and plans are approved for his removal to Prague. This is a city where, in the words of an abominable pop group with short haircuts who appear on TV, the sun always shines and life is always fun even when it is raining. Otík, however, faces another reality—a new flat in a soulless new apartment bloc where the toilet flushes but the

III–9   Zdeněk Svěrák as the visiting artist in Menzel's *My Sweet Little Village*

shower does not work. There are plans for Otík's village house to revert to his Prague-based boss who will, of course, import a flushing toilet and plastic thatching from West Germany. This piece of direct criticism, with its echoes of *Private Hurricane*, is clear but somewhat muffled by the film's happy ending.

There are several illicit affairs conducted and Otík is maneuvered into leaving his shared accommodation to leave the coast free for a friend's extracurricular activity (masquerading as the preparation of a lecture on livestock). Otík's fate is to go and see a Romanian film and to promise not to leave before the end. Another youth nurtures a passion for the local schoolteacher, only to have his hopes dashed when he spies through her window to see a visiting artist (Svěrák) with her panties on his head.

Rudolf Hrušínský, as the doctor, provides the film with "philosophical" reflection, rather like one of the aging Lotharios of *Capricious Summer*. As he drives his rusty old Škoda into ditches, his pseudo-romantic commentary continues and he sings about the "steadfast Czechs" of olden days. He reflects on the beauty of young girls (and the fashion for no bras), confronts the hypochondria of patients and jokes with a seriously ill patient about the merits of giving up both smoking and drinking at the same time ("a body should be partly decayed"). In a later conversation on what people could possibly want more than a television set and a car, he suggests a grave.

The film is full of neatly observed incidents—the avid interest in a U.S. film on television (titled *Harpoon*, it promises death and violence so the audience ignores the announcer's obligatory denunciation of U.S. corruption that precedes it), the discussion on how to address old ladies in the countryside (they are no longer called "auntie"), the full-sized plaster cast for an injured farmhand that resembles a socialist-realist statue to his immortality.

A carefully contrived and balanced script full of comic repetition, *My Sweet Little Village* continues Menzel's apparently conscious attempt to work within the major traditions of screen comedy. His love for Renoir is evident and, in the balance of his performing ensemble and use of music, so is the lyrical style of the Czech director Václav Krška.

The film has other senses in which it seems familiar. The manipulation of the party scene recalls Forman's *Loves of a Blonde* and, leaving aside Hrušínský and Svěrák, whose faces are familiar from many films, the presence of actors from films by Forman and Passer provide the sense of a continuing reality. The film is basically a satirical but "philosophical" reflection on the absurdity of the human condition. Its observation of the "small" events of everyday life place it not only in a tradition that permeated the *new wave* but extends back in literature to Jan Neruda and forward to writers like Škvorecký and Klíma.

Menzel's low-key satires have allowed him to maintain his artistic integrity without attracting the attention of Western critics that accompanied

Closely Watched Trains. This has been partly due to the "invisibility" of Czechoslovakia in the festival circuit in recent years, partly to a certain reluctance to promote the films (e.g., *The Snowdrop Festival*), and partly to changes in critical fashion.

A director less easy to ignore is Věra Chytilová. While Menzel has balanced his insights with order and good taste, Chytilová is not prone to compromise. Although her sixties work was not amongst the most politically controversial in the narrow sense of the word, she was the most formally radical of the filmmakers. In *Something Different* (*O něčem jiném*, 1962), she juxtaposed documentary and fiction in her portrait of two women and the choices offered them by society. With the iconoclastic *Daisies* (1966), her non-narrative montage of the destructive antics of two teenage girls, she provoked outrage and admiration. In *The Fruit of Paradise* (*Ovoce stromů rajských jíme*, 1969), she made an incredibly beautiful but, from the point of view of conventional narrative, obscure allegory on the relations between men and women. Had they been West European films, they would be regarded as among the key modernist works of the sixties.

It was precisely this kind of "unintelligible" and avant-garde work that was criticized in the late sixties and has been rigorously excluded ever since. In a sense, what Chytilová did was to assert the primacy of film as a visual art and to demand freedoms regarded as routine in painting, poetry and music. But as the "most important" (ideologically) and most popular art, cinema must abide by other rules.

As the most eminent exponent of this avant garde, Chytilová was unable to work for seven years. However, she mounted a personal campaign, appealed to the President, and affirmed her commitment to socialism. As a result of this, and backroom intrigues by others, she was able to make a return with *The Apple Game* (*Hra o jablko*, 1976) which was, unusually, a feature film produced by the short-film studios. Since then, she has made five features, all of which are relatively orthodox by her standards of the sixties.

The Apple Game is a feminist comedy about a nurse who is seduced by a philandering doctor (played by Jiří Menzel). She becomes pregnant, loses her lovesick illusions, and decides to have the baby out of wedlock. The film had a somewhat checkered career at the outset, being entered and then withdrawn from the Berlin Festival and promoted with seeming reluctance before finally enjoying both domestic and international success. Like the firemen who objected to their portrayal in *The Firemen's Ball*, some representatives of the health service were apparently not pleased. However, it is unlikely that many people seriously thought the service played doctors and nurses on the floor of the delivery room while patients waited for attention. Many people who remained unconvinced by her more experimental work thought it her best film.

Despite *The Apple Game*'s more orthodox form, it is still a film that pro-

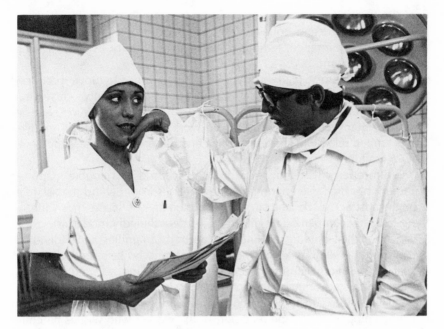

III–10   Doctors and nurses in Chytilová's *The Apple Game:* Dagmar Blahova and Jiří Menzel

vokes a sense of shock and surprise. It begins with a blank screen and the crying of a newborn baby. A sequence that includes various images of apples is accompanied by the breathing of a woman giving birth and the counting of a doctor. Red apples give way to the blood-covered head of a baby emerging from the womb and a rapid montage ends with a close-up of milk being expressed from a nipple. While the apples of the credits link the film to the imagery of her previous two films, to the themes of paradise and the game between men and women, the aesthetic shock of the opening also provides an intensely physical framework and a web of natural associations.

The film's feminist perspective hits some predictable targets—the position of women as housekeepers and "washing machines," male irresponsibility in the begetting of children combined with the need for the same doctor to be present during births at the hospital. The nurse also breaks the rules by seducing the male philanderer.

There is also a wider criticism of sexual behavior. Dr. John works with a colleague on a research project while sleeping with his wife behind his back. The wife is a willing participant and, in one of their scenes together, reveals that she likes "immoral things." Since she does not love him, it is vital that she have a climax every time.

Despite a few jokes at the expense of the economy and political jargon, the film is no wide-ranging dissection of the ills of society. Rather it presents a spirited and comic view of the battle of the sexes that convinces by its irreverence, feminine perspective, and (for its time) free approach to film form.

With *Prefab Story* (*Panelstory*, 1979), however, Chytilová produced what is quite probably the most critical film of the past twenty years. A satire on life in a contemporary housing project, it touches on such issues as theft, bad management, unprofessional work, and reified sex. It enjoyed only a limited release in Czechoslovakia and has never been screened publicly in Prague.

The film opens with shots of a building site and of a couple grappling on a bed in a high-rise apartment. The sun rises from behind the estate as a bright abstract globe and an opening montage of scenes from life on the estate is accompanied by music that is determinedly modernist.

Chytilová then opts for a multilevel portrait of families and individuals that is quite unrelenting—stories of the teenager who gets pregnant to the despair of the mother (only to hear her mother being seduced later by a TV star to the accompaniment of a discussion of morality), of the old woman who looks forlornly through the window of her apartment with her only companion, a tape recorder, of the worker who wishes he could sleep at night, of the child who engages in the willful destruction of nearly everything in sight.

Grafted onto this are smaller observations—the woman who sorts through the garbage dumpster complaining about what people throw away, the need to give bribes to get children into day care, competition for attention in the doctor's waiting room, the house painters who make love to the clients, the petty theft of a baby carriage, the cutting off of the water supply just before lunch, the problems of pregnancy, the lack of motivation ("Why should I study? I've got a flat and a new washing machine").

This observation is reinforced by blunt and aggressive imagery—a baby carriage stuck firmly in a morass of mud surrounding the site, the crosscutting of the painters' sexual conduct with images of construction and destruction. At the end of the film, another abstract globe (the moon) rises above the estate as a young couple meets. "Wouldn't you like to go to the moon?" says the boy. "No, it's so pleasant here," replies the girl. Kiss and fade out.

It is reasonable to take Chytilová's portrait of life in a contemporary housing development as a symbolic portrait of contemporary society. The housing developments are a reality and life in the various apartments provides her with a concentrated cross-section of society, from youth to age, from TV star to painter, or colored worker. Whether the film excited controversy for its symbolic level or because of what was construed as a literal attack on Prague building projects, one can only speculate. Surprisingly, there was a fairly positive review of the film in *Film a doba*.[22] However, it

III–11   Life in an apartment: Chytilová's *Prefab Story*

did add the rider that Chytilová had failed to maximize the positive aspects in the situation.

Here, of course, one touches on a basic problem of Czechoslovak film-making. Faults in society can be recognized but must form the basis of constructive criticism. The correctness of the system is beyond reproach, while the faults of individuals are not. But the wrapping up of criticism in permitted clothes only muffles it. The achievement of Chytilová lies in the fact that her film is designed for maximum impact—to force society to look at itself and the nature of its morality and material preoccupations. No one has ever accused Chytilová of being "anti-socialist," and *Prefab Story* can be seen as the work of someone who really wants to improve society rather than paper over the cracks. Her ironic "happy ending" is even more transparent than her "correct" conclusion to *Daisies* in exposing the artificiality of official optimism.

Chytilová has directed four further features, *Calamity (Kalamita,* 1979), *The Very Late Afternoon of a Faun (Faunovo příliš pozdní odpoledne,* 1983), *Wolf's Cabin (Vlčí bouda,* 1986), an underrated "morality" for young people, and the still-to-be released *The Jester and the Queen (Šašek a královna,* 1987). *Calamity* is the story of a young student who drops out of the university in order to become a train driver, his training for his job, and his sentimental education. Underneath it all, it seems, is a typical Barrandov moral tale, but the film is enlivened by philosophical discussions, virtuoso editing, and social comment. The couples frequently seen copulating in fields from the moving train seem to mark a continuation of the criticism of sexual morals that extends from *The Apple Game* and *Prefab Story*. And, for the allegory-conscious, the image of a train stuck in the snowdrift (the "calamity" of the film's title) might just mean something else.

The Very Late Afternoon of a Faun was adapted from a short story by the writer and animator Jiří Brdečka. It marks a renewal of Chytilová's collaboration with Ester Krumbachová (screenplay/artistic consultant) who had worked with her on *Daisies* and *The Fruit of Paradise*. A study in the life of a middle-aged man and "determined erotic" who preys on younger women, it provides some sitting targets for a female director. However, the portrait of the gap between desire and reality is not entirely unsympathetic and the humor is not only targeted on the man's physical decay. The young girls, who resolutely fail to conform to his romantic ideas with their shallow perceptions, chewing gum, refusal to shut the lavatory door, and casual attitude to sex, are hardly presented as positive models. Technically, the film employs a consistent but idiosyncratic use of subjective cam-

III–12   *The Very Late Afternoon of a Faun:* Leoš Suchařípa as Chytilová's Don Juan

era that is quite disconcerting. It is unusual in the context of an apparently commercial comedy and testifies to Chytilová's continuing commitment to experiment. Her film about Prague, made for Italian television about the same time, further developed her collaboration with cinematographer Jan Malíř in an intentionally experimental film that was very clearly the work of the director of *Daisies*.

In an interview following the U.S. premiere of *The Apple Game*, Chytilová spoke of her control of editing in her work and stated that this was a freedom shared by her colleagues. "But most of them have a conventional approach and edit the way they have been taught. . . . I want to give new meaning to a film with my editing—I want to put things together in a new way."[23] Her views differ little from those she expressed in the sixties. Basically, her commitment to the promotion of thought, of new ideas, of creation outside of prejudice and convention remains unchanged. "We live in a dark time, a film should be a little flashlight."[24]

It has often been pointed out that, in the fifties, when the political situation was at its darkest, Czechoslovakian animated film astonished the world. The feature productions of Jiří Trnka—*Old Czech Legends* (*Staré pověsti české*, 1953), *A Midsummer Night's Dream* (*Sen noci svatojanské*, 1959)—and Karel Zeman—*Journey to Primeval Times* (*Cesta do pravěku*, 1954), *An Invention for Destruction* (*Vynález zkázy*, 1958) and *Baron Munchausen* (*Baron Prášil*, 1961)—set a standard that has never been equaled. Precisely because the area of fairy tale and folk fantasy was acceptable, there was much less censorship. Likewise, small-scale production groups and the complex process of creation rendered day-by-day interference less of a possibility. Since the censorship of the seventies in some ways mirrored that of the fifties, it is worth considering the extent to which animation has followed a similar path to that time.

Unfortunately, the same claims cannot be made. This is not to suggest that the quality of animated films is low, merely that the possibly unique achievements of Trnka and Zeman have not been matched. Trnka himself died in 1969 while Zeman's features from this later period (*The Magician's Apprentice* [*Čarodějův učen*, 1977] and *Tales of Honzik and Marenka* [*Pohádka o Honzíkovi a Mařence*, 1980]) have not been of the same order. Feature animation has continued in the eighties, most notably in a sequence of coproductions with both West and East Germany. Stanislav Látal's *The Life and Incredible Adventures of Robinson Crusoe, the Sailor from York* (*Dobrodružství Robinsona Crusoe*, 1982) was followed by Jiří Tyller's *The Odyssey* (*Odyssea*, 1985), Jiří Barta's *The Pied Piper* (*Krysař*, 1986) and Ivan Renč's *Salar* (1986).

The Czech animation tradition remains strong and most of its best-known practitioners—Hermina Týrlová, Břetislav Pojar, Zdeněk Miler—have stayed active. However, it is the fate and perhaps the advantage of the maker of short films to be eternally ignored and underestimated.

Children's films are conventionally ghettoized, but Miler's *Mole* series had a great international success and set a standard of design and sensibility that has few equals in its field.

Amongst the most successful of the makers of short animated films has been the trio of Adolf Born, Jaroslav Doubrava, and Miloš Macourek, whose work goes beyond the simple moralities characteristic of the sixties' tradition. Macourek is a writer who is also active in features (his *Who Would Kill Jessie?* [*Kdo chce zabít Jessii?* 1966] attracted attention), but his ideas are rarely as well matched as in his collaborations with Born and Doubrava.

In *Hang Up* (*Mindrák*, 1981), for instance, we have the story of an intelligent dog that speaks French and reads Dostoyevsky in its spare time, a moral and intellectual superior to its beer-swilling, football-fan master. The dog's talents are only appreciated by his mistress. The master's plans to poison him or blow him up are frustrated and, finally, through a grim trick of fate, the master blows up his wife. Her arms and legs drop by the dog's kennel, rendering this a particularly black comedy. Finally, the master is sentenced for murder while the dog urinates on the leg of a court official.

The story is complemented by Born's caricatured vision—large men and women with fat legs, the dog more like a large bear—a specific style removed both from Disney and the matchstick abstractions of the "art" cartoon. The elements of fantasy and black comedy give both this and other films an edge that is missing from most of their competitors.

In puppet animation, Jiří Barta, one of the younger directors, should be mentioned not only for the considerable technical achievement of his films but also for his ambitious projects. His prize-winning film, *The Extinct World of Gloves* (*Zaniklý svět rukavic*, 1982) takes an array of gloves in different styles and from different periods of history, and animates them as a short history of the cinema—from silent cinema via pastiches of Buñuel and Fellini, to a futurist junkyard where tin cans become animated police cars in a city of urban decay. His feature film, *The Pied Piper*, attempts a gothic style based on carved walnut puppets, set against expressionistically carved sets and combined with live rats. There are no children in this tale, which draws on other traditions, including the work of the Czech poet Viktor Dyk. A vehement condemnation of a corrupt society, it involves images of rape and vengeance, recalling the black medieval epics of Bergman and Vláčil. However, in both films, the ideas at script level do not really match the invention of the superstructure, rather providing a trigger for a vision that is not totally integrated.

But integration is certainly an operative word in the case of Jan Švankmajer, not only the outstanding figure within Czech animation but also the one filmmaker whose work appears unrestricted by the political situation. No doubt, this was partly due to his making short films and also to the fact that "avant garde" work is more acceptable if contained within the generic term of the "trick film" (anything but live action)—a term which suggests, at any rate, a certain freedom. On the other hand, he was unable to complete any films between 1972–77 and his international success has been received in a mixed fashion. His best known film, *Dimensions of Dialogue/Possibilities for Dialogue* (*Možnosti dialogu*, 1982) has been condemned and he has become something of a film-maker "for export only."

One of the characteristics of the late-sixties phase of the *new wave* was an interest in the avant garde tradition. Surrealism was a strong influence and films directly inspired by its ideals included Němec's *Martyrs of Love*, Uher's film of Dominik Tatarka's *The Miraculous Virgin*, and Jireš' adaptation of Vitězslav Nezval's *Valerie and Her Week of Wonders*. Švankmajer began to make films at this time but, unlike the feature directors, he did not just make surrealist films but worked as a surrealist, joining the Prague surrealist group in 1969.

To make sense of this, it is worth recalling that the Czech forerunner of surrealism, known as poetism, was instituted in the twenties, the term being applied by the critic Karel Teige. According to Teige, "poetism" was a style of life that favored an art that was "playful, unheroic, unphilosophical, mischievious and fantastic."[25] Poetism led to surrealism in the thirties and one of its leaders, the poet Nezval, contributed to major films of the period—*Erotikon* (1920), *Extase* (1932), *From Saturday to Sunday* (*Ze soboty na neděli*, 1931), *On the Sunny Side* (*Na slunečni straně*, 1933). Many of the avant garde writers (Nezval and Vladislav Vančura, for example) were Communists, with the result that, despite the subsequent imposition of socialist realism, the thirties are a period that it has been difficult to completely disown. It was the surrealists who first published a Czech translation of Kafka's *The Trial*, subtitling it "a surrealist novel."

Paris and Prague have sometimes been described as the "twin poles of surrealism." While the significance of the Prague connection in the prewar period has not been fully appreciated, what is even less well known is the fact that surrealism has continued as an active force (albeit an underground one) until the present day.

Petr Král has pointed out that the poetist/surrealist tradition of the twenties and thirties did not share in the negative, apocalyptic, and utopian objectives of the French. Optimism, nostalgia, and romanticism were more vital—after all, the regaining of national independence provided an opportunity to participate in the building of a new culture and a new society.[26] Although the links with Marxism were not simple, a dialogue and interplay continued until the triumph of Stalinism in the fifties. The experience of Stalinism resulted in a plurality and relativism of approach within the movement and an emphasis on its critical role. However, the seventies ushered in a new era of cohesion and a greater emphasis on practice. But, argues Král, the other options are always present. The examination of the imaginative mechanism and the concern with games were inseparable from a reflection on the epoch and the way in which it conditioned individuals. "Humor, sarcasm, a sense of the absurd, traditional characteristics of the Praguers, always find a way of manifesting themselves."[27]

Jan Švankmajer has only recently attracted major critical attention and this is partly due to the obscurity within which makers of short/animation films conventionally work. His background is in the fine arts and he also studied in the Dramatic Art Faculty (or Marionette Faculty) of the Academy of Fine Arts in the fifties. It was not until 1964 that he made his first film, *The Last Trick (Poslední trik pana Edgara a pana Schwarzwalda)*, and while this and his other early films won awards, they could still be contained within the "invisible" world of the short film.

It was only with a remarkable sequence of films produced between 1968 and 1972 that the full force and originality of his vision could be felt. Some saw his Kafkaesque *The Flat (Byt*, 1968), *The Garden (Zahrada*, 1968), and *A Week in the Quiet House (Tichý týden u dome*, 1969) as sharing the atmosphere of the *new wave*. Yet Švankmajer has always denied any direct involvement and there is no reason to doubt this. Rather, it could be argued that a shared socio-political context often promotes a similar mood and concern among those with different points of departure. A further sequence of films ending with *Jabberwocky* (1971) and *Leonardo's Diary (Leonardův deník*, 1972) brought his film career to a virtual standstill, and he was only able to complete one short film in the next eight years. The fact that *The Flat, The Garden*, and *Jabberwocky* could not be shown indicates that someone somewhere disapproved.

It was only with *The Fall of the House of Usher (Zánik domu usherú*, 1981), *Dimensions of Dialogue* (1982), *The Pit, the Pendulum and Hope (Kyvadlo, jáma a naděje*, 1983) and *Down to the Cellar (Do sklepa*, 1983) that he finally established a major international reputation. Crucial to this were the Grand Prix awards to *Dimensions of Dialogue* in 1983 at both Berlin and Annecy and the retrospective of Švankmajer's work at Annecy. Predictably, *Dimensions of Dialogue* was not shown publicly in Czechoslovakia and the authorities were not keen to help in its international promotion.

Švankmajer has characterized his work as surrealist investigation—an attempt to liberate feelings of fear and anguish using the weapons of sarcasm, objective humor, and black comedy.[28] *Dimensions of Dialogue* consists of three sections: *Eternal Dialogue, Passionate Dialogue*, and *Exhausting Dialogue*. In the first, a human head consisting of cutlery, crockery, and kitchen implements devours another made of fruit and vegetables. The two then merge in a chaotic synthesis, reform, and undergo further conflict and transformation. Finally, a perfectly modeled human head emerges and begins to vomit replicas of itself. In *Passionate Dialogue* a male and a female figure touch and embrace in gestures of love but finally enter into conflict and tear each other to pieces. In *Exhausting Dialogue*, two heads are formed from the same matter and engage in complementary activities

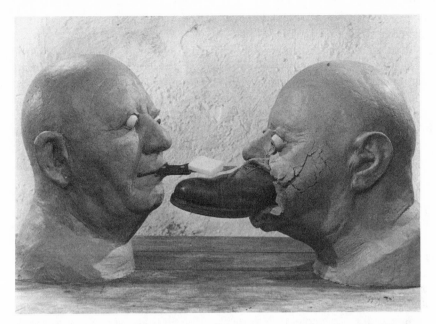

III–13   Exhausting dialogue: *Jan Švankmajer's Dimensions of Dialogue*

From the mouth of one emerges a toothbrush and from the other a tube of toothpaste to be squeezed onto the brush, a knife spreads butter on a piece of bread, a shoe is laced, and a pencil sharpened. But the process goes wrong, each head produces the wrong object, and chaos and destruction follow. Finally, the bulging eyes of the rather unpleasant heads give way to cracked and exhausted dissolution.

If one looks for a simple interpretation, we are faced with dialogue as an eternal fact and eternal conflict designed to produce a single uniform truth (*Eternal Dialogue*). However, dialogue between lovers is irrational and destructive, and the attempt at complementary dialogue easily converts into destructive conflict. An essentially negative, but perhaps realistic, view of human possibilities, it is a far cry from official optimism or simple-minded pacifism. Indeed, any conclusion one might reach would be anti-utopian and relativistic. The film could be interpreted as a demonstration of the surrealist view of life as dialectic, as a flux in which logic and abstraction can at best only envisage part of the totality.

While the importance of the film is grounded in a particular perspective, its force derives from its imagery. Here, it is important to recall Švankmajer's involvement with tactile experiments and his view of the resonance of objects. He sees objects as possessing a kind of "interior life" a content derived from their previous use. A good example is *Jabber-*

wocky, where old children's toys are animated to create a world of lost childhood.

There is certainly a strong resemblance between the object montage in Dimensions of Dialogue and the tactile combinations produced during his film silence between 1972 and 1980 (particularly the unusual tactile combinations of kitchen implements). His view that objects can provide an aesthetic "message" cannot be transferred to film, but his own sensitivity to textures and objects allows a selection and "total montage" that promote a tactile dimension. The qualities of materials are emphasized: of bristle and plastic when they are sharpened, of bread when it is tied with shoelaces, of pencil lead when it penetrates toothpaste.

With his two subsequent films, Švankmajer returns to a style closer to The Flat since both are live-action films employing animation techniques. In The Pit, the Pendulum and Hope, based on Poe and Villiers de l'Isle Adam, the audience is placed in the position of victim and the action is filmed entirely with a subjective camera. The central character is not seen at all; we are supposed to become him. We begin strapped to a bench as the pendulum swings and the knife blade comes closer to cutting us in half. However, with the aid of the remnants of a last meal, the containing straps are smeared with meat, attracting rats who come to nibble at the bonds. A last-minute escape—which is not permitted some of the rats, who are sliced in half by the blade—leads to a frantic and breathless stumble down a subterranean passage and a climb upwards towards the light. There we are confronted by a caped religious figure that blocks our escape in the name of "brotherhood."

A frightening and neurotic film capable of being seen politically, it also corresponds to the much more personal form of the nightmare and the fear of entrapment. The black and white photography has the murky and depressing quality of The Flat in a film totally without compromise in its black vision.

Down to the Cellar, made in Slovakia, is a little more upbeat and is filmed in color. A little girl is sent to the cellar to fetch potatoes but, in the process, encounters a sequence of nightmarish events. It is a film that has obvious links with Little Red Riding Hood or even Alice in Wonderland (his current project). In the cellar she meets an old man who makes a bed out of coal and offers her a place beside him, an old woman who bakes cakes from coal dust, an enormous cat that stalks her, shoes that fight for a piece of bread she is eating, and potatoes that follow a life of their own and escape from her basket. The man is seen as a possible child molester—he offers her a sweet—and an attack is heard on the soundtrack. Yet the film has a certain simplicity and the threats lack the quality of an omnipresent nightmare characteristic of The Flat and The Pit, the Pendulum and Hope. Finally, the girl escapes from the cellar but drops her basket of potatoes. She returns to the cellar but whether the ending implies a repetition of her nightmare or an ability to confront her fears remains open.

III–14   Little Red Riding Hood? Švankmajer's *Down to the Cellar*

If the focus of discussion so far has been largely restricted to the work of filmmakers who established their reputation in the sixties, this is entirely understandable. Whatever the limitations of their work in the seventies and eighties, it can frequently be seen as a continuation of tendencies present in their more substantial early works or defined in relation to them. Faced with restrictive policies, younger filmmakers have found it less easy to transcend their limitations. However, there is certainly a range of young directors who, if given their heads, could make some significant movies.

One director who has created a recognizable body of work is Jiří Svoboda, particularly with his *A Meeting with Shadows* (*Schůzka se stíny*, 1982), *The End of the Lonely Farm Berhof* (*Zánik samoty Berhof*, 1983), and *Scalpel, Please* (*Skalpel, prosím*, 1985). Characterized by a strong visual style, they also provide impressive dramatic roles for actors like Jana Brejchová, Radoslav Brzobohatý, and Miroslav Macháček. Although his style is more forcefully dramatic, his liking for simple themes capable of wider resonance is sometimes reminiscent of Vláčil.

One of his most impressive films is *A Meeting with Shadows*. Set against the background of an archaeological expedition, it concerns the relationship between the expedition's driver and the wife of an English archaeologist. The mystery is centered on the driver's peculiar, negative, and disturbed behavior. At times the film approaches its problems much like an exercise in Bergmanesque existentialism, with a similar use of symbolism and acting in depth. But it is less the solution to this psychological thriller (both protagonists had been involved in Nazi medical experiments on children) than the basic situation that gives the film its particular resonance.

Earlier reference was made to Zdeněk Svěrák's varied contribution to Czech cinema. Apart from his work with Menzel, he is best known for his collaborations with writer/director Ladislav Smoljak and, together, they are identified with a particular brand of black absurdist humor. In the sixties, they were the principal playwrights and producers of the Jará Cimrman Theatre. According to Škvorecký, it offered "a hugely sophisticated, irreverent, nonsensical and often socio-politically critical dramaturgy, with roots in the 'decadent' dada and pataphysical mystification."[29]

Jará Cimrman, who gave the theater its name, was an imaginary character and universal genius, equally adept as a writer, inventor, and filmmaker. The absurdist humor to which the plays gave birth has found its way to the screen in a variety of guises—not least through guest appearances by Svěrák and Smoljak in other people's films.

Together they scripted a number of films, including two for the veteran comedy director, Oldřich Lipský, *Joachim, Put It in the Machine* (*Jáchyme, hod ho do stroje*, 1974) and *Mareček, Pass Me a Pen* (*Marečku, podejte mi pero*, 1976). Their work for Menzel on *Seclusion Near a Forest*, though not typical, was the most successful from this period. More recently, since Smoljak himself turned director, their stage humor has transferred more successfully to the screen with *Run, Waiter, Run* (*Vrchní, prchni*, 1980), *Jára Cimrman, Lying Asleep* (1983), and *Dissolved and Let Out* (*Rozpuštěný a vypuštěný*, 1984).

Run, Waiter, Run concerns the exploits of a bookshop assistant and father of several illegitimate children, who impersonates head waiters in a number of Prague restaurants in order to supplement his income. As head waiters are the ones who collect the money, it presumably hit some predictable targets and was a great commercial success. In *Jára Cimrman, Lying Asleep*, set at the end of the nineteenth century, Cimrman is involved in a petition to change the Austro-Hungarian monarchy into an Austro-Hungarian-Czech monarchy. However, his quixotic manipulations of the Austrian state come to nothing when both the Archduke Ferdinand and the Emperor turn out to be doubles. The title of *Dissolved and Let Out* refers to a body dissolved in a bath of acid. A turn-of-the-century detective drama, it features a hero (sometimes represented by a clockwork replica) who is constantly frustrated by an unseen superior. Its strange, almost Kafkaesque mood and deadpan humor certainly make it unusual—and probably inaccessible—to a non-Czech audience. Svěrák and Smoljak can scarcely be categorized as new young filmmakers; they are more of a phenomenon—and a specifically Czech one at that.

Among younger filmmakers worth noting are Vladimír Drha, Karel

III–15   Jana Brejchová in Jiří Svoda's *A Meeting with Shadows*

Smyczek, Jaroslav Soukup, Zdeněk Flidr, Zdeněk Troška and, in Slovakia, Vladimír Balco. Both Drha and Smyczek have made sensitive films on the theme of youth and Drha's *A New Boy Started Today* (*Dneska přišel nový kluk*, 1981) attracted attention for dealing with inequalities in the education system and negative industrial practice. However, a comparison of Smyczek's *Just a Little Whistle* (*Jen si tak trochu písknout*, 1980) with Forman's *Black Peter/Peter and Pavla* (*Černý Petr*, 1964) reveals how much is still being missed. Soukup's *Love in the Arcade* (*Láska v pasáži*, 1984) addressed problems of teenage crime and drugs for virtually the first time, while Flidr's *They've All Got Talent* (*Všichni mají talent*, 1984) criticized the attitudes of a mid-level bureaucrat whose only interest in the fate of an amateur folk dance group lies in the prospect of foreign travel. Neither is world shaking, but both show considerable sensibility.

The work of Troška and Balco is of more interest for its for formal initiatives. Troška's *The Treasure of Count Chamaré* (*Poklad hraběte Chamaré*, 1985) adopted a freewheeling approach, rather reminiscent of a pop video, to a standard historical novel set in the seventeenth century. It looks quite unlike anything else produced in recent years and, if its interest is almost exclusively stylistic, it is important for all that. Balco's *Angle of Approach* (*Uhol pohladu*, 1985) achieves a mixture of form/content interest in its story of a young filmmaker who makes a "cinéma vérité" film about his girlfriend's father, a famous organist. It offers some quite sharp observation on materialist and careerist motivation, and not least that of the filmmaker himself.

In the last two years (1986–87) there has been a definite increase in the degree to which social problems, specifically drugs and delinquency, have been openly treated. Zdeněk Zaoral's *The Cobweb* (*Pavučina*, 1986), which began life as an independent film, was subsequently completed with official backing, and was the first film to confront the drug issue head-on. Despite a certain spontaneity and a convincing sullen performance by its leading actress (Eva Kulichová), it has some uncomfortably arty effects and presents an ultimately stereotyped analysis. Viktor Polesný's short film, *Half Time* (*Poločas rozpadu*, 1986), scripted by Radek John, who also wrote an influential book on the subject, avoids the stereotypes, but is more of an exercise in mass aversion therapy.

Altogether more successful is Karel Smyczek's *Why?* (*Proč?*, 1987), also scripted by Radek John, a drama documentary reconstruction of a riot by football fans in the early eighties. Avoiding a simple narrative, it takes six of the young people brought to trial and examines both their backgrounds and their involvement in the incident. A deliberately violent and sometimes shocking film, it significantly avoids simple moralizing or ready-made solutions. The young people are, in fact, quite ordinary and the roots of their behavior by no means obvious. The film suggests some explanations—and the image of a girl looking down over a deserted cityscape from a high-rise apartment speaks for itself—but is fundamentally an attempt to promote analysis and discussion.

Another interesting development in the same period has been some rather successful Western-style commercial films. Vít Olmer's *Like Poison* (*Jako jed*, 1985) analyzes the love affair between a middle-aged architect (Zdeněk Svěrák) and a young Slovak girl, while *Anthony's Chance* (*Antonyho šance*, 1986) is the story of a young widower who tries to bring up his daughter and create a new marriage. While touching on some genuine social issues, the prime focus is entertainment, achieved through attractive performances, atmospheric photography (Ota Kopřiva), and lively music scores from Jiří Stivín. If *Anthony's Chance* is Czechoslovakia's answer to *Kramer vs. Kramer*, Soukup's *Fists in the Dark* (*Pěsti ve tmě*, 1986) has been described (misleadingly) as the Czech *Rocky*. Despite its boxing theme, it is primarily an exercise in the nostalgic recreation of period (the thirties) with not a few stylistic nods in the direction of Clayton's *The Great Gatsby* and Polanski's *Chinatown*.

The most encouraging fact about the younger filmmakers is their obvious talent. But it is also sad that their films often acquire significance through simple or tepid points of social criticism or stylistic innovations that, in an international context, are quite unremarkable.

One of the ironies of the post-invasion period has been the international success of Czech literature. If most of the leading writers have been banned at home, many have at the same time acquired an international following. The critical recognition of the emigré writers Milan Kundera and Josef Škvorecký has had much to do with this, as did the winning of the 1984 Nobel Prize by Czechoslovakia's best-loved poet, Jaroslav Seifert.[30] However, the success of the emigré writers has not derived from any "dissident" quality and their work has remained resolutely Czech in its inspiration.

A discussion of whether the same might apply to filmmakers may seem odd since, unlike writers, they are forced to take their material from other cultures and to work within a non-Czech production context. Yet, just as German directors brought a new sensibility to Hollywood in the thirties, Czech directors have brought their own insights. To varying degrees, the European and North American work of Jasný, Kadár, and Passer can be seen to have links with their work in Czechoslovakia. Films based on Czech themes have, however, been nonexistent—unless one counts Stanislav Barabás's Comenius (from Kokoschka) and Ivo Dvořák's Metamorphosis (from Kafka).

Nonetheless, there is justification in the view that Miloš Forman has maintained a Czech tradition—particularly in his best-known films, One Flew Over the Cuckoo's Nest (1975) and Amadeus (1983). His first American film, Taking Off (1970) was, in many respects, like one of his Czech films transplanted.

While One Flew Over the Cuckoo's Nest, and Amadeus, are taken from very specific non-Czech sources, they contain many ideas that would fall on fertile ground in Czechoslovakia. These would include the rebellion of the individual against the restrictions of an asylum where the patients are voluntary inmates (One Flew Over the Cuckoo's Nest), the persecution of the talented by the mediocre, and censorship portrayed as total absurdity (Amadeus). Amadeus, of course, has the additional advantage of having been made in Prague with a largely Czech team that included Miroslav Ondříček (cinematography), Karel Černý (art direction), and Theodor Pištěk (costumes). Other collaborators included the opera designer Josef Svoboda, screenwriter Zdeněk Mahler, and the film directors František Vláčil and Jan Schmidt.

Not for the first time, the continuing theme of Czechoslovak cinema in the seventies and eighties has been the struggle of filmmakers to make good movies and to reconcile this with the ideological demands of the state. As David Anderman put it in a report from Prague in the New York Times, the seventies saw the growth of "an apparatus of censors, 'literary advisors' and bureaucrats whose sole purpose was to make certain that the system did not produce anything that could be construed as 'reactionary,' or even 'introspective'—anything that did not educate people to 'the socialist realities'."[31] Antonín Liehm wrote in 1976: "Every attempt at even the slightest originality is stifled at the screenplay stage, and the studio maintains a vigilant eye during the shooting to ensure that the style of the film remains faithful to the very worst traditions, now almost universally rejected throughout Eastern Europe. . . ."[32]

Luckily, such policies can ultimately be self-defeating. The production of screenplays designed purely to promote official ideology results not only in sterility but also in expensive and monumental flops that embarrass even those who demand them. In 1980 Radek John complained in *Film a doba* of directors' "fear of reality."[33] The answer was simple, of course: no one was allowed to confront it. When films within permitted ideological trappings do convince—*And My Greetings to the Swallows, Shadows of a Hot Summer, A Meeting with Shadows*, or Antonín Moskalyk's *Cuckoo in the Dark Forest* (*Kukačka v temném lese*, 1985)—they go well beyond the ideological brief and raise entirely different issues.

It is frequently asserted that few people in Czechoslovakia now believe the official ideology—that having made obligatory noises, people just get on with their daily work and their private lives. An exercise in practical materialism is encouraged, part of the unwritten exchange of affluence for acquiescence. Havel sees such consumerism in negative terms, but Ernest Gellner argues that it might have benefits, that the necessary level of affluence can only be attained by allowing a degree of honesty, efficiency, and liberty.[34] Pragmatism might, in the end, supersede ideological dogma and fear of ideological deviation.

A degree of pragmatism has certainly been evident in the film industry. The re-employment of important directors in the mid-seventies can be seen as evidence of this, as can the reorganization of the industry in the early eighties into new production groups and the deliberate promotion of more ambitious screenplays. An increasing number of foreign productions have been based in Prague (*Yentl, Amadeus, The Howling II, Rosa Luxemburg*), and coproductions with Western Europe have again become possible.

The situation within the film industry is clearly more flexible than it was and—without denigrating the achievements already made against the odds—it may not be long before Czechoslovakia's filmmakers again interest the world. Change is inevitable and there seems little reason to continue the paranoid vigilance that has prevailed since 1969.

All this depends, of course, on the situation of Czechoslovakia itself, on the fate of Gorbachev's reforms in the Soviet Union, on relations between the Great Powers. If it is truly possible to move beyond the ideological simplifications of Cold War politics, then the situation of Central Europe should be reviewed. Both sides may equate silence and acquiescence with the preservation of peace. Yet a stability based on demoralization and a developed use of police methods is no stability at all. Without some acceptance of the legitimate demands and freedoms of the "small" countries, there can be no genuine accommodation between the powers. While it may seem utopian, the recognition of such freedoms need not imply any threat to legitimate Soviet security interests. As Churchill said to Stalin at the Yalta Conference, "The eagle should permit the small birds to sing, and care not wherefore they sing."[35]

NOTES

I would like to thank Simon Field and Igor Hájek for valuable comments on the first draft of this chapter. I am grateful also to the North Staffordshire Polytechnic for financial assistance. Stills were supplied courtesy of the British Film Institute, Peter Cargin, and the National Film Archive.

1. Zdeněk Mlynář, a leading member of the Dubček government now in exile, was apparently a fellow student of Gorbachev, who was at that time already interested in the possibilities for reform. See Christian Schmidt-Häuer, *Gorbachev: The Path to Power,* trans. Ewald Osers and Chris Romberg (London: Pan Books, 1986), pp. 48–52, 59.

2. On the other hand, Yegor Yakovlev, the "arch-priest" of Soviet *glasnost,* has justified the Soviet intervention in Czechoslovakia in 1968 on the grounds that counter-revolutionaries were planning civil war. It remains to be seen how far the permitted democracy of *glasnost* will be allowed to go outside of the Soviet Union. See Mary Kaldor and Jonathan Steele, "Interview with Yegor Yakovlev", *END Journal* (London) 28–29 (Summer 1987), pp. 11–12. Hans Starek points out that while there is much debate on the subject of *přestavba* (restructuring), there is almost no media discussion of *otevřenost* (openness). *Přestavba* is not presented as contradicting the policies of recent years but as a natural progression from *Poučení* (Lessons from the Crisis Years). See Hans Starek, " 'Přestavba' Rules—But What Is It?," *Labour Focus on Eastern Europe* 9 (2) (July–October 1987), pp. 44–45.

3. Jiří Mucha, interviewed by Antonín J. Liehm, *The Politics of Culture,* trans. Peter Kussi (New York: Grove Press, 1973), p. 221.

4. Quoted in Michael Charlton, *The Eagle and the Small Birds: Crisis in the Soviet Empire: From Yalta to Solidarity* (London: British Broadcasting Corporation, 1984), p. 56.

5. Vladimír V. Kusin, *From Dubček to Charter 77: A Study of "Normalisation" in Czechoslovakia, 1968–1978* (Edinburgh: Q Press, 1978), pp. 239–240.

6. There is some dispute over the precise figures but, however constituted, the total number of those who left the party approaches half a million. See Kusin, pp. 85–87.

7. See Kusin, p. 97.

8. Milan Šimečka, *The Restoration of Order: The Normalization of Czechoslovakia,* trans. A. G. Brain (London: Verso Editions, 1984), p. 37.

9. Šimečka, p. 43.

10. Karel Kosík, *The Dialectics of the Concrete: A Study of Problems of Man and World,* trans. Karel Kovanda and James Schmidt (Dordrecht and Boston: Reidel, 1976).

11. Václav Havel, "The Power of the Powerless," trans. Paul Wilson, in John Keane (ed.), *The Power of the Powerless: Citizens Against the State in Central-Eastern Europe* (London: Hutchinson, 1985).

12. Havel, p. 90.

13. Havel, p. 93.

14. "Czechoslovaak Writers and Charter 77 Address the Budapest Cultural Forum" (Charter 77 Document No. 24/1985).

15. O. Sojka (pseudonym), "The Bounds of Silence," *Index on Censorship 5(3)* (Autumn 1976).

16. Although the work of Forman, Kadár, and Weiss has been partially reinstated, their names, unlike those of pre-war emigrés, are not included in recentfilm graphies and histories. Perversely, their films are acknowledged under the names of their cinematographers and art directors.

17. Ludvík Toman, "*Czech Feature Films: Variety of Genres and Subjects,*" *Czechoslovak Film 1–2* (1972), pp. 6–7.

18. Jan Žalman, "Question-Marks on the New Czechoslovak Cinema," *Film Quarterly* (Winter 1967–68), pp. 18–27.

19. Alfred French, *Czech Writers and Politics, 1945–1969* (Boulder: East European Monographs; New Yorki: Columbia University Press, 1982), pp. 372–373.

20. Despite his partial reinstatement, Hrabal's work was subject to censorship and many of his books have only been published outside the country. Similarly, the script for *Cutting It Short* was carefully vetted before production.

21. A point noted by the emigré critic Jan Uhde. See Josef Škvorecký, *Jiří Menzel and the history of the Closely Watched Trains* (Boulder: East European Monographs; New York: Columbia University Press, 1982), p. 91.

22. Miroslav Zůna and Vladimír Solecký, "Ještě k filmovému svetu Věry Chytilové," *Film a doba* 28 (5) (May 1982), pp. 266–271.

23. Věra Chytilová, in Harriet Polt, "A Film Should Be a Little Flashlight: An Interview with Věra Chytilová," *Take One* (November 1978), p. 43.

24. Chytilová, p. 44.

25. Karel Teige, "Poetism" (1924), quoted in Alfred French, *The Poets of Prague* (London: Oxford University Press, 1969), p. 39.

26. Petr Král, *Le Surréalisme en Tchécoslovaquie* (Paris: Flammarion, 1983), pp. 14–15.

27. Král, p. 63.

28. Jan Švankmajer, in Petr Král, "Questions à Jan Švankmajer," *Positif*, No. 297 (November 1985), p. 42.

29. Škvorecký, p. 9.

30. Other emigré writers to attract attention include Arnošt Lustig, Jiří Gruša, and Pavel Kohout. Ivan Klíma, who is unable to publish in Czechoslovakia, has also been translated along with other writers still in Czechoslovakia, including Havel, Hrabal, Miroslav Holub, and Ladislav Fuks.

31. David A. Anderman, "New Czech Film Has Drama in Its Own History," *New York Times,* March 12, 1978, p. 59.

32. Antonín J. Liehm, "Triumph of the Untalented," *Index on Censorship* 5(3) (Autumn 1976), p. 60.

33. Radek John, "Hlavní tendence v české filmové komedii" (part two), *Film a doba* 26 (5) (May 1980), pp. 274–281.

34. Ernest Gellner, "Between Loyalty and Truth," *The Times Literary Supplement* (London), October 3, 1986, p. 1090.

35. Quoted in Charlton, *The Eagle and the Small Birds,* p. 13.

4

Poland:
The Cinema of
Moral Concern

Frank Turaj

Any description of contemporary cinema in Poland begins, properly and inevitably, with the work of Andrzej Wajda, whose influence has been so deep and broad as to defy easy assessment. If there was one particular time rather than another when this became true, it was with the making of *Man of Marble* (*Człowiek z marmuru*, 1976), the film which launched the movement among filmmakers to undertake a moral examination of Polish life and modern Polish history.[1]

There was a certain antecedent to this provided by Wajda when he made *Ashes and Diamonds* (*Popiół i diament*, 1958), in which an anti-Communist is the hero. Brilliantly realized, that movie became a touchstone. Fifteen films later, Wajda created another important moment in the history of Polish cinema with *Man of Marble*. He had been trying for fourteen years to get permission to make this film, ever since he first read the screenplay by Aleksander Ścibor-Rylski, but the project was rejected by the Ministry of Culture. Then, in early 1976, permission came. The delay was not surprising, given the sensitive elements of the story: Stalinism, cynical manipulation, repression—all involved in recapturing the authenticity of the period. In fact, the script was inspired by an actual event.

During the early fifties, Polish workers were subjected to the Soviet-inspired *Stakhanovite* phenomenon: that is, certain workers were cultivated to exceed greatly the norms of production and then accorded publicity and rewards. It happened that the workmates of a particularly successful model bricklayer, angry at the pressure he created for them, passed him a hot brick, causing injury. Around this actual event Wajda and Ścibor-Rylski built a filmic tale of one Mateusz Birkut, an honest, good bricklayer who tries to do his best, is cultivated by the authorities, and is hailed and exploited as a national hero. After he is passed the hot brick, his friends are arrested and accused of sabotage. Birkut defends a friend he feels has been falsely accused with so much vigor that he finds

IV–1   *Man of Marble (Człowiek z marmuru)*

himself in trouble and then in prison. Publicity ceases. A marble statue of
him is removed to the basement of a museum.

Those Stalinist years, although officially called a period of errors and dis-
tortions, were not open to discussion; references in literature and history
were suppressed. It was Wajda's intention to educate the young, so, to
that end, he adopted the point of view of a young film student who, in
the course of making a documentary, discovers the marble statue and
sets out to learn the story behind it.[2] Played by Krystyna Janda,
Agnieszka, the student, encounters resistance among those originally involved with Birkut, but she perseveres.

Wajda thus has us following two stories at once, the bricklayer's and
the filmmaker's: related stories because one is about the manipulation of reality, the other about trying to find out what reality was. Although Birkut
and Agnieszka never actually meet, they meet thematically in their insistence upon integrity. They also meet at one remove when she finds his
son and learns that he is dead. There are oblique suggestions that he
might have been involved in the riots of 1970 and shot down. (A ceme-
tery scene which makes that plain was excised from the film, but later included in *Man of Iron*.) Ultimately, she does not finish her documentary, because a supervisor whose approval she needs is not willing to grant it.
Nonetheless the movie ends in an up-beat way through the use of music,
lighting, and camera-work to suggest that as long as there are people like
Agnieszka, there is hope for truth.

The authorities saw the finished product in the fall of 1976 and viewed it with consternation. Like *Ashes and Diamonds* it broke the norms. Since its production attracted notice in Poland and elsewhere, it would have been embarrassing to shelve it. It was released quietly to one theater and drew such crowds that it made the officials nervous. To thin the crowds, the film was released widely and was an enormous popular success. It was not, however, accorded the attention normal to such a hit. Positive criticism was spiked and a limit was placed on negative criticism in order not to attract notice. The annual awards festival at Gdansk was proscribed from giving it any kind of award, but following the official ceremonies an award was presented on the steps outside the hall by Wajda's colleagues: a brick tied with a red ribbon!

Whereas in *Man of Marble* cynical manipulation was one of the main subjects, in Wajda's next piece it became the total substance of the story. Because of *Man of Marble*, there were attempts to make the director into an unperson. He and his film unit were subjected to discrimination and no mention of him was found in the media. He was, as it were, being excluded from life. Agnieszka Holland's screenplay on such a theme fit his mood very well. *Without Anesthesia (Bez znieczulenia*, 1978) is a story of a journalist who returns from abroad and in an initial interview says something on television which for some reason is found to be offensive. While it is ambiguous what it is that he has said that was disturbing to the powers that be, he is made the victim of a bureaucratic freeze-out. He also discovers that his wife is leaving him for a younger man, whose views incidentally are politically orthodox. When he has essentially been deprived of the decencies of life, and even made the subject of malicious slander in a divorce hearing, he dies by burning. The implication is suicide.

How is it possible, *Without Anesthesia* seems to ask, to change the image of a man from positive to negative without anything noticeable happening to bring it about? How can the conditions of life be so manipulated as to make it seem that a man has almost ceased to exist? Whose fault is it? There is no answer. The journalist (played by Zbigniew Zapasiewicz, one of the finest actors in Poland) is caught in a society in which there is no moral framework, in which there are no dependable standards of good and evil, or even of quality and mediocrity. Anyone can suddenly be on the bottom of the pile. Since there are no solid or fixed values from which to form moral judgments, cynical manipulation becomes a way of life.

Both theme and narrative are direct. To accommodate this, Wajda switched styles. In *Without Anesthesia* there is nothing baroque, nothing spectacular, no structural complexity, little in the way of symbol and metaphor. This variation in style fit precisely with what younger directors were doing, directors who were concerning themselves with moral themes directly explicated and plainly presented. In *Man of Marble* Wajda broke new political ground from the angle of ethics and values. In *Without Anes-*

thesia he demonstrated that an older director, one used to a film language of greater complexity, could work superbly well in the new, plain mode.

As if to demonstrate his versatility further, Wajda switched again when he made *The Maids of Wilko* (*Panny z Wilka*, 1979), which was nonpolitical, lyrical, delicate, nostalgic, about time, memory, and love. This film will probably remain his most beautiful work. It was made as a kind of tribute to the writer Jarosław Iwaszkiewicz, author of the story on which the film is based, a story with delicately efficient portraits of a number of women, the multiple characterizations held together cinematically by milieu and visual atmosphere. In *The Maids of Wilko* the principal visual idea is contained in the concept of autumn. This is an autumnal film in the sense that it is about the way nature withers and changes colors, and relationships do also; autumn for all its beauty still diminishes what was once new, fresh, vibrant. The autumnal quality as realized visually is a breathtaking tour de force.

This film met with a universally positive, even avid, reception. Even those "official" critics who had attacked *Man of Marble* and *Without Anesthesia* praised *The Maids of Wilko*, calling it Wajda's masterpiece.

Wajda had less success with *The Conductor* (*Dyrygent*, 1980), perhaps because of production complications that came about with the limited availability of John Gielgud. The great British actor, whose family origins were Polish, was glad to accept the role, but his schedule was tight. The final script and background shooting were done in confusion, with the result that the seams in the movie are too evident. Manipulation was once again a theme, in this case the manipulation of people by a mediocre provincial music director whose tawdry character stands out starkly against the portrayal of an old, morally noble conductor (Gielgud). Some have assumed a political allegory in *The Conductor* (music director-regime vs. orchestra-society), but this interpretation makes no sense here. This a thoughtful, delicate rendering of art, love, maturity, integrity, and the destructive force of hatred. It actually had little impact in Poland; the attention of the public was turning to the drama of reality. Solidarity was about to come into existence.

During the critical strikes of August, 1980, Wajda went to Gdansk, the focal city of unrest, to see about making a documentary there, *Workers 80* (*Robotnicy 80*, 1980). At the shipyards the strikers were admitting no one, fearing provocateurs; nonetheless, when Wajda arrived he was admitted immediately and taken directly to the strike committee. Along the way, someone suggested to him, pointing to the metal hulls and cranes, that he should now make a film about a man of iron. Of course, that is what he did. Ścibor-Rylski wrote a script, completing the first draft in eight days. Time was crucial. Political circumstances might change, making such a film impossible.

The plan was to make a sequel to *Man of Marble*, in which the bricklayer's son, Tomczyk, would be an activist striker now married to Agniesz-ka, the documentarist from *Man of Marble*. The structure of the film had to accommodate the different time periods, remaining topical with respect to the then-current events. In addition there was the problem of obtaining quick approval. Józef Tejchma, Minister of Culture when *Man of Marble* was made, had been dismissed. During the liberal flare-up of 1980 and 1981 he had been once again appointed, and found the screenplay of *Man of Iron* on his desk. Once again he approved it and then later was dismissed. But *Man of Iron* (*Człowiek z żelaza*, 1981) started production in the early spring of 1981.

To tie the elements of the story together, Ścibor-Rylski created the character of an alcoholic journalist who is blackmailed into gathering information about the strikers for the security police. The more this man learns, the more he loses his cynicism. Finally, he turns his back on the official who had suborned him, but by then he has lost the trust of the strikers. As he leaves the yards following the victory of the strikers in their negotiations and the signing of the agreement, he runs into his old boss, an *apparatchik*, who dismisses the agreement with the workers as meaningless. This final scene was, as it turned out, prophetic.

Man of Iron has artistic deficiencies, not surprising given the intense production schedule. The hero, Tomczyk, is one-dimensional. The narrative is uneven. There are seams where the staged sequences, documentary material, and segments related to *Man of Marble* join; but the movie is unique in the way it uses all its different elements to give an impression of immediacy, suspense, and power. For effect it compares with Costa-Gavras' "Z" or *State of Siege*. At Cannes that year it received the highest award. *Man of Iron* opened in Poland on July 26, 1981, and quickly became the most popular Polish film of all time. The fact that millions were allowed to see it was a sign of new conditions. Since December 12, 1981, when a form of martial law was declared, it has not been seen again in Poland to the time of this writing.

Some found a gloss on post-martial-law political life in Poland in Wajda's next film, *Danton* (1983), which was made in France. Viewers saw Lech Wałęsa in the character of Danton and General Wojciech Jaruzelski, party chief and prime minister, in the portrayal of Maximillian Robespierre. The film does invite some comparisons; for example, the posture and carriage of Wojciech Pszoniak, who plays Robespierre, suggests he might be miming Jaruzelski. Given that *Danton* is about a country in upheaval it is not surprising to find political reference points in the dialogue, and to be sure, the Polish audience did find metaphors. In France, not surprisingly, the movie was read in terms of French politics. The Republican and Gaullist opposition identified with Danton and linked the ruling Socialists and Mitterand with the doctrinaire Robespierre. Wajda and his writers reject the linkages.[3]

Danton was a compelling drama because of very intelligent scriptwriting and brilliant performances by the leads, Pszoniak and Gérard Depardieu as Danton. The director succeeded in maintaining heavy suspense and an atmosphere of threat from start to end, partly by compressing events into three days but mainly because of his masterful control of his actors and his cameras.

Less successful aesthetically and dramatically was Wajda's *Love in Germany* (*Miłość w Niemczech*, 1984), with a screenplay by Bolesław Michałek and Agnieszka Holland from a book by Rolf Hochhuth. It is the documentary story of a Polish prisoner of war who is hanged for having an affair with a German woman. The movie, like the book, is concerned with mass psychology, Nazi paranoia and racial ideology, and it adds a special dimension of its own, the torrid performance of Hanna Schygulla as a woman who has lost emotional and sexual control of herself in a lusciously and sensuously convincing way. The script effectively evokes the complicity of ordinary people. For obvious reasons the film was not well received in Germany (it was a German-French coproduction). It has never been shown in Poland.

Relations between Wajda and the authorities were never very good. Things came to a head in 1983 when the regime dissolved Wajda's company, Unit "X," effecting in that way their intention to dismiss Wajda and Bolesław Michałek, his literary director. Once again his name was little used in the official media, but it is impossible to make him an unperson in Poland. His stature is simply too great, both as artist and as cultural hero.

It is fair to say that *Man of Marble* opened an important chapter in film culture in 1976, but that chapter had many other authors, none more important than Krzysztof Zanussi, previously known for *The Structure of Crystal* (*Struktura kryształu*, 1969), *Illumination* (*Iluminacja*, 1973), and *Balance Sheet* (*Bilans kwartalny*, 1975), alternatively titled *A Woman's Decision*. Zanussi made *Camouflage* (*Barwe ochronne*, 1976) in the same year that Wajda made *Man of Marble*. With it he made his own special contribution toward inaugurating the new mood: his technique and substance less spectacular, more philosophical, analytical, and precise, but with a deep respect for the ambiguities of existence. His is the quintessential cinema of intellectual morality.

The point of departure for Zanussi's *Camouflage* is, not surprisingly, philosophical rather than political. It brings together two views of life represented by the two main characters, one of them a naturalist, the other a humanist. To put it another way, they argue positions for life as it is versus life as it should be. But this is not just philosophy, and I suspect an irony in the title. Zanussi is playing at camouflage because the obverse side of the dialectic is clearly political and thus, implicitly, so is the film. The thematic duel is developed verbally and dramatically between a young assistant professor, an idealist and moralist, and on the other side a seasoned, worldly professor whose strength is in cynicism. The young man believes that life should be lived according to the values of veracity, justice, and loyalty, values which

IV–2   *Camouflage (Barwy ochronne)*

the older man believes to be naïve at best. For the latter, life is a game of survival in which we must learn from nature to adapt to our environment, to put on protective coloring as so many species do. There are clear social extrapolations here, and the professor sets out to convert the assistant to his view of life as an exercise in adjustment and accommodation.

Clearly Zanussi favors the young man's position, but just as clearly he intends no two-dimensional morality tale. His characters face critical choices, test those choices morally and psychologically, and make commitments. In the closing scene of *Camouflage* the protagonist and antagonist get into a physical fight when the assistant, seeing cynicism and duplicity successful, attacks the professor. They battle to a stand-off. That stand-off is part of the message.

The audience saw through the protective coloring of the movie and found in it a comment on political and social life. The professor is a rendition of a particular Polish type—the careerist, the manipulator, to whom idealism is naïve and moral rebellion stupid. By avoiding direct political reference, Zanussi made the personal moral issues more incisive. Wajda's *Man of Marble* addressed national integrity by referring to history. Zanussi's *Camouflage* speaks directly to the integrity of the individual soul. Both were seminal to the many films that came to be categorized as "the cinema of moral concern" (*kino moralnego niepokoju*).

The release of *Camouflage* prompted actions by enemies of the new cinema which exemplified the kind of manipulation that was a theme for many movies. The film was a success even though there were attempts at first to keep this from happening. Favorable reviews were suppressed, and, with no bad reviews, there was silence. The aura of the forbidden gave rise to more word-of-mouth information and enhanced the film's appeal. Then the approach was reversed in order to use *Camouflage* to divert popularity and attention from *Man of Marble*. Moreover, there was concern about the Gdansk awards and the officials were set against Wajda getting the prize. If, however, an inferior movie were rewarded, that would simply court ridicule. Since *Camouflage* was universally deemed important and was not well-liked by the regime, it seemed that the award could be shunted there without making the officials look too bad and the award could be kept from Wajda's politically explicit work. Zanussi turned the manipulation upon itself by declining to accept the grand prize.

Zanussi's next film carried him further into philosophy and psychology than any of his works to date. *Spiral* (*Spirala*, 1978) is distinguished in every way and may be his masterpiece. It is the story of a man who knows that he is dying and decides to end his life in the mountains by perishing of exposure. That decision, the meaning of it and of his life, of other lives, is measured by the relationships he begins the night before he goes into the mountains, where he is, in fact, rescued before he freezes.

IV–3   *Spiral (Spirala)*

The film is an existential confrontation with death. We see the dying man's relationship to the thing he now italicizes as *life* and his reactions to those who will go on living. We also see the reactions of those who feel compelled to respond to his dying.

Zanussi is brutal in maintaining focus even when we would rather turn our heads away. His is the forcefulness of a relentless thinker and an insistent artist, an insistence that we stay with the fundamental questions of life and death until we have worked our way through to some resolution or until we are defeated. It is not always clear which of these is happening.

In 1980, sensing the velocity of current events and anxious about future production conditions, Zanussi made two films at once, *Contract* (*Kontrakt*, 1980) and *The Constant Factor* (*Constans*, 1980). A single crew was organized to make both, sometimes shooting scenes from the two on alternate days.

Contract is the story of a wedding in which the bride says no at the ceremony. The cast of characters is an inventory of certain types familiar in contemporary Poland, filling out a bitter metaphor. There is the spoiled young would-be groom, son of a rich physician. The physician himself is a corrupt hospital director, somewhat reminiscent of the old Polish intelligentsia, not above taking special gifts from his patients. There is a business manager, rude, uneducated but shrewd, a product of the system, pushy, puffed up with success. There is a foreign relative, exotic, who turns out to be an embarrassment, and there are others.

No one is terribly put off by the fact that the wedding aborts. In any case the guests do not care much. They only attend such affairs to make contacts, do business, make their way among the privileged few of a socialist society. The bride's honest rebellion is insignificant, it seems. We are left with an image of a sleazy and corrupt world and a feeling that it must all collapse. So let it collapse! Zanussi seems to be saying.

The Constant Factor also took corruption as a subject, but this movie dealt with it seriously, from the highly intellectual orientation of a philosophical protagonist, a learner, a searcher trying to find underlying sense in life. He tries to find it in the pure form of mathematics by investigating constant factors, to find some method to see if his own life can be rationalized or if life itself can be rationalized. What is determined and what remains variable? Along the way he is employed in a corrupt situation but refuses to be corrupted himself. He is provoked, framed and fired. He finds new work on a high scaffold and is there when a dislodged stone falls toward a running child. We do not learn whether the child is killed or not, but the point is that in either case nothing is predictable, calculable, certain. There is always a variation lurking. Although a scientist and philosopher by training, Zanussi surrenders to the mystery of things. His art and his religion seem to fuse to express that if there is a constant factor other than God, or collateral with God, it is death.

Interpretation of *The Constant Factor*, which was shown in 1980, was skewed by the political and social climate; the philosophical dimensions were quite lost. The film was read by the Polish audience as the story of an honest man victimized by a corrupt system in which his coworkers are also victims, playing according to the rules as they know them, working within the system as it is. Internationally, it was appreciated for its intellectuality, taking the best director prize at Cannes and receiving the international film critics award, confirming Zanussi's stature as a world-class auteur.

His reputation was perhaps a little undermined by *Man from a Far Country* (*Z dalekiego kraju*; Italian title, *Da un Paese Lontano*, 1981), made as an Italian-British venture. Reportedly the Pope himself suggested Zanussi as director. Certainly a Polish director seemed the logical choice to film a life of John Paul II. Unfortunately, the docudrama had no dramatic center, little unity or cohesion. Perhaps the subject overwhelmed Zanussi, and he stayed too far from the personality of the Pope. Lacking intimacy and introspection, it hardly seems to be by Zanussi.

In contrast, *The Year of the Quiet Sun* (*Rok spokojnego słońca*, 1984) was Zanussi to the core. A Polish-American-German coproduction, it is the story of a love affair between a Polish woman (played by Maja Komorowska, a great actress) and an American soldier (Scott Wilson) that takes place in Poland immediately after World War II. With her aged and infirm mother, the woman ekes out a miserable life. Set against a bleak depiction of time and place, the romantic relationship is enhanced by the way its tenderness stands out against the visual atmosphere. Its depth is signified by the loving way the couple transcends the language barrier. He wishes to smuggle her out of Poland, but her mother's health will not permit her to go. The mother commits a kind of passive suicide, ostensibly freeing her daughter to go with the soldier. Ironically, she cannot leave because she cannot morally accept her mother's sacrifice and so does not keep her rendezvous with him in the West. Years later, old and debilitated, she learns of his death and his bequest which would now allow her to come to the United States in a way absolved of any connection with her mother's sacrifice. Death intervenes, but this time the irony is not bitter because she has been fulfilled by his gesture. Not able to join him in life, she joins him by dying in an ending lifted filmically to a bright, religious hope, suggesting redemption after tragic life.

Zanussi will never be popular with a mass audience. The intellectuality of his work precludes that, but emphasizing that he is an intellectual filmmaker must be balanced by pointing out that he is an artist of the secret heart as well. For him the human condition cannot be captured by reason alone; in fact, it cannot be captured at all. It must be illuminated. In essence his message is that when we are at the limits of thought, we must find intuition.

In 1978, one of Poland's most important directors, Jerzy Kawalerowicz, made a comeback with an excellent and important film, *Death of the President* (*Śmierć prezydenta*, 1978). Known for *A Night of Remembrance* (*Celuloza*, 1954), *Night Train* (*Pociąg*, 1959), *Mother Joan of the Angels* (*Matka Joanna od Aniolów*, 1961), and *The Pharoah* (*Faraon*, 1966), among others, he fell into a fallow period but returned with his best movie. Turning to politics and accurate history, in *Death of the President* he succeeded in making the ultimate docudrama, one in which the elements of tension, suspense, and story are not in the least hampered by a precise recreation of history.

The film presents an episode from the first years of the independent Poland, newly brought into being as a republic just after World War I. A political centrist is unexpectedly elected president by the senate with the support of the left and minorities. Ultra-rightists are furious, and one of them kills him just three days after the inauguration. The story is constructed by using the technique of the courtroom drama, with only the assassin visible, explaining his frame of mind, and by going to hour-by-hour, day-by-day dramatization of events in the senate, the streets, meetings, etc. Narrative momentum is remarkable. Elucidation of what might be confusing political issues is brilliant, largely because of a tight, intelligent script by Bolesław Michałek. As a period piece, it is visually a tour-de-force.

The public responded to *Death of the President* as something more than a historical drama. Young viewers noted the workings of a demo-

IV–4   *Death of the President (Śmierć prezydenta)*

cratic, multiparty process; the role of the majority in the light of—and even composed of—minorities; freedom of speech; and aggressive opposition. Political toleration and political morality are the central subjects.

After a psychological drama, *A Chance Meeting on the Ocean* (*Spotkanie na Atlantyku*, 1980) which was a failure in every way, Kawalerowicz made another fine film, *Austeria* (1981), which received attention at home and abroad. It is a story about life among Polish Jews in eastern Galicia before World War I. Kawalerowicz came from that region, so the project was for him a trip into memory to which he did justice by systematically collecting Jewish cultural facts, objects, songs, music, mores, and even authentic faces. In the film, a group of Jews gathers at the village inn to shelter together against troops from several armies marauding in the area. After a long night, dawn seems to bring hope and a promise of safety, but when the Jews leave to celebrate their survival with a cleansing bath in a pond, the pond turns red with their blood. In his depiction of this story Kawalerowicz succeeds in conveying the texture of a lost world of tradition, culture, and faith.

While *Austeria* was not exactly a film of the times, the times allowed it to be made. The subject of Jews in the territory of what is now the Soviet Union had been avoided, but in the liberal atmosphere of 1980–81 he was given permission to address it.

The works of Wajda, Zanussi, and Kawalerowicz were central and influential, of course. At the same time, leaders and influential figures are often simply the most prominent members of a movement. Sometimes they are in the current, not guiding it; sometimes they are either or both. Manifestly, young and veteran Polish filmmakers were feeling a moral reawakening, eager to express their concern for individual and social conscience.

In 1975, before *Man of Marble* had been made or the project approved, Krzysztof Kieślowski, a documentarist who had directed some TV movies, made his first full-length feature, *The Scar* (*Blizna*, 1975), demonstrating a gift for incisive revelation. This film adumbrated things to come. Many new factories were being built in the seventies. This movie tells of one such project and its basically decent director, who is played off against a conniving local official. The good man is naïvely unaware of his situation and ineffective against manipulation. The community is damaged. Although not an especially good film, *The Scar* will later be cited as a forerunner of a new tendency.

A better film was Marek Piwowski's *Foul Play* (*Przepraszam, czy tu biją?*, 1975). A more accurate title translation is "Pardon me, do they beat you up here?" This is a wry, sardonic piece, a rare occurrence of the gangster genre, one of whose subjects is the legality and legitimacy of police procedures. It is robustly entertaining, full of exaggerated characters, capers, and heists. Its hidden serious edge has to do with the limits of police conduct in carrying out the law.

After *Man of Marble* and *Camouflage*, no movie was more effective or more influential than Feliks Falk's *Top Dog* (*Wodzirej*, 1977). A little earlier such a film would not have been permitted, evidence that the authorities were willing to tolerate a greater scope of thematic expression for younger directors and not only for such giants as Wajda and Zanussi. The hero, or anti-hero, is a young master of ceremonies who makes a living presiding over parties, nightclub shows and fancy balls. To further himself he throws away friendship, loyalty, and honesty, indulging in every form of hypocrisy and manipulation. The narrative is tight and intense. The acting of Jerzy Stuhr (now one of Poland's top actors) is exceptional. *Top Dog* depicts weak social rules and immoral arrangements, yet the protagonist is not completely a monster. He is shown to be a creation of his corrupt milieu. He must play a kind of daily politics of manipulation. By reading between the lines, the public found an indictment of more than the little world of show business.

Also in 1977, Janusz Majewski—already well known for *The Lodger* (*Sublocator*, 1967), *The Criminal Who Stole a Crime* (*Zbrodniarz który ukradł zbrodnię*, 1969), and *Hotel Pacific* (*Zaklęte rewiry*, 1975)—made a splendid period reconstruction with *The Gorgon Affair* (*Sprawa Gorgonowej*, 1977), about a famous murder case of the thirties. It deals with systems of justice, the pressures put upon courts, and presumption of innocence. These themes all had topical reverberations. It is a riveting drama with rich visual qualities.

Bohdan Poręba, considered an establishment filmmaker, diffidently joined the mood of social commentary in *Where the Water Is Clear and the Grass Green* (*Gdzie woda czysta i trawa zielona*, 1977). In it he describes the disintegration of decent social conventions in a provincial town and provides a simplistic solution; a party secretary, with help from the head office, solves all the problems.

Fundamental individual responsibility is the subject of Janusz Zaorski's *Room with a View of the Ocean* (*Pokój z widokiem na morze*, 1978), in which a man prepares for suicide, intending to jump from a tall building. Society's servants—policemen, etc.—struggle for his life, seeking to dissuade him, even trick him. By contrast, one man is against forcing him to live. Instead, he wants the would-be suicide to take moral responsibility for whatever he will do—live or die. That approach succeeds. The man lives, but that is less to the point than his assumption of responsibility for himself.

That same year, Marcel Łoziński carried out a fascinating cinema experiment while making *How Are We to Live?* (*Jak żyć*, 1978). He brought together a number of young couples in a summer camp, all of them ordinary people, except for two planted by the director. They instigate a competition to determine the best married couple. The results are amazing: hypocrisy, lies, schemes, spying, all within the framework of camp life. To no one's surprise the film was regarded as a vicious caricature of Polish society. Officials were reluctant to release it and did not do so until the winter of 1980–81, the Solidarity period. It was withdrawn again after martial law was declared in December 1981.

Also in 1978, Edward Żebrowski made *Hospital of the Transfiguration* (*Szpital przemienienia*, 1978), based on an early novel by Stanisław Lem. In a mental hospital at the outbreak of the war, a group of people, including patients, from different walks of life, reveal their basic personalities and views. As a subtext, Żebrowski explores an old dilemma of the Polish intelligentsia: resignation or resistance.

About this time it became clear to the film community that they were in a new situation. A relatively open and optimistic mood prevailed. In a printed discussion, Feliks Falk said that what happened was the creation of "a new and unusual phenomenon, an unprecedented intensity and fresh perspective for social themes. . . ." He gave credit to colleagues in the documentary field like Kieślowski, Łoziński, Tomasz Zygadło and others who "without compromise were telling us as much as possible about Polish reality." Agnieszka Holland added, "We have set our standards high because [*Man of Marble, Camouflage, The Scar*] have raised them considerably. Those films were the first to discuss certain issues concerning us in a manner which was honest and mature."[4] It is impossible to overestimate how much had happened in two or three years. Adrenalin was flowing through the film community.

The following year, 1979, was even more spirited. Falk's *Top Dog*, embargoed since production, opened triumphantly. Wajda's *Without Anesthesia* continued to play to large audiences, as did other recent films of the moral concern tendency. Krzysztof Kieślowski made *Film Buff* (*Amator*, 1979), another landmark. A young factory worker and amateur filmmaker is encouraged to make a movie about his plant. He faces the basic question as to what constitutes an honest film. If he follows the wishes of his company sponsors, they become in a sense his censors. In any case, is the whole truth desirable, useful? There are traps in this world for truth-tellers. Compromise and conformity seem pragmatically sensible. *Film Buff* ends with a gesture: the would-be filmmaker throws away his footage and turns the camera on himself. The theme clearly has to do with integrity and social pressure, truth and restraint. *Film Buff* struck a chord and became an unqualified success.

His spirits raised by the success of *Top Dog*, Feliks Falk made *The Chance* (*Szansa*, 1979) about two teachers who struggle for their students' minds. One of them is humane and liberal but naïve and ineffectual. The other is autocratic, an advocate of rigor and discipline. Neither man wins this philosophical duel, and the film ends bitterly, ambivalent about the strengths of each orientation.

Janusz Kijowski came to prominence with *Index* (1978), and *Kung-Fu*, (1979). *Index* dealt with attitudes among students during the student unrest of 1968, a subject up until this time taboo. It was not well made and was notable mainly for its theme. *Kung-Fu* was better and stronger, although still short on deep exploration of psychological and moral motivations because it was so unremittingly journalistic, topical, and "Social," with a capital "S." Still, it tells a strong story about a nonconformist who is set up and framed. The hero refuses to surrender. With no faith in the system, he relies on his friends, who win a kind of justice for him using cunning and blackmail. The implications are stark. When the system fails, the only refuge is in friends, relationships based on loyalty and personal solidarity, these being more dependable than society.

The importance of authentic human relationships is, in a different context, also the subject of Krzysztof Wojciechowski's *Stress at the New Address* (*Róg Brzeskiej i Capri*, 1979). A better translation of the title is "The Corner of Brzeska and Capri Streets." This is a semi-documentary of life in a run-down neighborhood, populated by people who live on the margins of society. As bad as life may be there, is it not perhaps better than it would be in a huge housing project that is anonymous and devoid of character and texture? Wojciechowski treats the subject warmly even though his style is relentlessly realistic.

Great aesthetic distinction belongs to a film which departed from the dominant mode of docudrama and low style. Wojciech Marczewski's *Nightmares* (*Zmory*, 1979) is a debut film outstanding for both intelli-

IV–5   *Stress at the New Address (Róg Brzeskiej i Capri)*

gence of content and visual elegance. It deftly follows the spiritual, social, and sexual maturation of a young boy, while reminding us that cinema is a visual art. The film is intellectually iconoclastic, and at the same
time nostalgic and pleasing to the eye.

Another aesthetic success was Agnieszka Holland's *Provincial Actors*
(*Aktorzy prowincjonalni*, 1979), a film of searching realism, moral dissection, good structure, and rich visual properties. It depicts players in a provincial theater who are stifling in an atmosphere of conformity and mediocrity. One of them is given a chance for improvement when offered a role
in Stanisław Wyspiański's *Liberation (Wyzwolenie)*. He egoistically engages in an argument over the production and loses. Wyspiański's play is
full of meditations and reflections on the fate of Poland; Holland's use of
it as an allusion makes her film comparable in intention. This is particularly true when the actor declaims, after Wyspiański, "Let us finally do
something which depends on us." The film is a statement about lost confidence and moral paralysis and a call for boldness and integrity.

The cinema of moral concern was emulated by some directors who
were ordinarily defenders of orthodoxy and not at all sympathetic to liberal trends. For example, Ryszard Filipski, who together with Bohdan
Poręba took a point of view antipathetic to that reflected in the films mentioned above, made *High Flights (Wysokie loty*, 1980), in which he

IV–6   *Provincial Actors (Aktorzy prowincjonalni)*

lashed out at moral decay among the elite of the "Red Bourgeoisie." He draws a vicious caricature of excess and corruption, depicting orgiastic party officials throwing caviar at one another and dousing themselves with champagne. To salve his orthodoxy, he also shows an honest, if help- less, party official and his good son who, it is suggested, will eventually prevail.

In 1980, Agnieszka Holland made *Fever* (*Gorączka*, 1980), a gloomy por- trayal of life among the revolutionaries in the aftermath of the abortive re- volt of 1905, a picture of provocation, despair, and determination. These re- bels lived febrile, intense lives, so, to bring form to substance, Holland made her narrative fitful and pitched. It is a violent and moving film.

Feverish in its own way was *The Moth* (*Ćma*, 1980), by Tomasz Zygadło, about a radio host of a night time call-in show. His callers are neu- rotic, sometimes desperate night people. As he relieves them, at least for a few moments, of their pains and fears, he accumulates anxiety, remorse and fear himself. The part is played to perfection by the great Roman Wilhelmi. This is a film with strength and turbulent psychology laced with moral anguish.

In that year, 1980, events were occurring in the cities of Gdansk, Szcze- cin, and Gdynia whose effects were felt throughout Poland and followed keenly all over the Western world. A strike in the shipyards of Gdansk spread throughout the country. Mounting tension led finally to negotia- tions and an agreement between the workers and the state. It is signifi- cant that the last stages of negotiations took place in front of cameras held by documentarists, something rare—if not unprecedented. The cam- eras were there because of efforts by the Polish Filmmakers Association, chaired by Wajda, and resulted in the famous documentary, *Workers 80* (*Robotnicy 80*, 1980). The film captured not only the words and gestures exchanged but also the facial expressions and the strange atmosphere of happenings unique to Polish history. The agreement promised, among other things, radical reforms with respect to censorship. It was concluded just ten days before the annual Gdansk film festival; that is, the festival was held in the very city which was the focus of unrest and the site of the agreement.

On the opening night of the festival, *Workers 80* was seen for the first time in public, shown to an audience that included its protagonists. In con- nection with the festival there was a forum of the Polish Filmmakers Associa- tion at which Wajda read a report from the executive committee, "Some Thoughts on the Duty of Our Profession to Our Country and Our Epoch." Some of his comments go to the heart of the cinema of moral con- cern. Wajda read:

The impossibility of having a healthy society without having solid, commonly accepted, moral criteria is a problem that cannot be ignored. Just as pictured in many of our films, contemporary Polish society is imbued with a number of moral styles of which few can deserve to be called moral. . . . What is said at meetings is different from what is said in the family circle or among friends. What is read in the newspaper is not what the man on the street knows or talks about.

He argued the universal, not only intellectual, desire for free expression:

For many years it has been suggested to us that the idea of freedom of thought, conscience and beliefs is an invention of small groups of intellectuals who misunderstood the essential historical process. The opinion has been promoted that workers and indeed society are satisfied with intellectual mush like that on television, in the simplistic press, in popular culture. . . . Yet it was the workers who launched this fight for freedom of discussion, for freedom of expression of differing ideas to serve the good of the country.

Wajda concluded his remarks by focusing on his craft and its practitioners, suggesting that cinema is uniquely the place where an "equality of cultural opportunity is real every day, where discourse about Poland and the world takes place. No other medium can substitute, including television. It is up to us if and how a new consciousness for Poland will be born in the cinema."[5]

For a time a thoroughly liberal cultural atmosphere pervaded the country. In 1981 a number of films heretofore blocked were released. Among them was Marcel Łoziński's *How Are We to Live?* And finally, after fourteen years, Jerzy Skolimowski's *Hands Up! (Ręce do góry)*—its first version finished in 1968—was released. The director decided to update it first. He shot sequences in London and Lebanon which were supposed to broaden the film's perspective, and he reedited his earlier work. The added scenes were meant to give a new angle to the themes of narrow-mindedness and philistinism, but they proved extraneous and ineffective. The original portions, depicting the young characters' psychological and political adventures before they turned smug, remain original and interesting.

There continued to be a fascination with the Stalinist years, partly because that period is intrinsically interesting but also because Stalinism is a good target. It is a way of criticizing the system without being blamed for criticizing the system. It is permissible to denigrate Stalinism, as long as it is Polish Stalinism (any criticism involving the Soviets is the ultimate taboo), since it was officially acknowledged as an erroneous phenomenon. Yet since it is an important part of the history of Communist regimes, criticizing it is almost as good as decrying any manifestations of a police-controlled society that may still exist. Whatever the reasons they had, Marczewski, Falk, and Domaradzki picked Stalinist subjects.

Marczewski made *Shivers (Dreszcze,* 1981) from his own script. It was the story of a boy coming of age in the early fifties. His father is a politi-

IV–7   *Shivers (Dreszce)*

cal prisoner, but the boy is turning into a loyal activist in a state-run Young Pioneer establishment, and is almost at the point where he is ready to reject his father. *Shivers* is both strong as a political statement, and subtle in its psychological presentation.

Feliks Falk carried out a project he had had in mind for some time, *There Was Jazz (Był Jazz,* 1981), about a group of musicians who play the jazz music prohibited during Stalinist years. They work, love, hate to study, and face police repression, but jazz remains their most important preoccupation. At that time, jazz was more than a mode of music; it was an articulation in a syncopated code of dissent. That made it an escape from grim reality, and a gesture against the grimness of reality.

Domaradzki made a movie that was to be released five years later, in 1986. *The Big Race (Wielki bieg,* 1981) tells of a long-distance running event manipulated under cover of sport to be an occasion for hypocrisy and propaganda. The winners were not necessarily to be those who ran fast and finished first. The protagonist, on the other hand, does not run for sport either, but his motivation is noble. He wants to present to the President, who will congratulate the winner, a letter asking for the release of his jailed father. But he is cheated, and in the locker room he hears the President's voice and the ovation accorded the fake winner.

Toward the end of 1981, economic and political conditions deteriorated and all signs pointed toward a complete social collapse. During the summer and fall, filmmakers hastily finished their projects. Janusz Zaorski made *Child's Play (Dziecinne zabawy,* 1981) about a group of architects working against demoralization and bureaucracy. A workers' strike occurs

IV-8   *The Big Race (Wielki bieg)*

at a construction site. The architects join the strike. There appears to be an expression here of hope for solidarity and, through that, social harmony under principles of moral decency.

In spite of the conditions, Agnieszka Holland and Krzysztof Kieślowski made perhaps their most mature works in 1981. Holland's *A Woman Alone* (*Kobieta samotna*, 1981) is a stark story of a mail clerk who lives a life of ugliness and desperation. In conspiracy with a man, she decides to embezzle money meant for poor pensioners. The misadventure ends with her murder. This is an exploration of the dark byways of human misery, of destiny, and of a relentless environment within which moral perspective vanishes. Kieślowski's *Blind Chance* (*Przypadek*, 1981) is based on three versions of a banal event—catching a train. First, we see what happens if a man catches a train: second, if he misses it; third, if he never undertakes the trip. In one version he becomes a rebel dissident; in another, an establishment activist; in the third, no one of any consequence.

Even as Poland entered into the depth of the crisis, some ventures were initiated and, surprisingly, even allowed to finish. Ryszard Bugajski, after months of delay, obtained script approval for *Interrogation* (*Przesłuchanie*, 1982), a film with acutely sensitive elements, chief among them a searching and intimate portrayal of a member of the security police.

The story, again, is about the early fifties and involves a woman against whom false and distorted accusations are made. The setting is a prison run by the security police and the depiction spares nothing, portraying horrifying conditions and cruel tortures. The main role is played by Krystyna Janda who had already identified herself with daring films, including *Man of Marble, Man of Iron*, and *Without Anesthesia*. Her performance in *Interrogation* is extraordinary: it has to be classed among the greatest acting accomplishments in cinema history. With a strong script, sharp and forceful direction by Bugajski, and Janda's acting, this is perhaps the best of the films that took the fifties as a subject. The industry officials have refused to distribute *Interrogation*, but copies of the film and videotapes have circulated in the West.

Janusz Zaorski made a film from a novel by Kazimierz Brandys, *Mother of Kings* (*Matka Królów*, 1982). Zaorski's treatment of his material faithfully captures the spirit of the book about a working-class family, a mother and her sons, and how history affected their lives. The novel was written in 1957 and reflected perfectly the view of the left-oriented intelligentsia of the time, condemning the Stalinist years but hopeful for the future.

Tadeusz Chmielewski, a master of comedy who broke out of that genre with his detective thriller-tragedy, *In the Still of the Night* (*Wśród nocnej ciszy*, 1978), made another serious film from Stefan Żeromski's novel, *Faithful River* (*Wierna rzeka*, 1983). The novel was written in 1912 about a Polish uprising in 1863 which was brutally suppressed by the Czar's troops. Chmielewski's film was begun in 1981, but because of various delays the last footage was not shot until February 1983, when a snowfall finally made the shooting of certain scenes propitious. A story in which Russian troops mistreat Poles is still highly sensitive, even if the troops were Czarist.

On the night of December 12 going into the morning of December 13, 1981, a "state of war" was proclaimed in Poland. This was, in fact, a declaration of martial law, but since there were no legitimate provisions for declaring martial law, the term "state of war" was invoked. Political and social life froze in that cold repressive December. A curfew was declared. There was mass arrest of Solidarity activists. Phone links were cut, and domestic travel was restricted. Public places, including theaters and cinemas, were closed. Film production stopped.

Within weeks some efforts were made to promote activity, and slowly things began to move again in the film industry. First the movie houses were opened for children's films, then for other films. However, many movies which had already been widely circulated were now proscribed: *Man of Iron, Man of Marble, How Are We to Live? Shivers* was removed until 1984, *There Was Jazz* until 1985, *The Big Race* until 1986.

There was understandable anxiety that the "state of war" would be fatal to the most interesting aspects of Polish cinema and perhaps might undermine the industry as a whole. It was feared that the best directors would be silenced or muted and that those movies which awakened the strongest emotions among the public would be kept on the shelf. To add to the anxiety some notable young directors elected to emigrate: Agnieszka Holland, Piotr Andrejew, Zbigniew Kamiński, Witold Orzechowski, Ryszard Bugajski. As indicated above there were consequences, but they were not as dire as they might have been. Indeed, moderation seems to have been the policy adopted.

Leading directors continued working, at first outside Poland. While it is indicative of conditions after 1981 that work was undertaken outside the country rather than in it, it is also noteworthy that passports were granted and exit allowed, usually with some minor bureaucratic harassment. Clearly the regime had no intention of imitating the harsher practices of other Communist states. All along, Poland has been able to maintain its continuing relationships with its prominent artists, musicians, writers, actors, directors, by allowing rather free entry and exit. Irrevocable emigration was not necessary. In one way or another work went on.

In Poland, Juliusz Machulski made a striking debut with *Va Banque* (1981, released 1983). This is an enormously clever story of trickery and revenge, very much like the American movie *The Sting*. An aging criminal, played by the director's father, Jan Machulski, is released from jail and sets about retrieving loot from an old caper from a crooked banker who let him take the rap while also cheating him of the money. The story is set in the thirties and the film's visual evocation of mood and time enhances the production considerably. The acting is subdued, even delicate, allowing ingenious plot detail and aura of time and place to carry off a tour de force. A sequel, *Va Banque II* (1984) was equally popular. More popular still was Machulski's *Sex Mission* (*Seksmisja*, 1985) a comedy in the science fiction mode, a lesser film designed to appeal to young moviegoers.

Yesterday (same Polish title, 1984) by Radosław Piwowarski also had youth in mind but in quite a different way. This is a story of high-school students in a provincial town dominated, as such places can be, by the school, the church, and the moviehouse. Four boys are caught up in the Beatle phenomenon of the sixties and decide to start a similar band. This sets up a generational conflict the exposition of which proves how politically charged popular music can be even when no standard ideological issues are involved. One aspect of the plot involves the development of an intense triangle of young love that leads to serious consequences and ultimately to an ending that suggests how futile passions, drives, and commitments are in the perspective of the passing of time. Legal problems over music rights have blocked distribution in the West, where *Yesterday* would probably have been well received.

In 1985 Piwowarski made *My Mother's Lovers* (*Kochankowie mojej mamy*) with Krystyna Janda, whose excellent performance in tandem with the incredibly skillful acting of Rafal Wegrzynek, who plays her eleven-

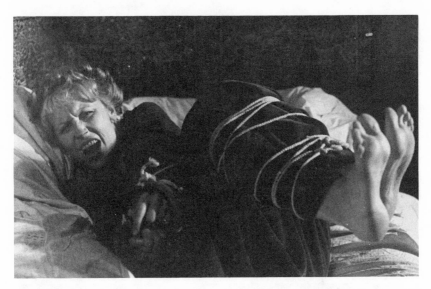

IV–9   *My Mother's Lovers (Kochankowie mojej mamy)*

year-old son, cements what might otherwise be a ragged script into a story that is loving, touching, degrading, and disillusioning, all at once. A slightly ambiguous, heartwrenching end seems aesthetically wrong but somehow fitting.

Barbara Sass made *The Scream* (*Krzyk*, 1982) about a woman released from prison and given work in a rather better-than-average home for the aged, where she confronts a malicious and contemptuous old man, a patient, whose treatment of her sets up a fatal and distorted conflict. Her life is generally abject and degrading; her only hope is marriage and the possibility of an apartment. The necessary bribe to get the apartment is impossible and hopes collapse. She focuses blame on the old man, whom she takes to be a representative of older forms of social corruption, one of those who had helped to create injustice and social despair. After an argument she kills him and only then discovers that his life story is not what she had thought at all. She has killed a person for no reason; he was no symbol. Overwhelmed by this realization she cries out and the film ends.

Janusz Zaorski followed *Mother of Kings* with *The Baritone* (*Baryton*, 1984), a lesser work. An opera singer returns triumphantly to his home town after twenty-five years abroad. The script is overloaded with betrayals, machinations, manipulations, and deals, all of which result in the capture of control of events by a pro-Nazi German pervert. The time is 1933. The obviously intended political parallel does not work well. Zaorski is much more effective with *Bodensee* (*Jezioro Bodeńskie*, 1985), a story of a young prisoner-of-war of French and Polish extraction in a

IV–10   *The Scream (Krzyk)*

Nazi internment camp used as a depot for prisoner swaps via Switzer-
land. The Polish-French connection has allegorical overtones with respect
to Polish history. The young man's sense of personal identification, however, is wholly Polish and his hopes and dreams are laden with Polish political and historical motifs.

The film made during the post-martial-law period most heavily laced
with political content is Krzysztof Kieślowski's *No End*, also known as *Without an Ending* (*Bez końca*, 1984). It is said to have been the high point of
the 1985 Gdansk Film Festival, though its screening was in doubt until
the last moment. It is about the attempt to free an imprisoned activist,
who eventually is released. The film interweaves complex themes of
death, bereavement, perseverance, heroism, spiritual, personal, and moral
dimensions, and even overtones of supernaturalism. One can see in the film
the influence of Wajda and Zanussi, but the film stands by itself as an original work, enriched by what came before it without yielding anything of its
impressive integrity and artistry.

Wajda returned to filmmaking in Poland, after two films abroad, with
Chronicles of Love (*Kronika wypadków miłosnych*, 1985), referred to as
A Chronicle of Amorous Accidents or *Chronicle of Love Affairs*, both awkward translations. It is from a novel and screenplay by Tadeusz Konwicki,
who also plays a role in the movie. In this case the script does not seem

to provide the kind of narrative mastery for which Wajda's films are renowned, but all his other gifts are very much in evidence, especially his gift for cinematic lyricism. Indeed, this film needs to be classified under his lyrical works. There is much in it that can be identified as having personal meaning to the director. The story takes place in 1939 when catastrophe is imminent, even as love is present and formative. There is a young boy whose fate we follow, partly through the appearances of an old man, a kind of chorus figure played by Konwicki, who is at the same time meant to be an aspect of the boy, either an alter ego or some strange secular angel. Time, love, fate, tragedy interweave, unravel and weave again. Although not one of Wajda's best films, *Chronicles of Love* is still a fascinating cinematic experiment.

Another lovely lyrical experiment is Andrzej Barański's *Woman from the Provinces* (*Kobieta z prowincji*, 1984). This is a simple story of a woman from a small town, her care for her children, her widowhood, her hard labors, her callous second marriage, her independence and determination. Several things set this simple story apart from many films which deal with such a tale. First of all, it does not follow a simple narrative line. The director has adopted a narrative structure which starts the tale more or less in the middle, and from that point it moves back and forth in time to show temporally disjunctured slices of her life. In the end, images of old age and infancy alternate on the screen. Because juxtapositions are not forced into a straight-time progression nor into the usual

IV–11   *A Chronicle of Amorous Accidents (Chronicle of Love Affairs)* (*Kroniak wypadków miłosnych*)

IV - 12   *Woman from the Provinces (Kobieta z prowincji)*

flashback device, they assume subtly shifting thematic relationships. Another extraordinary dimension of the film is the acting of Ewa Dałkowska, whose creation of this gentle woman is accomplished with many soft and delicate nuances. The artwork, camera work, settings and lighting are all strongly crafted and carefully integrated.

Witold Leszczynski, best known for his earlier film *Life of Matthew* (*Żywot Mateusza*, 1967), recently made his most interesting film of the eighties, *Axiliad* (*Siekierezada*, 1985), about a poet who leaves his lover in a personal quest for self-discovery. He goes into a forest, where timber is being cleared, to work among the rough woodsmen. As is often conventional in literature, a journey into a wood is an internal one, and this one participates in that convention. It is a story of psychological discovery within a landscape sometimes crude and primitive, sometimes rough but beautiful. The dramatic structure, the landscape, and the camerawork conspire to create an effect that suggests both seeking and foreboding. Eventually another man arrives to share the rented hut and functions in the film as an alter ego—reminiscent of Joseph Conrad's *The Secret Sharer*. The film is replete with images of this "doubleness." Ultimately what the protagonist discovers in the forest (and in himself) leads him to a shocking but, in a way, foretold suicide.

Tomasz Zygadło's *Childhood Scenes of Provincial Life*, also titled *Scenes of Childhood* (*Sceny dziecięce z życia prowincji*, 1985), received considerable critical attention. A character in the film—an old, retired, ruminative politician—is made to resemble the former head of the Polish Communist Party, Władysław Gomułka.

IV–13   *Axiliad (Siekierezada)*

IV–14   *Hero of the Year (Star of the Year) (Bohater roku)*

Feliks Falk, one of Poland's top-ranked directors, made *Hero of the Year* (*Bohater roku*, 1986), a sequel to his important film *Top Dog*. The accomplished actor Jerzy Stuhr is again featured as the character Danielak, the master of ceremonies in *Top Dog*. In this film, Danielak discovers the potential for a grand public relations scam based on a TV news report of a simple citizen who saves a number of his fellow citizens from a possible gas explosion and publicly criticizes the authorities for their carelessness and neglect. Danielak talks the authorities into allowing him to exploit this open and honest man by presenting him on various public platforms as a hero of the year and using him to promote a carefully guided program of ersatz public criticism, a deceitful democratic openness, a controlled *glasnost*. But the protagonist is not a simpleton and eventually walks off the stage. Unlike *Top Dog*, at the end of *Hero of the Year*, there is a clear change in Danielak's character, perhaps even a reversal. He has taken a good look into himself and seen something there to turn him around. Perhaps it is something personal; perhaps it is merely the realization that the shopworn schemes for manipulating individuals and the public will no longer work in the eighties. The film has been both a critical and box office success and the winner of several international film festival prizes.

What form Polish cinema will take and what strengths it will reveal in the next decade are uncertain. It is an encouraging sign of continuing vitality, however, that it has weathered the crisis of 1981–82 in rather good health. In Poland, more than in most countries, film is an important, serious and influential part of society, politics, and culture. As an art form it has not only mirrored contemporary Polish history, but has also played an important role in helping to make the very history it mirrors—to shape contemporary events, public moods and attitudes.

NOTES

1. The material in this chapter is based heavily upon the book which I coauthored with Bolesław Michałek, *The Modern Cinema of Poland* (Bloomington: Indiana University Press, 1988). While the present chapter is my own, it could never have been written without the benefit of Michałek's deep and intimate knowledge of Polish cinema. One of Poland's most influential and prominent film critics, screenwriters, and editors, Michałek was for many years the literary director of Wajda's Unit "X".

2. Conversation with Andrzej Wajda, October, 1981. The observations and interpretations in this chapter are based heavily and primarily upon interviews and conversations with leading Polish film writers, critics, directors, and other film artists, and upon years of viewing and studying the films themselves. Among the most important of these expert guides are Andrzej Wajda, Krzysztof Zanussi, Tadeusz Chmielewski, Feliks Falk, Janusz Majewski, Wojciech Marczewski, Edward Żebrowski, Jerzy Domaradzki, Jerzy Antczak, Witold Orzechowski, Filip Bajon, Krystyna Zachwatowicz, Daniel Olbrychski, Irena Olszewska, Jadwiga Barańska, Michał Misiorny, and Czesław Donziłło.

3. Nonetheless, there was no way to convince Poles that the film intended no double meaning. I saw the film twice shortly after its opening in a Warsaw theater in February, 1983. The remarks of the people waiting in line made it clear that they were expecting political/aesthetic sleight-of-hand. Comments overheard after the film's showing confirmed that the Polish audience was making political interpretations.

4. *Kino*, 4, 1978, Warsaw.

5. My translation from the original report. Also translated and reprinted in *Polish Perspectives* Vol. 24, No. 1 (Warsaw, 1981), pp. 49–54.

5

Hungary:
The Magyar on the Bridge

David Paul

THREE IMAGES

In the rain, a young woman walks along the center stripe of Budapest's Elizabeth Bridge. She pays no heed to the traffic rushing past her in both directions but continues to stride toward the camera. Across the frame, in large letters, appears the word MAGYAR (Hungarian).

This image, from the logo of the 1987 Hungarian Feature Film Festival, gives visual form to a popular self-impression. Smack in the middle of a continent forever riven by opposing forces, the Hungarian walks his or her own course. History has repeatedly demonstrated the perils of Hungary's geopolitical position, but Hungarian culture has not been swept away by the powerful momentum of others, nor has it been crushed in the collision of mightier forces.

There is a Hungarian joke that approaches the self-image from another angle. Two men board an otherwise empty streetcar, one through the front door and one through the rear. If the two are Italians, they both head for the same seat and fight over it. If they are Germans, they wait for the conductor to come on and tell them where to sit. If they are Hungarians, one sees the other and quickly gets off, preferring to wait for the next tram.

National self-images should of course be taken with a grain of salt, these included. Hungarians are perhaps less individualistic than they fancy themselves—that, indeed, may be the point of the joke—and their culture has hardly been immune to outside influences. Still, the Magyar on the bridge and the men on the streetcar can serve to introduce the Hungarian cinema, which frequently mirrors the qualities Hungarians like to see in themselves. That sense of individualism produces a range of formal diversity remarkable for such a small film culture, and that problem of geopolitics lends itself to some unique and daring scenarios.

Consider a second image. The setting is the outside of a prison on the *puszta*, that flat-as-a-table-top plain extending endlessly eastward from the Danube. Some peasant women have brought food for the prisoners. One prisoner, promised that he will be spared from execution if he informs on political outlaws, fingers a woman in the group. Panicking, all the women flee across the *puszta*. They grow smaller and smaller as they run toward the far horizon, and for a long moment no one bothers to pursue them. Suddenly horsemen sweep across the screen, and scant effort is required to round the women up. Throughout the scene there is little dialogue and no background music; the camera photographs the action as objectively as if it were recording a lion's kill for a PBS nature program. The viewer sees that oppression is a natural and impersonal fact of authority, and wide open spaces can be a prison from which escape is as unlikely as from Alcatraz.

The scene is from *The Round-up* (*Szegénylegények*, 1965), written by Gyula Hernádi and directed by Miklós Jancsó.[1] This film presents the earliest statement of Jancsó's characteristic style, with numerous long takes within which a slow but complicated *mise en scène* develops at an emotional distance from the viewer. *The Round-up's* subject matter, the plight of Hungarian rebels in the Habsburg empire, is typical of the early Jancsó stories, which are often historical pageants filled with political lessons that have relevance for Hungary's present.

Now a third image. Onscreen a baby is born, its birth photographed unflinchingly in close-up. We are watching not a documentary but the final scene of a feature film, and yet the actress Lili Monori is in fact giving birth to her own child. The scene ends in a blackout, a sudden and startling conclusion to this story about a woman's struggle for an independent identity in a society that wants to force her into a traditional, subservient role. Juli, unmarried, has been abandoned by her lover because he cannot bear the stigma of her earlier child, born out of wedlock; now she has two and must continue to face the hardships of single parenthood.

The film is *Nine Months* (*Kilenc hónap*, 1976), written and directed by Márta Mészáros. Two years ahead of Paul Mazursky's *An Unmarried Woman* (USA, 1978) and several other American movies praised for their feminist sensibility, *Nine Months* was by no means the first of director Mészáros's feminist stories. The uncompromising naturalism of the final scene is consistent with the film's realism throughout—as it is characteristic of Mészáros's feature work in general—and the subject matter, an intimate story about contemporary people, is also typical of Mészáros's *oeuvre*. Márta Mészáros and Miklós Jancsó know and respect each other very well, but their films are as different as those of Frederick Wiseman and Federico Fellini.[2] Nor do the styles of Jancsó and Mészáros represent the polar extremes of the Hungarian spectrum. Beyond Mészáros's realism are fiction films starkly in the style of *cinéma vérité*, such as Pál Erdöss's *The Princess* (*Adj király katonát!*, 1982),[3] and nonfiction films whose dramatic structures obscure the boundary between documentary and feature work, a good example being Sándor Sára's *At the Crossroads* (*Keresztúton*, 1986). Beyond Jancsó, at the other end of the spectrum, are films by directors working on the experimental edge, for example *The Dog's Night Song* (*A kutya éji dala*, 1983) by the late Gábor Bódy and *Lenz* (*Lenz*, 1986) by András Szirtes.

And yet this wide range of film styles, encompassing many that fall between the realism of Mészáros and the expressionism of Jancsó, would appear to be linked by a spirit of Hungarian otherness, a unity of diversity which, within the film culture as in the larger society, invokes a specific national quality as a source of pride. This quality, like that clichéed phenomenon of "national character" about which historians and others have long debated, cannot be easily described, but it will be evident as we survey Hungarian films.

BACKGROUNDS

History, Politics, and Film

The history of East Central Europe is long and tragic, and that of modern Hungary is perhaps even more tragic than that of its neighbors. The Hungarian kingdom lost its independence in the sixteenth century, overpowered by the Turks and the Habsburgs. In 1849, Hungarian nationalists revolted against the Austrian monarch but were decisively reconquered. In 1867 the kingdom was revived—but in a way that diehard patriots found humiliating; the Habsburg monarch formally accepted the Hungarian crown within what was thereafter called the Austro-Hungarian Empire. On the losing side of World War I, Hungary surrendered more than half its territory by the terms of the Treaty of Trianon (1919). A republican government soon gave way to the Communist rule of Béla Kun, the Republic of Councils, which in turn was overthrown after a few months of violent civil strife by right-wing forces loyal to Admiral Miklós Horthy. The country, nominally a kingdom again, never got a king and was in fact governed by Horthy as regent. Hungary drifted further to the right during the thirties and, in the end, found itself participating in the horrors of fascism. There followed another war and another defeat, another fierce competition for political power, and the triumph of a minority party supported by an army of occupation. Long dominated by foreign powers to the west and south, Hungary now fell under the influence of its giant neighbor to the east.

In Zoltán Fábri's film *Hungarians* (*Magyarok*, 1977), a group of peasants have left the abject poverty of their home village to work the fields of a German landowner far to the north; all the local men are off fighting

V–1   *Hungarians (Magyarok)*

Hitler's war. When news of Germany's defeat reaches the Hungarian farm-hands, the eldest among them says, "If [the Germans] hadn't joined up with the Hungarians, they wouldn't have lost."

The sense of forever being a defeated nation intensified over the first decade of Communist rule. Hungarians have long memories, and they had not forgotten that Russian forces helped the Austrian emperor crush their revolt in 1849. A hundred years later, Hungarian Communist Party chief Mátyás Rákosi styled himself after his master, Joseph Stalin, and his party's policies bore a distinct "made in Moscow" stamp: forced collectivization of agriculture, nationalization of industry, the suppression of churches, the rewriting of history to denigrate many national heroes and celebrate less familiar and often foreign socialist figures, the sealing of the borders against imperialist penetration, and the ruthless application of police-state measures complete with blood purges, mass arrests, and ubiquitous informants. Stalinism in Hungary lasted only half a decade, but its legacy has persisted ever since in the ongoing intraparty conflict between those who hold to strict authoritarianism and those who believe society can be trusted with one or another degree of democratization.

The death of Stalin, in 1953, released a stream of changes in Hungary. Opposition to Rákosi's extremism emerged, and the party went through a period of serious infighting. The goverment became unstable. Intellectuals, encouraged by a lessening of censorship, burst out of the constraints that had been imposed upon artistic and literary production by the norms of socialist realism. Imre Nagy, a popular Communist who had been imprisoned in the purges, became Prime Minister for some twenty months during which he and Rákosi, who continued to head the party, were locked in a policy conflict between the more liberal "New Course" of the former and the hard line of the latter. Ousted in the spring of 1955, Nagy made another comeback a year-and-a-half later in the heat of a mass revolt. That revolt of autumn 1956 marked the culmination of the liberalizing forces. Pressured by violence in the streets, Premier Nagy formed a multiparty government and announced the withdrawal of Hungary from the Soviet bloc.

Within days, Soviet tanks rolled across the countryside and Soviet guns fired on Hungarian soldiers, who had joined the populace in revolt. The Hungarian forces were no match for the superior firepower of their former and future ally, but much blood was shed before Soviet authority was reestablished. The major population centers, especially Budapest, added the scars of new property damage to those remaining from the previous war, and in the aftermath, 200,000 Hungarians fled across the border to Austria and points west. Under Soviet guidance a new government was formed, with János Kádár as the head of the party. Imre Nagy was executed. Hungary had suffered yet another defeat.

During the first decade after the Second World War, the Hungarian cinema had emerged from the disaster with difficulty. Owing to the scarcity of resources, only three movies were produced in each of the first several years after 1945.[4] Even so, some were of high quality, most notably Géza Radványi's *Somewhere in Europe* (*Valahol Európában*, 1947), a work which many outside critics believed signaled the beginning of a Hungarian neorealist wave. In 1948, however, the film industry was nationalized, and very soon it fell under the stultifying norms of Zhdanovism. Radványi emigrated, and other promising directors such as Frigyes Bán and István Szőts were obliged to apply the principles of socialist realism to their work. Not until 1954, with Fábri's *Fourteen Lives in Danger* (*Életjel*), did Hungarian filmmakers begin again to explore their own themes through fresh styles. Between 1954 and 1956, a number of directors, including Szöts, Fábri, and Félix Máriássy, abandoned socialist realism as a style while cautiously expanding the cinema's thematic repertoire.

In 1956, two films were made that dared to examine current political realities. Tamás Banovich directed *The Sneezed-Away Empire* (*Az eltüsszentett birodalom*), described by the Liehms as "a fairy-tale allegory about a tyrant whose entire kingdom had to bend to his will,"[5] and Zoltán Várkonyi filmed *Bitter Truth* (*Keserű igazság*), a hard-hitting story about a construction works manager whose ambition and pigheaded devotion to the overfulfillment of production quotas cause the collapse of an uncompleted silo and the death of a workman. *The Sneezed-Away Empire* was shown in theaters for a short while before the Soviet intervention, but *Bitter Truth* was shelved upon completion and not released until thirty years later.

The Kádár era began not only with the repression of literature and film but also with a period of generalized political retrenchment. One-party rule was quickly reinstituted, the Soviet alliance was reaffirmed, the regime's identifiable enemies were punished, collectivization—virtually abandoned after 1953—was resumed, and the full weight of censorship (though not the burden of Zhdanovism) descended once more upon culture.

The policies of repression affected the entire society, but they were by no means a return to Stalinism. Even so, many prominent intellectuals were temporarily silenced, and the film movement that had begun in 1954 came to a halt. In a sense, the years immediately following 1956 were an interlude between two generations of filmmakers, for it was during this time that the most important Hungarian directors of the current period began their careers. They included Jancsó, active in newsreel and documentary work for twelve years before settling into features with Cantata (Oldás és kötés, 1962),[6] and Károly Makk, who had debuted with Liliomfi (1954) and directed several more movies before completing The Fanatics (Megszállottak, 1961), the release of which signaled a positive change in the political environment, as the film told a story of bureaucratic misjudgment and indifference. István Gaál made his debut with Current (Sodrásban) in 1963, and István Szabó with The Age of Daydreaming (Álmodozások kora) in 1964. Márta Mészáros, like Jancsó, made documentary films for more than a decade before directing her first feature, The Girl (Eltávozott nap, 1968).[7]

Surrounding this new cinematic wave were changes in the political and social climate. Within a few years after the post-1956 clampdown, the Kádár regime felt confident enough of its authority that it began slowly to release the pressures on society. By 1968 the party put into effect a New Economic Mechanism (NEM) which liberalized the economy by decentralizing much of the planning apparatus, releasing some commodity prices to float with the forces of supply and demand, introducing wage incentives, allowing the establishment of small private businesses in carefully delimited areas of trade and services, increasing the role of private agriculture (though not de-collectivizing the major part of farming), and encouraging the formation of cooperatives. Development of the NEM halted under conservatives' pressure for a few years during the mid-seventies, but the momentum gathered speed upon the adoption of a new set of similarly minded reforms in the early eighties. By the middle of the decade, one could plainly see the impact in the proliferation of private shops, restaurants, taxicabs, and other services, as well as the encroachment of numerous Western firms in the form of joint companies and franchises; by 1985, among other examples, affluent visitors to Budapest could choose to stay in a Hilton, a Forum, an Intercontinental, or a Hyatt Hotel. It should be remembered that Hungary is a small and resource-poor country, and its economy continues to suffer from a number of serious structural problems, including the heavy trade obligations imposed by membership in the eastern bloc. However, as a result of the NEM and subsequent reforms, the Hungarian economy has outperformed those of most other Soviet-bloc countries, at least in providing creature comforts for its own citizens.

Along with the economic changes have come significant political changes as well. Multicandidate elections, albeit still under the watchful eye of the ruling party, have become standard for all levels of government. Restrictions on foreign travel have been substantially eased, and restrictions on foreigners visiting Hungary—including former citizens who emigrated without official permission—have been greatly reduced. Rare instances of public dissent exceeding the limits of official tolerance have resulted in harassment, punishment, or exile for the dissidents, whose numbers are very small, but on the other hand, the government has encouraged a modest degree of critical reporting by the press and an ever-expanding latitude for cultural intellectuals. In turn, intellectuals have by and large learned the limits of self-expression and, while sometimes courageously pushing against them, more commonly accept the boundaries and work within them. The result has been a lively activity within the cultural community, with literature and film profiting especially from the relaxed political environment.

HUNGARIAN CINEMA:
SOME GENERALIZATIONS

The effects of this long and rocky national history can be seen in several qualities of the contemporary Hungarian cinema. In the first place, one notices a marked preference for tragedy and a weak comedic tradition—true of Hungarian literature and drama as well. Humor is not absent in the films of Szabó and Gaál, for example, but it is a subtle humor that punctuates an overriding seriousness. Of today's major directors, only Péter Bacsó works consistently in comedy; his films—such as *The Witness* (*A tanú*, 1969, 1978), *Oh, Bloody Life!* (*Te rongyos élet!*, 1983), and *Banana Skin Waltz* (*Banánhejkeringő*, 1986)—present broad, slapstick plots overlying serious messages about political and social ills. They are very popular among Hungarian audiences who are starved for laughs, but they hardly represent a high level of comedy. Besides Bacsó, Károly Makk sometimes directs comedies, but with a humor that is sly and sophisticated, as in *A Very Moral Night* (*Egy erkölcsös éjszaka*, 1977) and the American co-production *Lily in Love* (1984).

Hungarian cinema appears to be changing gradually in this respect. Younger directors have developed individual comedic styles, though their comedy nearly always overlies or cuts through stories of an essentially serious or even tragic nature. Examples are Péter Gothár's *Time* (*Idő van*, 1985), Péter Gárdos's *Whooping Cough* (*Szamárköhögés*, 1986), and

András Jeles's *The Workers' Dream Brigade* (*Álombrigád*, not released).

The fact that even comedy tends to deliver a message emphasizes another quality of the Hungarian cinema: among filmmakers and critics alike, it is taken for granted that the cinema has a serious social and moral role to play. And its function has been radically transformed since the fifties, when filmmakers were required to paint pictures confirming the regime's view of reality. Today one finds propaganda films made, appropriately enough, by the State Propaganda Film Studio—but not by MAFILM, the feature film studio, or any of its four major production units. MAFILM's artists understand their social function to be that of critics, not sycophants, and within the rules of the prevailing censorship policies, they endeavor to play this role.[8]

Also running through the Hungarian cinema is a preoccupation with history. Historical themes are especially strong in the *oeuvres* of the veteran directors Jancsó, Szabó, and Fábri, but they also show up in some younger filmmakers' works. Examples are *Mária's Day* (*Mária nap*, 1983), directed by Judit Elek and set in the eighteen seventies; Ferenc Grünwalsky's *To See the Light* (*Eszmélés*, 1985), set in the eighteen nineties; and *A Fond Farewell to the Prince* (*Érzékeny búcsú a fejedelemtől*, 1986), a seventeenth-century period piece with contemporary implications, directed by László Vitézy. Hungarians, like other inhabitants of Central Europe, are very history-conscious, looking to the complicated past for clues about their complicated present-day identity—their sense of "Hungarity"—and in this question of past and present identity many filmmakers find a compelling source of subject matter.[9]

THE AUTEURS

In Hungary, as elsewhere in Europe, it is assumed that a film is primarily the product of its director. This is not to deny the input of screenwriters, cinematographers, actors, editors, and other obviously vital members of production teams; but the director, who typically develops the scenario for a screenplay, participates in or at least oversees its writing, seeks permission from studio officials to proceed with production, decides upon casting, directs the shooting, and supervises the editing, inevitably stamps a film with his or her mark.

This was not always so. Historically, the Hungarian cinema was strongly influenced by classical literature and drama; correspondingly, motion pictures were considered to be either for entertainment only or for the interpretation of works whose main value derived from another art form. Though both modern and classical literary works are frequently plumbed for cinematic subjects today, the autonomy of the motion picture as an art form is not questioned; adaptations from other media are crafted to suit the aesthetics of the cinema, and original screenplays are presumed to be of equal artistic potential. The director's preeminence as cinematic artist is well established.

The Giants

Four names stand out among the seventy or so directors employed at any given time by MAFILM: Jancsó, Szabó, Makk, and Mészáros. In the sixties and seventies, the name of István Gaál (b. 1933) would have been on this list. Gaál's earlier films were much acclaimed internationally; for example, *The Falcons* (*Magasiskola*, 1970) won awards in Cannes, Chicago, and Adelaide, and *Dead Landscape* (*Holt vidék*, 1971) captured prizes in Karlovy Vary and Milan. Since then, however, Gaál has received no major awards, and from 1972 to 1984 he completed only two theatrical features: *Legato* (1977), a complex story about a young man's probe into the wartime record of his father—a theme reminiscent of István Szabó's celebrated *Father* (*Apa*, 1966), and *Potsherds*, also known as *Buffer Zone* (*Cserepek*, 1980), a kind of Hungarian midlife crisis story. During this time Gaál also directed two documentaries and three television plays.

Gaál's films have a characteristic look, visually strong and painterly. The rhythms of his narrative tend to be unconventional, sometimes purposely invoking musical forms; Gaál has said that *Baptism* (*Keresztelő*, 1968), for example, is structured like a sonata.[10] Like Jancsó, he skillfully captures the flavor of rural Hungarian landscapes, but, unlike Jancsó, Gaál has often sought to contrast the lifestyles indigenous to those settings, stark, brutal, and yet beautiful, with those of urban life.[11]

In 1985, Gaál completed a six-year project, marrying his powerful visual style to his longtime interest in music. The result was a competent film version of Christoph Willibald Gluck's opera *Orpheus and Eurydice* (*Orféusz és Euridike*) in which choreographed motion parallels the rhythms of the music throughout.

Another filmmaker whose name deserves to be mentioned here is Zoltán Fábri. The oldest director working in recent years (b. 1917), Fábri displays a special feeling for rural life, where he finds the core of his nation's qualities, good and bad. Fábri's directing career began during the Rákosi years, but his second and third features, *Fourteen Lives in Danger* (1954) and *Merry-Go-Round* (*Körhinta*, 1955), were landmarks in the Hungarian cinema's break with Stalinist aesthetics.[12] More than two decades later, Fábri's *Hungarians* (1977) and *Bálint Fábian Meets God* (*Fábian Bálint találkozása istennél*, 1980) explored not only "Hungarity," which the two films treated with marvelous insight, but broader humanistic questions of community, conflict, and morality as well.

Miklós Jancsó

It was the work of Miklós Jancsó (b. 1921), more than that of anyone else, that brought the Hungarian cinema to the world's attention during the sixties. *The Round-up* (1965), Jancsó's fourth feature, won the FIPRESCI award at the Locarno Festival in 1966 and was named best foreign-language film by the British Film Critics Association in 1967. More international honors followed: in Paris and Adelaide for *The Red and the White* (*Csillagosok, katonák,* 1967); in Avellino for *Silence and Cry* (*Csend és kiáltás,* 1968) and Adelaide for *Confrontation* (also 1968); in Atlanta for *Winter Wind* (*Sirokkó,* 1969); and in Milan, Santiago de Chile, Paris, and Cannes (best director) for *Red Psalm* (*Még kér a nép,* 1971).

These films, together with *Agnus Dei* (*Égi bárány,* 1970), firmly established Jancsó's revolutionary style. Jancsó has named as his "masters" Ingmar Bergman, Jean-Luc Godard, Michelangelo Antonioni, and Andrzej Wajda.[13] From Bergman and Wajda he drew ideas about symbolism and iconography, though Jancsó's images are very much his own: a wandering violinist playing amid scenes of human brutality in *Agnus Dei,* a rose blossoming from the bleeding hand of a naked girl in *Red Psalm.* From Godard he learned much about narrative experimentation and the value of distancing audiences in the interest of dialecticism, but instead of Godardian narrative disjuncture Jancsó developed an approach based on the long take characteristic of Antonioni. In Jancsó's hands, a take often lasts five or six minutes, and in the cases of *Winter Wind* and *Elektreia* (*Szerelmem, Elektra,* 1974), each entire film consists of only twelve takes. Within one Jancsó take, peasants and soldiers might dance together around a maypole until, heeding the

V–2   Miklós Jancsó

trumpet's call to battle, the soldiers regroup into a larger circle around the peasants and slaughter them (*Red Psalm*); or the face of a young woman, in closeup, might give way to a long shot of militant students blocking the passage of an army jeep on a river bank, after which the apparent conflict fades as students and soldiers playfully join in some high-spirited dunking (*Confrontation*).[14] The camera may be still, though more commonly it tracks and pans; it may zoom several times from close-up to extreme long shot. Realistic episodes may alternate with stagy, ballet-like sequences. Motion is choreographed, acting stylized, dialogue ritualistic. The overall effect, clearly Brechtian, allows a scene to play itself out without drawing the viewer into it, thereby allowing him a space in which to reflect on what he sees.

In his early features Jancsó often drew from Hungarian history, whether recent or more distant: *The Round-up* from the time just after the Austro-Hungarian Compromise of 1867, *Red Psalm* from the eighteen nineties, *Silence and Cry* and *Agnus Dei* from the violent years after World War I, *My Way Home* from the last days of World War II, *Winter Wind* from the thirties, *Confrontation* from the first days of the Communist revolution. In a sense, the time settings are interchangeable; *The Round-up* is a comment on Nazi concentration camps or Rákosi-era political persecutions as much as on those of the Habsburg Empire, and *Red Psalm* is as much an allegory about Hungary's timeless geopolitical dilemma as a story of a peasant revolt in the last century.

During the seventies, Jancsó's career changed. He directed four films in Italy—*The Pacifist* (*La Pacifista*, 1970), *Technique and Rite* (*La tecnica ed il rito*, 1971), *Rome Wants Another Caesar* (*Roma rivuole Cesare*, 1973), and *Private Vices, Public Virtues* (*Vizi privati pubbliche virtu*, 1976)— and, between 1971 and 1977, only one MAFILM production (*Elektreia*). His international prizes dwindled to only one, a Silver Plaque at the 1975 Chicago Festival for *Elektreia*. Moreover, Jancsó's new work came under much criticism, both in Hungary and abroad. It was said that he had exhausted his artistic and intellectual originality, and that his films had become redundant; his depiction of nudity had led to increasing eroticism and even to pornography (this was said, in particular, of *Private Vices . . .* , a story about a prince who is enamored of revolutionary ideals but lost in a private world of kinky self-indulgence). On the other hand, those who defended Jancsó argued that, far from being caught in a muddle of stagnant ideas, Jancsó continued to build in more subtle ways upon his earlier aesthetics while expressing further his insistent concerns with questions of power, oppression, and the morality of revolution.[15]

In 1978, Jancsó finished *Hungarian Rhapsody* (*Magyar rapszódia*) and *Allegro Barbaro*, two controversial works originally intended to be part of a trilogy that he has never completed. *Hungarian Rhapsody* focuses on an idealistic young nobleman, István, caught in the political turmoil and moral confusion of the twenties; *Allegro Barbaro* continues the story about the same character during the Nazi occupation. They are beautiful films filled with mysterious, challenging images: a ceremonial cortege bearing the coffin of the nobleman's young lover, a floating funeral pyre; a ritual undressing of István's peasant bride, a marriage bed out in the open. As a new technique, Jancsó added the passing of time into his typical long takes so that a camera pan from one element in a scene to another signifies a time jump of indeterminate length.

In some circles, these two films were well received; Jancsó was given an award at Cannes in 1979 for lifetime achievement, the films picked up the audience's prize in Barcelona the same year, and Jancsó's cinematographer, János Kende, won the award for camera work at the 1981 Cartagena Festival. Elsewhere, however, Jancsó was again criticized for redundancy and meaningless formalism and, when his next feature, the Hungarian-Italian coproduction *The Tyrant's Heart* (*A zsarnok szíve*, 1981) was released, it also met with mixed reviews.[16]

So, too, have Jancsó's most recent works been greeted. In 1984 he filmed a rock concert (*Omega, Omega*), and critics wondered why. In 1985 he completed a French production, *The Dawn* (*L'Aube*), based on a book by Elie Wiesel; this film has been praised for its disciplined interior camera work and condemned as boring. His latest film, *Season of Monsters* (*Szörnyek évadja*, 1987), has drawn the usual charges.

It cannot be said, however, that *Season of Monsters* contains nothing

V–3   *Season of Monsters* (*Szörnyek évadja*)

new. The setting is contemporary and the opening scenes take place mostly within compact urban interiors: a hotel room, corridors, elevators, the inside of a speeding Volkswagen. There are two "stories," or, rather, story fragments: the first, told in a language near to realism, concerns Zoltai, an émigré professor who has returned home to Hungary to commit suicide, and his former classmate, Bardócz, called as a physician to the scene of the suicide. The second story, by far the longer and more complex, focuses on a weird birthday celebration which Bardócz attends. The setting shifts to an isolated rural location more typical for Jancsó, and the film language becomes nonrealistic, frequently surreal. The theme is no longer suicide, but rather the conflict between elitism and egalitarianism (as personified, respectively, by Bardócz and a new character, Komondi). The first story has not been entirely forgotten, for the image of Professor Zoltai, in an interview just before his death, intrudes upon the birthday celebration by appearing on a video monitor. Outside, monsters have been reported in the lake. The action is filled with such things as multiple fireballs, murders that do or do not take place, and resurrections. A police helicopter appears and causes nothing but chaos. At the end, a verse from Genesis is quoted with deep irony: "And God saw everything that He had made, and behold, it was very good." *Season of Monsters* presents a complicated, puzzling vision of impending doom depicted in Jancsó's unique cinematic language.

Such language has always been too esoteric for many audiences, and it may no longer have the freshness it possessed in the sixties. But it is unjust to accuse Jancsó of having lost his creative spark. In each new film he shows us something more, he continues to develop his style. It is a consistent, recognizable style which marks a film as uniquely and unmistakably "Jancsó." If he has failed to follow his revolutionary achievement of the sixties with further breakthroughs, he should be entitled to our forgiveness. After all, Jancsó's contribution to cinema is one that very few filmmakers can hope to equal.

István Szabó

In the seventies and eighties, István Szabó (b. 1938) came to be widely regarded as Hungary's foremost film director. Szabó's prodigious talent was apparent from the beginning of his career; even before *The Age of Daydreaming* (1964), three of his short films had won prizes, and *The Age of Daydreaming*, completed when Szabó was twenty-six years old, captured the award at Locarno in 1965 for best first feature. Since then, almost every time István Szabó has directed a film, it has won one or more awards in major international competitions, at the festivals in Cannes, Locarno, Moscow, and elsewhere. His greatest success to date has been *Mephisto* (1981), a Hungarian-West German coproduction which picked up two prizes in Hungary and seven abroad, including the American Acad-

V–4   István Szabó

emy Award (Oscar) for best foreign-language film and the prize at Cannes for best screenplay. Not a prolific filmmaker, Szabó chooses his projects with deliberation and prepares them meticulously.

Over the years, both his style and his stories have shown a clear, consistent progression.[17] Szabó's early works were strongly influenced by the French *new wave*. *The Age of Daydreaming* pays homage to François Truffaut in its explicit mimicking of Truffaut scenes, especially from *Jules and Jim*, and its gentle-painful story of characters from the filmmaker's own generation: *Daydreaming* is about young idealists who fall victim to the human failings of their elders. By the time of his third feature, *Love Film (Szerelmes film*, 1970), Szabó's style had come to resemble that of Alain Resnais as he interwove pieces of reality, memory, and fantasy, but in this work as well as in his second film, *Father*, Szabó proved that he can learn from others while still displaying his own originality.

These first three films tell very personal stories about young people maturing, struggling for self-identity, falling in love, and resolving the discrepancies between truth and fantasy. The stories are told with wit, but they are colored by the intractability of larger, impersonal forces which limit the scope of human efficacy. In *Father* the hero is a fatherless boy who grows up amid the postwar chaos of revolution and social turmoil. In *Love Film*, a young man whose childhood sweetheart has left Hungary travels to the West to see her, experiencing the passion of memories and the reality of permanent separation.

From this early phase of Szabó's filmmaking, *Father* is the most acclaimed work and *Love Film* the most underrated. Thematically, *Father* is an ambitious film; the boy Takó represents an entire generation of Central Europeans emerging, still children, from World War II. Growing up without a father and substituting fantasies for a real sense of identity becomes a metaphor for the experience of entire nations struggling through a time of insecurity. *Love Film*, in contrast, presents a specifically Hungarian story but tells it with a deeper attempt at probing the mysteries of human memory. Jancsi and Kata, the young lovers, have been separated by Kata's decision to emigrate during the national tragedy of 1956; in real life, thousands of Hungarian families were torn apart by such decisions.[18] *Love Film* shows us the images of Jancsi's mind—scenes of him and Kata sledding, hiding in a bomb shelter together, being reunited on a train platform in France; scenes of people he had known and events he had heard about—without distinguishing clearly between past and future or between "real" happenings and flights of fantasy. Szabó has edited the cuts between reality and memory/anticipation with exquisite delicacy, producing a narrative flow that is lovely in its complexity and yet not difficult for audiences to grasp.

In these first three films, Szabó developed a visual technique that moved the stories from the personal to the universal level. An example is a scene from *Father* in which the grown-up Takó resolves to swim across the wide Danube—something his father had never done; he swims hard, and just when we know he's going to make it, the camera tilts upward from the lone figure of Takó and the focus widens to show a river filled with swimmers. Szabó employs an analogous technique in the final scene of *Love Film*: back in Budapest, Jancsi sends a telegram to Kata and the camera pans across the post office to show other Hungarians also sending messages to loved ones abroad.

Szabó's next several projects led him into still more experimental narrative styles focusing on collective protagonists. In the segment "A Dream About a House," from a series of short films collectively titled *Budapest, Why I Love It* (*Budapest, amiért szeretem*, 1971), an impersonal camera captures the human events that have taken place over the lifespan of an old apartment building, showing them elliptically and in a jumbled time sequence.[19] In *25 Fireman's Street* (*Tüzoltó utca 25*, 1973), the camera assumes the viewpoint of the characters themselves, a small community of people who have lived in a building now undergoing demolition. Their memories pour onto the screen, and the narrative takes bewildering leaps in time and space as it recreates numerous overlapping stories about the Second World War, the occupation, the deportations, and the postwar changes. In *Budapest Tales* (*Budapesti mesék*, 1976), the community is made up of individuals who emerge, one by one and two by two, in the aftermath of an unidentified holocaust and take refuge together in an abandoned trolley car. As they push the car across an isolated landscape on tracks which they believe must lead to civilization, they play out characteristic human games of organization, power, and cruelty.[20]

Budapest Tales is a transitional film for Szabó. Its community point of view and the abstract quality of the story fit logically into the pattern of his work after *Love Film*. At the same time, there is in *Budapest Tales* a return partway to straight-line narrative, foretelling the greater narrative conventionality that would make Szabó's next three films successful with mass audiences abroad.

In *Confidence* (*Bizalom*, 1979), a man and a woman, strangers to each other, hide out together in a room amid the fierce combat raging in Budapest during the autumn of 1944. Wanted by the authorities because of their connections with the Resistance, they have been given refuge by sympathizers. They take assumed names, pretending to be husband and wife, entering a situation as unsettling as the hostile environment outside. Never knowing if they can trust each other, they nevertheless fall in love, only to realize the insecurity and transiency of their situation.

Confined to one room for almost the entire film, the setting has a stage-like ambience. Close camera work and exquisite subtlety in the acting performances by Ildikó Bánsági and Péter Andorai give the minimal plot an unexpected emotional charge. When Liberation Day arrives, the two protagonists suddenly confront the moment they have long awaited and yet come to dread—their reemergence from the womblike shelter to a world whose contours are now unfamiliar.

Identity and security, the twin themes running through *Confidence*, receive an even more powerful treatment in *Mephisto* (1981) and *Colonel Redl* (*Oberst Redl*, 1984). In *Mephisto*, the actor Hendrik Höfgen desperately seeks security through public acceptance and acclaim, but he discovers that the only way to achieve it in the increasingly vicious environment of Nazi Germany is to sell his soul, Faust-like, to the forces of evil. In *Colonel Redl*, a poor boy from a marginal ethnic background (Ruthene) seeks security and power in the upper ranks of the Austro-Hungarian Army—and discovers that he cannot forever escape the sentence imposed on him by his true identity.

In both films the central conflict, to use Szabó's own words, is the "clash between the soul of the protagonist and the realities of politics."[21] *Mephisto*'s Höfgen wants only to perform, to direct, to give the public art— and to be acclaimed as an artist; politics interest him only insofar as it provides a context for his art, and so he moves without compunction from the left-wing cabarets where his career begins to the directorship of the State Theater under Nazi rule. There he discovers that he cannot achieve the glory he so fiercely desires without subordinating his art to the policies of the state. Colonel Redl finds similar disillusionment. He has risen through the ranks of the army believing that loyalty to the emperor is the only politics required for success, but he discovers among the elites of the dying monarchy a maze of intrigue through which he cannot find his way.

V–5   *Colonel Redl (Redl ezredes)*

Szabó's narrative style in *Mephisto* and *Colonel Redl* has a more conventional look compared to his earlier films, but his imagery is no less complex. Numerous visual metaphors enrich the narrative. In *Colonel Redl*, a scene at the site of Roman ruins foretells the demise of the Austro-Hungarian Empire. In the final scene of *Mephisto*, as another example, Höfgen is blinded by bright lights: an allusion to the blinding of Faust at the end of Goethe's play, as well as to Höfgen's own moral blindness. Masks are another metaphor, occurring in both films. Actor Höfgen plays his greatest stage role as Mephistopheles in whiteface, a mask that haunts and dominates *Mephisto*'s imagery. Masks appear in *Colonel Redl*, too, at a New Year's ball that foreshadows Redl's downfall. In their lives, the protagonists mask themselves. Höfgen, masked as the servant of art, effectually serves the state. Redl, masked as a member of the ruling aristocracy with all its manners and morals, is in fact just a poor naïf with an even more perilous secret—he is a homosexual. His ultimate unmasking puts an end not only to his ambitions but also to his reason for living.

Throughout his career, István Szabó has been obsessed by history: history as understood in a Central European way—history as an intruder in human affairs, a destroyer of families, a brutish and impersonal antagonist locked in combat with the individual. It is this history that weaves its way relentlessly through Szabó's films. History treats his characters unkindly, whether they deserve it or not. But still they struggle for the security of self-identity, what Szabó considers "one of the great problems of the twentieth century."[22] The portrayal of that struggle gives Szabó's films a deep humanistic quality and marks him as one of Europe's most important contemporary film directors.

Károly Makk

In contrast to the measured consistency of Szabó and the perennial controversy of Jancsó, the long career of Károly Makk (b. 1925) has been characterized by peaks and valleys. In fact, it can fairly be said that Makk's international reputation has been earned by two films: *Love* (*Szerelem*, 1970) and *Another Way* (*Egymásra nézve*, 1982).

Makk was active in filmmaking as early as 1944 and assisted Géza Radványi on the set of *Somewhere in Europe* (1947), but he had to wait for his own first feature until 1954 *(Liliomfi)*. *Liliomfi* was popular in Hungary, and *The Fanatics* (1961) was notable for its political statement, but it was not until the appearance of *Love* that Makk's exquisite talent became clearly recognizable.

Love, adapted from two short stories by the important contemporary writer Tibor Déry, centers on an aged woman who is slowly dying and her vivacious daughter-in-law, Luca. It is set in the Budapest of 1953. Missing from the first scenes is János, the old woman's son and Luca's husband. Gradually it is revealed, through indirect dialogue and flash frames of a prison cell, that János is a victim of the Rákosi-era purges, but Luca valiantly attempts to humor her mother-in-law by making up stories to explain János's long absence. In the end, János is released without explanation and comes home to a bittersweet reunion with his wife: a small

V–6   Károly Makk

basket containing the old woman's eyeglasses and a few of her favorite possessions tells him that his mother has died.

The film displays Makk's craftmanship at telling a story of great emotional power with the restraint necessary, at the time, for treating the political realities with honesty and clarity. Luca, married to an "enemy of the people," loses her friends, her job as a schoolteacher, and most of her apartment—all revealed through scenes that are direct and ugly, but understated. The realism with which Luca's world is depicted stands in contrast to the soft tones of the room where her bedridden mother-in-law spends her last days and nights, surrounded by outdated furnishings and the knickknacks of a bygone day. The old woman "sees" flash frames of yesteryear, gallant men on horseback and ladies with parasols photographed with the slight distortion of a wide-angle lens, whereas Luca sees crisp images of her own era with its crumbling plaster and shortages of food. Filmed in black and white, the contrasts are very effective. There is humor in the depiction of the old woman and in Luca's sometimes playful, sometimes exasperated interaction with her, but the film never descends to ridicule. It is one of the film's outstanding achievements that we see in the old woman's increasing senility a profound dignity.

Superb acting performances by Mari Törőcsik, as Luca, and Lili Darvas, the widow of playwright Ferenc Molnár, combine with Makk's directing to make *Love* one of the most delicately beautiful films ever made. Not

V–7   *Love (Szerelem)*

only is it remarkable for its tender view of the old woman and her faithful daughter-in-law, but by opening up the subject of the purges it picked at one of the most painful sores in Hungarian history.

Makk's next cinematic peak was equally notable, but it did not occur for another twelve years. In between, Makk directed a creditable but not outstanding screen version of Isztván Örkény's well-known theater piece, *Catsplay* (*Macskajáték*, 1974); a soft-edged comedy, *A Very Moral Night* (1977), about a medical student who lives as a boarder in a turn-of-the-century house of prostitution; and *Two Stories from the Recent Past* (*Két történet a félmúltból*, 1979), which passed almost unnoticed. But in *Another Way*, the world was once again shown the power of Makk's talent as well as his willingness to take on sensitive political topics.

In *Another Way*, he in fact took on two hot topics, censorship and lesbianism, and, to make matters still more delicate, worked with a story set in 1958, when the messy political business of the 1956 revolt was still being cleaned up. The heroine, Éva, is a gifted journalist recently readmitted to the staff of a weekly called *Igazság* ("Truth") after having been disciplined for unspecified political indiscretions. On the job, she develops an obsessive attraction for a fellow reporter, Lívia, whose resistance is slowly broken down by the persistent Éva. The two roles are powerfully played by Polish actresses Jadwiga Jankowska-Cieslak (as Éva) and Grażyna Szapołowska (as Lívia).

On assignment in the countryside, Éva uncovers a story about a cooperative-farm chairman who is alleged to be a successful recruiter but turns out to have achieved his "success" by coercing peasants to join. Éva's editor judges her story too hot to publish as it is and assumes the task of editing it himself. A series of intense and realistic scenes reveals the workings of censorship, the delicate position of the editor, and the power of the publisher. Éva is fired (she has already resigned). The story ends tragically, with Lívia in the hospital recuperating from a serious gunshot wound inflicted by her outraged husband and Éva killed while attempting to cross the border.

Makk's visual style again alternates between the realistic and the lyrical. Tender scenes between Éva and Lívia are bathed in warm colors, and the mood is one of a gentle eroticism. Their love begins to blossom not in the springtime, but in the winter: an ironic omen. In keeping with the central theme of truth—truth about Éva and Lívia's feelings toward each other, truth about the reality which Éva as a journalist so fervently wishes to report—Makk's image system contains numerous indexes to *seeing*, such as mirrors, window panes, a reflection in a pool of water or on a shiny table top; scenes revealing Éva's lesbianism are viewed through curtains or obliquely around a bend, and vulnerability is revealed in the open (as, for example, a scene in which Éva and Lívia are caught by police while necking on a park bench). As Éva approaches the border, knowing that she will be shot, an owl spies on her.

At first glance the issues of lesbianism and censorship may strike one as unlikely twins, but a brilliant idea links them in this story. For Éva, sexual and political nonconformity are of one piece. Since she cannot accept the Party line on matters of sexual preference—the Party line being roughly as judgmental about homosexuality as typical American mores at the time—she can equally well reject the Party's line on journalistic standards. Falsehood is her enemy.

At the Cannes Festival in 1982, *Another Way* earned the FIPRESCI critics' award and Jadwiga Jankowska-Cieślak won the jury's prize for best actress. The film has been screened at several festivals in the United States, but it has not been well appreciated here and is not, at the time of this writing, in American distribution.

It is true that some of Makk's films are lightweight; *A Very Moral Night* and *Lily in Love* (1984), an English-language American coproduction starring Christopher Plummer and Maggie Smith as an aging show business couple, are representative examples. But Károly Makk's films, at least those of the seventies and eighties, always show the elegant touch of a mature director in control of his art. At their best, Makk's films are brilliant as they probe sensitive, emotionally charged issues. And though his best stories are set in the past, their lessons relate unmistakably to current political problems. *Love* reminded Hungarians in 1970–71 that the victims of Stalinism carry their pain with them. *Another Way*'s message, about nonconformity, tolerance, and truth, bears obvious relevance to the mid-eighties, when smug attitudes about the relative permissiveness of Hungarian society masked a continuing official starchiness about certain issues. Éva's editor, who argues the need for compromise in order to protect the limited gains of his day (compared to the stringencies of Stalinism), speaks for editors, publishers, and producers in the eighties.

Márta Mészáros

Márta Mészáros's work is almost as controversial as Miklós Jancsó's. With the exception of her newest pictures—the *Diary* sequence (see below) —her films have commanded much more favorable attention abroad than in Hungary. "All my previous work has been hated and despised," she has said, referring to her standing in Hungary,[23] whereas she has received awards for *Adoption* (*Örökbefogadás*, 1975) at the Berlin and Chicago festivals, for *Nine Months* at Cannes and Teheran, for *Just Like at Home* (*Olyan mint otthon*, 1978) at San Sebastian, and for *Diary for My Children* (*Napló gyermekeimnek*, 1982, 1984) at Cannes, Munich, and Chicago. Only *Diary* has won awards in Hungary.

Prior to the eighties, Mészáros's films told stories about women in search of fulfillment and individuality in a society that denies them the totality that they seek. In *The Girl*, the search is complicated by the conflict between peasant traditions and urban lifestyles. In *Nine Months*, the heroine is isolated by generalized societal prejudices and the intolerance of her man. In *Women* (*Ők ketten*, 1977),[24] a young woman and a middle-aged woman, both unable to solve their marital problems, form a deep friendship despite their different social backgrounds.

Mészáros's films insist that motherhood is an important part of the feminine identity, and conflicts between the role of mother and the drive for individuality are strongly played out. She has sometimes drawn criticism, however, for making stereotyped "heavies" out of the men in her stories, particularly in *Nine Months* and *Women*.

Between *Women* and the first *Diary* Mészáros directed three coproductions, none of which attracted much attention: *On the Move* (*Útközben*, 1979), a Hungarian-Polish collaboration, and two Hungarian-French productions, *The Heiresses* (*Örökség / Les héritières*, 1980), and *Anna*, also known as *Mother and Daughter* (*Une mère, une fille . . .* , 1981).

And then she embarked upon what would be her grandest, and most personal, project, the *Diary* sequence. By the time of this writing, two films have been completed: *Diary for My Children* and *Diary for My Loves* (*Napló szerelmeimnek*, 1987). Originally, director Mészáros had envisioned a trilogy, but her most recent plans—again, as of this writing—anticipate at least four installments of the story, each a full-length movie.

The heroine of *Diary* is Juli Kovács, a semifictionalized alter ego of Mészáros (b. 1931) herself, the daughter of a sculptor who fled Horthy's Hungary with wife and daughter to the Soviet Union, where he disappeared in Stalin's purge of the intellectuals during 1938. These story elements are told in flashback, as *Diary for My Children* begins with Juli's return to Hungary as a teenager in 1946. Her mother has died in Russia, too, so Juli takes up residence in Budapest with a family friend, Magda, who is an officer in the state security police. Hungary is drifting into Stalinism, and Magda is one of the chosen.

Living with Magda, Juli quickly recognizes the sinister political atmosphere descending over Hungary and watches as Magda increasingly personifies the hypocrisies of a new ruling caste. Juli becomes infatuated wth János, a friend of Magda's who reminds Juli of her lost father; when János falls victim to Hungary's political terror and Magda refuses to help, Juli packs her bags and breaks with Magda.

In the second installment of the story, *Diary for My Loves*, Juli is living on her own but cannot get away from Magda completely. Despite their ongoing conflict, Juli accepts Magda's help and receives a state scholarship to study in Moscow. There she enters the film academy and studies directing, following a movie obsession she had developed in the first installment of *Diary*. While in Moscow, she makes an effort to find her father and learns that he has died.

Diary for My Loves takes place between 1953 and 1956, and in the relaxed political atmosphere Juli aspires to make truthful documentaries about her country. So she returns to Hungary to begin her career. In the studios, however, censorship is still tight. Through János, who has been re-

V–8   Diary for My Children (Napló gyermekeimnek)

leased from prison, she meets people who are working for positive change. Filled with optimism, Juli makes a return trip to Moscow to receive her diploma. Once there, she learns that fighting has broken out in Hungary. The border is closed, and she cannot return home.

In its explicit treatment of political realities, Diary broke much new cinematic ground. Like her heroine, Director Mészáros set out to tell the truth about the times. Thus we are not spared the explicit information that Juli's father perished unjustly in the Soviet Union; that those who championed an egalitarian society of and for the workers were quick to assume the lifestyle of the bourgeoisie whom they had displaced; and that life for political prisoners was inhumanly brutal (seen in the second Diary as János emerges from incarceration with permanent internal injuries). In the second Diary there is some footage from a newsreel showing Imre Nagy speaking in parliament—the first such cinematic reference to the executed leader of 1956.[25]

Both films show Mészáros's characteristic preference for realism, spiced with many carefully chosen images captured by cinematographer Miklós Jancsó, Jr.: a sparkling chandelier in Magda's apartment indexes her position of social privilege; the abundant red banners display the political ebullience of the time while olive drab uniforms on the members of the Communist Youth League bear witness to the militarized atmosphere of everyday life.

The first Diary is filmed in black and white, with the happier flashbacks of Juli's childhood shot in a dream-like harsh light: one of the few deviations from strict realism. The second *Diary* is filmed primarily in color, with flashbacks in sepia tone and newsreel clips in the original black and white. In both films a deft, confident camera frames its scenes with care. Zsuzsa Czinkóczi, the young actress who plays the demanding role of Juli, does so adequately in the first *Diary* but lapses into an unsatisfying passivity in the second.[26]

In *Diary for My Loves*, Mészáros could not resist the opportunity to make a feminist comment, as Juli's teachers in Moscow scoff at her desire to enter the men's world of film directing. In most respects, however, the two *Diaries* mark a departure in Márta Mészáros's career, combining a highly personal story about a girl who loves movies and a commentary on broader political questions. They follow by more than a decade the first Hungarian films that looked critically back at the Rákosi years, but they do so in a way that removes virtually all remaining traces of euphemism. Mészáros's two projected sequels will carry the story through to approximately 1968.

Other Directors

One of the most popular directors is Péter Bacsó, most of whose films in recent years have been social and political comedies—a "genre" that, for Hungary, Bacsó invented. *The Witness*, completed in 1969 but withheld from distribution for political reasons until 1978, is an outrageous satire set during the Rákosi years. Its hero is a hapless bungler, but he has a

V–9   *Diary for My Loves (Napló szerelmeimnek)*

friend in an official position who gets him "important" jobs (the director-ship of a "people's amusement park," the managership of Hungary's first-ever orange grove) that are far beyond his competency. The film teeters be-tween humor and horror when the protagonist, compelled to give false testimony at a political trial, forgets his lines.

Bacsó tried to follow up the delayed success of *The Witness,* again pok-ing fun at the foibles of the Stalinists in *Oh, Bloody Life!* (1983), about an operetta singer banished to the countryside because she was formerly mar-ried to a count. In *What's the Time, Mr. Clock? (Hány az óra, Vekker úr?,* 1985), Bacsó filmed a tragicomic tale of a Jewish clockmaker in World War II whose ability to tell the time without a watch enables him to be-come a hero. *Banana Skin Waltz* (1987) is a contemporary story about a sur-geon whose life is turned topsy-turvy by a chance encounter with a de-ranged naked woman.

Bacsó's movies draw big crowds in Hungary, but few of them travel well; the Bacsó brand of comedy does not translate easily across cultural barriers. Some Hungarian critics deplore Bacsó's attempts to find humor amid tragedy, arguing that there was nothing funny about Stalinism or the Second World War and that Bacsó's satires trivialize history. Bacsó de-fends his work by arguing that his films do not poke fun at tragedy, they poke fun at those who hold power. One of the most important qualities

V–10   *The Witness (A tanú)*

about power, Bacsó says, is its humorlessness; accordingly, one of the most effective weapons with which to combat power is humor.[27]

Apart from the question of their appropriateness, one can justifiably ask whether Bacsó's films are *good* satires, relying as they do on stereotype and hyperbole. *The Witness* was certainly a daring venture into uncharted territory, and, partly because of its shock value, it worked. The other films mentioned, however, can be faulted for exaggerated situations, forced humor, or awkward balancing between comic and tragic elements.[28]

Still, there is no question about Péter Bacsó's importance. He remains well loved by his Hungarian fans, and his work has not gone unnoticed abroad; among other honors have been awards at Cannes (1981) for *The Witness* and Locarno for *Present Indicative* (*Jelenidő*, 1971), and the grand prize at Sanremo for *The Last Chance* (*Harmadik nekifutás*, 1973). It must also be mentioned that, as head of MAFILM's "Objektiv" studio unit, Bacsó fought for the right to produce and distribute Károly Makk's *Love* and succeeded—even while his own pathbreaking film, *The Witness*, languished on the censor's shelf.

Many additional Hungarian directors would deserve mention on the basis of at least one quality film since the late seventies. Some of the names and titles familiar in the West are Pál Gábor, who wrote and directed the much-honored *Angi Vera* (1978); András Kovács, *The Stud Farm* (*Ménesgazda*, 1978); János Rózsa, *Spider Football* (*Pókfoci*, 1976) and *Mascot* (*Kabala*, 1981); Ferenc András, *Rain and Shine* (*Veri az ördög a feleséget*, 1977)[29] and *The Great Generation* (*A nagy generáció*, 1986); Zsolt Kézdi-Kovács, *When Joseph Returns* (*Ha megjőn József*, 1975), *The Nice Neighbor* (*A kedves szomszéd*, 1979), and *Forbidden Relations* (*Visszaesők*, 1982); Imre Gyöngyössy and Barna Kabay, *The Revolt of Job* (*Jób lázadása*, 1983); György Szomjas, *Light Physical Injuries* (*Könnyű testi sértés*, 1983); Judit Elek, *Mária's Day* (1983); Pál Erdőss, *The Princess* (1982); and Péter Gárdos, *The Philadelphia Attraction* (*Uramisten*, 1984)[30] and *Whooping Cough* (1986).

Two promising film directors who emerged during the seventies are, unfortunately, no longer living. They are Zoltán Huszárik (1931–1980) and Gábor Bódy (1946–1985). Huszárik's *Sinbad* (*Szindbád*, 1970) has been widely praised for its visual beauty in the portrayal of an aging man who no longer lives the life of sensual pleasures he once did—but remembers it in poetic detail. In *Csontváry* (1980), Huszárik turned his visual flair to a portrait of Tivadar Csontváry Kosztka, an important *fin de siècle* painter.

Bódy burst upon the scene with *American Fragment*, also known as *American Torso* (*Amerikai anzix*, 1975). The grand prize winner at Mannheim in 1976, *American Fragment* is a psychological study of three Hungarian freedom fighters who find themselves fighting on the side of the Union in the American Civil War. Bódy shot the film in black and white and painstakingly edited it to make it appear like a complex series of sepia-toned period photographs somehow set in motion. He followed with *Narcissus and Psyche* (*Nárcisz és Psyché*, 1980), a resetting of the ancient myth in nineteenth-century Europe, and *The Dog's Night Song* (1983), one of the most original European films of the eighties. *The Dog's Night Song* tells the story of a fake priest (acted by Bódy himself) who suddenly appears in a Hungarian village and, by preaching a gospel of Christian love, sets himself apart from his community. The plot is full of twists and tangents, moving from the story of a strange friendship between the bogus priest and a suicidal, paraplegic Communist, to a soldier quarreling with his young wife, to a nonsense interview with a punk rock group called The Galloping Coroners (an actual group popular in Budapest at the time). It is an artsy film with radical color contrasts (blue scenes, red scenes) and experimental sound techniques in places, and the themes running through it boggle the intellect: human love and the lack of it in our time, punk nihilism as a response to moral chaos, the unfulfilled promises of an optimistic age (this message would appear to aim indiscriminately at both socialism and capitalism). The film's title connects to a segment of dialogue between a small boy and a learned astronomer: "Why do dogs bay at the full moon?"—"I don't know. Maybe they remember when the moon crashed and Atlantis sank . . . Or maybe they're just expressing the misery of being a dog."

Especially talented among the surviving members of Bódy's generation are Péter Gothár (b. 1947), Gyula Gazdag (b. 1947), and András Jeles (b.

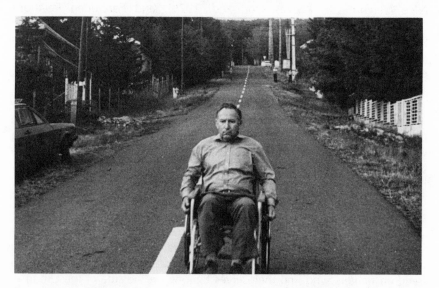

V–11   *The Dog's Night Song (A kutya éji dala)*

1945). Gothár worked with Hungarian Television during the sixties before entering the Academy of Theater and Film Art in Budapest. His first feature, *A Priceless Day* (*Ajándék ez a nap*, 1979), won a Gold Lion at Venice, as well as the Hungarian Film Critics' Prize for best direction. Gothár repeated this early success with *Time Stands Still* (*Megáll az idő*, 1981), capturing awards in Cannes, Chicago, New York, Brussels, and Tokyo. *A Priceless Day* tells a hard-hitting story about disintegrating family life and the nasty world of the black market housing business—two subjects the government had always treated with delicacy. *Time Stands Still*, sometimes superficially compared to George Lucas's *American Graffiti* (USA, 1973), paints a dusky, agonizing picture of Hungarian teenagers *circa* 1963, their family life still affected by the loss of loved ones from the 1956 revolt even as they struggle to find their way through the normal trials of adolescence. Gothár's third film, *Time* (*Idő van*, 1985), is a comic surrealist adventure that tells the story, as Gothár likes to describe it, of "a typical Hungarian family going on holiday."[31] The Hungarian title means "there is time," in the sense of "there's still time"—a reference to the mid-life anxiety of the protagonist, who despairs over not having accomplished anything in his thirty-five years. Western audiences find *Time* incomprehensible or puzzlingly amusing; Hungarian audiences find it uproarious, reading the subtext that is replete with references to Hungarian political obsessions, outrageous jokes about factory relations, and depictions of tragicomic family situations.

Time establishes Gothár as a director of versatility whose style has shown a remarkable pattern of development. His first film, *A Priceless Day*, is told mostly in the realist vein, though Gothár tinted some of his scenes with harsh color. In *Time Stands Still*, Gothár and his cinematographer, Lajos Koltai, created a pervading impressionistic aura, dark and somber, enveloping the young protagonists, who can only seek relief by grasping at the sympathetic music of American heart-throb, Paul Anka. One of numerous unforgettable images from this film is that of dancers in ducktail and bouffant hair-dos, their faces contorted with adolescent yearnings, crooning along with Anka's "You Are My Destiny," played by a phonograph in a murky makeshift ballroom.

The prolific Gyula Gazdag is not yet well known in the West, but he has been directing films since his documentary, *The Long Distance Runner* (*Hosszú futásodra mindig számíthatunk*, 1968), completed when Gazdag was twenty-one. His first feature film came three years later, *Whistling Cobblestone* (*Sipoló macskakő*, 1971), a remembrance of political disillusionment among kids at a summer camp—a story startling for its time. Gazdag moves freely from documentaries to features, and in both forms he shows much courage and originality. His *Package Tour* (*Tarsasutazás*, 1984) is a documentary about a return visit by survivors of Auschwitz to the death camp forty years later. Gazdag and his cinematographer, Elemér Ragályi, trained their disciplined camera on the members and organizers of the tour from a neutral stance, allowing the event to unfold without narrative comment, revealing the tour organizers as insensitive and poorly organized while the returnees, slowly at first and impassively, then with increasing emotion, recall their experiences at that horrible place. Gazdag's most recent film is *Hungarian Fairy Tale* (*Hol volt, hol nem volt*, 1987), a fable about an orphaned boy who, upon the death of his mother, sets out on a fantasy-like adventure in search of the man whose name was arbitrarily entered on his birth record as his father. Filmed in black and white, the story is told in a highly original style; keyed to the music of "The Magic Flute," the lyrical tones of the beginning evolve almost imperceptibly into the fantastical scenes toward the end, when the boy and two eccentric grown-ups he has met fly off on a large metal eagle. The fairy-tale tone masks ambitious intentions. The movie raises questions about love and family and the social welfare bureaucracy; it seems to suggest, in a clever but ultimately unsatisfying way, that the only escape from the absurdity of the case worker syndrome is through fantasy. Still, Gazdag's talent shows throughout this film, and he is a director whose work deserves more international attention.[32]

Even less known outside Hungary is András Jeles. As of this writing, Jeles had completed only two films, *The Little Valentino* (*A kis Valentino*, 1978) and *Annunciation* (*Angyali üdvözlet*, 1984). The first of these tells a story about one day in the life of a twenty-year-old drifter, told in the language of an absurd realism. *Annunciation*, equally simple in form, is Jeles's adaptation of a nineteenth-century work, Imre Madách's *The Tragedy of Man* (*Az ember tragédiája*). Madách's dramatic poem is a sweep-

V–12   *A Hungarian Fairy Tale (Hol volt, hol nem volt)*

V–13   *The Annunciation (Angyali üdvözlet)*

ing epic about the tragic follies of mankind; Jeles's adaptation loosely follows the original. The story begins with the fall of Adam and Eve, after
which Lucifer guides Adam through a dream in which he plays changing
roles: as Miltiades, the Athenian general unjustly condemned to death by
a mistaken public; as a crusader in Byzantium witnessing a conflict between Christian sects which sends thousands to the stake; as Kepler in service to the petty and eccentric emperor Rudolf; as Danton amid the Reign
of Terror; and so on. Coming out of the dream, Adam despairs about the future of his species, but just as he is about to commit suicide, Eve tells
him she is pregnant and he decides to live. Despite the complexity of the
story and the difficulties of adapting it to the screen, Jeles opted for a simple, stage-like approach and, in a stunning choice, cast the acting entirely with eight- to twelve-year-old children. The result is a remarkable,
unique piece of cinema which has unfortunately not been released outside Hungary.

Jeles's third film, *The Workers' Dream Brigade*, will be discussed below.

HUNGARIAN FILMS,
HUNGARIAN CONCERNS

Hungarian filmmakers cover a wide variety of subjects, but as one surveys their work, two themes recur with noticeable consistency. The first
is that quality that we have referred to as "Hungarity," the nature of the

Hungarian experience and the community identity. The theme raises questions that draw filmmakers into historical reflection, examining the myths of both the distant past and the more recent past. The second broad theme has to do with the quality of contemporary life. Subsumed under this theme are a wealth of specific issues—family life, the role of women, the realities of workers, morality, and others.

Hungarity

Somewhere in Europe, the title of Radványi's 1947 film, tells us that "Hungarity" has long been on the minds of filmmakers. The Hungary of Miklós Jancsó is a place drenched in history; its people dance in a timeless ballet enacting and reenacting a story of romantic delusions and unequal conflicts. In contrast, the Hungary of István Szabó's early films is a community that appears to have the capacity, singly and together, to find its identity; in Szabó's later films, however, the quest for identity frustrates his characters, who are ultimately swallowed by forces beyond their comprehension.

In *Mária's Day* (1983), written and directed by Judit Elek, the Hungarian condition is one of betrayed ideals; Elek's aristocrats, in-laws of the great poet Sándor Petőfi who was martyred in the 1849 uprising, sit around and mourn their country's subsequent compromise with the Austrians. The Hungarian aristocracy can only dream idle dreams of a new heroic epoch. In László Vitézy's *A Fond Farewell to the Prince* (1986), the seventeenth-century ruler of Transylvania, Gábor Bethlen, must chart a hazardous course between the Ottoman sultan, his protector, and the Habsburg emperor, whose designs extend to the prince's realm. Transylvania's position, like that of present-day Hungary, allows the prince to give his subjects a degree of prosperity and religious freedom (the prince himself being a Calvinist) that their Hungarian co-nationals living under the Habsburgs do not enjoy. But Don Diego, the resident historian summoned from Venice by the prince to write his memoirs, sees the truth: Transylvania's independence is limited, and the country's prosperity is fragile.[33]

In Sándor Sára's documentary *At the Crossroads* (1986), the Hungarian condition is one of marginality. Much favored by Hungarian film critics, *At the Crossroads* tells the story of a small community of Transylvanian Hungarians who have been repeatedly brutalized and displaced throughout the past two centuries.

Is a Jew also a Hungarian? Historically, Jews tended to fare better in Hungary than in most other Central European countries, but one sees few Jewish stories in Hungarian films. Those that one does see, however, can be extraordinary, such as Gyöngyössy's and Kabay's *The Revolt of Job* (1983), a softspoken World War II story about an elderly Jewish couple who, having no children to inherit their property and sensing the danger in the air, adopt a feisty Gentile boy to carry on after their departure. Two years after this film, Gyöngyössy and Kabay collaborated with Katalin Petényi to produce a moving documentary, *The Land of the Miraculous Rabbis* (*Add tudtul fiaidnak*, 1985), about the last few Jews living in a rural community of northeastern Hungary. These two films, together with Gazdag's *Package Tour*, make for an impressive trio of Hungarian films treating the subject of the holocaust. Less impressive, but worth seeing, is Erika Szántó's *Elysium* (1986), a story about the disappearance of a ten-year-old boy into the camps.

"Setting aside stupidity, . . . we are pure," reads the epigraph to Zoltán Fábri's *Hungarians*.[34] Because of the war, Fábri's dirt-poor peasants have a rare opportunity to earn a decent living in Germany. Their relative affluence comes at the cost of homesickness, but worse than this is the destruction of their innocence: they see prisoners of war, French and Russian, forced to work without adequate nourishment and shot if they do not maintain the pace; Polish women and children are brought to nearby barracks under armed guard, and later they disappear. At the end of the film the Hungarian migrants have returned to their home village, only to learn that their men are now being taken away to fight in the war that had, initially, brought them unexpected fortune.

Are they so pure? One foreign observer of the Hungarian cinema, writing in 1976, has chastised Hungarians for their unwillingness to accept any responsibility for historical tragedies. According to this viewer, Hungarian filmmakers always blame others—the Turks, the Habsburgs, the Nazis; Hungarians, the prisoners of geopolitics, are the victims of forces too great to be resisted.[35] Perhaps the argument is true for Hungarian films prior to the mid-seventies, but there have been changes since then. In *Mária's Day*, for example, Hungarian helplessness is a state of mind; in *At the Crossroads*, there is testimony that Hungarian governments have been just as insensitive as others to the plight of the displaced community that serves as the film's subject. In Fábri's *Hungarians*, the "pure" villagers are supervised by a Hungarian foreman who, by simply fulfilling his task on the farm, clearly plays a role of importance in the larger scheme of things.

There are hints of Hungarian responsibility in other films made since the mid-seventies. If *Budapest Tales* is an allegory about postwar Hungary, as some critics argue, then Szabó's Hungarians are capable of not just petty bickering but brutality as well. In Fábri's *Bálint Fábian Meets God* (1980), the parent generation of his *Hungarians* gets caught up in World War I, the Republic of Councils, and the white terror, and these "innocent" peasants turn out to be quite capable of committing atrocities. Gazdag's "package tour" participants acknowledge that there is still some antisemitism in Hungary forty years after the Holocaust. And finally, of course, in the many films that have been made about the Rákosi era, from Bacsó's satires to Mészáros's *Diary*, the finger of responsibility points backward; about the fifties, Hungarian filmmakers have chanted a chorus of *mea culpas*.

Contemporary Life

The seventies and eighties have seen a proliferation of films on contemporary problems that, as subject matter for the cinema, were previously considered taboo. Márta Mészáros's exploration of the woman's condition opened the more general question of family relations, beckoning filmmakers like Péter Gothár, Judit Elek, and Zsolt Kézdi-Kovács to enter this arena. Life among the working class, a delicate political topic in a workers' state, especially attracted Pál Erdőss, while issues of personal and social morality were taken up by Gábor Bódy in *The Dog's Night Song*, Károly Makk in *Another Way*, and several others.

Elek's *Maybe Tomorrow* (*Majd holnap*, 1979) is a story about two families racked by marital fighting, adultery, jealousy, and violence. Kézdi-Kovács's *The Nice Neighbor* (1979) tells an even uglier story about the residents of a condemned building; they will all be resettled into new flats, but the housing authorities will determine how large an apartment each household is entitled to. In their efforts to position themselves advantageously, the residents are not above bribery, lying, character assassination, marrying for the sake of obtaining more living space, and shunting unwilling parents into nursing homes.

Years ahead of their time, Tamás Andor and Pál Schiffer Jr. made a documentary about the lives of workers who commute by train from small towns and villages to work in the factories of Csepel Island (Budapest). The resulting film was *Black Train* (*Fekete vonat*, 1970), a Béla Balázs Studio production which exposed a laundry list of social ills: low wages, deplorable housing conditions, poor diets, alienated youth, and uncaring bureaucrats. *Black Train* was not widely viewed, but twelve years later, Pál Erdőss's fictional story about young workers, *The Princess*, was distributed both in Hungary and abroad, winning awards at the Budapest, Cannes, and Locarno festivals. *The Princess* focuses on a teenage girl, Jutka, who arrives from the country to work in a Budapest textile mill and lives in a women's hostel. Before long, the wonders of city life turn into a sad experience replete with unsafe working conditions, miserable housing, alienation, rampant alcoholism, black marketeering, conspicuous consumption among the socialist bourgeoisie, male chauvinism, violence, rape, and the community's prejudices against single parenthood. In the sequel, *Countdown* (*Visszaszámlálás*, 1985), Jutka marries a young man who sets himself up as a self-employed trucker only to discover that the private sector, encouraged by the economic reforms of the eighties, is full of shysters and manipulators.

Manipulation and exploitation are themes that run through *Pretty Girls*

(*Szépleányok*, 1986), a documentary by András Dér and László Hartai about the "Miss Hungary" pageant of 1985—the first national beauty contest in fifty years. The film tells a disgusting story of commercialism and disregard for the sensitivities of the contestants, some of whom were sold into the West European soft-core pornography market without being aware of their rights. The winner, a lovely seventeen-year-old named Csilla Andrea Molnár, committed suicide during the year of her reign.

Finally in this section, mention must be made of Ferenc András's *The Great Generation* (1986), for it connects themes of "Hungarity" and contemporary society into one of the best Hungarian films of the eighties. Its three male protagonists, one of whom (Réb) has returned for his first visit after eighteen years of living in America, remember their closeness in the sixties when they, like young people in many countries, thought of themselves as a special generation. They were not, of course, and their ordinariness is all too evident in what they have subsequently become, each quite miserable in his own specific corruption—Réb as an unsuccessful petty con man, Nikita as an affluent private entrepreneur, and Makay as a disk jockey lost in the rock 'n' roll of his youth. András's ambitious film paints an unflattering portrait of one generation, but it does not stop there; it also seeks to deflate the myth of emigration and dull the glamour of private wealth. Though told with wit and irony, *The Great Generation* is a sad story about people who have lost their purity and no longer have even their self-illusions to fall back on.

V–14   *Pretty Girls (Széplányok)*

Breaking Taboos

Increasingly during the late seventies and eighties, Hungarian filmmakers broke the old rules that had prohibited the direct portrayal of sensitive social and political questions. Just as Makk was making a film about a lesbian (*Another Way*), Kézdi-Kovács directed *Forbidden Relations*, a story of a man and a woman who fall passionately in love before learning that they are stepbrother and stepsister, separated since childhood. *Forbidden Relations* treats the subject of incest and community standards with a candor that is astonishing, yet it avoids the sensationalism into which films like this could so easily slip.

Political taboos have fallen gradually since the startling release of Makk's *Love*. Not only the nineteen fifties, but another revolutionary period became a target for cinematic demythification. Dezső Magyar (now working in the United States) led a team of young rebels from the Béla Balázs Studio in making *The Agitators* (*Agitátorok*, 1970), a story of unthinking fanaticism among the leaders of the 1919 revolution. *The Agitators* was shelved for fifteen years before finally being released in early 1986. Though the events of 1919 continue to be approached with some caution, further cinematic treatments of that period can be seen in *Bálint Fábián Meets God* and *The Red Countess* (*A vörös grófnő*, 1984). The latter, written and directed by András Kovács, tells the story of the ill-fated succession government led by Count Mihály Károlyi and its capitulation to Béla Kun and the Communists. Centering on Károlyi's wife, a progressive-minded daughter of the elite Andrássys, the film captures the milieu of the aristocracy not uncritically, but with much warmth and nostalgia.

Nor was *Love* the first film to deal with the Rákosi era. Other stories related to Stalinism in one way or another were Fábri's *Twenty Hours* (*Húsz óra*, 1964), Gaál's *The Green Years* (*Zöldár*, 1965), Ferenc Kósa's *Ten Thousand Suns* (*Tízezer nap*, 1965), and Sándor Sára's *The Upthrown Stone* (*Feldobott kő*, 1968). In the early seventies, political topics tended to be treated through metaphor, as, for example, Gaál's *The Falcons*, a stylized film about a bird farm where a benevolent but stern chief supervises the training of falcons for the purpose of keeping magpies and other local pests under control,[36] and Sára's *Pheasant Tomorrow* (*Holnap lesz fácán*, 1974), an ironic story about authority and order in a vacation campground.

Outside Hungary, these subtle films were either little known or poorly understood when *The Stud Farm* and *Angi Vera* (both 1978) were released abroad in 1979, drawing great international attention. *The Stud Farm*, directed by András Kovács, tells a story of conflict between the new manager of a horse-breeding farm and the villagers, resentful of the outsider's authority. Just below the surface lies the terror enforcing the Hungarian collectivization drive. When two stallions are led out for mating, they bolt and challenge each other in a savage battle that illuminates the real nature of the human conflict.

In Pál Gábor's elegant and understated *Angi Vera*, winner of more than a dozen awards internationally, an honest nurse who dares to criticize conditions in her hospital is chosen by the Party for political training. At the Party school, she metamorphoses from naïve young thing to alert Stalinist with an icy-cool understanding of the political environment. In a public self-criticism session, she admits having a love affair with a married teacher, costing him his position but gaining for herself a golden future in Party work.

These films opened the floodgates. By the mid-eighties, it seemed that every filmmaker had a story about Stalinism, and, encouraged by the regime's stated openness in confronting the misdeeds of the early fifties, they spilled their stories onto the screen. Good intentions do not always make good art, and some of the resulting films are not of high quality. Ironically, just when the Soviet cinema began at last to peel back the layers of restriction that had so long buried the past, Hungarian moviegoers considered Stalinism old hat.

Not so, or not quite so, with the national tragedy of 1956. The thirtieth anniversary of the uprising brought out many public discussions characterized by a cautious honesty (the uprising, for example, cannot be referred to in the public media as a "revolution," but on the other hand, it is no longer mandatory that it be called a "counterrevolution"). Filmmakers continue to treat the subject with delicacy,[37] as they have since as early as 1957, when György Révész's *At Midnight* (*Éjfélkor*) presented the dilemma of people having to decide between emigrating and staying in the homeland. Cinematic treatments, though few, have become increasingly bold, and recent benchmarks of candor can be seen in Mészáros's *Diary for My Loves* and Péter Gárdos's *Whooping Cough* (1986).

Whooping Cough is a personal story told from the viewpoint of a ten-year-old boy (Gárdos, who both directed and co-scripted the film, was eight in 1956). The boy and his younger sister are enjoying a holiday from school and do not quite comprehend their elders' anxiety. Fighting rages outside, and the adults' increasingly frantic behavior appears nonsensical and even funny. To the children, the atmosphere is one of unexpected freedom in which they can get away with all kinds of mischief. They escape from the house and, together with several other children, make their way to the outskirts of the city. There they find an abandoned handcar and figure out how to move it along the railroad tracks. Suddenly they are caught in a crossfire; they drop to the floor as the handcar rolls on, eventually passing out of the bullets' path. But one of the children has been killed, and all of them have had the reality of the fighting impressed upon them forever.

Whooping Cough is a clever and original film, its tragicomic irony reminiscent of certain works from the Czech *new wave*, particularly Jiří

Menzel's *Closely Watched Trains* (*Ostře sledované vláky,* 1966). *Whooping Cough* has received some attention abroad by winning the grand prize at the 1987 Chicago Festival. Hungarian audiences appear to be divided in their response, some finding it warm and moving, others criticizing it for its lighthearted beginning. But its production marked a bold new cinematic approach to the remembrance of an event that Hungarians will never forget.

Nor have contemporary political realities been overlooked by filmmakers, though in this area an even greater degree of caution prevails. The benchmark here is *A Fond Farewell to the Prince.* No Hungarian viewer will fail to recognize the resemblance of seventeenth-century Transylvania, kept on a relatively loose leash by the Ottoman empire, to current-day Hungary, the most successful social and economic innovator of the Soviet bloc. More daring still is the story's implication that the Transylvanian prince acceded to the throne after having his predecessor murdered—a not-so subtle allusion to the manner in which János Kádár, the Hungarian leader between 1956 and 1988, gained his position.

The boundary between what the authorities of the late eighties considered permissible and what they did not appears to lie somewhere between *A Fond Farewell to the Prince* and András Jeles's *The Workers' Dream Brigade. Dream Brigade* is a most unusual film, combining elements of absurd surrealism with a savage flair for satirical broadside. The story wanders hither and yon, narrated by an older man whose face and clothing are colored like marble, before eventually centering on a "brigade" of factory

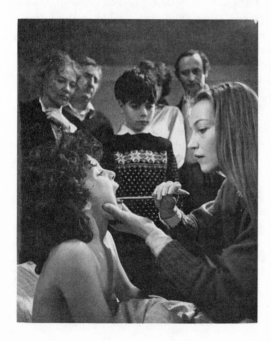

V–15   *Whooping Cough*
(*Szamárköhögés*)

workers organized, against their wishes, to perform a play before an audience of professional thespians. Throughout the scenes involving the workers, they are shown to be angry and resentful, constantly mouthing off in blistering obscenities about the quality of management, "the Party," and the privileged lives of the intellectuals, for whom the workers do not like being compelled to perform. Jeles's film, scripted, shot, and shelved in the mid-eighties, remains in rough cut while the director awaits permission to finish it. If permission is forthcoming, it will be a signal that yet another set of taboos has fallen.

HUNGARIAN CINEMA IN THE LATE NINETEEN EIGHTIES

Hungarian cinema, as a state-owned industry, is of course subject to censorship. And yet, many films have shown candor in their portrayal of Hungarian social and political realities. The Hungarian preference for decentralized authority is largely responsible for this, but the studio units' autonomy would not be possible but for a comparatively indulgent Ministry of Culture. Ordinarily, film censorship is self-censorship, and authorities of the state rarely interfere; filmmakers know the limits of what the state will tolerate and, for the most part, stay within them. Studio committees develop a special sensitivity to the ministry's standards, and, while their critics sometimes accuse them of conservatism, theirs is a realistic approach which has made possible a gradual, consistent expansion of the permitted territory.

Once in a while a film unit will reveal an uncanny sense of timing by producing a film that pushes the boundary of the permissible outward, as in the case of Another Way. In other cases, a fight must be fought; it took Makk and his studio more than five years to get permission to film Love. And then, there is always a possibility that a film project will be approved, the script will be developed, the shooting will take place, and maybe even the final editing will be completed—as with The Witness—but the finished film will be shelved by the judgment of a higher authority; for it is still true that the Ministry of Culture has final say on whether or not a film is fit for distribution.[38]

The process whereby a project is first proposed, then scripted, cast, shot, edited, and distributed involves consultations and even negotiations at every step, and at every step the filmmaker can be asked to make changes. This may seem intrusive, but in actuality the process is analogous to the Hollywood system except that the large commercial studio is replaced by a small noncommercial unit, the bankrolling producer is replaced by employees of the state, and the priority of commercialism is replaced by a mix of political and aesthetic judgments. Few Hungarian film artists, it appears, would trade their system for Hollywood's, despite the apparent advantage of Hollywood money.[39]

That hardly means the Hungarian system has no problems. Lacking a firm commercial base, the Hungarian cinema relies on subsidies from the state. The national budget has been under severe pressure during most of the eighties, and the film industry has been obliged to take its share of the cuts. MAFILM, which produced only twenty films in an average year during the seventies, has reduced its annual output to as few as sixteen. Similar cuts have hit Pannonia, a studio for documentary and animated films, and the Béla Balázs Studio, where young filmmakers fresh out of film school have an opportunity to practice their skills.

In the atmosphere of persistently tightening budgets, filmmakers have often sought international coproduction contracts, hoping to have the best of two worlds—the artistic freedom of their own country and the legendary bankrolls of the West. Jancsó enjoyed a modest success by working in Italy during the seventies, and Szabó has had a tremendous experience with both *Mephisto* and *Colonel Redl*. But it is not so easy. Mészáros's coproductions have not done well commercially or critically, Makk's *Lily in Love* was not successful, and less well-known Hungarians find it very difficult to sell their talents abroad.

Some, like Pál Gábor, have learned just how dangerous the risks of coproduction can be. Gábor, whose personal style made *Angi Vera* the international success it was, snapped at the lure of an American coproduction to direct *Brady's Escape*, also known as *The Long Ride* (*A hosszú vágta*, 1983). Suddenly he was no auteur but the employee of a producer. The script, by William Lewis, is about an American airman, J.T. Brady (John Savage), whose plane is shot down over Hungary in 1944. Forced to parachute, Brady gets away from the Nazis because the horsemen of the Hortobágy *puszta*, decked out in their colorful tourist-show costumes, consider the occupying Germans as much of an enemy as Brady does. The script is a catalogue of silver-screen clichés, culminating in the predictable escape of the American hero while the natives, obviously expendable, die like so many Comanches. Gábor, whose strength as a director lies in understatement, had not only to work with an overly sentimental Hollywood script, but also to use an American musical score and submit to American editing, surrendering the final cut to the American producer. The resulting movie was a disaster, good for nothing but late-night American television.

So what lies ahead? This question is on the minds of many cineastes. Some, like Miklós Jancsó, look back with nostalgia to the sixties, when Hungarian films captured so much world attention in a day when few small countries fielded notable cinematic teams. Today, the phenomenon of small-country cinema is not so unusual; the world knows quality films from places as far flung as Bolivia, Tunisia, and Hong Kong. Hungarian cinema, lost amid the crowd, no longer commands the respect it once enjoyed.[40]

Besides the now-chronic financial crisis, two major questions confront Hungarian filmmakers. The first concerns subject matter. Hungarian cinema, as the foregoing discussion makes clear, has always looked inward, drawing its themes primarily from the Hungarian experience. At their best, Hungarian films are capable of projecting that experience in ways that engage the world audience, but many films—including many good films—plainly do not interest foreigners. Most filmmakers consider it their primary responsibility to produce for the domestic audience (this is as it should be), but they also long to tell their stories and communicate their messages to the wider world. How can they do this without falling into the trap of *Brady's Escape*?

The second question concerns originality of form. Every film culture in the world feels the impact of Hollywood, whose technical virtuosity and glitzy style appeal to all audiences. Hollywood offers a Faustian bargain: popularity and fame in return for the artist's soul—that is, access to mass audiences through "professional" scripts and formulaic narrative structures. If Hungarian filmmakers are to attract international attention, must they adapt their styles to mimic the Hollywood look?

Some Hungarian critics charge István Szabó with just this offense, arguing that his move to big-money West German coproductions coincided with his retreat from formal experimentalism toward a greater realism. (At the time of this writing, Szabó was involved in the early stages of an American coproduction.) In fairness, it must be reiterated that *Mephisto* and *Colonel Redl* show a great deal of originality, even if their narrative lines have a conventional look.

The same critics point to examples like *The Fall* (*Zuhanás közben*, 1987), the debut film of Tamás Tolmár (b. 1950), in which they see the dangers of the Hollywood influence. *The Fall* is a big-city crime story filled with violence and climaxing with a car chase—a movie that appeals to mass tastes but, in the eyes of the critics, betrays the aesthetic purpose of Hungarian film. The critics fear that continuing financial pressures may push MAFILM more toward productions of this sort for the mass market, and they see it as their task to prevent this tendency from dominating the future of Hungarian cinema.

The critics are doing their job, but perhaps they exaggerate the danger. Hollywood presents not only a threat but also an alternative. Péter Gárdos, for example, admits to a Hollywood influence,[41] and his *Whooping Cough* demonstrates that the style can be employed to tell a Hungarian story—and tell it well. The same can be said about the recent films of János Rózsa (b. 1937). Rózsa's *Love, Mother* (*Csók, anyu*, 1986), was cowinner of the jury's main prize at the 1987 Hungarian Film Festival, indicating that some critics have an open mind on the question of the Hollywood style.

At the same time, the work of such promising younger directors as Gyula Gazdag, Péter Gothár, and András Jeles continues to resist any Hollywood tendencies. Moreover, the Budapest Academy of Theater and Film Art and the Béla Balázs Studio, the most important institutions that train Hungarian filmmakers, still encourage experimentalism as a way for future *auteurs* to develop their own styles.

In this context, and at least for the time being, the Hollywood threat does not loom large. The Hungarian cinema in the late eighties retains its pluralism and carries on its bold inquiries into Hungarian themes.

NOTES

The author gratefully acknowledges the support of the National Endowment for the Humanities and the generous assistance of Hungarofilm. He also thanks the American Philosophical Society for a supplementary grant during an early stage of his research. A word of personal thanks is due to János Huszár, and especially to Éva Kun and Katalin Vajda, for their always cheerful help, and to Anamária Róna for expert translating assistance.

1. A curious thing sometimes happens to the title when a Hungarian film goes into American distribution. In this case, the original title, more accurately translated as "The Hopeless Ones" or "Outlaws," was abandoned for one deemed to be more "catchy" and bearing a cultural reference that Americans would readily understand. Jancsó's films have been especially vulnerable to retitling in translation, probably because many of the original titles carry a culturally specific meaning; examples are *My Way Home* (*Így jöttem*, or, roughly, "Thus I Came," 1967), *Confrontation* (*Fényes szelek*, "Luminous Winds," 1968), and *Red Psalm* (*Még kér a nép*, "The People Are Still Asking," 1971). Though many of the titles discussed in this chapter have been significantly changed from Hungarian to English, I shall call the reader's attention only to those retitlings that are particularly amusing.

2. For a number of years Jancsó and Mészáros were married. Their son, Miklós Jancsó, Jr., is now a talented cinematographer who has directed the photography for Mészáros's two recent films, *Diary for My Children* (*Napló gyermekeimnek*, 1981/1984) and *Diary for My Loves* (*Napló szerelmeimnek*, 1987). The author adds this not to spread gossip but to illustrate the closeness of the Hungarian filmmaking community in which such a wide range of styles and approaches coexist.

3. The Hungarian title means approximately "King, Give Me Some Soldiers!"

4. Mira and Antonín J. Liehm, *The Most Important Art: East European Film after 1945* (Berkeley, Los Angeles, and London: University of California Press, 1977), p. 146.

5. *The Most Important Art*, p. 168.

6. *Cantata* was Jancsó's second feature. His first, *The Bells Have Gone to Rome* (*A harangok Rómába mentek*, 1958), was not particularly successful and was followed by several more years of working on documentaries and shorts.

7. For more detailed discussion of Hungarian film between 1945–1960, see Liehm and Liehm, *The Most Important Art*, pp. 146–73 and Graham Petrie, *History Must Answer to Man: The Contemporary Hungarian Cinema* (Budapest: Corvina Kiádó and London: Tantivy Press, 1978), pp. 1–20.

8. Of course, it might be argued that anti-Stalinist films, now common in Hungary, are in fact pro-regime films because the current regime has so strongly disas-

sociated itself from the policies of the Rákosi period. Contemporary filmmakers who continue to focus on the injustices of the fifties sometimes come under attack by Hungarian critics who consider it easy to take pot shots at the past and would prefer to see more contemporary problems portrayed on the screen.

9. The films just mentioned, as well as the subject of "Hungarity," will be discussed below.

10. O.W. Riegel, "What Is 'Hungarian' in the Hungarian Cinema (Part III)," *New Hungarian Quarterly* 18 (65) (Spring 1977), p. 208.

11. For a detailed discussion of István Gaál's films, see Petrie, *History Must Answer to Man,* pp. 138–74; cf. Liehm and Liehm, *The Most Important Art,* pp. 387–88, 401–402, and Eric Koopmanschap, *De Hongaarse Film* (Netherlands: Den Bosch, 1983), p. 51.

12. Liehm and Liehm, *The Most Important Art,* p. 166.

13. Interview with the author, February 26, 1987.

14. The foregoing *Red Psalm* sequence is described in detail by Roy Armes in *The Ambiguous Image* (Bloomington, IN and London: Indiana University Press, 1976), p. 152; the *Confrontation* sequence is described by Petrie in *History Must Answer to Man,* pp. 94–95.

15. By the mid-seventies, one critic—even without having seen *Private Vices*—expressed "irritation with [Jancsó's] symbol codifications, his manneristic style, the deliberate mystification, the endless marches and counter-marches, the casual killings, the obligatory nudes and horses, the hermetic never-never land of parading zombies." O.W. Riegel, "What Is 'Hungarian' in the Hungarian Cinema (Part II)," *New Hungarian Quarterly* 17 (64) (Winter, 1976), p. 207. For a spirited defense of Jancsó's work during the seventies, see Petrie, "Miklós Jancsó: Decline and Fall?" in David W. Paul, ed., *Politics, Art and Commitment in the East European Cinema* (London: Macmillan, and New York: St. Martin's Press, 1983), pp. 189–210.

16. Full title of the film is *The Tyrant's Heart, or Boccaccio in Hungary.* On its reception at the 1982 New York Film Festival, see, e.g., Janet Maslin's brief but scathing review in *The New York Times,* October 4, 1982, p. C14, and E. Stein's laudatory remarks in *Film Comment* 18 (6) (November–December, 1982), p. 68.

17. For discussions of Szabó's career to the mid-seventies, see Petrie, *History Must Answer to Man,* pp. 106–37; also Karen Jaehne, "István Szabó: Dreams of Memories," *Film Quarterly* 32 (1) (Fall, 1978), pp. 30–41.

18. Perhaps, by stretching the allusions, the story can be said to be about emigration and separation more generally, but its specifically Hungarian references nevertheless dominate.

19. "A Dream About a House," for which Szabó won the Main Prize at the Oberhausen Short Film Festival in 1972, is often shown by itself. The present author has not seen the other films in the series.

20. Petrie, (*History Must Answer to Man,* pp. 226–27) has pointed out that *Budapest Tales* contains allegorical references to specific Hungarian events between 1945 and 1956. I do not disagree, but my reading of the film is that it can be interpreted on many levels; accordingly, one can see it as a statement on reconstruction, political conflict, and the abuse of power in Hungary or as a study of community-building in something like a state of nature. The latter perspective is argued by Jaehne, "István Szabó," pp. 37–40. The film's title (which can also be translated as "Budapest Fables") suggests that Szabó had both intentions in mind.

21. Interview with the author, September 25, 1985; published in *Columbia Film View* 1 (2) (Winter, 1985), p. 4.

22. Ibid., p. 5.

23. Interview with J. Hoberman, *Village Voice,* November 6, 1984. One West-

erner who admires Mészáros's feminism but criticizes the quality of her films is Petrie, *History Must Answer to Man*, pp. 211–13, 228–33.

24. Sometimes a translation of the Hungarian title, "The Two of Them," is used to refer to this film in English, though it is distributed in the United States under the title "Women."

25. I am told that television programs commemorating the thirtieth anniversary of the 1956 revolt in the autumn of 1986 had made cautious mention of Nagy while airing similar newsreel clips.

26. Perhaps it is Director Mészáros's intent to portray her heroine as an observer, assuming the "objective" position of the young film student's camera, but, with the exception of only one or two scenes, the effect is to minimize the film's emotionality for no good reason.

27. Interview with the author, Budapest, September 25, 1985.

28. It should be said that Bacsó has directed more than twenty features, most of which I have not seen. Many of his earlier films were serious rather than comical or tragicomic and, according to Petrie, tended toward the style of cinéma vérité. See Petrie, *History Must Answer to Man*, pp. 187–89; also Koopmanschap, *De Hongaarse Film*, p. 50.

29. Hungarian title "The Devil Is Beating His Wife."

30. Hungarian title "Oh My God."

31. Interview with the author, September 28, 1985.

32. A Gazdag retrospective was shown at the Museum of Modern Art in New York and the Pacific Film Archive in Berkeley during the spring of 1987; one hopes more American screenings will follow.

33. This apparently corresponds to the facts about the Transylvanian principality, which tends to be idealized in Hungarian popular history. But, as an emigrant Hungarian writer has described Transylvania, "Her independence was limited, and her liberalism ambiguous." Paul Ignotus, *Hungary* (New York and Washington: Praeger, 1972), p. 36.

34. The citation was taken from a poem, "Hungarians," by Attila József (1905–1937).

35. Riegel, "What Is 'Hungarian'. . . ," (Part I), *New Hungarian Quarterly* 17 (63) (Autumn 1976), pp. 185–93.

36. It is not possible to do justice to this extraordinary film in a brief description. For a detailed discussion, see Petrie, *History Must Answer to Man*, pp. 158–67.

37. However, the irrepressible Péter Bacsó dreams of filming a tragicomedy about 1956, as indicated in an interview with this author (September 25, 1985).

38. For a brief explanation of the process by which a film is made, see Daniel Bickley, "Socialism and Humanism: The Contemporary Hungarian Cinema," *Cineaste* 9 (2) (1978–79), pp. 32–33.

39. In a conversation with the author (September 28, 1985), Zsolt Kézdi-Kovács, who is very familiar with the American cinema, expressed what numerous other Hungarian directors have also stated or implied when asked to compare their filmmaking milieu with that of the United States: "The kinds of films we make [in Hungary] are made [in the U.S.] with so little money, and in such unfavorable conditions of distribution and so on, that they haven't a chance to compete with the big films." Kézdi-Kovács admires American independent filmmakers like Jim Jarmusch and John Hanson who work against the odds of their native film culture.

40. Interview with Jancsó, February 26, 1987.

41. Interview, February 15, 1987.

6

Bulgaria:
The Cinema of Poetics

Ronald Holloway

Although Bulgarian cinema hardly catches the eye in North America, it has been known to enliven audiences at several ranking European film festivals. At the 1983 Venice festival, Vesselin Branev's *Hotel Central* (*Hotel Tsentral*, 1983) was hailed by knowledgeable critics as a discovery. Branev was making his debut as a feature film director, a fifty-one-year-old debutant who already had a distinguished career behind him as a screenwriter and and director of telefeatures.

Bulgarian animation is world class. No one attending the 1985 Varna World Animated Film Festival was surprised to see Donyo Donev's feature-length *We Called Them Montagues and Capulets* (*Narekohme gi Monteki i Kapuleti*, 1985) win the first prize in its category. Donev is a recognized master of the philosophical parable, honed in the traditions of Bulgarian folklore. Indeed, Bulgarian animation ranks high among the singularly progressive national cinematographies in Eastern Europe in this field.

At the recent tribute to Eastern European Cinema at the 1987 Pesaro festival (which offered a valuable cross-reference on what is going on in socialist production studios today), Rumyana Petkova's *Coming Down to Earth* (*Prizemyavé*, 1985) was recognized as a forthright feminist statement made by a collective of women filmmaking talent. That film alone exemplifies that the concerns of women in socialist countries on fundamental issues are no different than those of their counterparts in the West.

Bulgaria is often referred to as "the Prussia of the Balkans." It is a land of culture and traditions. As a country on the crossroads between Europe and Asia, it tends to absorb and reflect rather than promote or flaunt its own unique national character. One has to spend some time in Sofia, visit the rural communities, and partake of various festive celebrations to grasp the depth of its cinematic expression.

There have been two major periods of astonishing growth and maturity in Bulgarian cinema. The first occurred in the late fifties and lasted until the early sixties. It was a cinema of poetics, elements that have character-

215

ized the best in this national cinematography from practically the beginning. The second took place in the early seventies and continued to the series of epic productions celebrating the thirteen-hundredth anniversary of the founding of the Bulgarian nation in 1981. The cost alone of producing a series of super-spectacles induced a subsequent cutback within the film industry that was to affect it both aesthetically and commercially. This study will focus only on the second major period of Bulgarian cinema.

FIRST IMPRESSIONS

When I paid my first visit to Bulgaria—to the Varna Festival of Bulgarian Feature Films—in September 1969, the screenings were mostly in a modest outdoor arena for the general public, some Black Sea tourists, and a handful of selected foreign critics. But the opportunity to meet the country's leading film directors over the span of a week in easy-going surroundings made the invitation worthwhile.

The first Bulgarian film revival (1956–65) had followed pretty much the general course of the "thaw" during the post-Stalin years and the Krushchev era. One general director of Bulgarian film succeeded another in rapid succession during these questioning times: Alexander Dunchev (1965–67), Georgi Karamanev (1967–68), Filip Filipov (1968–69), and now, at the time of my visit, Hristo Santov (1969–71). The leading director in the country, Rangel Vulchanov, had practically given up feature filmmaking to work on documentaries. Binka Zhelyazkova's *The Attached Balloon (Privarzaniyat balon*, 1967) had been withdrawn from distribution shortly after its release and was thereafter relegated to the shelf until the present day. Three other feature films from this period were also on the shelf: Hristo Piskov's and Irina Aktasheva's *Monday Morning (Ponedelnik sutrin*, 1966), Lyubomir Sharlandjiev's *The Prosecutor (Prokurorat*, 1968), and Eduard Zahariev's *The Sky over the Veleka (Nebeto na Veleka*, 1968).

Still, there was much to get interested in. The first impressions need not only be related to the art of the cinema. Bulgaria is, after all, an archaeological trove: the tombs of the Proto-Thracians were being unearthed in the immediate vicinity of Varna, and diggings have been going on for over a decade at the nearby ancient Bulgarian capitals of Pliska and Preslav. Even more impressive are the restored examples of early Christian architecture at the peninsular city of Nesebur on the Black Sea coast. Many famous cloisters are but a short drive away, each significant for the preservation of Old Slavonic icons and manuscripts dating back to the ninth century.

Needless to say, in view of these outside but related interests, I was fascinated by one of the films in the Varna festival: Todor Dinov's and Hristo

Hristov's *Iconostasis* (*Ikonostasat*, 1969). For even though its narrative line was heavily theatrical—based on Dimiter Talev's *The Iron Candle-stick* (published in 1952) and set during the period of the Bulgarian Renaissance (the late nineteenth century under the Turkish Occupation)—its affinity to Andrei Tarkovsky's *Andrei Rublev* (1966, released 1969/71) was unmistakable. Indeed, the spiritual agonies suffered by the woodcarver, Rafe, in *Iconostasis* paralleled those of the great Russian icon painter in *Andrei Rublev* in thematic expression if not narrative content. And since Tarkovsky's film prompted a walkout at the Cannes festival by the Soviet delegation in May 1969, the appearance of this film only a few months later in a Bulgarian showcase stirred speculation among foreign critics. *Iconostasis* marked the beginning of a new era in contemporary Bulgarian cinema.

THE ARTIST SEEKS A WAY

In a cinema of poetics an artist can find his intended audience via the image rather than the word. This had happened in Bulgarian cinema. Back in 1956, two projects were approved by the State Committee for Cinematography: Rangel Vulchanov's *On a Small Island* (*Na malkiya ostrov*, 1958) and Binka Zhelyazkova and Hristo Ganev's *Partisans* (*Partizani*, never released), also known as *Life Flows Quietly By* (*Zhivotat si teche tiho*). Both films were completed approximately at the same time, but the Zhelyazkova/Ganev project immediately triggered heated discussion.

The theme of Partisan-heroes-turned-political-careerists was not new to socialist cinema at this time, but the more metaphorical and decisively poetic *On a Small Island* was considered more appropriate for release—even though the latter also blatantly circumvented the tenets of socialist realism. Although *Partisans* has yet to be seen to be properly appraised, the parallel projects can be viewed as two sides of the same coin. This is not to say that Rangel Vulchanov and his screenplay writer, Valeri Petrov, would escape running afoul of the authorities themselves. After two more poetic statements—*First Lesson* (*Parvi urok*, 1960) and *Sun and Shadow* (*Slantseto i syankata*, 1962)—the collaboration between the country's leading poet and Bulgarian cinema's most gifted director was brought to a forced close.

But the seeds of a poetic cinema had been sown. The tradition was to continue in other films: Konrad Wolf's *Stars* (*Zdezdi/Sterne*, 1959), an East German-Bulgarian coproduction; Binka Zhelyazkova's *We Were Young* (*A byahme mladi*, 1961), scripted again by Hristo Ganev; Vulo Radev's *Peach Thief* (*Kradetsat na praskovi*, 1964), costarring Nevena Kokanova and Rade Marković (respectively one of Bulgaria's and one of Yugoslavia's most popular actors); and Borislav Sharaliev's *Knight without Honor* (*Ritsar bez bronya*, 1966), a children's film scripted by Valeri

Petrov. And it was to surface again in Binka Zhelyazkova's *The Attached Balloon* (1967), scripted by one of Bulgaria's outstanding writers, Yordan Radichkov.

Thus, with the appearance of *Iconostasis* in 1969, a tradition of a national poetic cinema was confirmed again despite stylistic flaws by a pair of debut directors, Todor Dinov from the field of animation and Hristo Hristov from the theater. An allegory on the times, the story itself sketched in broad terms the dilemma facing the committed film artist whose projects have to be approved by bureaucrats committed to the staid formula of socialist realism in the scenario. A visual breath-of-life is particularly felt at the moment when the discouraged icon-painter, during the last days of the Ottoman occupation when a revival in Bulgarian arts and literature is badly needed, enters the Bachkovo Monastery near Plovdiv to receive inspiration from the frescoes painted on the refectory walls back in 1606.

A NEW START

Pavel Pissarev entered the picture as the new General Director of the Bulgarian State Cinematography in 1971. His appearance on the scene coincided with a short feature made by a talented graduate of the Moscow

VI–1   *Iconostasis*

Film School (VGIK): Georgi Djulgerov's *The Test* (*Izpit*), the second part of the omnibus film *Colorful World* (*Sharen svyat*, 1971). Both Djulgerov's film and Milan Nikolov's *Naked Conscience* (*Gola suvest*) were based on tales by Nikolai Haitov, a rural writer who took his stories from the legends of the Rhodope Mountains and the realities of simple peasant life. It is the moral tone in *The Test* that makes it a standout.

Unlike the socially engaged films that went before it, *The Test* does not preach. The film is about an individual wrestling with his own fate and following the dictates of his own conscience; it is not immersed in the polemics of a hero struggling for the greater good of the working class. Further, the story could have taken place anywhere at any time. Indeed, Djulgerov had made this very film twice over—first as a graduate film (*The Cooper*, 1969) at VGIK set in Armenia, and now as a debut director for Bulgariafilm looking for sources of inspiration in his own national traditions.

Although *The Test* skirted sociopolitical issues, two other films made at the end of the sixties, Grisha Ostrovski and Todor Stoyanov's *Sidetrack* (*Otklonenie*, 1967) and Metodi Andonov's *The White Room* (*Byalata staya*, 1968), offered "between-the-lines" statements on the ill effects of Stalinism and the Personality Cult. Their aim was a reckoning with the past in metaphoric or parabolic terms; by dealing with the issues at hand in this manner, the viewer had to decipher the message for himself. Also, Georgi Stoyanov's *Birds and Greyhounds* (*Ptitsi i hratki*, 1969) was noteworthy for attempting to offer a different perspective on teenaged resistance to fascism in a provincial village at the outbreak of the Second World War, but overall this amounted to a minor effort.

The beginning of the seventies heralded a breakthrough for native thematic material in Bulgarian cinema. Just as writers-scriptwriters Angel Wagenstein and Valeri Petrov set standards at the birth of a postwar national cinema, a new breed of storytellers drew inspiration directly from the lives of the people and the handed-down legends of times past. Among these were Nikolai Haitov, Yordan Radichkov, and Georgi Mishev.

Pavel Pissarev, as the new General Director answering to Cultural Minister Lyudmila Shivkova, inaugurated the new start in 1971 by dividing the state film industry into three independent production units, Haemus, Mladost, and Sredets—with a fourth one, Suvremenik, added in 1978. The filmmakers had now to answer principally to themselves and their artistic directors at the Boyana Studios (located a short driving distance from Sofia at the foot of Mount Vitosha). He also supported the founding of the Sofia Film Academy (VITIS) in 1973.

A commercial success confirmed the foresight of these structural changes almost immediately. Metodi Andonov's *The Goat Horn* (*Koziyat roz*, 1972), based on a Haitov story, was seen by more Bulgarians than any other national film production before or since. A tale of revenge set during the long reign of the Turkish occupation, the film attracted a vast audience primarily because it was a good simple story well told, with reference to a long-gone past still familiar to every viewer from childhood experiences at the family hearth. *The Goat Horn* did not find as enthusiastic response abroad as at home, but it did encourage a national cinema to look to its own audience for indices of production values.

In the same year, another film was made that proved to be even more integral to a maturing socialist cinema: Hristo Hristov's *The Last Summer* (*Posledno lyato*, 1972; released 1974), based on a story by Yordan Radichkov. On the surface, *The Last Summer* records the plight of a villager who refuses to abandon his traditional family home to settle elsewhere just as a newly constructed dam causes everything around him that he holds dear to disappear under the waters of a new man-made lake. The film is more than just a human drama; it is also a social analysis of village-to-town migration with all the ramifications that a newly formed industrial society must reckon. Further, the primitive free spirit of the film's hero gives way gradually to visionary surrealistic fantasies and stream-of-consciousness poetic passages alien to the usual socially engaged theme of this type. The film was shelved for two years before release—and when it was finally released in a cut version in 1974, critical themes of this nature were becoming more common.

More signs of a revival could be noted in the children's film genre and films for youth. Dimiter Petrov's *Porcupines Are Born Without Bristles* (*Taralezhite se razhdat bez bodli*, 1971) featured three novellas scripted by the Mormarev brothers, who over the years were to play a major role— together with directors Dimiter Petrov and Ivanka Grubcheva—in honing the specialized children's film to a fine art. Lyudmil Kirkov's *A Boy Becomes a Man* (*Momcheto si otiva*, 1972) also marked the beginning of a fruitful collaboration between a socially engaged director and a storyteller whose theme of integrity in an alien society made both his books and his screenplays popular entertainment among the masses. It was not long before Bulgarian cinema was internationally recognized for its unique and peculiar "Balkan" merits.

THE PAVEL PISSAREV YEARS

For approximately a decade between 1971 and 1980, during which time Pavel Pissarev served as General Director of Bulgariafilm, an era of prosperity descended upon the Boyana Studios that has not been seen before or since. Quite likely, the magic of the moment was ultimately due to the forthcoming thirteen-hundredth anniversary celebrations in 1981, for which the state shelled out millions in leva for cultural events and programming.

VI–2   *A Boy Becomes a Man (Momcheto si otiva)*

To honor the official anniversary of the founding of the Bulgarian state (20 October 1981), several traveling art exhibits and touring performance groups were scheduled in Western Europe, North and South America, and elsewhere around the world. Indeed, the Thracian Gold Exhibit was underway for more than a decade without returning home at all, while the same was true of the religious treasures—manuscripts, icons, religious vessels—preserved in the Rila Monastery. Theater, choral and orchestral performances, and a "Festival of Bulgarian Films" became common events abroad.

To breathe new life into a faltering national cinema, Pissarev worked closely with the newly elected First Secretary of Bulgarian Filmmakers, Hristo Hristov, whose own *Iconostasis* (1969) and *Hammer or Anvil* (*Nakovalnya ili chuk*, 1972)—an epic on the Leipzig Trial of 1933 and Georgi Dimitrov, coproduced by the Soviet Union and the German Democratic Republic—had thrust him into the foreground of the nation's directorial ranks. Hristov responded by both directing and creating the set design for the surrealist fantasy, *The Last Summer* (1972/74), a controversial film based on Yordan Radichkov's sociocritical novella (published in 1965). A milestone in contemporary Bulgarian cinema, it is arguably his best film.

The international film festivals responded almost immediately to the new line of artistic creativity emanating from the Boyana Studios. Lyudmil Staikov's *Affection* (*Obich*, 1972) won a Gold Prize at the 1973 Moscow Film Festival. Binka Zhelyazkova's *The Last Word* (*Poslednata*, 1973) was invited to participate in Cannes as an official entry. Festival invitations poured in for Eduard Zahariev's *The Hare Census* (*Prebroyavane na divite zaytsi*, 1973) and *Villa Zone* (*Vilna zona*, 1975), satires made in collaboration with Georgi Mishev; and his *Manly Times* (*Muzhki vremena*, 1977), based on a Nikolai Haitov story, won the Grand Prix at the 1978 New Delhi festival. That same year, Georgi Djulgerov won a Silver Bear for best direction at Berlin for *Advantage* (*Avantazh*, 1977).

Another welcome sign was the return of Rangel Vulchanov to form. After collaborating with Valeri Petrov again on *With Love and Tenderness* (*S lyubov i nezhnost*, 1978), parodying the purveyors of artistic taste and trendsetting, he pulled a script out of the drawer that had been lying there for fifteen years to make the nostalgic, bittersweet *The Unknown Soldier's Patent Leather Shoes* (*Lachenite obouvki na neznainiya voin*, 1979); it was chosen to open the London Film Festival.

Further, standards were set at children's film festivals throughout the seventies. Ivanka Grubcheva's *Exams at Any Odd Time* (*Izpiti po nikoe vreme*, 1974) and *With Nobody* (*Pri nikogo*, 1975), in particular, and also Rashko Ouzunov's *Talisman* (1978), were popular favorites. Bulgarian animation was hailed among the world's wittiest when the philosophical fables of Donyo Donev were singled out for an honorary retrospective at the 1979 Oberhausen Short Film Festival.

Young talent graduated from VITIS, the Sofia Film and Theater Academy, to make remarkable debut features during the late seventies: Kiran Kolarov's *Status: Orderly* (*Slouzhebno polozheniye: ordinarets*, 1978), Yevgeni Mihailov's *Home for Lonely Souls* (*Dom za nezhni doushi*, 1981), Ognyan Gelinov's *The Flying Machine* (*Letaloto*, 1981), Ivan Pavlov's *Mass Miracle* (*Massovo choudo*, 1981), and Rumyana Petkova's *Reflections* (*Otrazhenia*, 1982). For the first time, promising directors of theater and cinema did not have to journey abroad for their studies, for in Sofia their own teachers—Vulchanov, Djulgerov, Hristov—numbered among the best in socialist cinema.

Under Pissarev a filmmaker took full responsibility for his handling of approved thematic content. Rangel Vulchanov's *The Inspector and the Forest* (*Sledovatelyat i dorata*, 1975) made use of actual criminal records to expose a prostitution ring operating in the capital. Lyudmil Kirkov's *Matriarchate* (*Matriarhat*, 1977) expressed open doubts about abandoned villages peopled solely by women taking care of collective farms while their men preferred working in urban factories for long stretches. Ivan Andonov's *The Cherry Orchard* (*Chereshova gradina*, 1979) went even further by pitting an honest forester in a losing moral fight against a crooked di-

VI–3   *Matriarchate (Matriarhat)*

rector of a farm cooperative. Hristo Hristov's *The Truck* (*Kamionat*, 1980) and *A Woman at Thirty-Three* (*Edna zhena na trideset*, 1982) went so far in citing social ills that both films have received only limited release up to the present.

Pissarev's legacy, however, was the striking series of historical epics produced for the thirteen-hundredth anniversary year of 1981, some of them not fully completed until four years later. By Western standards, these super-spectacles would have cost a small fortune. Entire armies were conscripted to play extras in mass-orchestrated battle scenes; fortresses were built and costumes prepared to match originals; and all was photographed on Eastman-Kodak to assure archival longevity.

Taken together, these spectacles offer a picture-book review of Bulgarian history: Zahari Zhandov's *Master of Boyana* (*Boyanskiyat maistor*, 1981), Lyudmil Stalkov's *Khan Asparukh* (1981), Georgi Djulgerov's *Measure for Measure* (*Mera spored mera*, 1981), Georgi Stoyanov's *Constantine the Philosopher* (*Konstantin filosof*, 1983), and Borislav Sharaliev's *Boris the First* (*Boris purvi*, 1984). Save for the first named, each was conceived for release in two or three parts, and they all endeavor to render historical conflicts in distinctly modern terms. Even though the foreign critic may yell enough is enough upon seeing one of the epics, one cannot but be impressed by the desire of an entire people to relive on the screen the glories of the past— particularly as the Bulgarians had suffered under the Turkish yoke for five hundred years.

MEASURING A PAST HERITAGE

One of the four selected monuments set aside for UNESCO-sponsored preservation in Bulgaria is the Boyana Church near Sofia. No one knows who painted the frescoes in this royal chapel in 1259, but they are exemplary of the Turnovo School. They also anticipated Cimabue and Giotto a full generation later. One can therefore assume that Boyana is a key, indeed an essential bridge, between the rigid formula of the Byzantine icon and the humanism of the Italian Renaissance.

This historical footnote does not make a film. Zahari Zhandov's *Master of Boyana* (1981) leaves much to be desired as an integral work of cinematic art. However, that the film could be made at all in a socialist country wary of its own rich religious traditions speaks for itself—as well as for those officials in high government positions who allowed a project of this sort (together with others relating to the same religious heritage) to get off the ground in the first place. By way of comparison, the Soviet Union will be facing the same dilemma in 1988, when the millenium of Russia's conversion to Christianity will fall under similar artistic and cultural scrutiny.

Zhandov was undoubtedly the right Bulgarian film director to make *Master of Boyana*. He was one of the newsreel veterans who filmed the liberation of Sofia in September 1944, who later won several international prizes for documentaries about the land and its people in the immediate postwar years, and who directed the country's first major, artistically successful feature film: *Alarm* (*Trevoga*, 1951). Thirty years to the day after *Alarm*'s premiere—on 9 March 1981—*Master of Boyana* was presented in the headquarters of the Union of Bulgarian Filmmakers in Sofia. Although the screenplay had been written long ago (together with Yevgeni Konstantinov), the project had been approved only recently. The film was the first to celebrate the thirteen-hundredth anniversary.

In an interview, Zhandov himself admitted to two outside influences in the conception of *Master of Boyana*. His wife, an archaeologist and art historian, brought to the project a broad knowledge of the treasures still being unearthed, artifacts relating to the First Bulgarian Kingdom (681-1018) and the Second Bulgarian Kingdom (1186-1395). These helped to fortify certain fictional elements about the life and personality of the Boyana painter. The second influence was his friendship with the Georgian-Armenian director, Sergei Paradzhanov, whose own personal commitment to national religious traditions led to an open confrontation with Soviet authorities and imprisonment for his artistic beliefs. Georgian traditions, according to Zhandov, bear a direct relationship to Bulgarian.

Thus, in a sense, *Master of Boyana* prepared the way for the succeeding films dealing with the cultural and religious heritage of the country—particularly Georgi Stoyanov's *Constantine the Philosopher* (1983) and Borislav Sharaliev's *Boris the First* (1984). The very fact that both of these films were released long after the anniversary of the nation's founding attests to a measure of difficulty encountered in approving and distributing these films. Further, the untimely death of Bulgaria's cultural minister, Lyudmila Shivkova, in the very midst of the 1981 celebrations, added to the uncertainties plaguing Bulgarian cinema in general throughout the present decade.

Constantine the Philosopher deals with the conversion of the Slavs to Christianity. It is the story of the Greek missionaries Cyril (Constantine) and Methodius, who as monks journeyed first to Moravia and then to Bulgaria (the actual conversion in 864-65 taking place under their disciples). Cyril-Constantine (827-69) made his impact on history as a philosopher in the Byzantine court, succeeding the patriarch Photius as the head of the university's philosophy department in Constantinople while still in his twenties. Stoyanov's coverage of these years in Constantinople faced few outside hindrances of any kind. While shooting the second part, however, which dealt with the actual missionary activities, he found his proj-

VI–4   *Constantine the Philosopher (Konstantin filosof)*

ect stalled due to the untimely death of the cultural minister. For a time, in fact, the entire project ended up on the shelf.

Although reports conflict as to what exactly took place after the completion of the first part, a final decision was made to release the entire epic only as a television event for the national population. Subsequent requests from abroad to view the film as a theatrical production have met with little response. Many observers feel that the issue will be reviewed again in 1988, when Russia celebrates its own anniversary year. Indeed, the very question of the millenium celebrations of the conversion of Slavic peoples to Christianity is a controversial one among exponents of orthodox Marxist ideology. It has posed a problem to Poland and Czechoslovakia in the past, and now the Soviet Union is next in line. Bulgaria plays a key role in these ongoing discussions simply because the missionary spirit and subsequent Slavonic Orthodox liturgy emanated from Bulgaria. For this reason historians and political commentators have made it a point to visit the Rila Cloister in Bulgaria (near Sofia) and the Church of St. Clement in Ohrid in the Macedonian Republic of Yugoslavia (near Skopje) during the present decade to examine the roots of the dilemma.

As for Borislav Sharaliev's *Boris the First*, the question of Khan Boris's conversion to Christianity (in either 864 or 865) was narrowed down in the screenplay to a power struggle between the retiring khan and his wayward son, Vladimir, the latter preferring the principles of traditional Bulgarian paganism over suspect alliances with Orthodox Byzantium. Sharaliev, together with screenwriter Angel Wagenstein, treated the theme primarily in the context of a moral conflict. That in itself would have been sufficient to raise the film above the average, save that the director concentrated all his energies on the epic dimensions of costumes, action, and battle scenes. Further, one key personality is conspicuously absent from the story, and that is Simeon, Vladimir's brother, who left his monastic training in Constantinople to return to the ancient Bulgarian capital of Pliska to ascend the throne. Later, Simeon was to launch, at his own capital at Preslav, the Golden Age of the First Bulgarian Kingdom within the cultural tradition of a new Slavonic Christianity modeled on that of Byzantium.

These three films—*Master of Boyana, Constantine the Philosopher,* and *Boris the First* deserve, with all their faults, a special place in the history of Bulgarian cinema. Thematically, it is inconceivable that any of them would have been produced in this country up to a decade before, and it is only due to the occasion of the anniversary year that they have been attempted at all.

YARDSTICKS TO HISTORY

On the 20th of October, 1981 (the original day of the year an arbitrary one), Bulgaria celebrated its thirteen-hundredth anniversary as a state.

The usual festivities, complete with fireworks, marked the occasion, but the key cultural event was the national release of a film: Lyudmil Staikov's three-part epic, *Khan Asparukh*. The premiere of Part One was held on October 19th, followed by Parts Two and Three spaced a week apart. This was the most expensive film in Bulgarian film history, one that was to receive a second release three years later in shortened form for the foreign market: *681 A.D.—The Glory of Khan* (1984).

Part One, *Phanagoria*, deals with the migration of a Turkic people from the steppes of Middle Asia, a land referred to in the film as "Great Bulgaria." The emphasis here is on the life, customs, and traditions of a people. Part Two, *Migration*, is the story of the trek westward through the seasons and over a lengthy stretch of time until the tribe under the young khan reached the River Danube. There, they encountered stubborn resistance among the Slavs who had previously settled in this area. Part Three, *Land Forever*, highlights the unity of the Bulgars and Slavs to defeat a better equipped Byzantine army under Emperor Constantine IV Pogonatus. Naturally, for all these events, a cast of thousands arrayed in splendid costumes and armed with ancient weapons was required to lend an air of authenticity to the epic. *Khan Asparukh* was fittingly shot in Eastmancolor.

Despite the attention to production detail, however, the film has serious historical deficiencies. For one thing (as Bulgaria's neighboring countries, particularly Romania, noted), the very fact that the migrating Bul-

VI–5   *Khan Asparukh*

gars encountered only Slavs on their route to the Danube delta places much in question. Another deficiency is the fictionalized romanticism permeating the story from start to finish; indeed, the screenplay and the dialogue leave much to be desired.

What stands out are the action scenes and the landscapes photographed over the seasons. It was apparently for these reasons that a Warner Brothers' representative became interested in purchasing a shortened version of the film for exhibition abroad.

By contrast, the other historical epic to mark the anniversary, Georgi Djulgerov's *Measure for Measure*, rates as outstanding cinema in every respect. This is a film on the "Macedonian Question"—that is, the disputed area belonging today to Yugoslavia (the Macedonian Republic), but which was traditionally a part of ancient Bulgaria until the time of Ottoman occupation. That the film could be made at all is a bit of a production mystery, but Djulgerov does avoid open political statements and goes straight to the heart of a dramatic story that stands on its own merits.

Like *Khan Asparukh*, this is a three-part epic. Part One treats Macedonia still under the Turks (1878–1903), a time when the fate of the people in this area of the Balkans was still being determined by the Great Powers at the bargaining table. Part Two centers almost entirely on the Ilinden Day Uprising, on the Feast of St. Elijah (August 2), followed by the founding of the short-lived Krushovo Republic—all in the year 1903. Part Three then covers the final years of the revolution, 1906-12, when the Krushovo Republic was brutally crushed. Even the title, *Measure for Measure*, hints of an historical reassessment of the facts by way of a review of diaries and other chronicles by eyewitnesses.

The setting is a section of Macedonia in what is currently part of Greece, not at all Bulgaria or Yugoslavia. It is true, nonetheless, that Macedonians as a people are today found in these three bordering countries, a situation that has led to constant incidents in the past and present. Thus, the "Macedonian Question"—somewhat similar to the dilemma of Kurds inhabiting today's Iraq, Turkey, and the Soviet Union—is triggered whenever politically convenient either for pressing an issue or pressing an alarm button in the public forum.

The strength of Djulgerov's *Measure for Measure* is its blend of fiction and documentary. Far from being a dramatic epic or tied to a message of dubious sociopolitical worth, the film is rooted in the life experiences of real people in circumstances that require a personal decision to fight for human rights. As for the story line itself, the film depicts a "Viva Zapata" situation, one in which an illiterate peasant finds himself in the middle of something he does not quite understand, and does not wish to be a part of—until the revolution begins, and he finds a gun thrust into his hand. The outstanding performance by the film's screenwriter, Russi Chanev, in the lead role, as well as Radoslav Spassov's striking photography, adds to Djulgerov's directorial talent and augurs well for this filmmaking team.

However, following this production, Georgi Djulgerov dropped completely from sight as a feature film director. *Measure for Measure* thus became an unexplained caesura in his promising career, despite the director's trips abroad (one even to Moscow to show the film to former VGIK colleagues at the film school) to win support for both the project and the stylistic innovations it brought to Bulgarian cinema. In the end, however, it was these innovations that proved the undoing of both Djulgerov and *Measure for Measure*: indeed, the film had broken the mold for the formula-structured socialist (and Bulgarian) historical film.

One has only to make a comparison between *Measure for Measure* and *Khan Asparukh* to note the essential differences in the formula. Staikov offers little or no interpretation of history, while Djulgerov seeks to give reasons for the course that contemporary history took in the case of a new Bulgaria formed out of the remnants of the Ottoman Empire. Staikov's title figure is one-dimensional, a historical (almost legendary) icon emerging out of the mists of the past, while Djulgerov's hero is a stubborn, flesh-and-blood individual who grows into manhood while performing the tasks set before him. Staikov orchestrates his battle scenes, while Djulgerov shows the Ilinden Day Uprising as a confusing chain of events without much rhyme or reason.

Subsequent Bulgarian historical epics, particularly Borislav Sharaliev's *Boris the First* (1984) and Vladislav Ikonomov's *Day of the Rulers* (*Denyat na vladetelite*, 1985), returned to the typical formula for the socialist historical film.

THE METAMORPHOSIS OF THE PARTISAN FILM

Outside of the historical film, nothing is more sacred than the Partisan film in socialist countries. When Binka Zhelyazkova and Hristo Ganev attempted to show how corruption had tarnished the ideals of former Partisan heroes in *Life Flows Quietly By* (also known simply as *Partisans*) in 1958, shortly after the demise of the Personality Cult, the film was considered too explicit and was promptly shelved. Shortly thereafter, the writer-director pair made *We Were Young* (*A byahme mladi*, 1961), striking for its poetic realism but this time extolling the deeds of young resistance fighters in Sofia who were pursued by fascist authorities during the war years.

The same situation faced Rangel Vulchanov in the post-Stalinist years. His *On a Small Island* (1958), a personal statement rooted in the events following the 1923 uprising, is reported to have barely passed the censorship office, whereupon his next film (made together with poet-screenwriter Valeri Petrov) stayed well within the bounds of discretion in depicting, once again, the fate of young revolutionaries in Sofia during the war: *First Lesson* (1960).

It was not until Georgi Stoyanov's *Birds and Greyhounds* (1969) that lyrical statements on Partisan or resistance activities could be produced for a new, younger generation of viewers, for whom the years of resistance were now far removed. Scripted by Vassil Akyov and partially based on his own personal experiences as a teenager, this is the story of sixteen-year-olds in a small provincial village maturing into manhood on the eve of the Second World War. Compared with Zako Heskia's *The Eighth* (*Osmiyat*, 1969), the Grand Prix winner at the Varna festival, Stoyanov's approach to heroism in war was entirely different. By contrast, Heskia's "Eastern" was a pure adventure story, about parachute jumpers fighting to the death against overwhelming odds to defeat fascism on the home front before the Red Army arrived to liberate Bulgaria. Another "Eastern," Vulo Radev's *Black Angels* (*Chernite angeli*, 1970), also recorded in color (for the first time) the super-heroic deeds of a half-dozen teenagers training in the mountains for Partisan activity.

Within a few years (upon the appointment of Pavel Pissarev as film minister in 1971), the picture had entirely changed. Vassil Akyov collaborated with Georgi Djulgerov on *And the Day Came* (*I doyde denyat*, 1973), a Partisan film based on Aykov's autobiographical experiences that offers a fresh psychological approach to teenagers sacrificing their youth, and their lives, for a cause. The film's realism underscores the general thematic approach that events along these lines really might have happened during the resistance fighting as described in the midst of the Second World War. By the same token, a veteran "Eastern" director, Zako Heskia, presented an historical chronicle of a battle in March 1945 between a reorganized Bulgarian army and the retreating German army: *Dawn over the Drava* (*Zarevo nad Drava*, 1974). The same is true of Heskia's *The Last Battle* (*Boy posleden*, 1977), based on memoirs and dealing in semi-documentary form with the growth of the resistance in 1943 against the fascist government.

The key film in the metamorphosis of the Partisan resistance theme, however, occurred with the release of Georgi Stoyanov's *Panteley* (1978). This was Stoyanov's second collaboration with scriptwriter Vassil Aykov, and the absurdity of the situation alone makes it a standout. Picture an innocent, apolitical individual stumbling into the midst of a resistance movement, only to be mistaken by both sides, the fascists and the Partisans, as a suspect agent. It is the critical year 1944, not a time in which you would expect to find a Beckettian individual wandering the streets of Sofia in a bowler hat trying to find a way out of the mess he is suddenly immersed in without knowing how or why.

By the end of the seventies, the old-fashioned Partisan theme was relegated primarily to the television screen, with the more important films cut down for release in the theaters. One of these was Margarit Nikolic's *On the Tracks of the Missing* (*Po diryata na bezsledno izcheznalite*, 1979). A TV serial, it was exceptional for offering an historical account of threats, murders, and assassinations occurring in the Bulgarian Assembly during the White Terror of 1923–25 under Tsar Boris and his Prime Minister, Alexander Tsankov. The same general period of time had been covered earlier for the movie screen by Lyudmil Staikov in *Amendment to the Defense-of-State Act* (*Dopalnenie kam zakona za zashtito na darzhavata*, 1976), but by the end of the decade Staikov was content to summarize that crucial, troubled period in Bulgarian history in the lyrical, poetic, metaphorical *Illusion* (*Ilyuzia*, 1980). The 1923 uprising is now viewed symbolically through the eyes and experiences of an artist and an actress.

Occasionally a remake of the old theme with the same play on sacrifice and heroics appears on the scene. One of these was commissioned for the thirteen-hundredth anniversary celebrations: Borislav Sharaliev's *The Thrust* (*Oudarut*, 1982), chronicling the events in Sofia in August–September 1944, when the Soviet troops joined with Bulgarian Partisans for a triumphant entry into the city. While it seemed like ancient history to some observers, the film was produced for the masses in a slightly different context and with more technical finesse for a new generation of young moviegoers for whom the war is some distant dream.

TOWN AND VILLAGE

One of the real concerns of a progressive socialist society is the abandonment of peasant life in villages for resettlement in newly constructed industrial centers. The theme of building a new city was treated in one of the key films of the immediate postwar era: Nikola Korabov and Ducho Mundrov's *People of Dimitrovgrad* (*Dimitrovgradisi*, 1956). To show that same film today in conjunction with recent films (documentaries and features) within the context of a reassessment of the "town-and-country" issue would offer a clear index of just how far Bulgarian cinema has come over the past three decades.

For our purposes, in reviewing only the recent past, the key migration film is Hristo Hristov's *The Last Summer* (1974), a critical statement on the abandonment of villages (in this case due to the construction of a dam) that could not be released to the public until nearly two years after its completion. Even more significant than the power of imagery in this milestone production in Bulgarian cinema was the book (with the same title) on which it was based. Yordan Radichkov's novel explicitly mourns the passing of village life and its time-honored peasant traditions.

At approximately the same time as the release of *The Last Summer*, Hristov combined the stories of another recognized writer, Nikolai

Haitov, into a feature film with fundamentally the same theme as that of the temporarily shelved one: *A Tree without Roots* (*Darvo bez koren*, 1974). The two stories, "A Tree without Roots" and "Toward the Peak," describe in poignant terms the difficulties encountered by an old-timer who leaves a mountain village to visit his son's family in Sofia. There, he finds himself lost in a completely alien society—not so much because of the experience of a different pace of life, but because his son has changed his moral code. In effect, the son is now a member of the new cold and heartless middle class, a parvenu who wishes in fact to forget his roots.

Undoubtedly, the almost simultaneous release of the two films marked a change in production policy at the Boyana Studios. On one level, a review of the dignity of work itself was in progress at the end of the sixties. Lyudmil Kirkov's *Swedish Kings* (*Schvedskite krale*, 1968)— also known as *Steel Kings*—deals with a steelworker leaving his job for a brief excursion to the Black Sea coast to cavort on the beach with tourists and, as he states, "to live like a Swedish king" for a while. The situation was resolved by an underlying moral message.

Nikolai Nikiforov, the screenwriter for *Swedish Kings*, subsequently collaborated with Ivan Terziev on *Men without Work* (*Mazhe bez rabote*, 1972). Once again, the position on the dignity of work is rendered in satirical, humanistic terms. The setting is the construction of a road that is seemingly going nowhere; each of the laborers takes a contrasting position on life and his expectations as a member of the country's work force. It was not long before Terziev's sequel appeared on the scene: *Strong Water* (*Silna voda*, 1975), another tale of workers on a construction site—this time, however, they are drilling for water that does not exist in order to avoid work and to humor a local public official who has blindly ordered the project for political reasons.

Another gifted screenwriter found his best mode of expression in the "town-and-country" theme: Georgi Mishev. He collaborated with Lyudmil Kirkov on a two-film story about a youngster named Ran from the provinces who leaves his village to find his way in Lyudmil Kirkov's *A Boy Becomes a Man* (1972)—only to find his ideals as a schoolteacher tarnished in another provincial town: *Don't Go Away* (*Ne si otivay*, 1976). Between those two films, the team of Kirkov and Mishev collaborated on a pair of highly critical, yet humanly compassionate, films on the theme of migration and abandoned villages. The first, *Peasant on a Bicycle* (*Selyaninat s koleloto*, 1974), depicts a peasant who cannot get used to town life, and so he is off at regular intervals on his bicycle to visit his abandoned village—only to have a fatal relationship with a young girl assigned to work in the area. The same story, this time in a collective vein, is at the heart of *Matriarchate* (*Matriarhat*, 1977); it is social satire about a collective farm and nearby village inhabited entirely by women—whose men, ironically enough, are holding jobs in industrial towns described in Kirkov-Mishev's *Peasant on a Bicycle*.

AN INTERNATIONAL BREAKTHROUGH

Although the enormous box-office success of Metodi Andonov's *The Goat Horn* (1972) indicated that a new style of Bulgarian cinema had burst upon the scene after this promising national cinematography had been in the doldrums for more than a decade, it was not until recognition was accorded at international film festivals that a true international breakthrough could be accorded. Further, the opportunity for foreign critics to assess the revival-in-progress at Bulgarian Film Weeks added to the general interest and excitement.

The festivals in Moscow and Cannes provided the first festival platforms of note. Lyudmil Staikov's *Affection* (1972) won one of the main prizes at Moscow in 1973. A year later, Binka Zhelyazkova's *The Last Word* (1972) awoke some interest at Cannes, although this autobiographical tribute to the resistance was a pale echo of her earlier film *We Were Young* (1961).

At the same time, however, Eduard Zahariev collaborated with scriptwriter Georgi Mishev on *The Hare Census* (1973), one of the most popular films in Bulgarian history and a satire that has charmed European critics and filmmakers. Little else happens in the film other than a state inspector arriving on the scene in a provincial village to conduct a survey

VI–6   *Villa Zone (Vilna zona)*

on the number of hares in this rural area. As silly as everything sounds, similar surveys are welcomed by the local populace as an excuse for taking off work, having a picnic, and then sending the erstwhile inspector home in his car with the quaint bribery of a backseat filled with cabbages.

Zahariev and Mishev lost no time in turning out a second satire with even more absurd twists to score as a truly unique statement on Bulgaria's newly established middle class: *Villa Zone* (1975). This time they aimed their guns at the string of privately built "villas" encircling the capital of Sofia, and their satire is delightfully merciless. Much of the credit, however, goes not only to Zahariev and Mishev, but also to actor Itzhak Fintsi, whose deadpan facial expressions in both *The Hare Census* and *Villa Zone* made him a national figure. The entire film is little more than a garden party that runs amok, all of the characters outdoing each other in their petit bourgeois mentality and fumbling efforts at neighborly one-upmanship.

While these two social comedies were making their mark internationally, film festivals were booking Bulgarian films almost as a matter of course. Assen Shopov's *Eternal Times* (*Vechni vremena*, 1975), about villages abandoned in the mountain regions, was one of the standouts at Locarno. Vulo Radev's *Doomed Souls* (*Osadeni dushi*, 1975), based on Dimiter Dimov's novel with autobiographical aspects set during the Spanish Civil War, seemed to be programmed for entry at San Sebastian. And the two successive entries at Berlin, Rangel Vulchanov's *The Inspector and the Forest* (1975) and Hristo Hristov's *Cyclops* (*Tsiklopat*, 1976), drew more than favorable comment as unusual entries from a socialist country. Indeed, both Vulchanov and Hristov had now established themselves as two of the leading directors in East Europe.

Both *The Inspector and the Forest* and *Cyclops* were highly unusual films so far as their themes were concerned. Vulchanov opened the case records of a criminal seducing young girls who came from the country to the capital to seek employment or a new life. In order to lend more psychological intensity to *The Inspector and the Forest*, he chose two leading actors unknown to Bulgarian screens, relying almost entirely on realism and authenticity to carry the story. In fact, Sonya Boshkova as the young innocent was a nonprofessional altogether.

As for *Cyclops*, this science-fiction tale is set within the closed quarters of a submarine boat on a mysterious cruise into the unknown. The story bears an uncanny resemblance to a Soviet film set on a space mission, *Solaris* (1972), which was made by one of cinema's great directors, Andrei Tarkovsky. The similarities are particularly visible with regard to the fantasies and flashbacks experienced by the protagonist, the commander of the U-boat.

As festival programmers abroad sought a distinctly national production, Eduard Zahariev's *Manly Times* (1977) filled the bill to such a degree that, in time, the film became an official calling-card around the globe.

VI–7   Cyclops (Tsiklopat)

VI–8   Manly Times (Muzhki vremena)

Scripted by masterful storyteller Nikolai Haitov, the tale has its roots in folk-lore and ancient legends. An outlaw is hired by a rich man to kidnap a peasant girl whose heart he cannot win as a suitor; once this is done, the girl falls in love with the outlaw himself—and thus the situation is more complicated than before. As in the case of *The Goat Horn*, Haitov draws on legends as ancient as the Thracians and the Rhodope Mountains they once inhabited.

THE POLITICAL FILMS

By the end of the seventies, conditions had so improved in Bulgaria that a series of political films were approved for production and release. Many of them were projects stemming from the mid-sixties, when the first Bulgarian film revival was brought to an abrupt close. Others fit the atmosphere of the changing times. The movement extended over a period of approximately five years, from 1977 to 1981.

The first film to make its mark was Binka Zhelyazkova's *The Swimming Pool* (*Basseynat*, 1977), an entry at the Moscow film festival. Perhaps too wordy for a foreign audience, this film monologue was noteworthy for reviewing the period of the Personality Cult in a frankly open and morally consequential manner.

That same year saw Georgi Djulgerov's *Advantage* (1977). Winner of the Best Director Prize at the 1978 Berlin film festival, the film appeared on the scene at the very moment when Stalinism and the Personality Cult were being reviewed critically for the first time in the Soviet Union (Andrei Tarkovsky's *Mirror*), Poland (Andrzej Wajda's *Man of Marble*), and Hungary (Pál Gábor's *Angi Vera*). Djulgerov's compassionate, humanistic approach to the fate of a con man living by his wits during the period of the Personality Cult is unique in Bulgarian cinema, while his personal stylistic manner in handling the theme set him aside as one of the original talents working in East Europe. Another encouraging sign of an open policy at the Boyana Studios occurred when director Rangel Vulchanov was united with screenwriter Valeri Petrov to film a project that had been originally planned for the early sixties: *With Love and Tenderness* (1978), a sketch of an eccentric sculptor living in relative seclusion on the Black Sea coast who finds himself surrounded by philistines at a reunion of friends and acquaintances. Vulchanov followed this a year later with one of his most original and memorable films: *The Unknown Soldier's Patent Leather Shoes* (1979), developed from a script Vulchanov had written fifteen years earlier, but one that he never had the chance—until now—to adapt to the screen. This lyrical poem in an autobiographical vein to a peasant culture of the distant past features nonprofessionals in most of the roles, a factor that lends more honesty and integrity to the theme.

Several sociocritical films aimed at corruption and indifference in con-

VI–9   *The Unknown Soldier's Patent Leather Shoes (Lachenite obouvki na neznainiya voin)*

VI–10   *The Unknown Soldier's Patent Leather Shoes (Lachenite obouvki na neznainiya voin)*

temporary Bulgarian society were produced at this time, many of which were comparable to the best socially engaged films currently being produced in Poland, Hungary, and Yugoslavia. Among these were a series of films directed by a former actor and director of animation films, Ivan Andonov. His *Fairy Dance* (*Samodivsko horo*, 1976), made in collaboration with satirist Georgi Mishev, poked fun at the world of art lovers and would-be trendsetters. Then, at the Locarno festival, he attracted attention with the hard-hitting *The Roof* (*Pokriv*, 1978), a tragicomedy about a man trying to build a house by whatever illegal means available, while at the same time maintaining a love affair with a gypsy girl. And his *The Cherry Orchard* (1979), scripted by Nikolai Haitov, exposes the crooked dealings at a collective farm at the cost of a human life, that of an honest forester struggling to save an orchard from wanton destruction.

Guilt and corruption in the professional fields and among the well-to-do became a staple in Bulgarian cinema during the late seventies. Georgi Djulgerov's *Swap* (*Trampa*, 1978), despite its complex narrative line, explores the motives of an eminent writer and reporter in returning to a provincial town where he once compromised his principles (shown in flashbacks) during stormy meetings at the farm cooperative at the time of the Personality Cult. Ludmil Kirkov's *Short Sun* (*Kratko sluntse*, 1979), one of the best films of social conscience made during this period, describes how a university student, working a summer job as a well-digger in the "villa zone" surrounding the capital, meets a tragic end. This happens when the job threatens the villa owner with an uncomfortable delay due to the discovery of human bones—apparently the spot on which the well is being dug is where martyrs of the White Terror in the nineteen twenties were taken for execution and secret burial. And Ivan Nichev's *Boomerang* (*Bumerang*, 1979) makes no bones about corruption in the inner circles of the writers' profession, but even stronger is the director's attack on the wily tricks practiced by the younger generation. A graduate of the school of journalism tries using his connections to avoid an assignment to the provinces by offering to collaborate on the memoirs of an elderly writer who was once associated with the resistance.

Undoubtedly, Hristo Hristov, head of the Union of Bulgarian Filmmakers, committed himself more than any other director to the making of films of social responsibility and political conscience. He centered his attention primarily on individuals facing a mid-life crisis amid other psychological pressures. *Barrier* (*Barierata*, 1979), starring the talented Russian actor Innokenti Smoktunovsky, explores the fantasies of a composer suddenly finding himself confronted by a blithe spirit who believes she has the ability to fly. *The Truck* (1980) heightens the impending crises among several individuals from different social classes by placing them against a bare wintery background as the corpse of a young worker is brought back to a mountain village for burial. And *A Woman at Thirty-Three* (1982) takes pity on a middle-aged woman—a secretary, divorced, with a child, continuing her studies on the

VI–11   *Swap (Trampa)*

VI–12   *Short Sun (Kratko sluntse)*

VI–13   *Boomerang (Bumerang)*

VI–14   *Barrier (Barierta)*

side—whose prospects for fulfillment and happiness in a socialist society are little better, and perhaps worse, than they would be in a capitalist one.

Inevitably, the freedom to criticize would require self-searching on the part of the filmmakers themselves. Binka Zhelyazkova handled the situation commendably well in *The Big Night Bath* (*Golyamoto noshtno kupane*, 1980) within the context of a parable on artists and intellectuals playing a deadly ritual of Thracian-hanging games while on a vacation at a Black Sea resort. Another was the adaptation of Blaga Dimitrova's much-discussed critical novel, *Avalanche* (*Lavina*, 1982), a metaphor of social responsibility played out against the background of mountain climbing and an impending natural disaster.

As fascinating as these films were for the viewer who appreciates intellectual games, two other films made by veteran directors stated the case for social conscience in clearer and unequivocal terms. Lyudmil Kirkov, who had collaborated with moralist scriptwriter Stanislav Stratiev on *Short Sun* (1979), which was followed by a social satire on entertainment policies in resort hotels, *A Nameless Band* (*Orkestur bez ime*, 1982), made one of the best films of the decade: *Balance* (*Ravnovessie*, 1983). The focus here is on a film production unit on location on the Black Sea coast. The attention, however, centered on three minor figures in the unit whose fates are contrasted with the romantic excesses of the production itself. *Balance* deservedly won a Silver Prize at the Moscow festival.

The other film, Vesselin Branev's *Hotel Central* (1983), won broad critical praise at the Venice festival in 1983, the last occasion on which a Bulgarian entry at an international festival was welcomed with such critical unanimity. Branev, a screenwriter whose career was primarily in television, adapted two short stories by Konstantin Konstantinov on events related to

VI–15   *Hotel Central*

the 1934 *coup d'état*, the result of which was the dissolution of parliament and the imposition of totalitarian rule. An innocent young girl from the provinces is mistakenly arrested and brought to a hotel to serve as a chambermaid—to be used and abused as the town prostitute for all in power. She manages, however, to maintain her morals while exposing the corruption of those about her.

Both of these films featured outstanding performances by the female protagonists—Plamena Getova in Kirkov's *Balance* and Irène Krivoshieva in *Hotel Central*—a factor, in turn, that attested to the all-around depth in Bulgarian cinema after four decades of seeking its own way on the world production scene.

THE BOTTOM FALLS OUT

Why the bottom should have suddenly fallen out of Bulgarian cinema at a time when it had definitely reached maturity is solely a matter of speculation. Western observers have settled for the following reasons:

First, the unexpected death of the cultural minister Lyudmila Shivkova, in 1981, in the midst of the thirteen-hundredth anniversary celebrations, left too many things undone or still in the planning stage, among these, a number of promising film projects.

Second, the decision to appoint a new film minister, Nikolai Nenov, in 1980 to replace the able Pavel Pissarev (who was then given charge of theaters and stage performances), turned out to be an unproductive one. Until Nenov's own departure in 1986, filmmakers tended to be less willing to risk making sociocritical and sociopolitical films. As a result, fewer Bulgarian films were programmed at key international film festivals.

Third, Hristo Hristov stepped down as the head of the Union of Bulgarian Filmmakers in 1983, shortly after his production of *A Woman at Thirty-Three* (1982) was placed temporarily on the shelf. His elected replacement, Georgi Stoyanov, was also to have trouble receiving an authorized release of his *Constantine the Philosopher* (1983) until the completion of the film's second part.

Fourth, the high cost of producing the series of epic spectacles during and after the 1981 anniversary year depleted the country's film production coffers, particularly in regard to subsequent cultural events and film policies in general.

Fifth, some filmmakers—particularly Georgi Djulgerov—gave up film production altogether to work in the theater. In view of the fact that he was one of a handful of Bulgarian directors whose names commanded respect abroad, his abrupt departure from the scene heralded another creative drought in the Boyana Studios. Now that a filmmaking colleague, Lyudmil Staikov, has been appointed the new film minister (as of 1986), the general feeling is that Djulgerov and others will feel more at ease in making films of their liking.

Whatever the reasons, Bulgarian cinema has experienced its second decline after a period of feverish creativity. The creative well dried up completely by 1984. Thereafter, even the better films seemed "old hat" in comparison to those produced during the previous decade. Hristo Hristov's *Question Time* (*Subessednik po zhelanie,* 1984) and *Reference* (*Herakteristika,* 1985), the former about a man tidying up his life before he dies of leukemia, and the latter about corruption among taxi drivers, are commendable films but are without scope or vision. Eduard Zahariev's later films as well—*Almost a Love Story* (*Pochti lyubovna istoria,* 1980), *Elegy* (*Elegiya,* 1982), and *My Darling, My Darling* (*Skupi moi, skupa moya,* 1985)—are exercises in romantic sentimentality and strikingly the opposite of his former satirical masterpieces. Even the doyen of Bulgarian filmmakers, Rangel Vulchanov, appears to be biding his time with such minor excursions in poetic nostalgia as *Last Wishes* (*Posledni zhelania,* 1983) and *Where Are You Going?* (*Za kude putouvate?,* 1986).

By contrast, the films that have received an abundance of official support throughout the present decade, particularly at the Varna Festival of Bulgarian Feature Films, are thematically deficient (despite some praiseworthy stylistic qualities) in comparison with what had been produced in this country in the past. Among these are Borislav Sharaliev's *All Is Love* (*Vsichko e lyubov,* 1979), on juvenile delinquency, and *The Thrust* (*Oudarut,* 1982), on the liberation of Sofia. Another is Spanish director Juan Antonio Bardem's film biography of Georgi Dimitrov (1982 was the anniversary of his birthday) with an international cast, *The Warning* (*Predouprezhdeniyeto,* 1982). So too, Nikolai Volv's promising but script-heavy stories of the little man making good against odds: *King for a Day* (*Gospodin za edin den,* 1983), about a country bumpkin turning the tables on his village tormentors, and *All for Love* (*Da obichash na inat,* 1986), concerning a truckdriver who beats corruption on the job to measure up to the expectations and ideals of his teenaged son.

Hope for the future, many agree, lies primarily in the efforts of the younger generation of filmmakers to make a modest personal film or a stylistically challenging one. The founding of the Sofia Film and Theater Academy (VITIS) in 1973—whose teachers include Rangel Vulchanov, Hristo Hristov, and Georgi Djulgerov—meant that promising students no longer had to enroll at film academies in Moscow, Prague, Lodz, Babelsberg, and Budapest to get their training. And this "new generation" made themselves known before the decade was out.

Indeed, the debut by VITIS graduate Kiran Kolarov, *Status: Orderly* (1978), immediately made festival history. Produced as a telefeature, it portrayed a decaying Bulgarian nobility at the turn of the century. Kolarov's second feature, *The Airman* (*Vuzdushniyat chovek,* 1980), set in the period

of the Personality Cult shortly after the Second World War, was considered
too political and thus received only limited release. His latest film, Case
No. 205/1913 (Delo No. 205/1913, 1984), sketches the life, and suicide,
of Bulgaria's immortal poet, Peyo Yavorov (1878–1914), during the heady
period of a national literary revival. All these films are of more-than-passing
interest, yet they were looked upon by authorities as oddities rather than
realities.

Another VITIS director who made his mark shortly after graduation was
Yevgeni Mihailov, who collaborated with his camerawoman-wife, Elly
Mihailova (another VITIS graduate), on Home for Lonely Souls (1981),
which was about a theater actress (Plamena Getova) in the provinces who
has to come to grips with herself while wrestling with a role on the stage.
Their latest is a thriller set in the troubled thirties: Death Can Wait a
While (Smurtta mozhe da pochaka, 1985).

Still another newcomer to keep an eye on is Rumyana Petkova, who
worked with a crew of women collaborators on Reflections (1982), a film
about the problems facing a university student. The same feminist approach characterized her Coming Down to Earth (1985), the story of a
professional working woman and mother juggling her career and family obligations with unsatisfactory results on all sides.

Other films by newcomers include Ognyan Gelinov's The Flying Machine (1981), an amusing satire set during the Balkan Wars of 1912–13;
Ivan Pavlov's Mass Miracle (1981), a film-within-a-film story about the
misfortunes of a candidate trying to get into VITIS itself; and Docho
Bodjakov's Memory (Pamet, 1985), about a mother at the close of the Second World War seeking revenge for her son who was betrayed in the resistance movement.

A word should be said about screenwriter Konstantin Pavlov, who contributed the scripts not only for Ivan Pavlov's Mass Miracle and Docho
Bodjakov's Memory, but also for Lyudmil Staikov's Illusion (1980) and
Ivan Andonov's White Magic (Byala magiya, 1982). All of these are poetic statements on Bulgarian life and culture, its traditions and folk heritage. White Magic in particular captures, in colors and decor, the atmosphere of the nineteen twenties.

THE OTHER BULGARIAN CINEMA

Little has been said in this analytical survey of contemporary Bulgarian cinema about its production strength in children's films and animated cartoons. Such was not the scope of this survey. All the same, it should be
noted that when screenwriter Valeri Petrov was not collaborating with
Rangel Vulchanov on one of the milestones in Bulgarian cinema, he was
contributing delightful scripts for children's films: Borislav Sharaliev's

Knight without Armor (*Ritsar bez bronya*, 1966) and Zako Heskia's *Yo-Ho-Ho* (1981). Further, Dimiter Petrov (*The Captain/Kapitanat*, 1963), Ivanka Grubcheva (*Exams at Any Odd Time/Izpiti po nikoe vreme*, 1974), Rashko Ouzunov (*Talisman*, 1978), and Marianna Evstatieva (*Up in the Cherry Tree/Gore na chereshata*, 1984), as well as the scriptwriting pair of the Mormarev brothers (Petrov's *Porcupines Are Born without Bristles*, 1971, and Ivanka Grubcheva's *The Porcupines' War/Voynata na taralezhite*, 1979), set high standards in a genre that is by no means easy to master.

The same is true of animation. At least two animation directors will find a place of honor in film lexicons: Todor Dinov, the "Father of Bulgarian Animation," and Donyo Donev, whose *We Called Them Montagues and Capulets* (1985) marked the country's first venture into the realm of the feature cartoon. There is little doubt that both of these film artists have had an impact on the development and maturing of Bulgarian cinema as a whole, just as they will continue to do in the future.

In fact, film historians may argue that the Bulgarian animated film had matured into an art form while the Bulgarian feature film was still in its infancy. The reason is simple: Bulgaria, as did many countries in the Balkans, benefited from a long tradition of caricaturists. Thus, when a State Cinematography was founded shortly after the war, the first artists to be given a green light to create a native form of expression in the field of film animation were the caricaturists.

The first true Bulgarian cartoon was made in 1949, a collaborative effort involving many artists. At the same time, Todor Dinov, the most talented of the country's caricaturists, was studying film animation at the Moscow Film Academy. Upon his return home, he created overnight a national figure for the movie screens: *Brave Marko* (*Junak Marko*, 1953). Far from just being a cross between models of Disney and related Soviet animation, Marko was a pure product of the Bulgarian soul—a national hero imbued with the moral and philosophical dimensions of the legendary Balkan folk hero. Dinov's next test as a filmmaker was to wed satire to animation. He set to work tirelessly on producing a series of black-and-white line drawings related to a popular satirical magazine known to the majority of the population; the result was *Kino Prickles* (*Kinostarchel*, 1956–57).

From there, it was only a matter of time before he would become one of the central figures in socialist animation, an innovative artist whose best cartoons reached far beyond the visual limits of the medium to rank as sophisticated philosophical moral tales understood by all. These numbered *Little Annie* (*Malkoto Antsche*, 1958), *Prometheus* (1959), *The Story of the Pine-Tree Branch* (*Prikaska sa borowoto klontsche*, 1960), *Duet* (1961), *A Fable* (*Prikaska*, 1961), *The Lightning Rod* (*Gramootwodat*, 1962), *Jealousy* (*Rewnost*, 1963), *The Apple* (*Jabolkata*, 1963), and

The Daisy (*Margaritka*, 1965), some in collaboration with other artists. They are as fresh and stimulating today as when they were conceived and "breathed into life" on the drawing board.

As the recognized "Father of Bulgarian Animation"—whose best cartoons were noted for their graceful line, warm human characters, and an Aesopian twist in the narrative—Todor Dinov was to inspire and assist others on their way to improving the overall lot of Bulgarian cinema abroad. One of his collaborators was the animator Donyo Donev (codirector of *The Story of the Pine-Tree Branch*). Another was the theater director Hristo Hristov, with whom he collaborated on a key feature-film project in contemporary Bulgarian cinema: *Iconostasis* (1969).

The "Bulgarian School of Animation" was the talk of the short film and animation festivals of Europe by the sixties. In contrast to the "Zagreb School of Animation" in neighboring Yugoslavia—a studio that was to become world famous for its intellectual cartoons—the Bulgarians specialized in folk tales and the philosophical parable. Several artists working at the Sofia Animation Studio deserve mention: Donyo Donev, Stoyan Doukov, Hristo Topuzanov, Ivan Vesselinov, Ivan Andonov, Henri Koulev, Proiko Prokov, Gencho Simeonov, Radka Buchvarova, Zdenka Doicheva, Asparukh Panov, and Georgi Chavdarov. One of these, Ivan Andonov, progressed from acting to animation—and from there to making feature films. Another was to become as famous in his own right as Todor Dinov himself: Donyo Donev.

Indeed, Donev made the folkloric parable into a finely honed expression of philosophical truth focusing on the foibles of mankind. His cartoons of the seventies, in particular, literally charmed and amazed audiences at international film festivals. On the one side, his *Three Fools* series presented a trio of popular characters on both movie and television screens unsurpassed since the antics of Brave Marko: *The Three Fools* (*Trimata glupazi*, 1970), *The Clever Village* (*Umnoo selo*, 1972), *Three Foolish Hunters* (*Trimata glupazi lowzi*, 1972), and *The Three Fools and the Cow* (*Trimata glupazi i krawata*, 1974). Matched with these were three satirical gems on the suspect nobler aspirations of man: *De Facto* (1973), *The Musical Tree* (*Musikalnoto darwo*, 1976), and *Causa Perduta* (1977)—all of which belong in the annals of the best of world animation for their moral acerbity and intellectual wit.

Besides the genre of the children's film and the school of the animation cartoon, the Bulgarian feature film borrowed a great deal over the decades from the documentary. More often than not, this field functioned as a springboard to stronger thematic material in the Boyana feature film studios—and when the times were hard for a committed Bulgarian director, a return to documentary filmmaking supplied at least a safety valve for the troubled or sidetracked artist.

One can argue that the postwar Bulgarian cinema would never have gotten off the ground so quickly in the first place without the tireless input of newsreel cameramen and documentary filmmakers. Zahari Zhandov—whose *Alarm* (1951) is reckoned as the breakthrough feature film after the war—came to the feature film after winning recognition at international festivals in Brussels and Marienbad for *A Day in Sofia* (1946), followed by a major award at Venice for *Men amid the Clouds* (1947).

Rangel Vulchanov returned to the documentary field on occasions when work was not to his liking in the feature film studios, as did scriptwriters Hristo Ganev and Angel Wagenstein. Other filmmakers appear to have cut their directorial teeth on the documentary before venturing into the fiction film—Eduard Zahariev, in particular.

One director was to make a name in the documentary field alone: Hristo Kovachev. His prizewinning films include *Builders* (1974), *Agronomists* (1977), and *Shepherds* (1979). More recently, Georgi Djulgerov appears to be making a comeback on the Bulgarian production scene via two very fine documentaries with fiction elements: *Neshka Robeva and Her Girls* (1984) and its sequel *The Girls and Their Neshka Robeva* (1986), about the training and discipline involved in excelling in gymnastics. The materials of these two documentary films could easily be converted into a fascinating feature film. It remains uncertain whether these recent creative impulses in Bulgarian documentary production will help to re-energize feature film production and to restore the momentum which existed in the late seventies and early eighties.

7

Yugoslav Film in the Post-Tito Era

Daniel J. Goulding

The death of Josip Broz Tito on May 4, 1980, marked the end of an era in Yugoslavia's post-Second World War social and political development. Nearly 88 years old at his death, Tito had dominated Yugoslav domestic and international relations for nearly four decades, first as the Supreme Commander of the Communist-led Partisan resistance against enemy occupiers and domestic foes, and afterwards as the undisputed leader of the Party and State. His enormous prestige and astute political leadership had guided the young socialist state through a minefield of dramatic upheavals, international tensions, and domestic crises. On the other hand, the prestige and authority of his leadership had held in abeyance and left unresolved a number of deep and worrisome economic and political dilemmas and contradictions which burst into the open in the eighties and ushered in Yugoslavia's current "time of troubles."

At the center of Yugoslavia's current crisis are deteriorating economic conditions characterized by a high and persistent inflation rate which has reached 150 to 200 percent annually in the last few years, a huge balance of payments deficit, a precipitous drop in the living standards of many Yugoslavs, and the declining productivity of workers. Economic difficulties have been exacerbated by political paralysis at the federal level and the steady devolution of power to regional and republican centers whose interests do not always coincide with all-Yugoslav plans of social and economic stabilization and growth.[1]

Added to these woes have been the re-emergence of nationality problems and interethnic strife[2] and the multiple stresses carried in the wake of Yugoslavia's rapid transition from a predominantly agrarian economy at the end of the war to a predominantly urbanized and industrialized one today. Longstanding dilemmas in Yugoslavia's rapid urbanization and industrialization have been heightened by recent worsening economic and social conditions. The serious multiple crises which face Yugoslavia in the eighties have taken their toll on public confidence in the system and have led to an erosion of beliefs in the founding myths of the state and the inherent superiority of self-management socialism.[3]

This pessimistic litany of unresolved woes and dilemmas must be balanced against the resilience and independence of the peoples of Yugoslavia and the pride and resourcefulness they have shown in finding innovative solutions to seemingly intractable problems and crises in the past. The Yugoslavia of the eighties has been characterized by wide-ranging political and cultural expression and debate which sharply question received myths and which critically address the multiple dilemmas of contemporary social, economic, and political life. Yugoslav feature films have recently played a significant role in the present critical revisioning of Yugoslavia's revolutionary past and in imaginatively reflecting the subtle, complex, and changing contours of her evolving present.

Not since her "golden age" of the sixties has Yugoslavia's multinational film industry (with centers in all six republics and the two autonomous regions of Kosovo and Vojvodina) experienced such a fecund and vital period of film production and such a variety of meaningful film expression. The *new film* (*novi film*) period of the sixties is separated from the latest "resurgence" of Yugoslav feature films by a relatively low and flat profile of film production in the seventies.[4] Following the political suppression of *new film* tendencies in the late sixties and early seventies, Yugoslav feature films were characterized by a general lack of thematic boldness and cinematic experimentation. Heroic Partisan films (which had already begun to weary domestic viewers with their worn clichés, xenophobic excesses, and repetitive formulas), light comedies, action-adventure films, and historical dramas once again rose to the forefront, and *new film* radicalism receded to the vanishing point. It was not until the end of the seventies and the beginning of the eighties that the picture began to brighten considerably. Feature film production rose to levels which rivaled the high watermark of the late sixties,[5] and a new generation of film artists stimulated the revival of artistically and socially more interesting films.

RENEWAL AND RESURGENCE

The comeback of Yugoslav film in the late seventies and early eighties was initially spearheaded by a group of younger film directors, among the most important of whom are Srđan Karanović (b. 1945), Goran Paskaljević (b. 1947), Goran Marković (b. 1946), Rajko Grlić (b. 1947), and Lordan Zafranović (b. 1944). All were classmates, along with the talented cinematographer Živko Zalar, at FAMU, the professional film school in Prague, and became known collectively as the "Czech School" of Yugoslav directors. They shared and continue to share a common interest in making well-crafted films which communicate effectively with the audience as well as make sharp and meaningful comments on the complexities and contradictions of contemporary life in Yugoslavia.[6]

While the "Czech School" of Yugoslav film directors provided the yeast for leavening and quickening the resurgence of Yugoslav film expression in the late seventies and early eighties, numerous other creative sources have nurtured its continued maturation and growth during the last few years. Among the most promising and accomplished new feature film directors to emerge in the eighties are the Bosnian Emir Kusturica (b. 1954), who also received his professional film training at FAMU in Prague, and has directed two films which have received major international awards, *Do You Remember Dolly Bell* (*Sjećas li se Dolly Bell*, 1981) and *When Father Was Away on Business* (*Otac na službenom putu*, 1985); the Serbian Slobodan Šijan (b. 1946) who has directed four stylistically varied and critically acclaimed films, *Who's That Singing Over There* (*Ko to tamo peva*, 1980), *The Marathon Runner* (*Maratonci trče posčasni krug*, 1981), *How I Was Systematically Destroyed by an Idiot* (*Kako sam sistematski uništen od idiota*, 1983), and *Strangler Versus Strangler* (*Davitelj protiv davitelja*, 1984); the Macedonian Stole Popov (b. 1950) whose uneven first film, *The Red Horse* (*Crveniot konj*, 1981), was followed by his internationally successful film, *Happy New Year, 1949* (*Srećna nova, '49*, 1986); the Serbian Branko Baletić (b. 1946) whose relatively slight first film, *Plum Juice* (*Sok od šljiva*, 1980) was followed by his witty and accomplished film, *Balkan Express* (*Balkan ekspres*, 1983); the talented Slovenian cinematographer-turned-director Karpo Godina (b. 1943) whose successful first film, *The Raft of the Medusa* (*Splav meduze*, 1980) was followed by an interesting but comparatively less successful second film, *Red Boogie* (*Rdeči boogie*, 1983); and the Slovenian film scenarist and director Filip Robar-Dorin (b. 1940) whose debut film, *Sheep and Mammoths* (*Ovni in mamuti*, 1985) earned widespread critical praise.

Several directors who contributed substantially to *new film* tendencies in the sixties (the Serbians Živojin [Žika] Pavlović, Puriša Đorđević, Miloš Radivojević and Želimir Žilnik; the Croatians Vatroslav Mimica, Krsto Papić, Branko Ivanda, Ante Babaja and Zvonimir Berković; the Slovenians Boštjan Hladnik and Matjaž Klopčič; and the Bosnians Bora Drašković and Bato Čengić) have all directed films in the eighties, in some cases after a long absence from feature film production. Among the most significant of these recent films are *Body Scent* (*Zadah tela*, 1983) directed by Žika Pavlović, winner of the Golden Arena award for best film at the 1983 Pula feature film festival, which explores the dark underside of socialism in the characteristic style of Pavlović's most important films of the sixties; *The Inheritance* (*Dediščina*, 1985) directed by Matjaž Klopčič, featured in the *Certain Regard* section of the 1985 Cannes festival, a cinematically complex rendering of the period from 1914 to 1944 and the tragedy which overtakes three generations of the Vrhunc family; *Life Is Beautiful* (*Život je lep*, 1985), a dark metaphor of social breakdown in contemporary Yugoslavia, directed by Boro Drašković; and *Living Like the Rest of Us* (*Živeti kao sav normalan svet*, 1982), directed by Miloš

Radivojević, a compelling cinematic study of a talented and idealistic music student from the provinces who is progressively disillusioned by the subtle politics and corrupt lifestyles which he finds in the professional conservatory of music in Belgrade.

One of the foremost directors of the sixties, Aleksandar Petrović, has not directed a film in Yugoslavia since his controversial film, *The Master and Margarita* (*Majstor i Margarita*, 1972), adapted from the well-known and long-suppressed Russian novel of the same name by Mikhail Bulgakov. At the time of this writing, however, he has received French funding for a major film project, *Migrations*, which will be partially shot in Yugoslavia.[7] Dušan Makavejev, the best-known Yugoslav film director internationlly (*Sweet Movie, Montenegro, The Coca-Cola Kid*) has not made a film in Yugoslavia since *WR: Mysteries of the Organism* (*WR: Misterije organizma*, 1970). He has, however, recently returned to Yugoslavia for guest appearances, and *WR: Mysteries of the Organism* has enjoyed special screenings in Yugoslavia with enthusiastic audience responses. At the time of this writing, Makavejev is directing a U.S.- Yugoslav coproduced feature film, *For a Night of Love*.

International recognition of Yugoslavia's second coming of age as an important source of world-class films was most dramatically confirmed at the 1985 Cannes film festival, where the Yugoslav film, *When Father Was Away on Business*, directed by Emir Kusturica, won the coveted *Palme d'Or* for best feature film, and has since enjoyed widespread international critical and popular success. Major retrospectives of Yugoslav films have recently been organized by the prestigious Georges Pompidou Center in Paris (spring, 1986), the National Film Theater in London (fall, 1986), a series of retrospectives in the U.S. by the American Film Institute (1987), and in special sections devoted to Yugoslav films at major international film festivals. Several films which were either banned or not picked up for distribution in the late sixties have been re-released for domestic viewing, and recent critical film scholarship in Yugoslavia has made important strides in restoring the significance of the *new film* movement of the sixties and its relationship and continuity with recent developments.[8]

Unlike the sixties, the recent creative ferment in Yugoslav cinema has not coalesced, however loosely, around a "movement" or discernible set of collective or republican-centered sociocultural and aesthetic tendencies.[9] There is a common interest in making professionally well-crafted films with dramatically interesting story lines which communicate effectively with the contemporary audience. Free of political dogmatism, the *new Yugoslav cinema* is informed by a broad humanism which depicts the foibles and contradictions of human nature and explores the regions of human imagination and freedom playing against the labyrinthine, sometimes coercive, and infinitely complex surfaces of Yugoslav reality. While there is comparatively less experimentation with film form than in the six-

VII–1   Internal exile. *When Father Was Away on Business (Otac na službenom putu)*

ties, there are several recent films which blend social realism with magical realism, surrealism and comic invention—ranging from the situational and slapstick to the absurd, surreal and Kafkaesque.

Paradoxically, some of the boldest avant garde experiments in visual form and what Yugoslav critics call the "new narrativity" have taken place in the usually more conservative realm of television drama, especially in Belgrade.[10] The internationally renowned Zagreb school of animation has also continued to experiment with a wide variety of visual styles and graphic design. Among the most significant of these recent animated films are *Satiemania*, 1978, directed by Zdenko Gašparović, and inspired by the mocking, lyrical music of Erik Satie. Sketches, reminiscent of the best impressionistic drawing of the twenties, integrate graphic movement with humor and detached spleen: *Fisheye (Riblje oko*, 1982), directed by Joško Marušić, depicts a cruel reversal of nature when monster fish invade and demolish a fishing village. This macabre vision is executed with woodcuts creating a vivid black and white pictorial effect. *Obsession (Opsesija*, 1983), directed by Aleksandar Marks, uses exaggerated expressionistic drawings to create a nightmarish world based on Edgar Allan Poe's short story *The Black Cat*; and *House No. 42 (Kuća br. 42*, 1984), directed by Pavao Stalter, employs a cinematic reconstruction of a daguerreotype showing an old building in downtown Zagreb. Using soft focus and subtle time-lapse, the stationary picture turns into a peopled city scene which nostalgically captures petit-bourgeois behavior and a turn-of-the-century romantic atmosphere.

It should also be emphasized that liberated cinematic tendencies in Yugoslavia, as in past periods, exist at the thin edge of a much larger politically conformist and commercially oriented cinema. The most popular films with the domestic audience in the eighties have been light social comedies with contemporary settings. The most successful director of the genre, Zoran Čalić, has made seven films based on a continuing cast of characters, beginning with *Crazy Years* (*Lude godine*, 1977), which have all been enormous box office successes. Another film in this genre which broke all previous domestic box office records is *The Tight Spot* (*Tesna koža*, 1983), directed by Mića Milošević.[11] Several commercially oriented imitators of this trend, however, have failed to reach even the relatively low level of audience taste at which these films are aimed. There have also been sporadic attempts, usually not very successful, to expand the repertoire of popular films into such genres as science fiction, gangster films, murder mysteries, and *film noir*. More clearly established genres in Yugoslav feature film production (i.e., literary-historical films and feature films made especially for children) have recently been on the wane.

The current advance of Yugoslav feature film production in both qualitative and quantitative terms has moved against the grain of overall deteriorating economic conditions. A tax on film admissions constitutes one important source of film funding, but the price of film tickets, as a matter of cultural policy, has been kept low, despite spiraling inflation. The Yugoslav film industry is therefore faced with the paradox of having greatly increased the audience for domestic films while at the same time realizing a dwindling income from the tax on ticket admissions as measured in real terms. Inflation has also taken a heavy toll on the material infrastructure for film production, making it difficult to invest properly in film equipment and new technologies. Gifted film artists often work against the constraints of low production budgets and aging film equipment.

The Yugoslav film industry is also faced with the problem of adapting to the complexities of new and evolving self-management structures introduced by the Constitution of 1974 and the Law on Associated Labor passed in 1976. One consequence of these reforms has been to complicate greatly the overlapping levels of decision-making required to realize a film project. Another consequence has been the formation of autarkic regional and republican markets which make it more difficult to achieve interrepublican coproduction agreements and interrepublican film distribution. Every year there are new cries of alarm from major production studios and technical film enterprises in the various republics that the present level of feature film production cannot long be sustained and may be on the verge of collapse.[12]

Weighed against these negative developments has been the increasing reliance on creative and financial collaboration with republican-centered television enterprises, improved export earnings, and improved prospects
for coproductions with foreign film enterprises as well as recourse to
bank loans and alternative sources of republican financing. Undergirding
these efforts to maintain a viable film industry against serious financial obstacles is the profound social and political commitment which has been
made, and repeatedly confirmed, to sustain an independent, indigenous
film industry capable of expressing the remarkable cultural diversity and
languages of Yugoslavia's five nations and more than twenty nationalities
and ethnic minorities. What redeems and infuses this complex system
with life and vitality, of course, are the creative efforts, ambitions and personal dynamics of a seasoned and articulate vanguard of artists, critics,
and technical workers, who often chafe against the boundaries of the allow-
able to produce works of enduring artistic and sociocultural interest. This
chapter will focus on a thematic and sociocultural analysis of recent Yugoslav fiction feature films which represent "liberalizing" tendencies in both
form and content, and which reflect critically and imaginatively upon
Yugoslavia's revolutionary past, and upon her richly textured, complex
and troubled present.

CRITICAL REVISIONING OF
YUGOSLAVIA'S REVOLUTIONARY PAST

One of the noticeable thematic trends in Yugoslav feature films of the
eighties is the steady reduction and virtual disappearance of films dealing
with the Partisan war experience, either as action-adventure entertainment or as a source of artistic critical reexamination. Recently, the critical
focus has shifted to inter-war Yugoslavia, the Stalinist aftermath of the war,
and the dramatic period following Yugoslavia's break with the Cominform
on June 28, 1948.

The Tito-Stalin Split

Within a year after Tito's death on May 4, 1980, a spate of articles, novels and plays began to appear in Yugoslavia which sharply reexamined the
most controversial aspects of the anti-Stalinist purges carried out by the Tito-
led government following the anathema and expulsion of Yugoslavia from
the Cominform on June 28, 1948, with special attention focused upon the
Gulag-type concentration camp set up on the arid and desolate northern
Adriatic island of Goli otok (Naked Island). The most important of these
novels was *Tren* (*The Moment*) written by one of the Yugoslavia's most distinguished writers, Antonije Isaković, and based upon interviews of survivors of Goli otok. The novel was completed in 1979 but not released for

publication until after Tito's death, when it became an instant bestseller and generated widespread controversy.[13]

The most important play dealing with this same theme was Dušan Jovanović's The Karamazovs, which premiered in Slovenia in 1980, opened in Zagreb in 1982, and subsequently played to packed houses all over Yugoslavia.[14] Isaković's novel, Jovanović's play, and other literary works dealing with the same theme[15] provoked widespread controversy and polemics in Yugoslavia which reached their greatest intensity in 1982–1983. Some top officials and journalists argued that the extreme measures taken at Goli otok must be placed in the context of a time in which Yugoslavia's very existence was being threatened. One official stated, "Had we not sent the Cominformists to a place like Goli otok, the whole of Yugoslavia might be a Goli otok today."[16] Isaković acknowledged the weight of this historical argument, but reasoned that numerous innocent victims had been caught in the purge either because they were mistakenly arrested or were victims of witch hunts and of petty officials settling old scores. He also argued that the ends do not always justify the means: "We were fighting Stalinism with Stalinist methods when the real weapons against Stalinism are greater freedom and greater democracy."[17]

More conservative polemicists and party apologists inveighed against "people in Yugoslavia who specialize precisely in unearthing the errors of the past; i.e. the errors of the party," and a number of Yugoslav dramatists, novelists, poets, filmmakers, and other intellectuals were criticized for "fomenting counterrevolution, demystification of society, negativism toward socialism, and negative portrayals of Yugoslavia's revolutionary past."[18]

More recently, several important Yugoslav feature films have critically revisioned the dramatic period following Yugoslavia's expulsion from the Cominform (i.e. the period from 1948 to Stalin's death in 1953). The most significant of these films are The Balkan Spy (Balkanski špijun, 1984), When Father Was Away on Business (Otac na službenom putu, 1985), and Happy New Year, 1949 (Srećna nova '49, 1986).[19] The best known of these recent films is When Father Was Away on Business,[20] directed by Emir Kusturica in collaboration with the Bosnian writer-scenarist Abdullah Sidran. The film vividly depicts the tensions and the moral and political ambiguities which prevailed in Yugoslavia after the break with Stalin, as these impacted on a Moslem family living in Sarajevo. The time of the film is condensed from the summer of 1950 to the summer of 1952, a period in which Yugoslavia weathered the harshest diplomatic, economic, and military threats against her independence, and steadily gained in strength. The dramatic structure of the film mirrors and reflects this steady progress toward reconciliation and transcendence.

In the beginning of the film, the father, Meša, a petty Communist official in the labor department, makes the offhand comment that an anti-Stalinist political cartoon appearing in Yugoslavia's leading newspaper

Politika "goes too far."[21] Meša's remark is made to Ankica, his mistress, who is travelling with him on a train. Ankica, in a jealous pique because Meša will not divorce his wife and marry her, reports this comment to the local Party official Zio, who is the brother of Meša's wife and who covets the sexual favors of Ankica and subsequently marries her. Zio uses Meša's negative comment about the political cartoon to interrogate him, arrest him as unreliable, and send him off to a forced labor camp at Lipnica. As the film progresses, Meša achieves partial rehabilitation by being sent to a crude provincial outpost at Zvornik where his family is permitted to rejoin him. He finally achieves full rehabilitation near the end of the film when he is freed to return to his beloved Sarajevo. In the meantime, his wife Sena remains intensely loyal to Meša despite his infidelities, holds the family together, and develops an implacable hatred toward her brother Zio, and his wife Ankica, when she discovers that they are the cause of her family's misfortune.

In the complex marriage celebration which occurs at the end of the film, a sometimes bitter and tentative reconciliation takes place among estranged members of the family and with the political circumstances which had pried the family apart. Images of family renewal are captured in Sena's pregnancy with a third child and the marriage of her younger brother Faro to Natasha, the daughter of a close neighbor. Zio and Ankica present Malik, the youngest son, with a leather soccer ball which he has coveted throughout the film and which he happily and innocently accepts, not knowing the grief that Zio and Ankica have caused the family. Despite her husband's urging, Sena refuses to be reconciled with her brother Zio. He becomes quite drunk, and in a stereotypically Balkan gesture, deliberately smashes his head against an empty wine bottle which he has placed on the table and, not unexpectedly, suffers a nasty wound. After he is carried to a room to recover, Sena makes the first reluctant and tentative steps toward reconciliation. Meša, in the meantime, takes his own vengeance by beckoning Ankica to the cellar where he callously takes her sexually. At first reluctant, Ankica eventually gives way to her passion. At the conclusion of their sexual coupling, Meša leaves Ankica lying on the straw-covered earthen floor and contemptuously turns his back on her. In this act Meša has achieved a double vengeance; the sexual humiliation of Ankica and the cuckolding of his brother-in-law Zio. Ankica is so overcome with shame that she tries to hang herself from the rope of an old-fashioned privy. Alas, the rope is too long and she lands on her feet—succeeding only in flushing the toilet!

There are also images of separation and loss in the sequence. The querulous grandfather Mustafir is fed up with family politics and the larger politics of the time, packs his bag, and removes himself to a rest home. Young Malik follows his soccer ball to the window of their cellar, and is shocked to witness his father coupling with Ankica. This rude revelation, combined with the "loss" of his grandfather and the earlier loss of his

VII–2   Young love: Malik and Maša. *When Father Was Away on Business (Otac na službenom putu)*

first sweet love for Maša, a young girl suffering from a fatal blood disease, prompts Malik's last magical sleepwalking sequence which concludes the film.

Reconciliation with the larger political order is signaled by the "mock" interrogation scene conducted by the pragmatic and "enlightened" Communist official and *bon vivant* Čekić, who breaks the initial tension of the interview by joyfully announcing to Meša that he has been fully rehabilitated and is free to return to Sarajevo. Hope is also engendered by radio coverage of the famous three-to-one victory of the Yugoslav soccer team over the Soviet team in the final Olympic qualifying round held in Tampere, Finland, on Tuesday, July 22, 1952. Malik excitedly repeats the names of this legendary team: Beara, Stanković, Crnković, Čajkovski, Horvat, Boškov, Ognjanov, Mitić, Vukas, Bobek and Zebec, names which are a part of the fabric and myth of the times.[22]

Such a brief synopsis scarcely does justice to the aesthetic richness and complexity of the film. Structurally, Kusturica achieves one level of complexity by subtly shifting the narrative focus of the film from the innocent, precocious and mischievous perspective of the six-year-old child narrator Malik, to the "objective" camera which records scenes outside Malik's knowledge and experience. In an illuminating interview in Yugoslavia's leading weekly *NIN*, Kusturica explains, "I wanted to make a film which would talk about the period through the eyes of a boy who lives through all the consequences of his father being arrested. It is on his back and through his consciousness that history is refracted, although here, history is presented through emotions rather than facts."[23]

While Kusturica's film is not concerned with historicity and semi-documentary reconstruction, it nonetheless provides a realistic and richly detailed evocation of the material and cultural conditions of the time, and the clash between the traditional values and rituals of a Moslem family and the new socialist order which took shape after the Second World War. The circumcision ritual of Malik and his older brother Mirza, the wedding party at the end of the film, the Orthodox funeral for the father of Malik's best friend Jožo, are blended and seamlessly wed with the scene of the staged outdoor aviation exercise in which the "New Socialist Woman," Ankica, performs her daring loop-the-loops in a glider plane accompanied by pompous political ceremonies and speeches, and the scene of young Malik, representing the Communist Young Pioneers, forgetting and mixing-up his little public speech in such a way that he innocently commits the political heresy of downgrading Tito.

The film is filled with humor, ranging from the situational to the satiric and mordant, which serves to undercut and punch holes in official as well as personal solemnities. The Orthodox funeral, for example, is held for a neighbor, Vlado, who had also been arrested for Stalinist sympathies and presumably had committed suicide. But his body was not returned. In its place in the casket, resting on the pillow, is a photograph of the presumed dead Vlado. Peering into the casket, Malik observes, "I know when someone dies, he disappears, but he doesn't just vanish."

Kusturica also subtly blends social realism with Chagallian surrealism in Malik's sleepwaking sequences. In these sequences the rich earth tones of the cinematographer's palette (Vilko Filać who, like Kusturica, received his professional film training at FAMU in Prague) shifts to a softly focused magical luminosity. Each of the four sleepwalking sequences in the film is prompted by psychological conflicts in young Malik, and is dominated by images of aspiration and transcendence. In the first sequence, Malik walks across the narrow upper beam of a bridge across the Drina River. In the second sequence, he walks to the top of a tall cliff where he stands precariously until rescued by his father. In the third sequence he walks across the darkened streets to the home of his beloved Maša, ascends the stairs, and is tucked into bed beside Maša by her Russian émigré father, who comprehends the mystical union that has developed between his fatally ill daughter and Malik. In the final sleepwalking sequence which ends the film, Malik is miraculously levitated above the rooftops and trees. He turns to face the camera directly with the softly focused mountains surrounding Sarajevo in the background, and smiles enigmatically as the frame freezes.

Kusturica's film is obviously not a didactic or overt political tract. It is a film in which the cruel ambiguities of the time and the face of repression are countered with humor, magic, lyricism, and the elasticity of the human spirit, with all of its foibles and contradictions. In the final scene, young Malik has transcended the particularities of his family and of the times, and has entered what Eliade calls the "sacred" time of myth—a time which is recurrently present and which exists both in and out of history.

In the film *Happy New Year, 1949*, the director Stole Popov and his gifted and well-known scenarist Gordan Mihić punctuate the period of the Tito-Stalin split at a very different juncture than Kusturica's film. The film takes place during the fateful six months following Yugoslavia's expulsion from the Cominform on June 28, 1948, to the eve of Yugoslavia's blackest year since the end of the war, 1949. Near the end of the film, a group of forlorn revellers, framed in long shot, huddled together on the platform of a small provincial Macedonian train station, ironically ring in the new year, 1949, a year which was anything but "happy" in Yugoslavia.

During the months immediately following the Cominform expulsion, Yugoslavia suffered severe economic disruptions created by the Cominform-imposed economic blockade. Western economic aid and trade did not develop until several months into 1949, and the Tito-led leadership initially attempted to counter the anathema pronounced against it by proving what good Stalinists they were, using measures that included the imposition in 1949 of a disastrous policy of farm collectivization which further exacerbated an already escalating problem of food production and distribution. Moreover, Yugoslavia faced serious military buildups on her borders, and was diplomatically isolated by Stalin-directed purges and mock trials carried out against so-called "Titoists" in East European socialist countries.[24]

Popov's film vividly captures these dark days, and the dramatic progression of his film, as contrasted with Kusturica's, is one of disintegration, defeat and tragedy. The film is set in Skopje, the capital of Yugoslavia's Republic of Macedonia, and like Kusturica's film, focuses upon the dynamics of a family caught up in the maelstrom of the times.

In the opening of the film, the aging father is trying to hold the family together. The mother is gravely ill in a hospital and dies shortly afterwards. The father, his youngest son Kurla, and his young daughter Nada, are living at the brink of bare subsistence. The oldest son, Bota, is returning from the Soviet Union by train when the shocking news of Yugoslavia's expulsion is announced. Some passengers decide to return to the Soviet Union, others are induced by the KGB to act as informers inside Yugoslavia, and a friend of Bota's, who cannot resolve his conflicting loyalties, commits suicide on the train shortly after it crosses the Yugoslav border. Bota remains steadfastly loyal to Yugoslavia and resolves to start a new life with Vera, whom he met in the Soviet Union and who is returning with him on the train.

Bota's younger brother Kosta is completely alienated from the new socialist Yugoslavia and is engaged in smuggling activities and in protecting his territory from rival thugs. Bota attempts to reunite the family upon his arrival in Skopje, but is arrested and interrogated as a suspected Soviet agent. He is imprisoned, later cleared of the charges, but is further detained as an inducement to become an informer for the Yugoslav secret police. Bota resists intense pressure to become an informer, and is finally released.

In the meantime his brother Kosta has provided assistance and protection to Vera and they become sexually involved. Upon his release from prison, Bota learns of Vera's infidelity and that she has been compromised by the KGB in order to protect a brother still in the Soviet Union. After a complex moral struggle, Bota informs on Vera to the Yugoslav police authorities. Vera commits suicide before she is arrested. Bota, his personal integrity shattered, also commits suicide by quietly pointing a gun to his head and firing. Kosta, who has been savagely beaten by his rivals and returns to discover Vera's dead body in his apartment, gathers his waning strength to hop a train heading for Greece. The last sequence of the film intercuts overhead shots of the speeding train with shots of Kosta, half-frozen, clinging to the undercarriage of the train, to his life, and to the hope of escape.

Popov's film provides a tougher-edged evocation of the period and one less tinged with nostalgic remembrance than Kusturica's more celebrated film. An atmosphere of material deprivation, oppressive tension, swift betrayals, and harsh police tactics is mirrored and reflected in the betrayal and dissolution of family relationships. The irony of the film's title is given a bitter edge in the final sequence in which Kosta, who totally rejects the new social order, is the only one with enough remaining vitality to seek escape from the "madhouse" that Yugoslavia had become. The film won first prize at the 1986 Pula festival of Yugoslav feature films and received widespread critical acclaim from both Yugoslav and foreign critics.

The film *Balkan Spy*, codirected by the talented cinematographer Božidar Nikolić and the gifted comedy playwright and scenarist Dušan Kovačević, deals with Yugoslavia's Stalinist legacy in a very different way than the two films just discussed. In this film, the paranoia of the past is projected into a contemporary setting and the film mixes broad humor, farce and black comedy to underscore its absurdities and contradictions. The protagonist of the film, Ilija Čvorović, lives on the outskirts of Belgrade with his wife and daughter and enjoys the blessings of contemporary bourgeois socialism. Ilija is a Serbian provincial who spent two years in prison for shouting a popular slogan praising "Stalin and the Glorious Revolution" at a time when it was no longer fashionable to do so. His brother Djura was even more passionately devoted to Stalin and spent four years in jail. Ilija and the other male members of his family gave their all to the National War of Liberation and naïvely believed in the Stalinist slogans they had learned during the war and its aftermath. Ilija is satirized as an unredeemed Stalinist troglodyte who keeps his old loyalties, consisting of a large portrait of Stalin and guns from the Second World War, buried in the cellar.

The other major character in the film is Petar Jakovljević, who has rented a room from Ilija. Petar is cultivated and worldly, and has just returned from Paris where he has achieved success as a fashion designer. He is attempting to reestablish himself in Belgrade and moves within a small circle of sophisticated and educated friends.

At the beginning of the film, Ilija is summoned to the police station and asked routine questions about his tenant. This encounter with the authorities resurrects all of Ilija's old fears and anxieties, and he develops a full-blown conspiracy theory concerning the presumed nefarious activities of his tenant. He decides to redeem his past and fight for the good of the country by personally investigating and exposing Petar as a spy, as a part of a ring that reaches "all the way to the White House and the cowboy." His naïve interpretations of the innocent meetings of Petar and his friends gradually build into a paranoiac preoccupation which alarms his wife and threatens the security of their comfortable existence. Gradually Ilija convinces his wife Danica that he is fighting for a great cause and enlists the help of his brother Djura and four other male members of his family who dress in old-fashioned suits and snap-brim hats.

The initial farcical and lighthearted tone of the film, however, turns de-

VII–3   Ilica and Djura in hot pursuit. *The Balkan Spy (Balkanski špijun)*

cidedly darker as the film progresses. Ilija and his brothers capture Petar, tie him to a chair, and interrogate and beat him. While Djura and the others are out of the room, Ilija reveals the depths of his psychological scars from the past, and his uncomprehending and primitive feelings of despair at the injustice done to him while his tenant Petar had spent thirty successful years abroad. Ilija's poignant and passionate speech brings on a heart attack. Petar struggles to the phone, calls for an ambulance, and then escapes from the house still handcuffed to the chair, knowing that if Djura returns he will simply shoot him.

The last scene of the film shows Ilija clutching his chest and crawling on the road in pursuit of Petar, who is running as best he can with the chair held over his head. Both men are symbiotically bound together and handicapped by life and the past. Achieving the good life had not prepared Ilija for the complexities of modern living in urbanized Yugoslavia, and Petar is a diabetic expatriate with little prospect for finding his roots again.

Of the dozen feature films dealing with this theme over the past few years, two others deserve special mention. The accomplished and internationally respected director Lordan Zafranović—Sunday II (Nedelja II, 1969), Dalmatian Chronicle (Dalmatinska kronika, 1972), The Matthew Passions (Muke po mati, 1975), Occupation in 26 Scenes (Okupacija u 26 slika, 1978), The Fall of Italy (Pad Italije, 1981), The Angel's Bite (Ujed Anđela, 1984)—in his stylistically most mature film, Evening Bells (Večernja zvona, 1986), based on the award-winning novel by Mirko Kovač, provides a complex rendering of the period from 1926 to 1948 in which the protagonist Tomislav K., in the final sequences of the film, senselessly loses his life in prison after being falsely arrested as a Stalinist sympathizer. The film Dancing on Water (Bal na vodi, 1986), directed and written by Jovan Aćin and released in the U.S. under the curious and maladroit title Hey, Babu Riba, provides a nostalgic and witty evocation of the early fifties in which Yugoslavia was struggling to emerge from the Stalinist pall and move toward greater normalcy.

All of these films evoke the ambiguities and contradictions of the past and, in differing ways, critically reexamine the official mythology of Yugoslavia's socialist founding and evolution from heroic Partisan war to early Stalinist orthodoxy to the "progressive" break with Stalin to a system of enlightened "self-management" socialism. The tensions and dilemmas created in Yugoslavia by a self-managing, participatory, polycentric form of decision-making which stresses consultation and consensus on the one hand, and a one-party, hierarchically organized state apparatus in which decision-making flows from the top down on the other, have never been satisfactorily resolved to the present time.[25] These films rework the substrata of collective experience into critical filmic visions which infuse the present with the haunting contours of the past.

The Old Order Revisited

One of the brightest and most inventive films of the eighties is Slobodan Šijan's debut film *Who's That Singing Over There* (*Ko to tamo peva*, 1980) directed in collaboration with the scenarist Dušan Kovačević and the cinematographer Božidar Nikolić. The film wittily portrays a group of provincials making their way to Belgrade in a rickety bus, owned by KRSTIĆ AND SON, unaware of the tragedy that awaits them on that fatal day, Sunday, 6 April 1941, when Nazi Germany launched its savage bombing attack on Belgrade under the code name "Operation Punishment." Although the distance to Belgrade is only 100 kilometers, it takes the antique bus, fired by a coal-burning steam engine with a stack protruding from the roof, a full two days to make the journey. The bus travels over two-rut roads which sometimes disappear altogether and is diverted in its short journey by army maneuvers, a ploughed-up section of the road, and an unsafe bridge.

The passengers on the bus are a microcosm of the predominantly rural Yugoslavia which existed between the wars. There is a maladroit hunter from Belgrade returning from an unsuccessful hunting trip, a young married

VII–4   A provincial bus station. *Who's That Singing Over There (Ko to tamo peva)*

couple eager to consummate their nuptial vows at every opportunity, a village official dressed in black who is a Nazi sympathizer, an old Serbian soldier, a tubercular man, a local crooner on his way to Belgrade for an audition, the bus conductor and his not-very-bright son who drives the bus, and two Gypsy singers—a man and a young boy. The trip is filled with comic, sometimes slapstick episodes in which all of the characters reveal their motivations for going to Belgrade, and their general unpreparedness and lack of awareness of the destruction that awaits them.

The film vividly captures and satirizes the primitive conditions of the times, the narrow provincialism, the ineffectuality of the once-proud Yugoslav Army, and the petty quarrels and concerns of the passengers. The tone of the film turns darker when the bus arrives in Belgrade. The passengers verbally abuse and beat the two Gypsies who are falsely accused of stealing the wallet of the old Serbian soldier. In the chilling conclusion, the bombs fall, destroying the bus and killing all of the passengers except the two Gypsies who stand in the rubble and sing of the terrors to come.

This cinematic portrait-in-miniature of pre-war Yugoslavia is informed by tolerance and a humanistic embrace of all of the colorful characters who share this last fateful ride together. Sharp satire blends with nostalgic remembrance of a time past, a more innocent time, a decaying epoch which ends in flames and rubble.[26]

Another stylistically inventive and imaginative film dealing with interwar Yugoslavia is *The Raft of the Medusa* (*Splav meduze*, 1980), directed by Karpo Godina in collaboration with one of the most influential scenarists of the *new film* period, Branko Vučičević. Eschewing conventional narrative development, the film presents a visually stylish portrait of Yugoslavia in the twenties imbued with the spirit and style of Dada and surrealism. It focuses on four young avant-garde male cosmopolitans and two female school teachers who join up with a strongman and his assistant to form a "living theater" troupe traveling through the northern provinces of Yugoslavia and spreading radical ideas to uncomprehending audiences. An ironic modern counterpoint to those adrift on Géricault's raft in the classic painting of the French Romantic period, they move, in Vučičević's words, "on a sea of mud, shish-kebab, poverty, corruption and crazy Serbian chauvinism."[27]

Stalinist Aftermath

One of the most interesting and original recent films dealing with Yugoslavia's immediate post-war period of reconstruction is *You Only Love Once* (*Samo jednom se ljubi*, 1981), released under the English title *The Melody Haunts My Memory*.[28] Directed by Rajko Grlić—*Whichever Way the Ball Bounces* (*Kud puklo da puklo*, 1974), *Bravo Maestro*, 1978, *The Jaws of Life* (*U raljama života*, 1984), *Three's Happiness* (*Za sreću je potrebno troje*, 1986)—who also wrote the scenario in collaboration with

VII–5   Preaching to the unconverted. *The Raft of the Medusa (Splav meduse)*

Branko Somen, the film focuses upon a young Partisan hero, Tomislav, a bright, passionately intense but untutored provincial, who energetically joins two youthful wartime companions in administering a small town and rebuilding its local industry. He meets and falls in love with Beba ("baby"), a sensitive, cultured young ballerina, who has been sent to the small town from Zagreb as part of a work brigade. Her father is under heavy suspicion as a wartime enemy collaborator, and her sister had earlier run off with a German soldier. The more passionately Tomislav becomes involved with Beba, the more estranged he becomes from his close companions and fellow political commissars. Against their solemn warnings, he marries Beba in the new way, a Communist civil ceremony. On their wedding night, Tomislav introduces the shy and initially reluctant bride to the joys of sexual fulfillment. As the film progresses, there are several erotic scenes of lovemaking in which Beba becomes increasingly liberated and inventive. The lovemaking is imbued with an almost desperate intensity, as if the two lovers were attempting by sheer force of physical desire and passion to burn through the social barriers which separate them and the negative forces arrayed against their union. Beba's parents, members of the pre-war well-educated middle class, come for a prolonged visit. Their disdain for their daughter's choice of a husband and the rude conditions in which she lives is barely masked by civility and refined manners. In the meantime, suspicions mount concerning Tomislav's political reliability, and he is dismissed from the Party and his post. After losing his place in the new order, Tomislav follows a downward spiral of mental anguish and despair.

In the final sequence of the film, Tomislav follows Beba (who has returned to Zagreb) to a tawdry music hall where he discovers that she is dancing as a showgirl, having found no opportunity to pursue her career as a ballerina. Making his way to the dressing room, an exhausted, disillusioned and emptied Tomislav is momentarily soothed and reassured by Beba, who then leaves him alone in order to perform her next dance routine. Sitting alone in the crowded and tacky dressing room, Tomislav shoots himself in the head and slumps over dead in the chair.

The film imaginatively captures the spartan existence of the times and the political and social contradictions which eventually tear Tomislav apart. On one level there is the political contradiction of revolutionary idealism and youthful elan rubbing up against the emergence of special privileges and an increasingly intolerant new social and political structure. At another level there is the class conflict between Tomislav's peasant upbringing and the professional middle-class refinements of Beba's family. It is the complex cinematic representation of these class and sociopolitical vortices which lifts the love story above the level of melodrama, and makes the suicide at the end of the film both poignant and dramatically effective.

CONTEMPORARY REALITY:
CRITICAL VISIONS

In the more than four decades since the end of the Second World War, Yugoslavia has accomplished a remarkable transition from a predominantly rural and small-town culture based on an agrarian economy to a modern, urbanized, and industrial state. Despite backward areas, poverty, unemployment and inequalities, the general lot of the nations and nationalities constituting Yugoslavia has, until recently, steadily improved. New towns and suburbs have sprung up around the major cities to accommodate the steady influx of people from the countryside, consumer goods have proliferated, the university system has been greatly expanded, new roads and improved transportation and communication systems have been established, and political and economic freedoms have remained greater than in any other Communist state.

Along with the progress, as indicated in the beginning of this chapter, have come problems and contradictions carried in the wake of rapid material development. Contemporary Yugoslavia is now blessed with blocks of concrete high-rises, a high and persistent inflation rate, political stagnation, a huge balance-of-payments deficit, housing shortages, the inability

VII–6   Beba's sensuality. *You Only Love Once (Samo jednom se ljubi)*

VII–7   Tomislav's downward spiral. *You Only Love Once (Samo jednom se ljubi)*

to absorb increasing numbers of university graduates and professionally educated young people into the economy, stymied or neglected agricultural
development, the erosion of traditional values, and the breakdown of civility and personal relationships in the cities (exemplified by rising divorce
rates, drug problems, and violent crime). A proper balance or equilibrium
has not always been struck between the needs of town and country, agriculture and industrialization, the underdeveloped South and the more prosper-
ous North, local or individual initiative and central control and, in the international sphere, between East and West.

Such tensions and contradictions have offered fertile material for filmic
expression. Once again, as in the sixties, filmmakers are reflecting critically on *savremene teme* (contemporary themes) and expressing sometimes jolting and somber images of society's stresses, disruptions, disloca-
tions and social ironies.

One of the most inventive recent films dealing with urban malaise is
Strangler Versus Strangler (*Davitelj protiv davitelja*, 1984), directed by
Slobodan Šijan from an original script which he wrote with Nebojša
Pajkić. The film is both an elaborate parody of a Hitchcockian psychological thriller and a witty, bizarre, surrealistic and mordant satire on urban decadence, moral relativism, youthful iconoclasm, and the breakdown of public civility.

The principal strangler in the film, Pero, is etched with black humor as
a sad-eyed, timid, middle-aged man who lives with his tyrannical mother
and makes a living peddling carnations. He gorges himself on sweets,
loves the opera where patrons still buy "old-fashioned" carnations, is
bathed by his mother at night, and is punished by her when he fails to
sell his daily quota of carnations—she canes him across his outstretched
open palms. For entertainment, Pero hand-pumps an old-fashioned organ
while his mother sings traditional songs loudly and off key. They live in
an apartment filled with old furniture and Orthodox icons.

Pero's first victim is a chic, cool, contemporary young woman who
wears slacks and a mannishly styled hat. At a cafe in the evening she contemptuously dismisses Pero and refuses to accept his carnations even
though her male friend had offered to buy them for her. Pero is incensed,
dates himself by muttering "Some flower children!" and follows the
young woman to her apartment. She refuses to be intimidated, turns and
confronts Pero, and angrily berates him for following her. More in self-
defense than anger, Pero reaches for her throat, discovers his considerable strength, and strangles her.

Pero's second victim is an accomplished opera singer who also dis-
dains carnations and orders Pero out of her dressing room. She expires before reaching high C.

The deeds of Pero capture the imagination of a slender, neurotic young
new wave composer, Spiridon (Spiro), who despises beautiful women because his father had remarried a sexy younger woman who torments

Spiro with a superheated sexuality which he cannot handle. He becomes telepathically linked to Pero who answers his own neurotic need to grab the world by the neck. He deflects his urges into a *new wave* composition celebrating the deeds of the strangler which catches on with new wavers and punkers and leads to an anarchic concert at the "Brewery." Sofija, a sophisticated and coolly intellectual TV commentator, dissects the new piece on her show "Rockalade," and dismisses it as pseudo avantgarde, inspired by immaturity and misogynism. She satirizes both the composer-singer Spiro and his composition as sick extensions of "Nazi Punk" and other anarchic musical aberrations of the eighties.

Pero is enthralled by the new song about his deeds and becomes a follower of *new wave* concerts where he sells his carnations and applauds Spiro's performances with the same zeal he once reserved for his favorite operas. He is outraged by the negative review of the work given by Sofija. While he is watching her program on TV his mother is singing loudly behind him. He reaches back to silence her and without realizing it, ends her off-key renditions forever. He does not accept that his mother is dead and leaves her propped in her rocking chair for the remainder of the film. He imagines that she talks to him and eventually dresses as his mother and takes on her guise.

The third major character in this triangulation of strangulation is the aging, conventional police inspector Ognjen Stahinjić, who is under increasing public pressure to apprehend the strangler, and becomes so obsessed by the case that he works himself into depression and a nervous breakdown. At one point in the film, he is saved from hanging himself only by the imagined good advice of his pet cat Đorđe (George). The inspector's behavior becomes as deranged and surrealistic as that of Spiro and Pero.

Both Pero and Spiro are in pursuit of the TV commentator Sofija to avenge themselves for her negative review. In a bizarre three-way confrontation, Sofija spiritedly fights off Pero by biting off one of his ears before losing consciousness. When she revives, she mistakenly believes that Spiro is her rescuer. They discover a strong attraction to one another and embrace passionately. The inspector arrives late as usual, and is elated to discover his first piece of physical evidence in the case, Pero's ear, which he proudly displays on TV.

Sofija and Spiro are married in a conventional Orthodox ceremony and eagerly consummate their love on their wedding night. Sofija assumes the dominant one-up position, and as their lovemaking becomes more passionate she reaches for Spiro's throat and begins playfully strangling him. Spiro is seized by the same urge, and strangles her back. Alas, Spiro gets carried away and Sofija expires at the point of orgasm.

The film concludes with a series of intricate plot twists and Hitchcockian surprise endings. In the summary battle of the film, fought among the rafters of an old building, Pero and Spiro (now antagonists) en-

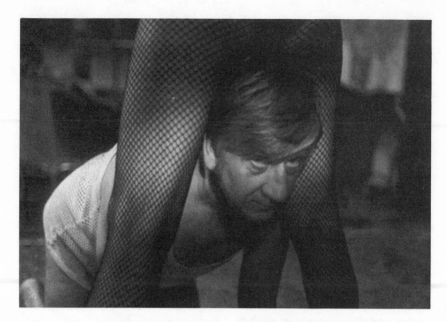

VII–8   Ambiguity in sexual roles. *Strangler Versus Strangler (Davitejl protiv davitelja)*

gage in mortal combat. Spiro manages to wrap a rope around Pero's neck. Pero slips backwards and hangs himself, clinging to one of Spiro's ears which is severed by the force of Pero's backward fall. The mad inspector arrives on the scene, assumes incorrectly that Sofija is Pero's last victim, and declares Spiro a hero.

In the epilogue of the film, Spiro is enjoying a romantic interlude on the Adriatic with the voluptuous young former wife of his recently deceased father. This idyllic scene is followed by concluding shots of Pero's darkened and decrepit apartment with the rotting bones of his mother still poised in the chair. Spiro has also been propelled into respectability and fame by transposing his *new wave* composition into the avant-garde orchestral composition which opened the film—framed with a back shot of one-eared Spiro conducting the piece. The film concludes with Spiro's avant-garde composition playing on the soundtrack celebrating the mordant message: "Some stranglers are born under a lucky star—and others are not."

Šijan's film is a mordant satire on the breakdown of traditional society and the replacement of old norms by a pervasive relativism, youthful iconoclasm, urban decadence, and sexual ambivalence. Especially well captured is the anarchic and inconoclastic spirit of a segment of Yugoslavia's youth which is radically disaffiliated from mainstream values and sacred

myths. Unlike the politically explicit radical youth movements in Yugoslavia during the late sixties, youthful disaffection in the eighties has often
been deflected into various rock, *new wave* and punk styles. The most radical of these new styles celebrate the values of anarchy, surrender, decline, and societal exile, voluntarily assumed.[29]

Šijan's film also adopts a satirical and ambivalent attitude toward new
sexual identities, the emergence of the modern liberated woman, and recent doubts concerning traditional Balkan virility and male chauvinism.[30]
Sofija personifies the strong, independent, intellectually astute woman,
but is also portrayed in the film as cool, "bitchy" and emasculating. The
proverbial "war between the sexes" is given a surrealistic twist in Spiro's
and Sofija's synthesis of copulation and strangulation.

A film which deals more explicitly with ambiguities in contemporary rela-
tionships between the sexes is *The Jaws of Life* (*U raljama života*, 1984),
directed by Rajko Grlić from a script written in collaboration with
Dubravka Ugrešić, the author of the novel upon which the film is based.
The film satirically interweaves the fate of Stefica Cvek, the heroine of a
TV series which parodies kitschy romantic love stories, and that of
Dunja, the creator and director of the series. The TV series "Stefica Cvek
in the Jaws of Life," opens with the theme song:

> I've met a gaze divine
> In the jaws of life.
> My love, kiss me please,
> In the jaws of life.

The heroine Stefica works as a clerk, is shy and slightly overweight, and
lives in a modest apartment with her aunt. Stefica takes her cues of modernity from empty chatter on the TV set which emphasizes the importance
of being slender and attractive. This message is underscored by Stefica's
aunt who advises her that, in order to catch a man, a girl must have the
"muscles of a panther ready to leap." Stefica yearns for sexual liberation
and tenderness. Her worldly but shallow older friend Marijana (who has
been married five times) gives Stefica advice on how to come out of her
shell, and while Stefica's aunt is out of town, arranges for a series of three
unlikely suitors to call on Stefica and introduce her to the joys of sexual
fulfillment. Stefica is hopeful and fully prepared to offer herself to each of
the motley threesome. The first is a taciturn, world-weary young man who
ejaculates prematurely and promptly falls asleep. The second is an over-the-
hill Serbian provincial whose macho pretensions ("I will screw you for
twenty hours straight") mask a flagrant case of impotence. He fails even to
enter the portal. The last is an alcoholic quasi-intellectual whose wife has
just left him for a plumber. He lapses into an alcoholic stupor before he
can satisfy Stefica's tender longings.

In the meantime, Dunja, the creator of this TV parody, is not faring
much better than her heroine. She is a warmly attractive, ambitious, inde-

VII–9   Stefica's alcoholic suitor. *The Jaws of Life (U raljama života)*

pendent and successful woman who lives in a well-appointed terrace apartment and moves in sophisticated circles. Her current lover, Sale, with
whom she shares her apartment, is a bored, chauvinistic Marxist polemi-
cist and TV commentator. On his TV program, he delivers a stinging indictment of a book critical of Yugoslavia's Stalinist past—without ever having read it! He becomes especially tiresome when Dunja permits an old
male friend, a down-and-out sixties rock musician, to camp out on her terrace. She mercifully delivers herself from Sale by throwing him out of her
apartment.

Dunja finds friendship and amusement with a male friend, Pipo, who
masks feelings of desperation and angst with gentleness and humor. In
his mid-thirties, he is impotent, lives with his mother, who is a well-
travelled and successful opera singer, and complains of making five times
less in salary for his technical expertise than he would earn in America. He
half-yearns to go to America, but uses his mother's presumed need for him
as an excuse for inaction. Pipo spends a platonic night in bed with Dunja,
and later makes a blundering and unsuccessful attempt at suicide. In the
meantime, Stefica comes to a similar decision in the TV series, with equal
lack of success.

Under pressure from her male producer, Dunja provides a sentimental
happy ending for her TV heroine. In the series, Stefica is inspired by a
pitch on TV to learn English. At the language institute, she meets the interested and tender gaze of a nice young man. They overcome initial shy-

ness by addressing each other in halting, textbook correct English and mutual happiness is snatched from the jaws of life.

Having contrived a happy ending for her heroine, Dunja decides to snatch some happiness in her own life. She tenderly leads Pipo out of his impotence and the film ends on an upbeat note. Pipo has further liberated himself by firmly resolving to go to America—a decision which fails to ruffle a hair on his mother's head. The kitsch ending of both the film and the film-within-the-film involves a double irony. It ironically suggests that life among the "sophisticated" may not be as far removed from kitsch as sometimes assumed. It also suggests that "contrived" happy endings do not address the multiple issues which the film raises. It may not be so easy to snatch happiness from the jaws of a life trivialized by television and fragmented by the inchoate pressures and anomie of urban living. Sentimental endings do not resolve the pressures on women who work as hard and as long as men, and who are also expected to assume the major burden of child-rearing and homemaking. They do not resolve the dilemma of well-educated, professional women who find themselves trapped at middle levels of organizational structures hierarchically dominated by men. At a deeper level, the film may implicitly convey the defensive patriarchal message that females grow stronger (i.e., take their rightful and equal place in society) only at the expense of weakening males—sending them into alcoholic stupors, spiritual angst, and genital flaccidity.

One of the most consistently original and cinematically inventive of the "Czech school" of Yugoslav directors, Srđan Karanović—Social Games (Društvena igra, 1972), The Scent of Wild Flowers (Miris poljskog cveća, 1978), Petrija's Wreath (Petrijin venac, 1980)—has made two recent films which critically evoke the tensions, contradictions and sense of crisis and inertia which have characterized Yugoslavia in the eighties. Something In-Between (Nešto između, 1983), for which he also wrote the scenario in collaboration with Milosav Marinović and the American Andrew Horton, is an engaging portrayal of a young American woman journalist who, in a brief six-week stay in Belgrade, finds herself caught "in-between" her sexual and sentimental attachments to two Yugoslav men. At a deeper level, the film explores the ambivalent posture of Yugoslavia, herself trapped "in-between" the political tensions of East and West and the cultural and economic collisions of North and South. Karanović was awarded first prize for best direction at the Pula Festival in 1983. The film received high critical praise at Cannes, and won the top prize at the fourth International Film Festival in Valencia, Spain.

Karanović's more recent film, A Throatful of Strawberries (Jagode u grlu, 1985), for which he wrote the script in collaboration with Rajko Grlić, conveys a somewhat more somber image of contemporary malaise. The film is built around the reunion of four old friends in their late thirties who have followed different paths since their student days of the sixties. The precipitating event for the reunion is the return of Miki Rubirosa, who has achieved material success abroad and is stopping over in Belgrade for a few days before going on to Vienna. He rents a Mercedes with a chauffeur to impress his friends and throws a party in a run-down boat cafe on the Sava river, complete with musicians and abundant drink and food. All of his friends have reached a critical point in their lives, and none have achieved the hopes they had formed in the relatively more optimistic and politically committed days of the sixties. Branislav (Brane) has managed to hustle the system, secure a nice apartment, marry his old sweetheart, sire two children, and dabble in infidelities. But his marriage is coming apart and dissolves completely during the course of the film. One of the friends is slipping into alcoholism, working at a low-paying job below his qualifications, is separated from his wife, and brings a young girlfriend, Vesna, to the party. Another of the friends, Boca, has achieved minor celebrity status as a TV commentator by delivering searing critiques of Yugoslavia's troubled political and economic situation. He drinks heavily despite a bad ulcer and delivers a litany of popular complaints: "They cannot pay me less than I work;" "People are getting mean, testy;" and "We can discuss anything without being thrown in jail, but nothing changes."

As the film progresses, Miki sheds his surface polish and sophistication and vainly attempts to recapture the *joie de vivre* and companionship of

VII–10   Brane's perfunctory infidelity. *A Throatful of Strawberries* (*Jagode u grlu*)

past days. He makes an attempt to seduce Vesna, but is deflected by her resistance and his own impotence. The unmerry merrymaking ultimately degenerates into a mindless game of tag played out on the boat, across the plank, and on the shore. Standing aloof from these disillusioned and desperate games is the young chauffeur, who rescues Vesna, unties the boat from its moorings, and watches it drift aimlessly down the Sava carrying its drunken cargo. He drives off with her in the Mercedes.

The pervasive mood of the film is one of malaise, fragmentation, and drift. The four companions in the film were all born in 1945, the "beginning of a new era," and have grown into disillusioned and troubled middle age, along with the social system of which they are a part.

The darkest cinematic metaphor of a disintegrating social order is evoked in the film *Life Is Beautiful* (*Život je lep*, 1985), directed by Boro Drašković from a script based on a controversial novel by the talented writer Aleksandar Tišma. Passengers on a train are trapped in a remote village because the engineer refuses to go on. Tired and disillusioned, he stops the train as a way of protesting the stasis and lack of direction in the whole social system which he describes as "falling apart." The passengers are self-absorbed, spiritually depleted, and confronted by the pent-up frustration and alienation of the local young men who are trapped on a flat plain and in a barren life. The animosity of the provincials towards the passengers reaches its highest pitch of cruelty in the local inn where the most varied

VII–11   Forced joie de vivre. *A Throatful of Strawberries* (*Jagode u grlu*)

and pessimistic sentiments are expressed and indifference to human values is brutally revealed. The leader of the young locals, Zaro, takes special delight in tormenting a pretty young provincial singer, Ana, and the two untalented musicians who accompany her. Zaro intimidates Ana into singing over and over again the song "Život je lep" ("Life Is Beautiful") until it becomes a harsh, ironic and discordant refrain. He further humiliates her by hanging a cowbell around her neck and forcing her to ring it as she sings. At one point he offers the exhausted musicians wine—but instead of wine the glasses are filled with vinegar.

A quiet and brooding presence in the film is a disaffected young man, Vita, who has returned to the village after failing in the larger world. He is attracted to the shy and sensitive young singer, Ana, and attempts to protect her from the brutalities of Zaro and the other locals. In the chilling conclusion of the film, Zaro leads Ana to a back room and takes her sexually while other men are lined up waiting their turns. Vita discovers Zaro in the act of sexual intercourse, takes out a gun and shoots him twice in the back. He further expresses his cold rage by firing repeatedly into the onlookers. The film concludes with a long shot of Vita, standing on the barren plain silhouetted against the first rays of dawn. He points the gun to his head and takes his own life.

Drašković succeeds admirably in preserving the literary integrity of the

VII–12   Ana's song. *Life Is Beautiful (Život je lep)*

text upon which the film is based while, at the same time, creating a brooding and menacing cinematic ambience. The film won the Silver Medal at the 1985 Venice film festival, and provoked widespread critical discussion and controversy in Yugoslavia. Drašković's film is a somber warning against the dangers posed by prolonged social crisis and political stagnation. As Pedro Ramet has suggested: "In conditions of profound social stress, the edifice of political culture crumbles and feverish creativity appears. But the cost of transcending the crisis may be abandonment of a lot of old political baggage."[31]

Enhancing the resurgence of an artistically and socially more relevant era of Yugoslav filmmaking are several feature films which comment sharply on contemporary problems of mismanaged self-management, alcoholism, care for the aged, youthful drug addiction, juvenile delinquency and medical care. Among the most significant of these films are *Days on Earth Are Flowing By* (*Zemaljski dani teku*, 1979) and *Special Treatment* (*Posebni tretman*, 1980), directed by Goran Paskaljević, which deal respectively with institutional approaches to caring for the aged and the treatment of alcoholics, and *Variola Vera*, 1982, directed by Goran Marković, which depicts personal venality and corruption in the medical and public health professions when a virulent outbreak occurs of a rare and fatal strain of smallpox with the medical name "Variola Vera." Marković, who both wrote and directed the film, was awarded first prize for best director and best screenplay at the 1982 Valencia film festival.

Several recent feature films have illuminated current dilemmas through the refracted lens of the immediate past. The most effective of these is *Do You Remember Dolly Bell* (*Sjećas li se Dolly Bell*, 1981), directed by Emir Kusturica in collaboration with the scenarist Abdullah Sidran. The film is set in the early sixties, when Yugoslavia was poised to enter her "second revolution"—a time of unprecedented cultural liberalization, economic growth, modernization, and innovative experimentation with self-management socialism. In a richly detailed portrayal of the period, Kusturica's film vividly depicts the forces of modernity and Western cultural influences colliding with traditional cultural norms and values, and of older forms of Marxist political orthodoxy clashing with steadily strengthening forces of socialist pragmatism and political and economic experimentation. The play of these larger sociocultural and political forces is framed against a skillfully drawn portrait of a sixteen-year-old boy, Dino Zolje, who lives with his poor family on the outskirts of Sarajevo, and whose painful process of growing into young manhood is poignantly assisted by a tender sexual liaison with a young prostitute, Dolly Bell. Kusturica's debut film was an enormous popular and critical success, and captured the Golden Lion for best first film at the 1981 Venice film festival.

Three of the most recent films produced in Yugoslavia at the time of this writing strongly confirm the artistic maturity and continued sociocultural vitality of her resurgent cinema. Živko Nikolić, one of the most rest-

VII–13   A better future? *Do You Remember Dolly Bell (Sjécas li se Dolly Bell)*

lessly inventive and experimental of the film directors to emerge in the seventies—*The Beasts* (*Beštije,* 1977), *Luka's Jovina* (*Jovana Lukina,* 1979), *The Death of Mr. Goluže* (*Smrt gospodine Goluže,* 1982), *Unseen Wonder* (*Čudo neviđeno,* 1984), *The Beauty of Vice* (*Lepota poroka,* 1986)—has recently made his most accessible and provocative film with the ironic title *In the Name of the People* (*U ime naroda,* 1987). The film combines hauntingly evocative scenes of underdevelopment with a searing examination of a mismanaged industrial enterprise upon which the local economy depends. Based upon an actual case, Nikolić's film transcends the particularities of self-management corruption to create a Kafkaesque fable of abusive power mysteriously exercised and built upon the willing complicity of its victims. In the final sequences of the film, perpetrators and victims alike conspire to cover up gross perversions of power, sexual exploitation, and secret manipulation. The honest protagonist of the film is physically cast out of this closed society, the gates are locked behind him, and the film ends with his forlorn figure framed in isolation.

Goran Paskaljević, whose film *Beach Guard in Winter* (*Čuvar plaže u zimskom periodu,* 1976) began the series of films by the "Czech School" of Yugoslav film directors in the late seventies, recently completed his most important film of the eighties, *Guardian Angel* (*Anđeo čuvar*, 1987). The film is a sensitive, cinematically rich, and compassionate dramatization of the real-life plight of young Yugoslav Gypsy children sold into bondage in Italy as beggars and petty thieves. Shot on location in Italy and in the Gypsy settlement of Ciganmala near Niš, Yugoslavia, the film paints an unromanticized and ethnographically authentic portrait of Gypsy life in a region where Gypsies lead a sedentary, segregated and economically depressed existence. The film depicts the unsuccessful efforts of a well-intentioned journalist to expose the inner workings of this modern trade in white slavery, and to gain the love and acceptance of a young Gypsy boy, Šaina. In the brutal conclusion of the film the journalist is savagely and fatally beaten by members of the Gypsy community and his dead body tossed on a rubbish heap outside the settlement. The rich imagery of the film is significantly enhanced by the skillfully edited musical sound track created by the versatile and talented Zoran Simjanović.

In his latest film *Déjà Vu* (*Već viđeno*, 1987), one of the most highly regarded of the "Czech School" directors, Goran Marković, departs from the sharp social commentary and satire which characterized his earlier films—*Special Education* (*Specijalno vaspitanje*, 1977), *National Category*

VII–14   Death of a journalist. *Guardian Angel* (*Anđeo čuvar*)

up to 785 cm (*Nacionalna klasa do 785 cm*, 1979), *Majstori, majstori* (1981), *Variola Vera* (1982), *Taiwan Canasta* (*Tajvanska kanasta*, 1985)—to create a tautly conceived and stylistically compelling psychological portrait of a once-brilliant pianist, Mihailo, who is haunted by childhood psychosexual traumas. A love affair with a beautiful young woman, Olga, prompts him to relive these tortured memories, shatters his fragile facade of "normalcy," and leads him to brutally murder Olga and her father. Olga's younger brother witnesses these murders from his hiding place and the cycle of neurotic disturbance is repeated in him. Marković's film exemplifies the high level of technical and artistic mastery which characterizes the best of the *new Yugoslav cinema* and the steadily ripening relationships which have developed between the writer-director Marković, the cinematographer Živko Zalar, the music director Zoran Simjanović, and a seasoned cast of excellent actors and actresses.

CONCLUSION

It is difficult to assess whether the cinematic accomplishments of Yugoslavia's recently touted *new Yugoslav cinema* can be sustained. There has perhaps never been a period in Yugoslavia's post-war film development in which there have been so many seasoned, artistically gifted, and professionally well-trained film directors, cinematographers, scenar-

VII–15   Sexual repression and openness. *Déjà vu* (*Véc viđeno*)

ists, actresses, actors, and other film artists and technicians eager to further strengthen the artistic integrity of Yugoslav films and to expand the international audience for them. Levels of feature film production have remained high despite very serious economic problems, creating healthy opportunities for new and relatively untried directors and other film artists to express themselves.

Film projects, however, must be guided through an increasingly fissiparous system, with film production enterprises (many of them small and underfinanced) spread throughout Yugoslavia's six republics and two autonomous regions. They must also be realized within the context of a unique and constantly redefined blend of socialist-determined market incentives and a complex multitiered and sometimes overlapping self-management organizational structure which seeks to prescribe the broad social roles and "collective responsibilities" of film artists. As a result, film projects are buffeted and sometimes shaped by contradictory pressures which emphasize box-office success on the one hand, and adherence to shifting sociopolitical definitions and restrictions on artistic expression on the other.

Finally, the fortunes of Yugoslav film are inevitably held hostage to the complex drama currently being acted out in the larger socio-cultural and political arena. It is difficult, if not impossible, to predict whether Yugoslavia will find a way out of her present quandaries. There are strong and opposing forces at work for fragmentation and unity; devolution and centralization; liberality and repression; openness and closure; a multi-candidate system, a multi-party system, and continuance of the status quo; economic liberalization of privately owned businesses and farms and opposition to any further liberalization; and contending and rival views of the meanings and lessons to be derived from Yugoslavia's often turbulent and dramatic past. It is a remarkable tribute to a relatively small film industry that each year some films are produced which not only reflect Yugoslavia's unique cultural and political experience, but which also transcend republican and national boundaries to imaginatively address filmgoers everywhere.

NOTES

1. For an astute and well-documented analysis of Yugoslavia's current economic and political difficulties, see Pedro Ramet, ed., *Yugoslavia in the 1980s*. See also, George Schöpflin, "Yugoslavia's Uncertain Future," "The Yugoslav Crisis," and "Yugoslavia's Growing Crisis," in, respectively, *Soviet Analyst* XI no. 13, 30 June, 1982, XII, no. 2, 26 January, 1983, and XIV, no. 25, 19 December, 1984.

2. Dennison Rusinow, "Nationalities Policy and the 'National Question,' " in *Yugoslavia in the 1980s*, pp. 131–165.

3. Sharon Zukin, "Self-Management and Socialism," in *Yugoslavia in the 1980s*, pp. 76–99.

4. The period from 1973 to 1977 marked Yugoslavia's lowest ebb of domestic feature film production since the early sixties, with nineteen films completed in 1973, seventeen in 1974, eighteen in 1975, sixteen in 1976, and eighteen in 1977. "Jugoslovenska kinematografija u brojkama," (Beograd: Institut za film, n.d.).

5. In the eighties, feature film production has remained steady at twenty-five and thirty per year. There was, however, a drop in production in 1987 to twenty-two feature films, only eighteen of which were screened at the annual feature film festival at Pula. Whether this drop signals a trend toward lower levels of production in the next few years is impossible to predict. "Jugoslovenska kinematografija u brojkama."

6. For a more detailed description and analysis of the earlier films directed by the "Czech School" of Yugoslav film directors, see Daniel J. Goulding, *Liberated Cinema: The Yugoslav Experience,* (Bloomington: Indiana University Press, 1985), pp. 143–172. See also Andrew Horton, "The New Serbo-Creationism," *American Film,* XI, no. 4, Jan./Feb., 1986, pp. 24–30.

7. Aleksandar Petrović, personal correspondence, 12 January, 1987.

8. See, for example, Bogdan Tirnanić's ten-part series on Yugoslav films in the sixties which appeared in *NIN* (May 18, 25; June 1, 8, 15, 22, 29; and July 6, 13 and 20, 1986).

9. A notable exception to this generalization is Slovenian film which has followed a distinctive line of development. See Ronald Holloway, "Slovenian Film," *Kino,* Special Issue, 1985, pp. 1–63. For a more complete definition and analysis of *new film* tendencies in the sixties and the controversies surrounding their development, see Goulding, *Liberated Cinema: The Yugoslav Experience,* pp. 62–84.

10. Nenad Puhovski, "Avant-Garde Television Drama and Video Art," unpublished lecture (delivered at a special conference on "Visual Media in Contemporary Yugoslavia") UCLA, February 6, 1987.

11. I am grateful to Milomir Marinović, Head of the International Films Department of Jugoslavija film, for providing me with information concerning the ten top domestic box-office draws for the years 1982–1986. These figures reveal that domestically produced films have regularly captured from five to seven of the top places. This substantial achievement has occurred in competition with such popular foreign imports as *Raiders of the Lost Ark, An Officer and a Gentleman, Terms of Endearment* and others (Milomir Marinović, personal correspondence, 10 December, 1986).

12. One of the most extensive recent analyses of the financial difficulties facing the Yugoslav film industry occurred in a Round Table Discussion at the 1985 Festival of Yugoslav Feature Films at Pula. For an extensive summary of this discussion, see *Bilten, 32. Jugoslovenskog igranog filma,* 20 July, pp. 9–11; 25 July, pp. 11–13; 26 July, pp. 4–8; 27 July, pp. 8–11.

13. Isaković provides vivid accounts of the harsh measures employed at Goli otok to "re-educate" or "resocialize" Stalinists and suspected Stalinist sympathizers which were compared by some Yugoslav critics to Dante's *Inferno* and Dostoevsky's *House of the Dead.* Prisoners at Goli otok were broken psychologically and physically by techniques in which the persecuted became the persecutors. Isaković describes a technique in which new arrivals to the camp, together with inmates deemed still unrepentant, were forced to run through a corridor of fellow prisoners who were wielding sticks and whips. The guards stood back and watched as the victims were beaten and verbally abused. Some victims collapsed, bleeding, to the ground. Those who made it to the end were required to point out which of the prisoners had not beaten them hard enough, and these men were then forced to run the gauntlet themselves.

14. Jovanović's play dramatizes the experiences of the protagonist Svetozar

Milić, a devoted Communist who had learned to identify Tito's accomplishments with Stalin's inspiration. When the break comes, Milić speaks in perplexity: "This has hit us overnight. How can something which was always pure white suddenly become black?" Milić's honest wavering is guilt enough. He is sent off to Goli otok where he is physically tortured and trained to recite "I am a bandit, a deserter, a scoundrel, without worth or honor, without pride, a chameleon, a sectarian, a provocateur, a stowaway on the ship of history of the Yugoslav people. I am a Cominform pig." Milić is broken psychologically and dies in prison. Ironically, the judge at his mock trial goes on to become a professor of philosophy.

15. Among the most important of these are Branko Hofman, *Noć do jutra (Night to Morning)*, Ferdo Godina, *Molčeči orkester (The Dumb Orchestra)*, Jure Franičević-Pločar, *Generalna proba (The General Trial)*, and Žarko Komanin, *Prestupna godina (Leapyear)*.

16. *International Herald Tribune*, 28 July, 1982.

17. *Ibid.*

18. Quoted in Pedro Ramet, ed., *Yugoslavia in the 1980s*, (Boulder and London: Westview Press, 1985), p. 15.

19. Only one feature film was made on this theme in 1987 and any further thematic and cinematic variations on the period of the Tito-Stalin split seem temporarily exhausted.

20. The title of the film is a reference to the euphemism used to explain to young Malik the reason for his father's absence.

21. This famous caricature by Zuko Džumhur depicts Marx in his study dominated by a large portrait of Stalin, which suggests the reversal of ideological roles that Stalin arrogantly assumed.

22. For an interesting discussion of the impact of this soccer victory on the popular imagination of the time, see Vladimir Dedijer, *The Battle That Stalin Lost*, (New York: Universal Library, 1972), pp. 306–310.

23. *NIN*, 27 January, 1985.

24. For a recent scholarly analysis of the Tito-Stalin split and its historic implications, see Wayne S. Vucinich, ed., *At the Brink of War and Peace: The Tito-Stalin Split in Historic Perspective*, (New York: Columbia University Press, 1982). See also, Dedijer, *The Battle That Stalin Lost*.

25. Slobodan Stanković, *The End of the Tito Era: Yugoslavia's Dilemmas*, (Stanford: Hoover Institution Press, 1981), pp. 3–5.

26. For this film, Šijan won the coveted Georges Sadoul award for best debut film by a foreign director. His second film, *The Marathon Runner (Maratonci trče počasni krug*, 1981) is also an accomplished and witty film set in inter-war Yugoslavia. A somewhat lighter but comically inventive film set in 1918 on the barren plateau of Lika is *The Small Train Robbery (Mala pljačka vlaka*, 1984), directed by Dejan Šorak.

27. Quoted in Ronald Holloway, "Slovenian Film," *Kino*, p. 43.

28. A more recent film dealing with the same theme, *Officer with a Rose (Oficir s ružom*, 1987), written and directed by Dejan Šorak, portrays a more sentimental love story than Grlič's film and considerably softens the harsh material and ideological conditions which existed immediately after the war. An impressive and inventive film on the immediate post-war years is the black comedy *Nothing But Words of Praise for the Deceased (O pokojniku sve najlepše*, 1984), the promising debut film of Predrag Antonijević.

29. In his intellectually provocative analysis of the original punk movement in Great Britain in the late seventies, Dick Hebdige summarizes its meaning in a way that has relevance to the distinct variants which have emerged in Yugoslavia in the eighties:

the punks turned towards the world a dead white face which was there and not "there." Like the myths of Roland Barthes, these "murdered victims"—emptied and inert—also had an alibi, an elsewhere, literally "made up" out of vaseline and cosmetics, hair dye and mascara. But paradoxically, in the case of the punks, this "elsewhere" was also a nowhere, a twilight zone, a zone constituted out of negativity. Like André Breton's Dada, punk night might seem to "open all doors" but these doors "gave onto a circular corridor."

Once inside this desecrated circle, punk was forever condemned to act out alienation, to mime its imagined condition, to manufacture a whole series of subjective correlatives for the official archetype of the crisis of modern life.

Dick Hebdige, *Subculture: The Meaning of Style,* (London and New York: Methuen, 1979), p. 65.

30. Feminist theory has only recently made an impact in Yugoslavia. See, for example, Slavenka Drakulić-Ilić, *Smrtni griješi feminizma: Ogledi o mudologiji* (Zagreb: Znanje, 1984) and Vjeran Katunarić, *Ženski eros i civilizacija smrti,* (Zagreb: Biblioteka Naprijed, 1984). For an interesting overview of new feminist thought in Yugoslavia, see Barbara Jancar, "The New Feminism in Yugoslavia," in Ramet, *Yugoslavia in the 1980s,* pp. 201–223.

31. *Yugoslavia in the 1980s,* p. 20.

SELECTED BIBLIOGRAPHY

GENERAL

Cameron, Ian et al. *Second Wave*. New York: Praeger, 1970.
Cook, David A. *A History of Narrative Film*. New York: W.W. Norton, 1981.
Graham, Peter. *The New Wave*. Garden City, N.Y.: Doubleday, 1968.
Hibbin, Nina. *Eastern Europe: An Illustrated Guide*. Screen Series. Cranbury, N.J.: A.S. Barnes, 1969.
Ionescu, Ghita. *The Politics of the European Communist States*. New York: Praeger, 1967.
Liehm, Mira, ed. *Il cinema nell'Europa dell'Est 1960–1977*. Venezie: Marsilio, 1977.
Liehm, Mira and Liehm, Antonín J. *The Most Important Art: East European Film After 1945*. Berkeley, Los Angeles and London: University of California Press, 1977.
Nemes, Károly. *Films of Commitment: Socialist Cinema in Eastern Europe*. Trans. András Boros-Kazai. Budapest: Corvina, 1985.
Paul, David W., ed. *Politics, Art and Commitment in the East European Cinema*. London: Macmillan and New York: St. Martin's Press, 1983.
Stoil, Michael. *Cinema Beyond the Danube: The Camera and Politics*. Metuchen, N.J.: Scarecrow Press, 1971.
Whyte, A. *New Cinema in Eastern Europe*. New York: Dutton, 1971.

SOVIET UNION

Aktual'nye problemy sovetskogo kino nachala 80-kh godov. Sbornik nauchnykh trudov VNIIK Goskino SSSR. Moscow, 1983.
Doder, Dusko. *Shadows and Whispers*. New York: Random House, 1986.
Drobashenko, D. et al., eds. *Sovetskoe kino, 70-ye gody*. Moscow: Iskusstvo, 1984.
Ferro, Marc, ed. *Film et Histoire*. Paris: Editions de l'Ecole des Hautes Etudes en Sciences Sociales, 1984.
Film URSS '70: Materiali critici e informativi, Vol. 1. Venice, Italy: Marsilio Editori, 1980.
Film URSS '70: La critica sovietica, Vol. 2. Venice, Italy: Marsilio Editori, 1980.
Film URSS: Il cinema delle repubbliche asiatiche sovietiche, Vol. 3. Venice, Italy: Marsilio Editori, 1986.
Film URSS: Il cinema delle repubbliche transcaucasiche sovietiche, Vol. 4. Venice, Italy: Marsilio Editori, 1986.
Fomin, V. I., ed. *Kinopanorama: sbornik statei*. Moscow: Iskusstvo, 1977.
—, ed. *Zhanry kino*. Moscow: Iskusstvo, 1979.
Golovskoy, Val. *Behind the Soviet Screen*. Ann Arbor, MI: Ardis, 1986.
Iurenev, R. *Kratkaia istoriia sovetskogo kino*. Moscow: Biuro propagandy sovetskogo kinoiskusstva, 1979.

Pankin, Boris. *Demanding Literature*. Moscow: Raduga Publishers, 1984 (two chapters on cinema).
Passèk, Jean-Loup, ed. *Le cinéma russe et soviétique*. Paris: L'Equerre, Centre Georges Pompidou, 1981.
Pogozheva, L. *Iz dnevnika kinokritika*. Moscow: Iskusstvo, 1978.
Tiurin, Iu. *Kinematograf Vasiliia Shukshina*. Moscow: Iskusstvo, 1984.
Vorontsov, Iu. *The Phenomenon of the Soviet Cinema*. Moscow: Progress Publishers, 1980.
Vronskaya, Jeanne. *Young Soviet Filmmakers*. London: George Allen and Unwin Ltd., 1972.
Zhdan, V. N., ed. *Kinematograf segodnia*. Moscow: Iskusstvo, 1983.
Zlotnik, O. Ia., ed. *Kinematograf molodykh*. Moscow: Iskusstvo, 1979.

GERMAN DEMOCRATIC REPUBLIC

Books

Bisky, Lothar and Wiedemann, Dieter. *Der Spielfilm—Rezeption und Wirkung: Kultursoziologische Analysen*. Berlin: Henschelverlag, 1985.
Blum, Heiko, et al. *Film in der DDR: Reihe Hanser 238*. München: Carl Hanser Verlag, 1977.
Emmerich, Wolfgang. *Kleine Literaturgeschichte der DDR*. Sammlung Luchterhand 326. Darmstadt und Neuwied: Luchterhand Verlag, 1985.³
Gaus, Günter. *Wo Deutschland liegt. Eine Ortsbestimmung*. dtv 105661. München: dtv, 1983.
Helwig, Gisela. *Frau und Familie: Bundesrepublik Deutschland—DDR*. Köln: Verlag Wissenschaft und Politik, 1987.
Jäger, Manfred. *Kultur und Politik in der DDR. Ein historischer Abriss*. Edition Deutschland Archiv. Köln: Verlag Wissenschaft und Politik, 1982.
Plenzdorf, Ulrich. *Filme*. Rostock: Hinstorff Verlag, 1987.
Richter, Rolf, ed. *DEFA-Spielfilm-Regisseure und ihre Kritiker*. Bd. 1 und 2. Berlin: Henschelverlag, 1981, 1983.
Rülicke-Weiler, Käthe, ed. *Film- und Fernsehkunst in der DDR. Traditionen. Beispiele. Tendenzen*. Berlin: Henschelverlag, 1979.
Schmitt, Hans-Jürgen ed. *Hansers Sozialgeschichte der deutschen Literatur. Bd. 11. Die Literatur der DDR*. dtv 4353. München: Carl Hanser Verlag, 1983.
Sontag, Susan. *Under the Sign of Saturn*. New York: Farrar, Straus and Giroux, 1980.
Staritz, Dietrich. *Geschichte der DDR. 1949–1985*. Neue historische Bibliothek, edition suhrkamp 260. Frankfurt/M: Suhrkamp Verlag, 1985.
Wuss, Peter. *Das offene Kunstwerk*. Dissertation (Humboldt Universität). Sonderdruck in der Reihe: *Aus Theorie und Praxis*, 1985.

Annual Periodicals

Filmobibliographischer Jahresbericht (GDR).
Prisma. Kino- und Fernseh-Almanach (GDR).
Studies in GDR Culture and Society. Selected Papers from the Annual New Hampshire Symposium on the German Democratic Republic (USA).

Monthly and Quarterly Periodicals

Aus Theorie und Praxis des Films (ed. Betriebsakademie des VEB DEFA Studio für Spielfilme) (GDR).

Beiträge zur Film- und Fernsehwissenschaft (Filmwissenschaftliche Beiträge) (GDR).
Cinéaste (USA).
Cinéma (France).
Film und Fernsehen (GDR).
The Journal of Communist Studies (USA).
Podium und Werkstatt. Schriften des Verbandes der Film- und Fernsehschaffenden der DDR (GDR).
Progress. Pressebulletin Kino DDR (GDR).
Sinn und Form. Beiträge zur Literatur (DDR).
Weimarer Beiträge. Zeitschrift für Literaturwissenschaft, Ästhetik und Kulturtheorie (GDR).

Newspapers and Weekly Magazines

Federal Republic of Germany

Christ und Welt
Frankfurter Rundschau
Der Spiegel
Süddeutsche Zeitung
Der Tagesspiegel (West Berlin)

German Democratic Republic

Berliner Zeitung
Forum (Berlin)
Freiheit (Halle)
Junge Welt (Berlin)
Leipziger Volkszeitung
Märkische Volksstimme
Neue Zeit (Berlin)
Neues Deutschland
Sonntag
Thüringische Landeszeitung
Tribüne
Das Volk (Erfurt)
Wochenpost (Berlin)

CZECHOSLOVAKIA

Books

Bartošková, Šárka, and Bartošek, Luboš. *Československé filmy, 1972–1976.* Prague: Československý filmovy ústav, 1977.
— *Československé filmy, 1977–1980.* Prague: Československý filmovy ústav, 1983.
— *Filmové profily.* Prague: Československý filmovy ústav, 1986.
Boček, Jaroslav, *Looking Back on the New Wave.* Prague: Československý Film-export, 1967.
Brož, Jaroslav. *The Path of Fame of the Czechoslovak Film.* Prague: Československý Filmexport, 1967.
Charlton, Michael. *The Eagle and the Small Birds: Crisis in the Soviet Empire from Yalta to Solidarity.* London: British Broadcasting Corporation. 1984.
Dewey, Langdon. *Outline of Czechoslovakian Cinema.* London: Informatics, 1971.
Hames, Peter. *The Czechoslovak New Wave.* Berkeley and Los Angeles: University of California Press, 1985.

Heneka, A., Janouch, František, Prečan, Vilém, and Vladislav, Jan, eds. *A Besieged Culture: Czechoslovakia Ten Years After Helsinki.* Translated by Joyce Dahlberg, Richard Fisher, Erazim Kohák, Peter Kussi, Káča Poláčková-Henley, Marian Šling, George Theiner, Ruth Tosek. Stockholm: Charta 77 Foundation; Vienna: International Helsinki Federation for Human Rights, 1985.

Keane, John, ed. *The Power of the Powerless: Citizens Against the State in Central-Eastern Europe.* Translated by Paul Wilson and A. G. Brain. London: Hutchinson, 1985.

Král, Petr. *Le Surréalisme en Tchécoslovaquie.* Paris: Flammarion, 1983.

Kusin, Vladimír V. *From Dubček to Charter 77: A Study of "Normalisation" in Czechoslovakia, 1968–1978.* Edinburg: Q Press, 1978.

Liehm, Antonín J. *Closely Watched Films: The Czechoslovak Experience.* New York: International Arts and Sciences Press, 1974.

— *The Miloš Forman Stories.* Translated by Jeanne Němcová. New York: International Arts and Sciences Press, 1975.

Schmidt-Häuer, Christian. *Gorbachev: the Path to Power.* Translated by Ewald Osers and Chris Romberg. London: Pan Books, 1986.

Šimečka, Milan. *The Restoration of Order: The Normalization of Czechoslovakia.* Translated by A. G. Brain. London: Verso Editions, 1984.

Skilling, H. Gordon. *Chapter 77 and Human Rights in Czechoslovakia.* London: Allen and Unwin, 1981.

Škvorecký, Josef. *All the Bright Young Men and Women.* Translated by Michael Schonberg. Toronto: Peter Martin Associates, 1971.

— *Jiří Menzel and the History of the Closely Watched Trains.* Boulder, Colorado: East European Monographs; New York: Columbia University Press, 1982.

Vladislav, Jan, ed. *Václav Havel or Living in Truth.* Translated by A. G. Brain, Paul Wilson, Erazim Kohák, Roger Scruton, J. R. Littleboy, D. Armour, Derek Viney, M. Pomichalek, A. Mozga, K. Seigneurie, George Theiner. London: Faber, 1987.

Žalman, Jan (Antonín Novák). *Films and Filmmakers in Czechoslovakia.* Prague: Orbis, 1968.

Articles

Ash, Timothy Garton. "Does Central Europe Exist?" *The New York Review of Books* (9 October 1986), pp. 45–52.

Elley, Derek. "Ripples from a Dying Wave." *Films and Filming,* 20 (July 1974), pp. 32–36.

Gellner, Ernest. "Between Loyalty and Truth." *The Times Literary Supplement* (London), 3 October 1986.

Hames, Peter. "Czech Mates." *Films and Filming,* 20 (April 1974), pp. 54–57.

—"The Return of Věra Chytilová." *Sight and Sound,* 48 (Summer 1979), pp. 168–173.

Král, Petr. "Questions à Jan Švankmajer." *Positif,* No. 297 (November 1985), pp. 38–43. English translation by Jill McGreal in *Afterimage,* No. 13 (Autumn 1987), pp. 22–32.

Liehm, Antonín J. "Triumph of the Untalented." *Index on Censorship* 5 (3) (Autumn 1976), pp. 57–60.

O'Pray, Michael. "In the Capital of Magic." *Monthly Film Bulletin* 53 (July 1986), pp. 218–219.

Polt, Harriet. "A Film Should Be a Little Flashlight: An Interview with Věra Chytilová." *Take One,* (November 1978), pp. 42–44.

Škvorecký, Josef. "What Was Saved from the Wreckage" *Sight and Sound,* 55 (Autumn 1986), pp. 278–281.
Žuna, Miroslav, and Solecký, Vladimír. "Jeste k filmovému svetu Věry Chytilové." *Film a doba* 28(5) (May 1982).

POLAND

Books

Ascherson, Neal. *The Polish August.* New York: Viking, 1982.
Bereda, Jerzy, et al. *Twórcy Polskiego Filmu: Leksykon.* Warsaw: Redaksja Wydawnictw Filmowych, 1986.
Brumberg, Abraham, ed. *Poland: Genesis of a Revolution.* New York: Vintage, 1983.
Fuksiewicz, Jacek. *Film i Telewizja w Polsce.* Warsaw: Interpress, 1981.
— *Polish Cinema.* Warsaw: Interpress, 1973.
Janicki, Stanisław. *The Polish Film.* Warsaw: Interpress, 1985.
Kuszewski, Stanisław. *Contemporary Polish Film.* Warsaw: Interpress, 1978.
Michałek, Bolesław, and Turaj, Frank. *The Modern Cinema of Poland.* Bloomington: Indiana University Press, 1988.
Polska Akademia Nauk: Instytut Sztuki. *Historia Filmu Polskiego.* Warsaw: Wydawnictwo Artyzstyczne i Filmowe. Five volumes published to date covering film history to 1967.
Steven, Stewart. *The Poles.* New York: Macmillan, 1982.
Weschler, Lawrence. *Solidarity.* New York: Simon and Schuster, 1982.

Selected Film Periodicals

Cinéaste. Published in New York, *Cinéaste* publishes occasional interviews with Polish filmmakers and reviews of Polish films, as well as reports and reviews of the annual Gdansk festival.
Film. Published in Warsaw, this weekly journal provides current and valuable information and critical reviews.
Kino. A valuable film monthly published in Warsaw, whose contents vary from popular reports to theoretical articles.
Polish Film. An English-language publication by Film Polski—Poland's official film distribution organization—which includes film synopsis, stills and filmographies, but is devoid of historical or critical significance.

HUNGARY

Books

Balázs, Béla. *Theory of the Film: Character and Growth of a New Art.* London: Dobson, 1952.
Estève, Michel, ed. *Le nouveau cinéma hongroise.* Paris: Reinhard, 1969.
Koopmanschap, Eric. *De Hongaarse Film.* No. 29, VNFI Verkenningen. Hilversum, Netherlands: Verenigd Nederlands Filminstituut, 1980.
— *De Hongaarse Film.* Den Bosch, Netherlands: Hungarofilm (Budapest), 1983.
Nemes, Károly. *Sadrásban ... a magyar film 25 éve, 1945–1970.* Budapest: Gondolat, 1972.

Nemeskürty, István. _Word and Image: History of the Hungarian Cinema._ Budapest: Corvina, 1968.

Petrie, Graham. _History Must Answer to Man: The Contemporary Hungarian Cinema._ Budapest: Corvina Kiádó and London: The Tantivy Press, 1978.

Szalay, Károly. _Mai magyar filmvígjáték; beteljesülések és elszalasztott lehetőségek._ Budapest: Magveto, 1978.

Articles and Essays

Armes, Roy. "Miklós Jancsó: Dialectic and Ritual," pp. 141–53 in _The Ambiguous Image; Narrative Style in Modern European Cinema._ Bloomington and London: Indiana University Press, 1976.

Bachmann, Gideon. "Letter from Hungary." _Take One_ 4(10) (June, 1975), pp. 24–26.

Bickley, Daniel. "Socialism and Humanism: The Contemporary Hungarian Cinema." _Cineaste_ 9(2) (1979), pp. 30–35.

Biró, Yvette. "The Hungarian Film Style and Its Variations." _New Hungarian Quarterly_ 9(32) (1968), pp. 3–8.

Budgen, Suzanne. "Hungary," in Peter Cowie, ed., _A Concise History of the Cinema,_ vol. 1. London: A Zwemmer, 1971, pp. 157–58.

Czigány, Lóránt. "Jancsó Country." _Film Quarterly_ 26(1) (Fall, 1972), pp. 44–50.

Hoberman, J. "Budapest's Business." _Film Comment_ 22(3) (May–June, 1986), pp. 68–71.

"Hungary." In _The Oxford Companion to Film._ London: Oxford University Press, 1976, pp. 343–45.

Jaehne, Karen. "István Szabó: Dreams of Memories." _Film Quarterly_ 32(1) (Fall, 1978), pp. 30–41.

Paul, David. "The Esthetics of Courage: The Political Climate for the Cinema in Poland and Hungary." _Cineaste_ 14(4) (1986), pp. 16–22.

— "István Szabó" (interview). _Columbia Film View_ 1(2) (Winter 1985), pp. 4–6.

Petrie, Graham. "New Cinema from Eastern Euorpe." _Film Comment_ 11(6) (November–December, 1975), pp. 48–51.

— "Two Years of Hungarian Cinema 1975–1977." _New Hungarian Quarterly_ 19 (72) (1978), pp. 210–21.

— "Why the Hungarian Cinema Matters." _New Hungarian Quarterly_ 18(68) (1977), pp. 215–18.

Riegel, O. W. "What Is Hungarian in the Hungarian Cinema?" Three-part article in _New Hungarian Quarterly_ 17(63) (Autumn, 1976), pp. 185–93; 17(64) (Winter, 1976), pp. 206–15; and 18(65) (Spring, 1977), pp. 201–10.

Periodicals

Hungarofilm Bulletin. Budapest, 1960–.
New Hungarian Quarterly. Budapest, 1968–.

BULGARIA

Bayer, Eduard, and Endler, Dietmar. _Bulgarische Literatur im Überblick._ Leipzig: Verlag Philipp Reclam jun., 1983.

Brossard, Jean-Pierre. _Aspects nouveaux du Cinéma bulgare._ La Chaux-de-Fonds: Editions Cinédiff, 1986.

Cervoni, Albert. _Les écrans de Sofia._ Paris: Filméditions Pierre L'Herminier Editeur, 1976.

Holloway, Ronald. *The Bulgarian Cinema*. London and Toronto: Associated University Presses, 1984.
Ignatovski, Vladimir. *Der bulgarische Film*. Berlin: Henschelverlag, 1985.
Lang, David Marshall. *The Bulgarians: From Pagan Times to the Ottoman Conquest*. London: Thames and Hudson, 1976.
Micheli, Sergio. *Cinema di animazione in Bulgaria*. Bologna: Cappelli Editore, 1975.
— *Il Cinema Bulgaro*. Padua: Marsilio Editori, 1971.
Ratschewa, Maria, and Eder, Klaus. *Der bulgarische Film*. Frankfurt: Kommunales Kino, 1977.
Stoyanovich, Ivan, ed. *The Bulgarian Cinema Today*. Sofia: Bulgariafilm Publication, 1981.

YUGOSLAVIA

Books

Banac, Ivo. *The National Question in Yugoslavia*. Ithaca: Cornell University Press, 1984.
Bass, George, and Marburg, Elizabeth, eds. *The Soviet-Yugoslav Controversy, 1948–1958: A Documentary Record*. New York: Prospect, 1959.
Benes, Vaclav L., Byrnes, Robert F., and Spulber, Nicolas, eds. *The Second Soviet-Yugoslav Dispute: Full Text of Main Documents*. Bloomington: Indiana University Press, 1959.
Clissold, Stephen. *Djilas: The Progress of a Revolutionary*. New York: Universe Books, 1983.
Cohen, Lenard, and Warwick, Paul. *Political Cohesion in a Fragile Mosiac: The Yugoslav Experience*. Boulder, Colorado: Westview Press, 1983.
Čolić, Milutin. *Jugoslovenski ratni film*. 2 vols. Belgrade: Institut za film, 1984.
Dedijer, Vladimir. *Dokumenti 1948*. 3 vols. Belgrade: RAD, 1979.
— *The Battle Stalin Lost*. New York: Universal Library, 1972.
Denitch, Bogdan Denis. *The Legitimation of a Revolution: The Yugoslav Case*. New Haven: Yale University Press, 1976.
Djilas, Milovan. *Conversations with Stalin*. New York: Praeger, 1958.
Doder, Dusko. *The Yugoslavs*. New York: Random House, 1978.
Drakulić-Ilić, *Smrtni griješi feminizma: Ogledi o mudologiji*. Zagreb: Znanje, 1984.
Goulding, Daniel J. *Liberated Cinema: The Yugoslav Experience*. Bloomington: Indiana University Press, 1985.
Hebdige, Dick. *Subculture: The Meaning of Style*. London and New York: Methuen, 1979.
Holloway, Ronald. *Z is for Zagreb*. Cranbury, N.J.: A. S. Barnes, 1972.
Ilić, Momčilo, ed. *Filmografija jugoslovenskog filma,* 1945–1965. Beograd: Institut za film, 1970.
— *Filmografija jugoslovenskog filma,* 1966–1970. Beograd: Institut za film, 1974.
Kosanović, Dejan. *Počeci kinematografija na tlu jugoslavije 1896–1918*. Belgrade: Institut za film, 1986.
Kutarnić, Vjeran. *Ženski eros i civilizacija smrti*. Zagreb: Biblioteka Naprijed, 1984.
Maclean, Fitzroy. *Tito*. New York: McGraw-Hill, 1980.
Munitić, Ranko. *Jugoslavenski filmski slučaj*. Split: Marjan film, 1980.
Obradović, Branislav, ed. *Filmografija jugoslovenskog igranog filma, 1945–1980*. Beograd: Institut za film, 1981.

— *Filmografija jugoslovenskog igranog filma, 1981–1985.* Beograd: Institut za film, 1987.

Petrović, Aleksandar. *Novi film.* Beograd: Institut za film, 1971.

Ramet, Pedro, ed. *Yugoslavia in the 1980s.* Boulder and London: Westview Press, 1985.

Rusinow, Dennison. *The Yugoslav Experiment, 1948–1974.* Berkeley and Los Angeles: University of California Press, 1977.

Schöpflin, George, ed. *Censorship and Political Communication in Eastern Europe: A Collection of Documents.* New York: St. Martin's Press, 1983.

Sher, Gerson S. *Praxis: Marxist Criticism and Dissent in Socialist Yugoslavia.* Bloomington: Indiana University Press, 1977.

Stanković, Slobodan. *The End of the Tito Era: Yugoslavia's Dilemmas.* Stanford: Hoover Institution Press, 1981.

Stojanović, Dusan. *Velika avantura filma.* Beograd: n. p., 1970.

Volk, Petar. *Istorija jugoslovenskog filma 1896–1982.* Belgrade: Institut za film, 1986.

Vucinich, Wayne S., ed. *At the Brink of War and Peace: The Tito-Stalin Split in Historic Prespective.* New York: Columbia University Press, 1982.

Articles, Reports, Documents

Binder, David. "A Return to Yugoslavia." *New York Times Magazine* (December 25, 1983), pp. 20–24.

Boglić, Mira. "O ambasadorima, špijunima, anđelima, daviteljima, pokojnicima: Pula 84." *Filmska kultura,* no. 151–152 (September, 1984), pp. 22–35.

— "U sjeni Zlatne palme: Cannes 85." *Filmska kultura,* no. 154–155–156 (September 1985), pp. 78–95.

"Festival of Yugoslav Feature Films in Pula." *Bulletin* (1965–1987).

"Le Film Yougoslave en 1985" (Special French Edition) *Filmograf* XI(34) (Spring, 1986).

Holloway, Ronald. "Slovenian Film." *Kino* (Special Issue, 1985).

— "Yugoslavia." In Peter Cowie, ed., *International Film Guide.* New York: A. S. Barnes, 1987.

Horton, Andrew. "The New Serbo-Creationism." *American Film* 11(4) (January–February 1986), pp. 24–30.

— "Yugoslavia: Multi-Faceted Cinema." In William Luhr, ed., *World Cinema Since 1945.* New York: Ungar, 1987.

"Jugoslovenska kinematografija u brojkama." Beograd: Institut za film, n.d. (foldout sheet prepared by Dejan Kosanović).

Kalafatović, Bogdan. "Godina odluke?: Pula 84." *Filmska kultura,* no. 151–152 (September, 1984), pp. 6–21.

Mikić, Krešimir. "Filmska fotografija na pulskom ekranu." *Filmska kultura,* no. 157–158–159 (April 1986), pp. 44–55.

Miletić, Nenad. "'Posuđena' i anonimna glazba u pulskoj Areni." *Filmska kultura,* no. 162–163 (December 1986), pp. 64–71.

Munitić, Ranko. "Trideset prvi festival: dvadeset devet paradoksa: Pula 84." *Filmska kultura,* no. 151–152 (September 1984), pp. 36–41.

"News" (published by Jugoslavija film, Belgrade, 1958–).

Ramet, Pedro. "Yugoslavia and the Threat of Internal and External Discontents." *Orbis* 28(1) (Spring, 1984), pp. 103–121.

"Rezutati filmske 1986. godina." *Filmska kultura,* no. 162–163 (December, 1986), pp. 72–81. (Report of a round-table discussion involving Mira Boglić, Cvetan Stanoevski, Ranko Munitić, Milan Damnjanović, Milan Cvijanović, Ivan Salečić, Miša Novaković, and Fawsi Soliman.)

Salečić, Ivan. "Model filma: Čovjek filmska trilogija Lordana Zafranovića." *Filmska kultura,* no. 162–163 (December, 1986), pp. 88–99.

Schöpflin, George. "Yugoslavia's Uncertain Future," "The Yugoslav Crisis," and "Yugoslavia's Growing Crisis." In, respectively, *Soviet Analyst,* XI, no. 13 (30 June 1982), XII, no. 2 (26 January 1983), and XIV, no. 25 (19 December, 1984).

Shaplen, Robert. "A Reporter at Large: Tito's Legacy—I." *The New Yorker* (5 March 1984), pp. 110–25.

— "A Reporter at Large: Tito's Legacy—II." *The New Yorker* (12 March 1984), pp. 79–119.

Tirnanić, Bogdan. "Paralelna istorija Jugoslovenskog filma." (a ten-part series on Yugoslav film in the sixties) *NIN* (May 18, 25; June 1, 8, 15, 22, 29; and July 6, 13 and 20, 1986).

Film Periodicals

Ekran. The major film journal of Slovenia, begun in 1962 under the editorship of Vitko Musek. Publishes ten numbers annually in Ljubljana.

Filmograf. A well-produced and informative film quarterly whose first number was issued in 1976. Published by the Institut za film in Belgrade, the journal is edited by Božidar Zečević and Predrag Golubović.

Filmska kultura. A quarterly journal published in Zagreb. The first number was issued in 1957 under the editorship of Stevo Ostojić and Fedor Hanžeković.

Filmske sveske. A quarterly journal dealing with film theory and aesthetics. Published by the Institut za film in Belgrade. The journal was begun in 1968 under the editorship of Dušan Stojanović.

Sineast. The major film journal of Bosnia-Hercegovina begun in 1967 under the editorship of Nikola Stojanović. Published by the Kino Klub in Sarajevo.

CONTRIBUTORS

Anna Lawton, Associate Professor of Russian Literature and Film at Purdue University, has published widely on Soviet cinema and related arts. Her book *Vadim Shershenevich: From Futurism to Imaginism* was published in 1981 (Ardis) and her book *Russian Futurism Through Its Manifestoes: Literary Theory 1912–1928* is in press with Cornell University Press. She has served as a Fellow at the Hoover Institution and has participated in the IREX Senior Scholar Exchange program.

Sigrun D. Leonhard, Assistant Professor of German at Carleton College, is a gifted young scholar who earned her doctorate in German Studies at Stanford University, and has published important articles on both German literature and film.

Peter Hames, Principal Lecturer in Film Studies in the Department of History of Art and Design at the North Staffordshire Polytechnic in England, wrote the critically acclaimed book *The Czechoslovak New Wave* (University of California Press, 1985) and organized the first major retrospective of Czechoslovak films at the National Film Theater in London. He has written articles for *Sight and Sound, Films and Filming, The Movie, Film* and other journals.

Frank Turaj, Professor of Film and Literature at American University, has recently co-authored with Bolesław Michałek *The Modern Cinema of Poland* (Indiana University Press, 1988). He received a medal from the Ministry of Culture in Poland for special contributions to Polish Cinema (1981) and was elected to the Fellowship of the Ring by the Polish Filmmakers Association in 1984.

David Paul, writer and film critic, is the editor and a contributor to *Politics, Art and Commitment in the East European Cinema* (London and New York, 1983), and his articles have appeared in recent volumes of *Film Quarterly, Film Comment, Cinéaste,* and other film journals. Paul's earlier writings include two books and numerous articles on politics and society in Eastern Europe. He received his doctorate in Political Science from Princeton, taught political science for nine years at the University of Washington, and has since served as a Lecturer and Scholar-in-Residence for the Washington Commission for the Humanities.

Ronald Holloway, freelance journalist and writer, is a film historian with a doctorate in theology from the University of Hamburg. He is author of numerous articles and monographs and several books: *Z is for Zagreb* (1972), *Beyond the Image* (1974), *O is for Oberhausen* (1979) and *Bulgarian Cinema* (1984). With Dorothea Holloway, he is coeditor of *Interfilm Reports* and *Kino.* His permanent residence is in West Berlin.

Daniel J. Goulding, Professor of Film Studies and Theater Arts at Oberlin College, has lectured and published widely on film and related subjects. His book *Liberated Cinema: The Yugoslav Experience* (Indiana University Press, 1985) received the first "Close-up" award from the Yugoslav Film Institute for "outstanding scholarship and promoting the value of Yugoslav film art internationally."

INDEX OF FILM TITLES

Numbers in italics indicate a photograph from the film mentioned.

INDEX OF NAMES

Numbers in italics indicate a photograph of the person mentioned.

SUBJECT INDEX

Action-adventure films, in Yugoslavia, 249. *See also* Thrillers

Aging as theme, in Yugoslav films, 277

Alcoholism as theme, in Yugoslav films, 277

Allegory: in Bulgarian films, 218; in Czechoslovak films, 108, 110, 113, 124, 128; in Hungarian films, 176, 182; in Polish films, 166

Animated films: in Bulgaria, 215, 222, 245–46; in Czechoslovakia, 129–31, 134; in Yugoslavia, 252–53

Anniversary celebrations, in Bulgaria, 220–21, 223, 224, 226–27

"Archaic school," in Soviet Union, 23–25

Aristocrats, The (Pogodin), 49*n*.45

Armed forces as theme. *See* Military as theme

Armenian film studio, and Soviet films, 6

"Arsenal," 43

Artists, role of, in East German films, 61, 62, 63–64, 82, 92, 94–95

Audiences, and Soviet films, 5, 6

Austro-Hungarian Empire, 174

Avalanche (Dimitrova), 241

Avant-garde films. *See* Experimental films

Bait Size 46, Medium Short (Shchekochikin), 48*n*.32

Biographical films, in Czechoslovakia, 111

Bitterfeld conference, 52, 83

Black Cat, The (Poe), 252

Black market as theme, in Soviet films, 27–30

Blindness as theme, in Hungarian films, 188

Bourgeoisie, role of. *See* Social criticism as theme

Boyana Church, 224

Bulgarian films. *See specific headings*

"Bulgarian School of Animation," 246

Bytovoy films, in Soviet Union: creativity as theme in, 12–13, 17; defined, 6; emigration as theme in, 13–14; experimental nature of, 11; factory problem as theme in, 6–8; fairy tale elements in, 9; humor in, 8–9, 12; satire in, 9–11; social criticism as theme in, 11; women's role in, 15–17; youth as theme in, 14–15

Capitalism as theme, in East German films, 93–94

Cartoons. *See* Animated films

Catsplay (Örkény), 191

Censorship: of Bulgarian films, 216, 217, 220, 229; of Czechoslovak films, 108, 115, 117, 124, 129, 131, 132, 134, 135, 139–40, 142*n*.20; of East German films, 52–54, 71, 73–74, 76, 95*n*.8, 99*nn*. 71, 73, 100*n*.92; of Hungarian films, 176–77, 179, 206, 209; of Polish films, 145, 147, 148, 150, 155, 156, 159, 160, 163–64; of Soviet films, x, 26, 28–29, 37, 38, 40

Censorship as theme, in Hungarian films, 191, 192

Chamber films, in Soviet Union, 30–31

Charter 77, 106–107

Children's films: in Bulgaria, 220, 222, 244–45; in Czechoslovakia, 130. *See also* Youth as theme

"Cinema of moral concern," in Poland, ix-x

City vs. country as theme. *See* Rural-urban dichotomy as theme

Classicism, in East German films, 79–80

Cold War, 4

Comedy. *See* Humor; Irony; Parody; Satire

Commercial films. *See* "Popular" films

Community as theme, in Hungarian films, 202

Condemned films. *See* Censorship

"Country prose," in Soviet Union, 25

Country vs. city as theme. *See* Rural-urban dichotomy as theme

Creativity as theme, in Soviet films, 12–13, 17

Crime and Punishment (Dostoevsky), 41

Czechoslovak films. *See specific headings*

"Czech School," of Yugoslav directors, 249–50

Dead Souls (Gogol), 28, 48*n*.31

Dear Elena Sergeevna (Razumovskaya), 48*n*.32

Detective films: in Czechoslovakia, 107, 136; in Poland, 163; in Soviet Union, 34

Detente, 3, 4

Dialectics of the Concrete (Kosík), 106

Diamonds of the Night (Lustig), 114

Docudramas: in Hungary, 174; in Poland, 152, 153. *See also* Documentaries

Documentaries: in Bulgaria, 247; in Hungary, 203, 204, 205; in Poland, 146, 157, 159. *See also* Docudramas

Does the Positive Hero Have a Bad Reputation in Our Films? (booklet), 55, 75–76, 96*n*.12

313